THE ICE HOCKEY ANNUAL

2003-04

EDITED AND COMPILED BY STEWART ROBERTS

First published in Great Britain by
Stewart Roberts
The Old Town Hall
142 Albion Street
Southwick
Brighton BN42 4AX

Cover Design by **Channel Graphic Communication**

Digital Artwork by **James "Big Jimmy" Mansell**

British Library Cataloguing-in-Publication Data.
A catalogue record for this book is available from the British Library.

The Ice Hockey Annual 2003-04

ISBN 0-9536410-4-X

The Ice Hockey Annual's official website is at www.graphyle.com/IHA.
Past editions of *The Ice Hockey Annual* are archived in the Hockey Hall of Fame,
London Life Resource Centre, Toronto, Canada.

Printed in Great Britain by **L & S Printing Co Ltd**
Hazelwood Close, Hazelwood Trading Estate, Worthing, West Sussex BN14 8NP

CONTENTS

COVER - *top* Coventry Blaze celebrate adding the *Findus* British National League playoff championship to their league title; *bottom* **Kevin Riehl** of Belfast Giants beats Superleague's player of the year, **Joel Laing** of Sheffield Steelers, for the winning penalty shot in the semi-final of the Superleague Playoff Championship.

Photos: Chris Valentine (top), Roger Cook.

ACKNOWLEDGEMENTS

Welcome to the 28th edition of *The Ice Hockey Annual*, the sport's longest running publication.

If the power of the pen really were mightier than the sword, then we would have had one strong, sponsored national league and a GB team in the elite group of the World Championships long ago!

Anyway, down to business, though saying thanks comes at the pleasurable end of business. When the going gets tough, the tough get going, they say, so the *Annual*'s contributors must be a sturdy lot, keeping this printed effort going on a mostly voluntary basis. A big thanks to every single one of you for that.

Some individual contributions have inevitably been larger than others so we must single out a few folk for public approbation (ransacking the old thesaurus already!).

Gordon Wade has been the *Annual*'s chief stats man for more years than either of us care to remember and his detailed coverage of Superleague has been legendary. As well as all the league competitions, Gordon compiled the GB Player Register and much of the Roll of Honour. We're just crossing our fingers that he sticks around for whatever follows Superleague.

His opposite number in the British National League is newbie **Craig Simpson**, of whom we know little, but thanks for all the stats, mate.

As the English Leagues keep expanding so does the workload of husband and wife team, **Sue** and **Steve Tomalin** from Romford. Fortunately, they seem to thrive on it. Likewise, **Malcolm "Sonic" Preen** whose website www.homepages.tcp.co.uk/~sonic/british.html is a must for everyone needing results from all British leagues. We freely admit to compiling the results and standings for the Scottish and women's leagues with the invaluable help of Malcolm's exhaustive research.

Another essential website is www.iihf.com where readers (and your editor) can find everything on world championship ice hockey - seniors, juniors, men and women.

Though the *Annual* does not pretend to be big on pictures, we are particularly proud this year of our photographs. Our 'snappers' have excelled themselves by capturing some of the game's most dramatic moments - last-minute game winners and crucial penalty shots.

Photographing ice hockey, often in poorly lit rinks with the players moving at what must seem like 100 mph is not easy. So an especially warm thank you goes to **Chris Valentine, Diane Davey, Tony Boot, Roger Cook, Kieran Galvin** and **Dave Page**.

Our appreciation, too, goes to all the club photographers for their team pics.

While we're also grateful to you, dear reader, for buying this book, this enterprise would be almost impossible without the generosity of our advertisers. Please support them with your custom whenever you can.

Kevin Barker is one of the *Annual*'s most loyal backers. His *Igloo Trading Company* supplies your local rink shop with a variety of skating items. *Airport and Road Equipment* supply and maintain the world famous *Zamboni*, now the NHL's official ice resurfacing machine.

Stiga's products are used for the Table Hockey World Championships and are also recognised by the NHL, while the *North American Sports Network* (*NASN*) enables you to watch live NHL games.

Powerplay is a good weekly read about our sport and there's hardly anything skatewise you can't find at *Skate Attack* in north London.

For mail order goodies, go to www.*crazykennys*.co.uk or their shop in Worksop. *D&P Trophies* will look after all your trophy needs, *Miras Sports* distribute some of the sport's best known brands of equipment, and there must be a *Specsavers*, sponsors of GB and Cardiff Devils, in your town.

You can now find the *Ice N Easy* skate shop at the superb new *IceSheffield* while **Ian Green**'s *Armchair Sports* is in Hull but often hits the road to bring you his books, magazines, trading cards and lots more. Former goalie **Jim Graves**, who was Belfast Giants' sales manager, is the man to speak to at *Big Stick Management* if you're thinking of organising an event.

Another handy website is www.*TA-Sports.net* where you will find a host of useful services. Talking of websites, there's not a more comprehensive one than www.*azhockey.com*, the web 'bible' for our sport. **Phil Stamp** masterminds this site as he does The Ice Hockey *Annual*'s site at www.*graphyle.com/IHA* where you can complete your collection of *Annuals*.

Finally, thanks to our new printers, *L&S Printing*, for putting everything together in a smart package, and to **James "Big Jimmy" Mansell** for not ruining it.

The Ice Hockey Annual

FOREWORD

Pro game over

JO COLLINS

British ice hockey has a rich if somewhat chequered history. Its popularity as a spectator sport has risen and fallen several times over the decades, first cresting just before the Second World War when GB won the 1936 World Championships and a Olympic Gold Medal.

There was another wave in the 1950s when, although not reaching quite the same heights internationally, we did have a national league that, unlike other professional sports, embraced Scotland and England.

But during the deep trough of the 1960s, the sport's very existence hung by a thread for many years until it was revived by a handful of fans some of whom, like our beloved editor, are still involved today.

They dedicated time and effort in trying to resurrect the game and I was fortunate to see the early days of this. Exciting times they were, too, as it began to prosper again. Many of us felt that ice hockey had a place on the same stage - or in the wings - as professional football, cricket, rugby union and other more traditional sports.

SPORT AND BUSINESS EXPLOSIVE MIX

But even after the successes of the 1980s and 1990s, ice hockey only got as far as a supporting role. Now it seems unable to decide which roles to accept. Sorry, this theatrical metaphor is getting out of hand. What I mean is, it's in a mess. Why? Well, I've been involved with the Players Association since its formation in 1993, before the professional game had shown any signs of taking off, so I've seen at first hand the ability of ice hockey to, if not quite self-destruct, to have a good go at it.

If anyone ever says that sport and politics don't mix, you can tell them they're right, but the harsh reality in the professional game is that sport and business is the really explosive mix.

Superleague was a business when it came along in 1996. It was created on the back of an under-funded governing body, the BIHA, who had a well-intentioned but weak leadership. And when the league exploded due to greed, clubs' self-interest, over-ambition, lack of working capital and an unrealistic idea of where the game could stand within British sport, it led directly to the present fractured situation.

I don't need to go into all the sordid details of the financial destruction inflicted on ice hockey over the last six or seven years. Having had to deal with the problems generated by well-heeled, high-flying businessmen with a flair for believing they could make money out of thin air, I am only too conscious of their other naive belief: that sport is just like any other business. It isn't. Normal rules do not and cannot apply.

I can't resist pointing out here that over that same decade, the IHPA has maintained itself financially on a sound footing. We are proud that of all the organisations involved in the sport today, the IHPA stands alone in having reached ten years with a clean financial bill of health.

The final collapse of Superleague was a long and painful process, if inevitable. It's easy to say now that it had disaster written all over it from the start. Certainly some of their early ideas - "we're a fledgling NHL", I recall one of them telling me - were straight out of a *Disney* fantasy. Having a make-over by calling themselves Elite League will not fool many.

ICE HOCKEY MUST FIND ITS NICHE

If nothing else, Superleague's failure has proved that ice hockey here can never be as popular as the mainstream sports. But the game does have a place, and it must find it quickly if it is not to disappear. The only way this can happen is for like-minded people, with the good of the sport at heart, to come together, even though they may have slightly different agendas.

My own view is that a 12 to 16-team semi-professional league with feeder leagues is the only system that the UK can realistically support. That and a greater domestic player base from which clubs can draw their rosters, plus a national team composed of players competing, playing and training as often as is practicable.

We have all learned that artificial financial restraints such as wage capping will only work after a fashion; some clubs will always have a bigger fan base than others with better and bigger facilities.

But that's not the real issue. To turn my theatrical metaphor into a cinematic one, unless we all work together, the sequel to Superleague will not be the Elite League but *Terminator*.

Jo Collins is the executive director of the Ice Hockey Players Association (GB).

HONOURS & AWARDS

HONOURS ROLL CALL 2002-03

SUPERLEAGUE Playoff Championship
BELFAST GIANTS
Superleague
SHEFFIELD STEELERS
The Challenge Cup
SHEFFIELD STEELERS

BRITISH NATIONAL LEAGUE Playoffs
COVENTRY BLAZE
British National League
COVENTRY BLAZE
Findus **Cup**
NEWCASTLE VIPERS

ENGLISH LEAGUES
Premier Playoff Championship
MILTON KEYNES LIGHTNING
Premier League
PETERBOROUGH PHANTOMS
Premier Cup
PETERBOROUGH PHANTOMS
National League North
SHEFFIELD SCIMITARS
National League South
BASINGSTOKE BUFFALO
National League Playoffs
BASINGSTOKE BUFFALO

SCOTTISH NATIONAL LEAGUE
EDINBURGH CAPITALS
Caledonia Cup
FIFE FLYERS

WOMEN'S LEAGUE
CARDIFF COMETS

Top League Points Scorers
Superleague
LEE JINMAN, Nottingham
British National League
TONY HAND, Dundee
English Premier League
GARY CLARKE, M Keynes
Best Goaltending Percentages
Superleague
JOEL LAING, Sheffield
British National League
STEVIE LYLE, Cardiff
English Premier League
ALLEN SUTTON, M Keynes

BRITISH ICE HOCKEY WRITERS' ASSOCIATION AWARDS

ALL-STAR TEAMS

SUPERLEAGUE
First Team
Goal   JOEL LAING, Sheffield
Defence   ROBBY SANDROCK, Belfast
     MARC LANIEL, Sheffield
Forwards   LEE JINMAN, Nottingham
     DAN CEMAN, Bracknell
     PAXTON SCHULTE, Belfast
Second Team
Goal   RYAN BACH, Belfast
Defence   DION DARLING, Sheffield
     JIM PAEK, Nottingham
Forwards   GREG HADDEN, Nottingham
     RHETT GORDON, Sheffield
     KEVIN RIEHL, Belfast

BRITISH NATIONAL LEAGUE
First Team
Goal   JODY LEHMAN, Coventry
Defence   STEVE CARPENTER, Coventry
     JAN KRAJICEK, Edinburgh
Forwards   TONY HAND, Dundee
     ASHLEY TAIT, Coventry
     KEN PRIESTLAY, Dundee
Second Team
Goal   STEPHEN MURPHY, Dundee
Defence   PAUL DIXON, Guildford
     NEIL LIDDIARD, Basingstoke
Forwards   TEEDER WYNNE, Dundee
     DAVID CLARKE, Guildford
     STEVE CHARTRAND, Coventry

OTHER AWARDS

Best British Defenceman (Alan Weeks Trophy)
NEIL LIDDIARD, Basingstoke
Best British Netminder (BIHWA Trophy)
JOE WATKINS, Bracknell
Best British Forward (BIHWA Trophy)
ASHLEY TAIT, Coventry
Top British Scorer (Ice Hockey Annual Trophy)
Not awarded

AWARDS TO OFFICIALS
Micky Curry Memorial Trophy - Most Improved
MORAY HANSON
Keith Franklin Memorial Trophy - Most Dedicated
Information not available.

ALL-STARS

JOEL LAING *top left* Sheffield Steelers' goalie set a record of seven Superleague shutouts; Belfast coach **DAVE WHISTLE** *top right* steered Giants to their second major trophy in three seasons; Nottingham Panther **LEE JINMAN** *bottom left* was Superleague's top points scorer; Edinburgh Capital **JAN KRAJICEK** was voted the best defenceman in the British National League.

Photos: Chris Valentine, Diane Davey

SUPERLEAGUE PLAYER OF THE YEAR *Sheffield Steelers' netminder **JOEL LAING**
*one-on-one with London Knights' **Dennis Maxwell**.*
Photo: Kieran Galvin

BRITISH ICE HOCKEY WRITERS' ASSOCIATION AWARDS, contd.

PLAYERS OF THE YEAR

Superleague JOEL LAING, Sheffield
BNL JODY LEHMAN, Coventry

Being a netminder from Saskatchewan, in your first season in this country, with an East Coast Hockey League background and having the initials JL seemed to be the Writers' requirements for their Player of the Year.

Only joking, but it was some coincidence that Sheffield Steelers' **JOEL LAING** and Coventry Blaze's **JODY LEHMAN** had so much in common. But then both leagues recruit quite heavily from the ECHL and hockey is a way of life out on the Canadian prairies.

The real reason for them being honoured was that each was the key man as the two clubs picked up four trophies. Laing chalked up a remarkable ten shutouts - seven in Superleague - to break **Trevor Robins'** two-year-old record.

We should not be too surprised at this superb performance as the 28-year-old was runner-up in 1999-2000 for the prestigious Hobey Baker Award as the best player in American college hockey. This earned him a trip to Pittsburgh Penguins' NHL training camp and a place on their ECHL farm team. His stats - save percentage of 94.2 and goals against average of 1.49 - were the best of any stopper in the league's seven seasons. No wonder his coach, **Mike Blaisdell**, said: "I never dreamed we'd get a guy this good on our budget."

Lehman, 27, with six-and-a-bit shutouts (one was shared) for the Blaze, had to fight off strong competition from Devils' Welsh keeper **Stevie Lyle** while the voters also liked Edinburgh's skilful Czech defenceman, **Jan Krajicek**.

COACHES OF THE YEAR

Superleague MIKE BLAISDELL, Sheffield
BNL PAUL THOMPSON, Coventry

In **Mike Blaisdell**'s fourth successive term at the House of Steel the former NHL forward from Moose Jaw, Saskatchewan once again recruited and created a league and cup winning side.

The odds were against him at the start when his budget was drastically trimmed and he was able to persuade only three of his Playoff-winning team to return.

His signing of netminder **Joel Laing** was perhaps his master-stroke - though he cheerfully admitted it was a happy accident - and he built his squad around the goalie who won several awards on his own account.

This is Blaiser's third Coach of the Year title in his 13 seasons in Britain, and his second with the Steelers. Under his leadership, Sheffield have won a Grand Slam, two league titles, two Playoff championships, three Challenge Cups and a *B&H* Autumn Cup.

Paul Thompson took a bit of stick when his Coventry Blaze finished as runners-up in all three 2001-02 competitions. So he quit his day job and his post as assistant coach to the GB team and went full-time with Blaze as their coach and commercial manager. His dedication was rewarded with the BNL's league and Playoff titles, the first trophies in their short history. Blaze lost only five league games and went through the Playoffs with an unblemished record.

'Tommo' has been with the team since their formation in 2000, though he actually joined the club four years earlier during their previous incarnation in Solihull. He is widely credited with their success in building a substantial following and becoming one of the sport's powers.

EDITORIAL

An important message

I regret to announce that *The Ice Hockey Annual* lost over a million pounds last year. But it's not my fault. My agent failed to negotiate a £5 million advance sales deal with *Waterstones* and an exclusive interview with **Jeremy Paxman**.

And I don't want anyone writing negative stories just because the *Annual* has refused to merge with the *NHL Guide*!

The *Annual*'s staff are looking forward with enthusiasm to our new edition which has at least 50 pages devoted to junior ice hockey and hardly any mention of Canadians (you can watch them on *NASN*).

I have restructured the business by hand-writing all the pages, then photocopying them and stapling them together. And my staff took a big cut in wages (only too true, sadly).

In the hope that you won't notice any difference, the book has been re-titled *The Elite Ice Hockey Annual*.

Unfortunately, this means it has been banned from sale in the shops and you will have to call at our office and collect your copy.

I just hope your *Elite Annual* doesn't fall apart before the end of the season.

Great arenas, shame about the clubs

Enough satire, I wonder how many of you realise that the UK's arenas are among the best in Europe. Well, they are. While new buildings are going up all over the continent now, we had a head start on our neighbours. Yet last year four of our five teams that ran out of money (or patience) were arena-based sides - Belfast, Glasgow, London and Manchester; another arena club, Newcastle, just survived in the British National League; and the arena-based Superleague went into liquidation.

We can forgive any fans who are still in denial over the collapse of the pro game because the standard of Superleague was probably the highest we've seen here for 50 years. But in the last three seasons, Superleague's crowds dropped alarmingly from 880,057 to 583,575, partly due to the league's reluctance to ice home-grown players.

The bewildered fans were then forced to spend the summer listening to the surviving clubs begging the governing body to affiliate their new league, dubbed Elite, all the while blaming them - and/or the rival BNL - for mismanaging the

game! To complete this surreal scene, the Elite kicked and screamed against being asked either to join the affiliated (and mostly financially stable) BNL, or to provide financial guarantees to cover the chance that some Elite teams might not finish the season.

The guarantees were essential partly because the Elite eight included a handful of non-Superleague teams of very mixed pedigrees that the arena clubs apparently agreed to subsidise. There was also the tricky question of the Elite's responsibility for Superleague's debts. (You can read the full horrors on page 21.)

Ice Hockey UK - not to mention the Ice Hockey Players Association - are sick and tired of picking up the pieces left by club owners for whom the word 'sport' might as well be Chinese. The demands were only what any right-thinking governing body would insist on to encourage financial prudence on those running the leagues.

Foolishly, however, Ice Hockey UK overlooked putting in place the paperwork for enforcing these ideals. With a variety of legal threats flying around and time fast running out, they were embarrassingly overruled by the world body, the International Ice Hockey Federation, who insisted that the Elite League be recognised to allow the season to be played. You can read about the negotiations elsewhere in the *Annual*.

The IIHF's interest in the UK is partly due to those marvellous arenas of ours. They yearn to stage the World Championships here - probably in Nottingham and Sheffield - by the end of the decade. They were so concerned about the British organisation that they were to take the lead in bringing the warring parties together and guide them in a restructure of the sport, with the prime aim being one national league in 2004-05.

A national league? Hmm, that would almost make this summer of discontent worth enduring.

More Brits or more bull?

While few emerged with any credit after yet another wacky off-season, it was good to read that the arena clubs have finally accepted the need for realistic budgets and home-grown players. For those of you who care about youth development and would like to see how far the clubs keep their promise, feel free to use the lists of players on pages 171 and 184 of this *Annual*.

Enjoy your hockey and tell your friends. (The game needs you more now than ever before.)
August 2003   **Stewart Roberts**
stewice@aol.com

QUOTES OF THE YEAR

Be Ware-y

"I'm told it took around three weeks and a good solicitor to draw up Mike's contract to play for Cardiff last year. It took me ten seconds to rip it up in front of him and get him to sign my new one on my terms! Mully [**Glen Mulvenna**] was terrified. He said we would both die if I did that to Waresy. I told him to sit still. If I made for the door, don't sit around and try to reason with the bloke, just bloody run! My first signing [for 2003-04] if it were up to me. Top bloke." *Paul McMillan, Devils' owner, recalling his 2002-03 negotiations with team captain Mike Ware.*

Headlines of the Year

'I won't sack the lotto'. *Reading Evening Post over interview with Bracknell Bees' coach,* **Enio Sacilotto***, after Bees lost 11-3 at home to Belfast Giants.*

'But you're the one that I want, Darling'. *From The Star over a story about other Superleague teams picking on Steelers' enforcer,* **Dion Darling***.*

'Geordie Longstaff is ice cream of the crop'. *The Newcastle Evening Chronicle.*

'Hand held by long arm of law.' *In the Coventry Evening Telegraph over the story of* **Tony Hand***'s brush with uniformed authority.*

Ol' time hockey

"I started head-butting his fist a few times to warm him up..." **Kurt Irvine** *of Coventry Blaze explaining what really happened in his altercation with Hull Thunder's Eric Lavigne.*

No cliché like an old cliché

'Coach **Clyde Tuyl** knows that Vipers must play for the full 60 minutes and turn up for the first period and ... require a league victory to push them up the table.' *From a newspaper report.*

Scottish? No thanks

"I realised there was nothing in Scotland for me if I wanted to be a hockey player. Anywhere other than Scotland is the place to be. You don't get a fair chance at home. Most teams will bring in Canadians or Americans rather than Scottish kids." **George Murray***, 15, who decided his hockey future would be better catered for in the Czech Republic where he plays for Znojmo.*

No pressure, but plenty of whacks

"Back home, there's so much pressure. There's none of that here. No politics whatsoever. I play more than I ever have, probably more than I should! Hockey's fun again. I don't mean to make it sound like it isn't serious because winning is still what it's all about, but it's almost like playing with a bunch of friends." *Paul Kruse, captain of Belfast Giants, a former Calgary Flame, talking to the Calgary Herald.about life in Superleague.*

Minimum wage for young Brits

"What chokes me is you get some teams spending 75 per cent of their wage bill on imports, 20 per cent on experienced Brits and then they need a few young players who get £40 or less a week. Those young players play because they love it. The leagues call themselves professional so they should be paid a mimimum wage." **Paul Simpson***, coach of Kingston Jets in the English National League, turning down the chance of coaching the BNL's Hull Thunder.*

Well organised kids

'[Swindon's] Link Centre does not open for business on Sunday evenings or bank holidays... the Swindon Junior Ice Hockey Club run matches on a Sunday evening.' *From the Evening Advertiser, Swindon. [Now we know why Swindon has one of the finest junior organisations in the country - ed.]*

Stanley Cup winners

"No one likes getting hammered every week, but the support we've been given by the crowd has been great. Every time we scored a goal in the last two months you'd have thought we were winning the Stanley Cup." **Stephen Foster***, Hull Thunder's goalie, on the fans' reaction to the team's all-British squad.*

The best is yet to come

"The standard was frighteningly good. All team owners should be telling their coaches to go out and find these players and bring them on. They might not be as mature but there was more talent on show than what we have at the moment." **Paul Thompson***, Coventry Blaze's coach, after his July 2003 visit to the EIHA's School of Excellence.*

Quotes on the attempted formation of the Elite League start on page 30.

PLAYERS IN THE NEWS

Brebant retires with 1,000 goals

Sheffield Steelers' GB international centreman **Rick Brebant** finally called it a career at the end of 2002-03 after playing over 800 games in major competitions in his adopted country.

Always a fierce competitor, Brebant, 39, broke the 1,000 goals mark - like his former Steelers' teammate **Tony Hand** - and ended his 16 seasons in Britain with 2,407 points.

All his points were scored at the highest level, either in the old Premier Division of the British League or, more recently, the Superleague. He led the league three times in points and the playoffs twice. He was top goal scorer in the Premier Division with 146 for Durham Wasps in his second season.

Between 1994 and 2002, he was capped 32 times for Britain scoring ten goals and 23 points. The '94 championships in Pool A were among the highlights of his career. "My favourite goal was a short-handed one for GB against Canada's NHL goalie [Quebec's **Stephane Fiset**]," he recalled.

He spent his last four campaigns in Sheffield and Steelers' coach, **Mike Blaisdell**, whom Rick played with in Durham, was full of praise for him. "He's one of the most intense guys I've ever come across," he told the Sheffield *Star*. "I've always respected the way he's the first one on the puck and it doesn't matter if the biggest guy in the league is coming into the corner to kill him, he'll go in every time."

When Brebant arrived here from his native Canada in 1987, he spent six seasons with Durham. "I was fortunate when I first came here that hockey was on the up," he said. "I've seen it grow to what it has become in the past few years. Now, hopefully, the game can be rebuilt with British-born talent and some good imports."

Rick has always hankered after coaching. He took charge of **Sir John Hall**'s Newcastle Cobras for two seasons and was Blaisdell's assistant in Sheffield. So it was little surprise when he joined Manchester Phoenix of the new Elite League as their coach in May 2003. He played with Storm during their most successful years.

Phoenix owner, **Neil Morris**, described Rick as "one of the hardest working, grittiest, skilful and most driven players I've ever had the privilege of watching. It is exactly these qualities we feel he will bring to our team."

Greg Hadden - Super sniper

Greg Hadden, who retired at the end of 2002-03, was Superleague's all-time leading goal scorer with 129 goals in 259 league games. The centreman broke **Ed Courtenay**'s record of 122 goals, though 'Big Eddie' tallied his in 60 fewer games. He ended his time in Britain with the most goals, 173, in all major competitions. (See *Superleague* section.)

Hadden, 32, played all his seven seasons here with Nottingham Panthers - also a league record - joining them from the ECHL's Richmond (Virginia) Renegades in the first Superleague campaign. He was the club's leading points scorer in 1998-99 with 29 goals and 55 points in 33 games.

SUPER IRON MAN

Rob Stewart of Belfast Giants took over the mantle of Superleague's Iron Man when he played his 251st consecutive league game on 20 September 2002.

The only player never to miss a game since the league began in 1996, the 5ft, 10in defenceman completed his league career by playing in 286 consecutive league games and appeared in a further 130 games in other official competitions.

"The whole seven years has been a blast," he told the *Nottingham Evening Post.* "The team, the city, the fans, eveything about it has made it the best place I've ever played in. It's weird but I probably know more about Nottingham than my own place back in Vancouver."

Though small in stature at only 5ft, 7in, Greg never worried about the rough stuff. "I've seen him fight **Mike Ware**, who's 6ft, 5in, and **Corey Beaulieu**, who's a man mountain," said **Steve Carpenter**, his teammate and an old friend from their Vancouver days. This attitude earned him respect around the circuit and he only picked up a modest 216 minutes in penalties, less than a minute a game.

Hadden, who is married with two children, returned to Vancouver to become a fire-fighter.

• Hadden finished as runner-up to **Vezio Sacratini** on the league's all-time points scoring list with 250. (See *Superleague* section.)

• The first of Hadden's two goals on 18 January 2003 in Panthers' 5-3 defeat of Belfast Giants gave him 167 in all major tournaments, breaking Ed Courtenay's record again.

THE BIG GUNS GO SILENT

GREG HADDEN *left* returned to Vancouver as Superleague's all-time top goal scorer with Nottingham Panthers; **RICK BREBANT** retired from Sheffield Steelers with over 1,000 goals in British ice hockey. *Photos*: Roger Cook, Chris Valentine.

The fickle finger points at Hand

Tony Hand, generally agreed to be the finest player ever produced in these islands, endured a torrid time in 2002-03. He was put on trial following an alleged assault on a spectator at Coventry's SkyDome, and parted company with Dundee Stars in unexplained circumstances.

The first British born and trained player to be drafted by the NHL, Hand, 35, was featured in last year's *Annual* after becoming the first player to break through the 1,000-goal barrier in British league play. He is also GB's highest scorer.

He returned to Stars for a second season as their player-coach in 2002-03 after taking them to the British National League and playoff double in their first season. In both years, he was the league's top points scorer, their Best British Player and an All-Star forward.

The assault allegations were made after **Joe Featherstone**, a Coventry Blaze fan, was hit in the face at the SkyDome on 15 February. His glasses were broken in the incident.

Hand was serving a two-minute minor at the time and he gave his version of events to the Scottish *Sun*: "I was sitting in the penalty box when this guy came in from behind me. It could have been anyone...he could have had a bottle in his hand, or a knife, anything. I was concerned for my safety so basically I gave him a defensive push out of the box and that's all."

Tony denied assault when his case came to trial at Coventry magistrates court in August. After a hearing lasting several days, he was cleared of the charge with the judge stating that she was "satisfied that there was neither intent nor recklessness in the act of Mr Hand who reacted to something that took him by surprise."

Featherstone, 33, was banned by the club from all Blaze games and junior matches at the SkyDome.

Stars refused to comment on Hand's sudden departure from the club. He was suspended only hours before their first playoff game at Fife, just a couple of weeks after the Coventry incident. His place as coach was taken by **Ken Priestlay**, his former team-mate at Sheffield Steelers who, ironically, Hand had brought back from Canada to join the Stars.

As far as the *Annual* can discover, Tony was the highest paid player in Britain last season and it seems reasonable to assume that Stars felt that such a salary could no longer be justified after they failed to repeat as league champions and their crowds went down by almost ten per cent compared to their first season.

Rumours that the team had lost confidence in Hand's abilities as coach were firmly denied by Priestlay.

In the off-season Tony, who was in the second year of his three-year contract with Stars, was reportedly contacted by Panthers' owner **Neil Black** to be the player-coach of Black's proposed Elite League team at Glasgow's Braehead Arena.

The Ice Hockey Players Association confirmed that they were advising the player on his contract position and 'a number of other issues'.

There was a happy ending of sorts for the Scot when he signed for his home town team, Edinburgh Capitals, in July 2003. Capitals are run by Tony's cousin, **Scott Neil**, who is a director of the Murrayfield rink where Tony made his senior debut at the age of 14. He last played in the Edinburgh suburb in 1994-95 before joining Steelers and then Ayr Scottish Eagles in the Superleague.

In the press release announcing the move, Capitals thanked **David Sim** of Capital Car Hire and **Raymond Lumsden** of Thomson's Televisions for their 'substantial sponsorship agreement which has specifically provided the financial resources to sign Tony'.

Hand, who turned down the opportunity to play in North America after he was drafted, said: "I want to be part of the club for the long term and I am keen to allow my young family to grow up in Edinburgh close to their relatives and friends."

'Lobby' goes to Switzerland

Another highly talented Brit, the globe-trotting Geordie, **David Longstaff**, who played in the Swedish elite league in 2001-02, racked up more air miles last season.

After playing only a dozen games for **Gary Cowan**'s ill-fated Manchester Storm (he scored five goals and nine points), the GB skipper joined Newcastle Vipers in the British National League

His 19-game stay in the 'Geordie capital' was just long enough for him to play a key role in Vipers' *Findus* Cup victory, the team's first ever trophy. Apart from that weekend, though, the 28-year-old rarely looked comfortable with the difference in style and standard from his season in Stockholm.

Early in the New Year, he followed up GB coach **Chris McSorley**'s recommendation and joined Swiss second division side, HC Sierre. Vipers' manager, **Alex Dampier**, admitted the move came "as a bit of a shock. But he came here on the understanding that if he got a good offer from Europe then we wouldn't stand in his way."

Sierre finished fifth in the National B League and when they were knocked out of the playoffs by the middle of February, it left him with a good six weeks to kill before the World Championships. Unfortunately, the paperwork was not in place for him to re-join the Vipers.

RICK BREBANT - 1,000 Goal Scorer

Forward. 5'9" 13st 0lb (182 lbs)   Born: Elliot Lake, Ontario. 21 February 1964

Season	Club	Lge	Major Competitions					League					Playoffs				
			GP	G	A	Pts	Pim	GP	G	A	Pts	Pim	GP	G	A	Pts	Pim
1987-88	DUR	BLP	31	91	88	179	32	25	77	75	152	18	6	14	13	27	14
1988-89	DUR	BLP	52	146	157	303	95	36	99	119	218	67	5	12	10	22	6
1989-90	DUR	BLP	46	93	101	194	80	31	64	70	134	44	4	4	8	12	6
1990-91	DUR	BLP	54	135	194	329	120	35	93	116	209	72	8	18	34	52	16
1991-92	DUR	BLP	53	115	119	234	147	35	78	82	160	99	8	17	16	33	26
1992-93	DUR	BLP	43	72	80	152	118	34	59	62	121	84	6	12	18	30	18
1993-94	CAR	BLP	63	119	154	273	130	44	88	120	208	98	8	16	19	35	8
1994-95	NOT	BLP	59	85	156	241	106	39	58	95	153	78	7	6	18	24	4
1995-96	DUR	BLP	41	41	92	133	96	24	19	60	79	56	7	3	11	14	20
1996-97	NEW	ISL	29	17	27	44	101	22	9	20	29	68					
1997-98	NEW	ISL	16	7	12	19	18	4	1	1	2	14					
1997-98	MAN	ISL	42	11	29	40	58	19	6	15	21	22	9	1	6	7	8
1998-99	MAN	ISL	60	19	34	53	76	39	13	19	32	40	7	3	5	8	18
1999-00	MAN	ISL	29	11	23	34	30	18	8	12	20	20					
1999-00	LON	ISL	28	13	22	35	42	19	9	14	23	32	8	3	8	11	10
2000-01	SHE	ISL	67	18	41	59	181	45	10	32	42	94	8	3	4	7	8
2001-02	SHE	ISL	52	16	40	56	49	42	13	30	43	36	8	1	8	9	13
2002-03	SHE	ISL	47	8	21	29	113	23	6	9	15	24	17	1	7	8	46
ISL Totals			370	120	249	369	668	231	75	152	227	350	57	12	38	50	103
Major Comps			812	1017	1390	2407	1592	534	710	951	1661	966	110	102	167	269	203

1988-89   most points & goals BLP, most points Autumn Cup

1990-91   most points BLP, Playoffs and *B&H* Cup .

1991-92   most points BLP, Playoffs and Autumn Cup

1994-95   most points *B&H* Cup

1999-2000   most assists Playoffs

Major Competitions - league, playoffs, B&H *Cup, Autumn Cup and Challenge Cup*

BLP - British League, Premier Division   ISL - Superleague

statistics by **Gordon Wade**

He was GB's second highest scorer in Zagreb, but he was the first to admit that he didn't play well, though he offered no excuses. He received several offers to play abroad again but decided to return to the Vipers' nest, signing a two-year contract with **Darryl Illingworth**'s ambitious club.

Then in June, disaster struck. The former Sheffield Steeler and Whitley Warrior broke one foot and dislocated the other after he dropped training weights on his feet and he was expected to miss the start of the season.

■ **Roy Harnett**, the Brighton Tigers, Sussex and Southampton Vikings forward, was the first Englishman to play in Switzerland. The GB international had a spell with Basle in the Swiss National League in 1950-51.

Shields in Maine

Colin Shields is the best British born player never to have appeared on a senior club side in this country, apart from a handful of games for Paisley Pirates in his early teens.

Shields, 23, was the second Brit to be drafted by the NHL when he was chosen by Philadelphia Flyers in 2000. Last season was his second with the University of Maine Black Bears in the USA where he continued to combine his academic and hockey careers.

Voted Bears' rookie of the year in 2001-02, he averaged a goal a game through the first two months of last season. But after sustaining a broken rib that knocked him out of action for four games, the right winger failed to score in his final 15 games.

Maine went out early in both the Hockey East and NCAA playoffs with Shields' below-par performances being a major factor. He finally scored again in Black Bears' 2-1 loss to Michigan in the first round of the NCAA playoffs. In 34 league games, he scored 14 goals and 27 points, and added a goal and an assist in three playoff games.

He looked strong in the Zagreb World Championships and his deft touch around the net brought him four goals in GB's five games.

He has one season of NCAA eligibility left before the Flyers have to decide if they should sign him or relinquish his rights. The scouting reports say he's weak defensively and not physical enough for the big league. His offensive talents might, however, attract the interest of an AHL team.

Brit Watch

Here are snapshots of how some of our top youngsters spent 2002-03.

• **MARK RICHARDSON** was the youngest player ever called up for the GB senior team when he played in their Euro Challenge games in the Ukraine in December 2002 at the age of 16.

Already six feet tall and the scorer of 18 goals and 38 points for the English Premier League's Swindon Lynx, he must have set another record by being picked for GB's senior squad before he played for their juniors.

He went to Romania in January with the under-20s when he scored a goal and an assist, and two months later he was off to Latvia with the under-18s where his three goals made him GB's second highest marksman.

Mark was snapped up by the BNL's Bracknell Bees in July 2003. Bees' coach, **Mike Ellis**, was keen to take the teenager under his wing and fast-track him into an American college. "He's a strong, skating forward, the best for his age and for the year above," said Ellis. "I'm going to throw him right in the deep end."

Richardson was the first school leaver to join the Bees' Young Stars In Training scheme, which is backed by the club's sponsor, *Paxton Ward*.

His elder brother **LEE RICHARDSON**, 20, played for Coventry Blaze as did **RUSS COWLEY**, 19. All three are products of the prolific Swindon youth organisation which is reckoned to be among the best in the country.

• **GREG OWEN** scored Bracknell Bees' first goal and was voted man of the match on his Superleague debut at London Knights on 19 September 2002. The 21-year-old Brit was on a contract which allowed him to train and play with Bees during the week, and join Milton Keynes Lightning in the EPL at weekends.

He was played sparingly in 23 games for Bees, tallying two goals and three points, but he went on a scoring spree in Milton Keynes with 50 goals in 53 games. Super sniper **GARY CLARKE** was the only Brit to outscore him with a league leading 110 goals.

The 5'11" forward, who was born in Northampton and first played for Milton Keynes juniors at the age of ten, was capped 14 times for GB last season. But his World Championship debut was spoiled when he was thrown out of GB's tempestuous game against their hosts.

Greg gained his first international cap with GB under-16s in 1996. In 1997 he joined Notre Dame Hounds, the renowned Canadian hockey school in Saskatchewan. He was re-signed by Bees in June 2003, this time to a full one-year contract. Coach Mike Ellis said: "He impressed me in Croatia with the GB squad and he will be a vital part of this year's Bees."

COLLAPSE OF THE SUPERLEAGUE

Slow death of pro league

Like toppling dominoes, five of Superleague's seven teams either collapsed or joined the rival British National League over a nine-month period in 2002-03. Only **SHEFFIELD STEELERS**, which had gone through a traumatic take-over in 2001, and **BELFAST GIANTS** - narrowly - survived the carnage.

The league itself, the first professional circuit in Britain for almost 50 years, went into liquidation after seven seasons of mis-management. The usual suspects for the demise were over-ambitious planning, reliance on foreign players and reluctance to work with a blue-chip sponsor who could help them to market the game nationally. The directors tended to make more enemies than friends with their fiercely guarded independence and insistence on treating everything as 'business'.

They left a mountain of debts to their players, tax authorities and local organisations from which the sport could take years to recover.

The milestones on the road to ruin:

5 November **MANCHESTER STORM** pull the plug after playing only 12 games (six in the MEN Arena). Storm Entertainment Ltd - managing director **Gary Cowan** - owed around £1 million, though this included a £282,000 fine by the league for not completing the season.

8 November **SCOTTISH EAGLES** fold after playing 14 games (five in Glasgow's Braehead Arena). [The first time a senior league has lost two teams before the end of a season.]

Eagles Hockey Ltd, whose directors were **Bob Zeller** and **Albert Maasland**, ran up debts of £153,839 after trading for less than six months.

30 November **John Nike OBE** announces that his **BRACKNELL BEES** will join the British National League for the 2003-04 season. Bees' home rink has the league's smallest capacity.

26 March **LONDON KNIGHTS** play their last game in London Arena after five seasons. The team's owners, Anschutz Entertainment Group, fail to inform the fans for a month, on 29 April.

The move is understood to be part of a Europe-wide cost-cutting exercise by the Los Angeles-based group. (See later.)

29 April Three weeks after the playoff final, **Superleague** put the company into liquidation. The Inland Revenue and Customs & Excise are owed £22,567 and unsecured creditors are owed £510,044, including £28,551 to Ice Hockey UK.

The directors are listed as **Bill Barr** (Ayr), Albert Maasland (Belfast), **Detlef Kornett** (London) and John Nike. (**Neil Black** (Nottingham) and **Norton Lea** (Sheffield) resigned before the liquidation meeting.)

3 July At a meeting in Belfast, managing director Albert Maasland persuades the creditors of **Belfast Giants** Ltd to accept payment of 20p in the £ so that the club can continue. Giants piled up debts of over £1 million after playing for barely three seasons.

The wake

Three of these directors, Messrs Black, Lea and Maasland, bounced back by creating the Elite Ice Hockey League. This was to have a lower wage cap than Superleague but still be of a higher standard than the BNL.

Left out in the cold were the supporters of the Knights and the Eagles. The fans of the Scottish club which, incidentally, was still owned by Bill Barr, realised that though the Braehead Arena was one of the UK's best, it was not in an ideal place for a hockey team. Glasgow, like London, has historically been indifferent to the sport.

Instead, they formed the Friends of Eagles Hockey, raised £21,000 to pay off the outstanding players' wages and lobbied Barr Holdings, SportScotland and their local MP for the team to return to the seven-year-old Centrum Arena in Ayr-Prestwick. Livewire former Eagle, **Angelo Catenaro**, even had plans to put together a new squad and enter them in the BNL.

Sadly, all came to nought in time for season 2003-04 but FoEH have high hopes that a team can be re-formed in time for 2004-05.

The tale of the London Knights was a longer and sorrier saga, as befits a side belonging to the world's largest owners of sports teams. Unfortunately, the Anschutz Entertainment Group behaved like any faceless, American corporation when they let the league's 'flagship' team slide beneath the waves without a trace.

With London Arena having already been sold to a property developer, the loyal and frustrated fans were left with two equally unpalatable choices - wait a couple of years (probably more) for the Millennium Dome to be refurbished as the world's largest entertainment centre (sorry about the superlatives but AEG are huge), or trot along to Alexandra Palace and watch London Racers in the Elite League. Or both, of course.

Seven fans decided not to leave everything to the whims of big business, and on 23 May 2003 they set up the London Knights Supporters Trust. Their stated aim was to work with AEG to ensure that the Knights were relaunched and meanwhile, keep the flame burning, so to speak. More details on their website at www.lkst.co.uk.

Knights' five seasons were ones of mixed fortunes, from the glory years of coach **Chris McSorley** and a Continental Cup silver medal, to the disasters of opening night and the theft of equipment which caused an important televised game to be cancelled.

Knights' average crowd of just over 3,000 was not to be sniffed at, but the failure of Superleague to create a national interest in the sport and the yawning gaps in the 10,000-seat arena meant the Knights were never a commercial success. Their refusal to ice local players was simply bad marketing. **Ian Cooper** (78 games), **Nicky Chinn** (26) and **David Clarke** (12) were their only Brits in five years.

There was little attempt at creating fan favourites among the players, though this was a league-wide mistake. The team went through four coaches and over 100 players with virtually the entire squad being replaced after each of the first three years.

> Ever wanted to go into space? Ever wanted to know what an astronaut feels like? Then go to the London Arena, and experience a lack of atmosphere for yourself! *- seen on the web*

Their last home game - London whitewashed fierce rivals Bracknell Bees 6-0 with **Sean Blanchard** scoring the final goal - was as controversial as their first. The club gave out mixed signals about their future, playing a highlights video on the big screen but flashing signs saying 'see you in Nottingham' [for the Playoff Championships]. The crowd of 3,502 gave them a standing ovation at the start and end of the game but was otherwise only a little more animated than usual. (We noticed one failed attempt to start a 'Mexican wave'.)

Many fans insisted that the Docklands arena - a building quite unsuitable for ice hockey even after its multi-million pound facelift in 1998 - was the wrong place for a professional ice hockey team. Wembley, a venue synonymous with the sport since the 1930s and designed after Toronto's Maple Leaf Gardens, was considered the ideal.

Detlef Kornett, AEG's managing director, was reported in a Berlin newspaper in the summer as saying that the group was selling off its shares in four of their six European clubs, including Knights. "As far as ice hockey is concerned, we want to concentrate on the German market. Apart from that, our interest lies in our arenas in London and Berlin."

As well as the Millennium Dome, AEG will retain the Berlin Polar Bears for whom they are constructing the Berliner Halle, a 16,000 capacity, 150 million Euro (around £100 million) arena next to the German capital's East railway station. The group already own 70 per cent of the German Elite League's Hamburg Freezers.

Chris McSorley, an AEG employee as coach of Geneva Eagles, told the *Annual* that his club would also remain part of the group. But rumours persisted that AEG have quietly buried their grandiose, if undeclared plan for a European league.

TRETIAK MEETS TROF

A dream came true for London netminder **Dave Trofimenkoff** on 2 March as his childhood hero, Russian goalie **Vladislav Tretiak**, watched the Knights' victory over Belfast Giants after the hockey legend dropped the puck in a pre-game ceremony.

Ice hockey is the least of his worries for the group's main shareholder, American multi-billionaire, **Philip Anschutz**. Since his European investments began in 1999 on the back of the telecomms boom, Anschutz, 63, has seen shares in his telecomms company, Qwest, slump from US$64 to $2. According to the US financial magazine, *Forbes*, this cost him personally US$8 billion and he fell from sixth to 54th on their list of the world's richest men.

☒ Two of Knights' classiest players, forward **Steve Thornton** and goalie **Trevor Robins**, suffered severe complications after routine knee operations. Thornton, the MVP of the 2003 World Division One Championship, needed 15 months to recover. Robins, once rated the finest netminder in Europe, was forced into retirement.

☑ Former Knights' coach, **Bob Leslie**, joined Basle Dragons in the Swiss National A League where his team will meet Chris McSorley's Geneva Eagles.

• Superleague's media manager, **Alyson Pollard**, left the organisation on 31 October 2002 and joined the staff of the new football stadium at Hull. Her departure left the league with just two full-time staff - **Brian Storey**, the chief admin officer, and his secretary. Hockey manager **Frank Dempster**, the league discipline chief, and officials manager **Andy French** were employed on a part-time basis. At the league's height in 1997-98, they had five full-time staff.

Manchester Storm - the last team

left to right, *back row*: Mike Perna, Ryan Stewart, David Longstaff, Dwight Parrish, Dan Hodge, Pasi Neilikainen, Geoff Peters, Joe Cardarelli, Dan Preston, Colin Pepperall, Alyson Bugg (physio); *front row*: Stevie Lyle, Mark Bultje, Pierre Allard, John Crawley (equipment), Ivan Matulik, Daryl Lipsey (coach), Rob Wilson, Shawn Maltby, Mike Torchia.   *Photo*: Andy Yates

---

CATCH ME IF YOU CAN 2

Hollywood will soon be coming to Holywood and other parts of Belfast when work begins on a feature film - *The Neutral Zone* - telling the story of the Belfast Giants and their founding father, **Bob Zeller**. The story is based on Zeller's idea of setting up a professional ice hockey team in, of all places, Belfast, and will recount the trials and tribulations of the team set-up process and culminate with the puck hitting the ice at the first home game in the Odyssey.

The makers, Crusader Entertainment, hope to deliver an inspirational feel-good movie for all the family.

Crusader's CEO, **Howard Baldwin** [former owner of the NHL's Pittsburgh Penguins and Hartford Whalers], set the company up with American billionaire **Philip Anschutz** (owner of the London Knights and LA Kings) three years ago. Baldwin's previous company produced another feel-good hockey film, *Mystery, Alaska*, starring **Russell Crowe** and **Burt Reynolds**.

In Belfast on a location-finding mission was the producer of *The Neutral Zone*, **Ginger Perkins**, who explained: "The story first came to our attention when Howard read all about the team's success in the fantastic coverage it got in the North American media. He showed it to me and asked if I thought there was a movie in it and I said 'yes.' So we contacted Bob Zeller and here we are. Our aim is to meet the standards set in *Mystery, Alaska*."

The company hope to start shooting in Belfast later this year and to use local talent as much as possible. With a budget estimated at US$10-20 million it will be a substantial release, and in addition to telling the story of Zeller's hockey crusade, should help to put Belfast on the movie map.

The movie is scheduled for release sometime in 2004 but for now the rumours surrounding who will play the leading parts are gathering momentum. **Nicholas Cage** as **Dave Whistle** anyone?

- Belfast Giants' press release, February 2003

THE GREAT ICE WAR 2003

The sport was split pretty well down the middle in 2003 in the wake of the collapsed Superleague. Here's a rundown of the major arguments and the personalities involved.

these lines for many years, with little success, or that the pro game had just collapsed.

There was also the fear that the fans - especially those in the large arenas which had hosted Superleague teams - would vote with

The Combatants

ELITE LEAGUE (EL)

Basingstoke Bison (BNL)
Belfast Giants (ISL)
Cardiff Devils (*Bob Phillips'* version) (New)
Coventry Blaze (BNL)
London Racers (New)
Manchester Phoenix (New)
Nottingham Panthers (ISL)
Sheffield Steelers (ISL)

2002-03 league shown in brackets.

BRITISH NATIONAL LEAGUE

Bracknell Bees (ISL)
Cardiff ?? (*Paul McMillan's* version) (BNL)
Dundee Stars (BNL)
Edinburgh Capitals (BNL)
Fife Flyers (BNL)
Guildford Flames (BNL)
Hull Stingrays (New - *Thunder played in BNL*)
Newcastle Vipers (BNL)

Whose side were they on?

English IHA
Ken Taggart, *chairman*
Public comment on 27 June: "An affiliation in principal [sic] has been made between the EIHL professional clubs and the EIHA clubs...there now exists a strong association and support structure between the professional arena-based clubs and the junior clubs."
Public comment on 1 August: "The EIHA recognises the Elite League as part of the EIHA."
Tony Oliver, *deputy chairman*
Public comment on 12 August: "The EIHA's board will continue to support the Elite League's application to affiliate to Ice Hockey UK. The EIHA has no intention of trying to take over the agreed functions of the IIHF, IHUK, FBNL, SIHA or NIIHF."
Northern Ireland IHF
John Lyttle, *chairman*
Public comment on 8 July: "No such sanction [of the Elite League by IHUK] has been given at this time by either the NIIHF or any of its sister organisations, the EIHA or the SIHA."
Scottish IHA   No public comment made.

Why an Elite League?

The question puzzling many fans during the long, hot summer was why did the EL clubs think the sport needed an Elite League, especially after the ignominious collapse of the Superleague? For all its faults, the BNL is still here after six years with seven perfectly sound teams (or as sound as you'll ever get in a minority sport) and three more if the EL hadn't come along.

The Elite claimed that it was all being done for the good of the game. **Roger Black,** the owner of the Alexandra Palace-based London Racers, said: "The objectives are to create a stable platform for the professional game and fully integrate youth development into the plan." He seemed unaware that the BNL had been trying to work with the English Ice Hockey Association on

their feet if the standard of ice hockey dropped.

Roger Black's cousin, Nottingham Panthers' owner **Neil Black,** was the most vociferous over this. [Read his views in our *Elite Quotes* section.] While we believe his worries on this score to be unfounded as Panthers' fans are passionate about the sport, the team were probably the most profitable in the country (our sources indicate a regular six-figure profit), so Mr Black had a lot to lose.

He had a second worry which would be neatly solved by the formation of an Elite League which could be sold as Superleague II. His contract with the NIC - drawn up under Lottery grant conditions imposed by Sport England - called for Panthers to play only in Superleague (see later).

But with only three old Superleague teams left, how could he persuade others to help him form a

WHO RUNS WHAT IN BRITISH ICE HOCKEY

ICE HOCKEY UK (IHUK)

The governing body of the sport in the United Kingdom, founded in July 1999 to replace the British Ice Hockey Association which had folded. Ice Hockey UK are the only UK organisation recognised by the world governing body, the International Ice Hockey Federation (IIHF), to whom IHUK pay fees for each world championship the GB teams enter.

The Board of Directors of IHUK comprises a finance director and nine elected members - two from the major league, the British National League; two from each regional association, England, Scotland and Northern Ireland; and one player. [The names of these directors are listed under *Governing Bodies* at the back of the *Annual*.] Each of these subsidiary organisations has only one vote, irrespective of the number of Board members.

IHUK is responsible for organising the sport in this country insofar as they have not delegated such authority to other bodies (see below). In addition, they are responsible for organising the GB teams at all levels, for men and women; for authorising International Transfer Cards (ITCs) for overseas players; dealing with national funding bodies; and representing the sport on the British Olympic Committee and other national sports bodies.

ENGLISH ICE HOCKEY ASSOCIATION (EIHA)

The national governing body for England and Wales responsible for organising, promoting and developing ice hockey in those countries. Its primary function is organising development leagues, tournaments and training camps for players from under-10 years to under-19 years, and officials up to the age of 19.

The EIHA also manages a semi-pro league, the English Premier League, and an amateur league, the English National League. Both are open to junior and senior players.

The EIHA is run by their member clubs who elect an executive committee (EC). [The names of the EC members are listed under *Governing Bodies* at the back of the *Annual*.] Each member club pays a registration fee at the start of each season, together with all necessary players' fees. Their annual income is estimated to be something over £250,000.

Two members of the EC are put forward by the EIHA to sit on the Board of Ice Hockey UK of which they are then directors. The EIHA has only one vote on the Board.

The EIHA contributes £13,000 annually to Ice Hockey UK to support the GB national teams.

SCOTTISH ICE HOCKEY ASSOCIATION (SIHA)
NORTHERN IRELAND ICE HOCKEY FEDERATION (NIIHF)

These bodies have the same responsibilities in Scotland and N Ireland as the EIHA do in England and Wales. Each body has one vote on the governing IHUK.

Fees to IHUK are £4,250 from the SIHA and £500 from the NIIHF.

BRITISH NATIONAL LEAGUE (BNL)

The only independent league recognised directly by IHUK. They pay an annual fee of £20,000 to the governing body for the commercial rights to the sport in return for which they can sell their league to TV and sponsors and keep any fees accruing from the sales. The current five-year contract expires in 2005.

The league is run by a Board of Directors comprising one member from each club. Each club holds shares worth £500 in the league which entitles them to membership. The BNL has two directors on Ice Hockey UK on which it is entitled to one vote.

new one? Sheffield Steelers' owner **Norton Lea** gave us the answer on the club's website in July, when he told fans that the league's arena clubs - Steelers, Panthers, Belfast Giants and Manchester Phoenix - were prepared to subsidise the rest of the eight-team circuit.

We can believe that Steelers and Panthers would do this as they are the most successful sides in Britain. But we're not so sure about the others. Giants barely escaped the biggest financial collapse in British ice hockey history, and Manchester were going to need all their funds to keep a team alive for a full season in one of Europe's largest and presumably most expensive arenas.

However, we can understand that Neil Black would be willing to help his cousin Roger's London Racers, as the league needed a side in the capital to enhance its standing.

This odd financial structure, along with the connections of some owners to the liquidated Superleague, were the main reasons that Ice Hockey UK insisted on financial guarantees before they agreed to affiliate the Elite League.

What were they fighting over?

Simply, getting the Elite League recognised. Norton Lea seemed surprised that club owners couldn't just go out and form a league and get the governing body to rubber-stamp it.

Other owners took a more aggressive view of Ice Hockey UK's unexpectedly tough stance. On Racers' website, Roger Black accused them of being "an annoyance [whose] chairman has not acted in an impartial and professional manner."

EIHA chairman, **Ken Taggart**, couldn't resist exploiting the flaws in the sport's structure which were exposed by the row. In his 1 July press release, he 'called into question Ice Hockey UK's ability to act as a governing body of British ice hockey' and accused it of damaging the sport and 'vastly overspending its budgets'.

Taggart may well have a case against IHUK for the gross under-representation of the EIHA on the governing body. They have only one vote, the same as the tiny Scottish and Northern Irish associations, despite the EIHA having 257 teams and almost 5,000 players.

Neither of these gentlemen appeared to realise how much they were setting back their cause with such inflammatory remarks.

• Roger Black took over Haringey Racers during season 2001-02 after his return from a long spell in Canada. Last year the team finished 11th out of 12 in the English Premier League.

• Ken Taggart is an American who returned to live in the States after several years in Britain playing and refereeing before taking control of the EIHA in the mid-Eighties.

NEIL BLACK

Why can't Ice Hockey UK get a grip on the clubs?

The governing body is basically an amateur one. It has little independent income and is almost entirely reliant on monies from the leagues and the regional associations, especially the EIHA.

The government, which is the source of income for many sports through the regional and national sports councils, has a strictly limited amount to spread around for minority sports. These quangos have strict criteria for dishing out the dosh and ice hockey rarely qualifies, anyway, for all sorts of reasons.

This in turn means that much of the power in this sport is in the hands of the clubs through their deep-pocketed owners. Great for the clubs but not healthy for the game. Even the English Ice Hockey Association is prospering with an annual income of over £250,000, derived from fees paid by their member clubs. (See panel.) Ironic, isn't it, that after years of poverty, the game's stability is now threatened by the rich!

IHUK's biggest mistake was to have no rules or regulations to clarify who did what. When push came to shove, there was nothing to prevent the Elite eight from forming a league. This didn't stop the governing body from obstinately refusing to affiliate them.

In the end it was the IIHF's decision - after a July fact-finding mission by their Council member **Frederick Meredith** - that the Elite clubs should be recognised as a league, pending a meeting of all parties early in the new season.

While the main fight was between the Elite League and the governing body, IHUK, there were other skirmishes, some of which could scar the face of the sport for a long time.

The Battles

BRITISH NATIONAL LEAGUE v PLANET ICE

Planet Ice own Basingstoke Bison and the lease of Coventry Blaze's home rink, the SkyDome. One of the earliest signs of friction in the BNL came with Planet Ice's dislike of the way the league is run, even though each club had a vote on the league's ruling Board. Among their concerns were distribution of prize money and sponsorship funds, and TV coverage.

The company was also behind the withdrawal from the BNL of the Milton Keynes and Peterborough clubs who joined the English Premier League in 2002-03.

Bison are understood to have joined the EL after receiving assurances of substantial financial assistance from the league, and the ambitious owners of the Blaze needed little urging to join a 'higher' league.

ELITE LGE v BRITISH NATIONAL LGE

The Elite League was created on 1 April 2003 to replace Superleague which formally went into liquidation a month later. The BNL, effectively a semi-pro league, began life in 1997-98.

Negotiations for a merger between the two organisations began in earnest soon after Scottish Eagles and Manchester Storm crashed out of Superleague early in the 2002-03 season.

Meetings were held in November (during the BNL's *Findus* Cup finals in Newcastle) and May (chaired by IHUK's **Stuart Robertson** at Heathrow) but there was little meeting of minds. The eight (originally nine with Glasgow) EL clubs were never fully represented and the BNL accused them of not negotiating in good faith.

Among the problem areas were mid-week games, definition and use of 'British' players, and the disparity between arenas and rinks, but the real stumbling blocks were (a) several Elite clubs did not wish to have Brits at all as they believed they would lower the standard of play too far for their fans, (b) what the EL perceived to be the BNL's weak and short-sighted administration and (c) the personal animosity between each league's more influential owners.

Two further meetings were held but nothing was resolved.

ELITE LEAGUE v ICE HOCKEY UK (and IIHF)

Early in 2003, Ice Hockey UK sent the Elite League a contract - believed to be similar to the one they had with Superleague - but the parties were not able to agree terms.

The league are understood to have originally offered £20,000 a season for the sport's commercial rights on the grounds that they were a new organisation and that this is all the BNL pay. The EL claimed they offered £175,000 but it was unclear when this offer was made or over how many seasons.

In any case, on 30 May the IHUK Board declined to affiliate the league. The *Annual* understands that one reason was that some of the EL clubs had been members of the liquidated Superleague which still owed more than half of their £40,000 affiliation fee from 2002-03.

IHUK repeated their appeal for the Elite League clubs to join the BNL. They also quashed the league's threat to bypass the British governing body and apply straight to the IIHF for recognition. A letter dated 2 June from the IIHF's secretary was published which made clear that such an approach would not be permitted.

PANTHERS v THE NATIONAL ICE CENTRE

All the other battles of the Great Ice War were just side-shows compared to the titanic clash waged between the Elite League's Panthers, owned by Neil Black of Aladdin Management, and their home arena, the National Ice Centre, represented by chief executive, **Geoff Huckstep**, and chairman, **Mich Stevenson**.

The NIC, being funded by public money, refused to entertain the idea of a team in their rink playing in an unauthorised league. But Panthers have turned a healthy profit almost every year under Black and the venture capitalist fought all summer to renew his contract.

The ground over which this battle was waged was outlined in Huckstep's open letter in mid-July. He explained that the NIC had asked Neil Black to supply the following -

+ financial guarantees from Panthers in case the league folded in mid-season,

+ more information on the viability of the EL teams (a regular complaint by many critics was that the EL never answered key financial questions satisfactorily),

+ details of the protection that Panthers have in place for their season ticket holders should the league not survive the full season,

+ an answer to how the league could operate without official sanction from IHUK,

+ an answer to why the BNL was considered an inferior league when the work permit limit [five per team] and wage caps were the same or very similar for both leagues.

The chief exec. was also concerned at 'reports that some owners may have financial interests in two or three clubs'. These questions were being asked, he said, because of the "appalling financial mismanagement" of Superleague. In other words, Neil Black was claiming that the Elite League replaced Superleague; that was a bust, so prove that the EL won't be as bad.

The NIC offered the league one answer - 'take Superleague out of administration and honour your debts'. Then, Geoff Huckstep concluded, Panthers could play in Superleague, and the NIC and Sport England would be happy.

Another alternative - a new owner with the team in the BNL - was avoided when agreement was reached at the eleventh hour, on 22 August, just three weeks before the first scheduled game, but only after Panthers had made contingency plans to play at the new iceSheffield centre.

CARDIFF DEVILS v CARDIFF ??

See our *News Round-Up* section later in the *Annual* for details of the battle between **Bob Phillips** and **Paul McMillan**.

ICE HOCKEY UK v ENGLISH ICE HOCKEY ASSOCIATION (EIHA)

The EIHA were a late entrant, joining the fray only after IHUK had declined to recognise the Elite League. Their chairman, Ken Taggart, issued a statement on 1 July saying that the EIHA had agreed to the 'affiliation in principal' of the Elite League. The problem was that it was unclear immediately whether or not the EIHA's ruling executive committee had given their full authority to their chairman's action.

The move infuriated Ice Hockey UK who claimed that the EIHA had no authority to do this. Unfortunately, to our knowledge, no contract exists between the bodies setting out just what they can and can't do. The EIHA is supposedly a 'development league' but their ambitious chairman has been content for the English Premier League teams to employ paid imports.

The Elite League claimed that the Scottish IHA also backed their affiliation. If the SIHA's chairman, **Frank Dempster**, a former Superleague employee, was sympathetic to the EL, his association did not issue a statement. IHUK's chairman, Stuart Robertson, is a member of the SIHA.

NORTHERN IRELAND ICE HOCKEY FEDERATION v BELFAST GIANTS

Despite having only two ice rinks, Belfast has several people who play an influential role in the sport.

On one side was Giants' beleaguered Canadian owner, **Albert Maasland**, who in July 2003 successfully fought off creditors demanding nearly a million pounds. Despite this catastrophe, he remained as one of the driving forces in setting up the Elite League.

On the other side were the NIIHF and its chairman, **John Lyttle**, who sits on the board of IHUK with **Andy Gibson**, who represents the Province's only other rink in Dundonald. They also created the Belfast Ice Warriors and attempted to join the BNL. (See *New Rinks News*.) Mr Lyttle felt moved to issue a press release on 8 July putting the NIIHF firmly on the side of Ice Hockey UK and accusing the EIHA of issuing 'misleading statements'.

In the middle, as it were, was Irishman **Eamon Convery** who is the lucky owner of Superleague's Dublin franchise. Though he's the chairman of the Elite League, he seemed more confused than anybody with the summer's near-farcical goings-on. "Our teams have joined the English Premier League," he told the *Nottingham Evening Post* after Taggart's announcement. "That league is recognised by Ice Hockey UK. What's the problem?"

ELITE QUOTES

Now tell us what you really think

"The BNL appears to be in a downward spiral and if they don't aspire to be more successful then their teams are going nowhere.

"OK, I admit we have made mistakes at Superleague level, mainly that we didn't include enough British players in our teams and we will be putting that right.

"We offered BNL teams the chance to play a cup tournament against Superleague teams and they turned us down, saying they didn't want to lose. They'd only play if we left out half of our imports and brought in British players to give them a chance. That's like Notts County telling Manchester United we won't play you because we will lose - unless you don't bring half your star players. It's that ridiculous.

"But there are some BNL teams with ambition and we want them on board.` We may have to make some amendments but we are not interested in downsizing or dropping down to BNL standard. Our fans will not put up with it.

"With that in mind, we are already looking at bringing in teams from leading European leagues to keep the interest alive. I think our supporters would sooner be watching the likes of Milan rather than Hull or Basingstoke on a Saturday night. We'd sooner be playing to 20 packed houses with a competitive six or seven team league than 30 only half-full - and so would the arena management." **Neil Black**, *the owner of Nottingham Panthers and the driving force behind the formation of the Elite League, in November 2002.*

Why Vipers wouldn't join the Elite

"I ˙ had listened to the arguments and the proposals, and I was all set to sign up when a throwaway line from one of the other directors changed my mind. He said 'You don't want to play the likes of Edinburgh and Hull, do you?' and I got up and walked out because I do want to play Edinburgh and Hull, as well as Nottingham and Sheffield." **Darryl Illingworth**, *owner of Newcastle Vipers.*

Cynical, moi?

'I suspect a thousand years from now, archaeologists will be unearthing a very strange site containing 15 skeletons slumped in a circle, their hands tightly grasped around their neighbours' throats!' *Seen on the web in February 2003 after an ISL/BNL merger rumour.*

Storm over Manchester

"I've not got a clue where we will go from here but I will fight to the death." **Gary Cowan**, *owner of Manchester Storm, on being told by arena operators, SMG Europe, that they were cancelling Storm's next home game as he had not paid the rent.*

...and over the Eagles

"Some players asked **Bob [Zeller]** if, as a wealthy man, he would show a bit of dignity to the players and compensate them. But that is just not going to happen." **Paul Heavey**, *Eagles' coach, after the team's collapse.*

Bad deals at the Odyssey

"They didn't make a cent from parking or the concession stores at the Odyssey. I find it quite incredible that the Giants didn't demand a cut. They're the only club I've been involved with who haven't taken money from these outlets." **Paxton Schulte**, *Belfast Giants, on the financial crisis which enveloped the club in 2003.*

The turning point

"The turning point was two seasons ago when more arena clubs [National Ice Centre and Odyssey Arena] came in throwing their weight about. They were pushing for expansion to go on to greater things. I don't blame them, we just cannot join them." **John Nike**, *owner of Bracknell Bees and a founder member of Superleague, on pulling Bees out of the league.*

BNL is the new Superleague

'This move [to the BNL] should be embraced as being...positive. The product is still good (you will see ex-Superleague players, possibly some of our own), it will include talented British players, it will attract a wider audience, attendances will rise, local rivalry will be back, we will be competing on a more level playing field, televison coverage is posible, you will see good competitive ice hockey, there will be more opposition teams and more excitement.' **Martin Weddell**, *Bracknell Bees' CEO, extolling the virtues of the BNL so hard, you wonder why it took Bees so long to make the move.*

Another view

'It should be remembered that individuals like **John Nike OBE** set up the Ice Hockey Superleague because ice hockey under the auspices of the British Ice Hockey Association was in a complete mess. It needed enlightened people like John Nike to save the sport...' *Bracknell Bees' match night programme..*

Don't need Ice Hockey UK

"We have heard nothing official from Ice Hockey UK about why they have refused to recognise us, but the fact is we don't need to be sanctioned by them. We will be appealing to the International body (IIHF) and if necessary will affiliate directly to them. We want to be part of the IIHF family." **Brian Storey**, *spokesman for the Elite League, on hearing of Ice Hockey UK's decision not to affiliate them.*

Blaze prefer to be rogues

"If the options are rogue league or BNL (and only those) then I will support the rogue league option. The sport has to move forward and improve..." **Grant Charman**, *a director of Elite League founder members, Coventry Blaze.*

US cavalry, er, Taggart to the rescue

"Now we no longer have to worry about affiliation to Ice Hockey UK. We are the Elite Conference of the Premier League." **Neil Black**.
"The affiliation is unambiguous. It is done, set in stone. The EIHA can affiliate and oversee any league it wants to...." **Albert Maasland**, *owner of Belfast Giants [not, the last time we looked, in England - ed.].*

Can't wait

"I haven't looked forward to a new season with so much anticipation for so long - new league, new teams, and for me, coaching new players. September 12 [scheduled date for first Elite League game at Alexandra Palace] can't come quick enough for me. All I can tell both Steelers and Racers fans is that this will be a special night and I am sure one that will announce the Elite League as a strong, stable and exciting league." **Mike Blaisdell**, *coach of Sheffield Steelers, in a press release written by team publicist **Dave Simms** in May 2003.*

World Championships "a holiday"

"At the end of the day, the players are worried about how much they will be paid, not if they go off for two weeks' holiday with Great Britain at the end of the season." **Paul Thompson**, *coach of Elite League club, Coventry Blaze, and former assistant coach of GB, on the problems of signing players if the league is not sanctioned by Ice Hockey UK.*

Never mind the debts, feel the Elite

"It is unfortunate that Giants have made huge losses. But at a time when we are trying to promote the aims of the Elite League in a positive manner, these negative stories really annoy me." **Eamon Convery**, *chairman of the Elite League.*
"It's no secret that all the [Elite League's] directors knew about Belfast. This isn't something new." **Neil Morris**, *owner of Manchester Phoenix.*

The Phoenix arises

"I'm going to be very honest with you...there are no other investors. The two other guys walked away. They read the press, they read what the fans were printing on the websites and they said I would never get the fans back. They said I would never bring commercial sponsors to the table and that hockey was dead in Manchester. So I went to the bank and I borrowed the money. I am the only guy.
"I can tell you something. It won't be long before we've got more than 4,000 hockey fans back in Manchester." **Neil Morris** *owner of Manchester Phoenix, at a meeting in July 2003.*

Never let the facts get in the way...

'London Racers - playing ice hockey since 1936'. *Legend on the home page of the new Elite League team's website, using poetic licence on their 2003 formation. The 1936 team was actually Harringay Racers which played at the long demolished Harringay Arena in Green Lanes and ceased operations in 1958.*
'The London Racers, with hockey roots that date back to 1936, play out of the Alexandra Palace, a historic Victorian recreation centre near Piccadilly Circus that opened in 1873 as The People's Palace. "It's literally a palace they've got a hockey rink in over there," Carr said.' *Romantic view of old London Town from* The Standard, *an Ontario newspaper, quoting Canadian **Gary Carr**, Racers' new coach.*

Loads-a-players

"Hey guys, what's the rush? There's plenty of good hockey players around and signing bus loads is easy." *Carr again, interrupting his California holiday in July 2003 to reassure fans.*

With grateful acknowledgements to the *Coventry Evening Telegraph, The Star* (Sheffield), *Manchester Evening News, Nottingham Evening Post, Hull Daily Mail, Reading Evening Post, Evening Chronicle* (Newcastle), *The Journal* (Newcastle), *South Wales Echo, Belfast Telegraph, Evening Advertiser* (Swindon), *Scottish Sun, The Herald* (Glasgow) and numerous websites..

NEWS ROUND-UP

Ice Hockey UK

Stuart Robertson was voted interim chairman of the sport's governing body on 6 November 2002, following the resignation of his fellow Scot, **Jim Anderson**, due to work commitments.

Mr Robertson is chairman of the SIHA's junior development committee and previously represented the Scottish Ice Hockey Association on the Board. His wife, Aileen, was the SIHA's secretary for many years.

The governing body restructured themselves in June 2003 and confirmed Mr Robertson as chairman. When the body was originally created in 1999, the members of the Board had been elected by votes from every club in the country, senior and junior.

After discussions with UK Sport, it was agreed instead that each regional association (England, Scotland and Northern Ireland) and affiliated league should hold elections for two people to go forward to represent them on the governing body. It was also agreed that the players should have one representative on the Board.

Ice Hockey UK's ten directors are listed under Governing Bodies at the back of the *Annual*. Each body represented has one vote on the Board.

The referees' referee

Ice Hockey UK appointed leading referee **Simon Kirkham** as their new Director of Officiating in October 2002.

An official for 16 years, he will oversee all officiating matters for the governing body. This involves working with the International Ice Hockey Federation and with the chief referees of the senior leagues.

Kirkham, 40, has officiated over 900 league and cup games in the UK, receiving his international licence in 1990. He learned to skate at the age of three at the old Nottingham Ice Stadium and went on to play for their second team, coached by the legendary **Les Strongman**.

Cardiff still be-Devilled

The good news in 2002-03 was that Cardiff Devils got through the season with some success, finishing in mid-table of the British National League and reaching the playoff finals.

The bad news was that the club's ownership went through more turmoil. The take-over by

Chris McSorley soon ran into problems. The workaholic manager-coach of Geneva Eagles doubles as the GB coach and at the time his deal was completed in July 2002, on top of his Geneva duties he was also trying to cope with planning GB's Euro Challenge series, not to mention an addition to his family.

All this persuaded him that he had to hand over responsibility for the day-to-day running of the team to his partner of ten weeks, **Paul McMillan**, with Chris retaining only a nominal one per cent of Devils.

McMillan, 43, who was previously the owner of Peterborough Pirates, understands the game and McSorley's decision proved a wise one. The new man steered Devils through a respectable season and increased their crowds. He was also fortunate in being able to attract former Devils, **Ivan Matulik** and **Stevie Lyle**, back to the WNIR when Manchester Storm collapsed.

THE SQUEALER RULE

Superleague and the BNL, perhaps wisely, have been shy about publicising their use of the 'squealer' rule which we revealed in last year's *Annual*.

Briefly, this encourages players to report, in confidence, suspected breaches of the wage cap by their team. If the breach is proved, the player is entitled to a percentage of the club's fine.

The rule was just one of the methods both leagues have been using to try and police their wage restrictions which, as some fans may have noticed, can be difficult to enforce.

But it didn't last. The club's troubles erupted again at the end of the season when a rift developed between McMillan and the rink's leaseholder whose contract with the club owner 'to run a BNL team' out of the Wales National Ice Rink still had a year to go.

The leaseholder, we should explain, is actually Reds Wales Properties Ltd (RWPL), a company controlled by **Bob Phillips** who ran Devils in Superleague in 2000-01. That team collapsed with heavy debts, infuriating many fans who stayed away the following year.

Phillips, or rather RWPL, bought the club's logo and trademark from McSorley and entered Devils in the new Elite League. Former Devils' favourite, **Shannon Hope**, was appointed director of hockey, and coach **Glen Mulvenna** was retained. McMillan was sidelined.

ENGLAND UNDER-13

The team that won the highly rated Canadian pee-wee tournament in Quebec in February 2003. (*See* Youth Internationals *for full details.*) *left to right, back (standing)*: Brett Perlini, Stephen Lee, James Neil, Danny Moore, Robert Farmer, Tom Duggan, Tom Squires, James Francis, Aaron Nell, Richard Bentham, Ryan Handisides; *front (kneeling)*: Joe Graham, Jamie Milton, Jonathan Tindall, Danny House, Robert Lachowicz, Joe Wiggell, Matthew Davies, Mark Thurman.

Hull Thunder

There was turmoil for the umpteenth time in Hull when the team owner, **Martin Jenkinson**, pulled out in January 2003. Player-coach **Mike Bishop**, captain **Scott Young** and forwards **Paul Ferone**, **Mike Morin** and **Jonathan Weaver** were all sacked with the team's streak of 12 defeats in 16 games being blamed.

Jenkinson with his director, the former player **Mike O'Connor**, had only taken over Thunder at the start of the season after losing his battle to buy Sheffield Steelers. He denied the sackings were a cost-cutting exercise to keep the club going, but admitted he wasn't getting value for money from the Canadians and wanted to introduce more home-grown players.

When Canadians **Eric Lavigne, Marc West** and **Domenic Parlatore** quit, crisis talks were held between the club and the British National League. Sheffield businessman and team sponsor, **Sid Butt**, agreed to underwrite the cost of running the club for the rest of the season and Hull's junior coach, the veteran Durham Wasps player and coach, **Peter (Jonker) Johnson**, was appointed as Thunder's coach.

The team duly completed the season with an entire line-up of British born and trained players. but they won no further games.

At an employment tribunal in July, six Thunder players had their claims for £12,000 in unpaid wages upheld. Drinkprize Ltd, whose directors were Jenkinson and O'Connor, did not contest the proceedings.

Meanwhile, senior ice hockey in Hull was taken over by **Mike** and **Sue Pack**, who renamed the team Stingrays. Mike, a London diamond merchant, and his wife had steered Solihull MK Kings through the 2002-03 BNL season in spite of having the league's smallest crowds of under 400 a game.

Solihull's coach, **Rick Strachan**, a former GB international defenceman and an assistant GB coach, was appointed coach of Stingrays.

Ice hockey on TV

Hockey Night in Canada live! What more could any armchair ice hockey fan want?

Last season's telly was like being back in the Seventies when **Dickie Davies** and ITV's *World of Sport* first brought the NHL to British viewers. There was more NHL hockey than British hockey on the box. At least back then the excuse was that there was very little British hockey to show. Nowadays with all these leagues....

Superleague did a deal for a 30-minute highlights package once a week during the season on *Sky Sports*. Imaginatively entitled *Face Off*, it started on 26 September. Former player **Richard Boprey**, Basingstoke Bison's PR man, and Guildford Flames' player-coach **Stan Marple** were the commentators. Like many viewers, we missed 'Bopes' regular commentating mate, **Paul Ferguson**.

The game tapes were made for the league by a specialist video company, Black Diamond Productions, who sent them to *Sky* for transmission. Some reports put the cost at £10,000 per club for the season. The commentary team were studio-bound.

From our couch the results looked poor and reinforced our long held belief that it's a mistake to economise on TV's presentation of ice hockey. Frankly, ours is not a TV-friendly game and to be done properly it needs a substantial investment of time and money. For the best example, think of those *Sky Sports* shows when *Benson and Hedges* were footing the bill.

LOOK MA, NO GOALS

The scoreless Challenge Cup draw in the MEN Arena on 19 September 2002 was only the third recorded in the top flight of UK ice hockey since 1953.

Storm's **Stevie Lyle** saved 24 shots and his opposite number, **Ryan Bach**, made 32 saves for the visitors, Belfast Giants, in a game that couldn't be settled even after five minutes' overtime.

All three double whitewashes came in the Superleague era.

Moreover, *Face-Off* was designed strictly for Superleague fans and of limited interest to supporters of other leagues' teams, let alone the casual sports viewer. This was a pity as there was no TV coverage anywhere of BNL games. The BNL issued a press release saying that *ITV1* cameras would be at their playoff final on 30 March, but added that it would only be shown as part of a documentary 'a little later in the year'.

The English Premier League's Slough Jets trumped all the other clubs by putting two games on the box in October 2002 - and doing it well. *Sky Sport's SportNation* screened 20 minutes of highlights from Jets' 19 October league game against Swindon Lynx in the Hangar. A week earlier Jets' coach **Warren Rost** and team captain **Rob Coutts** had featured in another 20-minute *SportNation* programme which amply lived up to its billing of 'giving viewers a brief introduction to ice hockey, showing how important sponsorship and junior development are to the sport's success in this country...'

Jets paid the production costs of the two shows with generous assistance from their new sponsor, finance company *Invesco Perpetual*.

Channel 5's weekly live NHL shows (plus every Stanley Cup final game) continued to be the sport's only appearance on terrestrial TV. But from 7 December 2002, they had competition from a new cable and satellite digital station, the **North American Sports Network (NASN)**.

NASN, a 24/7 operation, screened five or six games a week, either live or re-live (that's 'recorded highlights' in British English). The broadcasts came direct from North America with no British analysts in a London studio as at *Channel 5*. However, *NASN* could not show the Stanley Cup final games live as *Channel 5* owned the British screening rights.

NASN more than made up for this by becoming the first TV channel here to show the legendary *Hockey Night in Canada* show, complete with the ebullient **Don (Grapes) Cherry** and his straight man, **Ron MacLean**.

The channel, which is funded by *Microsoft* founder and sports fan **Paul G Allen**, is designed to appeal to the estimated 500,000 expatriate North Americans in the UK and Ireland. But it also has great appeal to all ice hockey fans and the presentation, not to mention the standard of play, poses serious competition to any programmes featuring British games.

The *Annual* was told that *NASN* had 11,000 subscribers by the end of March 2003 and was aiming to have 25,000-30,000 by the end of the year. The company has been active in creating partnerships with various hockey organisations, notably the new Manchester Phoenix club.

NASN is available from £9.99 per month, via *Sky Digital*, *Telewest* and *ntl*.

No more life with the Lions

Matt Bradbury, whose Nottingham Lions won only 35 of 166 league and playoff games under his guidance, resigned at the end of the season.

Bradbury, one of the country's only level 3 coaches, declared that his work and family commitments left him no time to run the English Premier League team. He is employed in the Sports Development Dept at Nottingham's National Ice Centre, Lions' home rink.

He took over the all-British team in 1998 and in their first two seasons, Lions competed in the league's northern conference, winning 13 of their 34 games. When they moved into the state-of-the-art National Ice Centre in 2000, the EIHA allowed them to move up to the Premier League. This league allows teams to use a limited number of overseas players but as Bradbury preferred to ice an entirely 'pure Brit' side, Lions were often beaten by double figures.

"I have always remained committed to my team, my principles and an all-British, professional organisation, even though the team is run on a voluntary basis," he told the club's website (www.lacecitylions.com). "I've always enjoyed coaching and I've always sought to help my players be the best they can be in their hockey careers."

Bradbury's resignation and difficulties with ice time at the NIC (Lions were forced to cancel four home games last season) led to the team not re-applying to the league for the new campaign.

Last trump sounds for Aces

The first ice hockey game at Altrincham was held on 4 February 1961. Just over 42 years later, on 30 March 2003, the last puck was dropped at the Devonshire Road ice rink when the building closed to the public. To mark the sad occasion the rink hosted a four-team Reunion Tournament, in which over 60 players from past and present Altrincham teams took part.

The organisers brought in three players from the original 1961-62 team - **Alan Watson, Harry Todd** and **Johnny Salt** - and among the others who made the nostalgic trip back to the Manchester suburb were **Don Jamieson** who flew in from Spokane, Washington State; **Jeff Epps** from Orillia, Ontario; **Brian Waddington** from Vancouver; **Jon Little** from Houston, Texas; and **Fred Kuster** and **Bruno Gresser** from Switzerland.

Others came from Blackpool, Bradford, Liverpool, Nottingham and Whitley Bay.

Somehow, the rink closure inspired Aces to their best season in years as they qualified for the playoff finals of the English National League. (See *English Leagues* section for details.)

Despite protests from local skaters including British ice dance champion **Nicky Slater**, the Thompson family, who owned the rink, sold the site to *Barratt Homes* for housing.

Sudden death in Varsity Match

Oxford University forward **Mark Sproule** etched his name into the long history of inter-varsity ice hockey rivalry on 15 March 2003 at Peterborough when he scored the winning goal in overtime of the 83rd Varsity Match. This was the first time the century-old contest had gone into sudden death OT.

Sproule's goal at 7:36 of the extra period gave his team a 4-3 victory and wrested the Patton Cup away from Cambridge University who had held the trophy for the last two years. Sproule, an American taking an MBA degree at Templeton College, was voted the game's MVP while Oxford's man of the match was Canadian forward **John Quong**, a politics student at Nuffield College.

The win was the Dark Blues' 55th since the series began in 1900, but only their second since 1997. Cambridge have won 26 games and two have been drawn. (The full list of early results is in *The Ice Hockey Annual 1986-87*.)

The ceremonial face-off was conducted by the Canadian High Commissioner, the **Rt. Hon Mel Cappe**.

• *The Annual is grateful to* **Prof. Bill Harris**, *the Cambridge coach, for these details of the game.*

■ Oxford's **Joy Tottman** was the star of the women's Varsity Match as Oxford University beat Cambridge 9-1, writes *Lee Power*. Defender Tottman was named player of the match after netting twice in the first period as Oxford raced into a 4-0 lead. The 20-year-old, who is studying Politics and Philosophy at New College, is probably better known to fans as the only female linesman in senior ice hockey. She was down to referee in this year's Women's World Championships before it was cancelled.

■ The solid silver trophy awarded to Cambridge University for their 1913 Varsity Match triumph has been presented to the Hockey Hall of Fame in Toronto after being found in the attic of one of the player's sons.

RECORDS

When Belfast Giants beat the Bees 11-3 in a Superleague game in Bracknell on 22 September, several records were set -

- Eleven was the highest number of goals ever scored in a game by the Giants and equalled the league record for goals by an away team,

- The eight-goal winning margin was the highest in Giants' short history and matched Cardiff's record 11-3 win at Manchester in January 1997.

- **Paxton Schulte**'s and **Rod Stevens**' hat-tricks were the first time two Giants' players have scored these in one game.

CREDIT SUISSE FIRST BOSTON SUMMER CUP

Rich man's plaything

London Arena, 15-18 August 2002.

Teams: **Berlin Eisbären (Polar Bears) and Hamburg Freezers** (German DEL), **Geneva Eagles** (Switzerland), **Sparta Prague** (Czech Rep.) **Stockholm Hammarby** (Sweden), **London Knights**.

American billionaire, **Phil Anschutz**, the owner of six European sides, brought them all to London Arena on a long, hot weekend in August 2002 for nine games watched by around 5,000 people a day for four days.

Perhaps only the head of the huge transatlantic corporation, Anschutz Entertainment Group, could have persuaded a merchant bank and similar blue-chip businesses to sponsor a glorified four-day training camp for his players.

As the annual event was held a week earlier than usual due to London Arena's non-availability, Knights had only 13 players and had to borrow six - four from their opponents plus **Boe Leslie**, a son of Knights' coach, **Bob Leslie**. Knights lost all their three games and finished last. Czech Extraleague winners, Sparta Prague, retained the trophy they won a year earlier in Geneva. Player of the tournament was Geneva goalie, **Reto Pavoni**. Full results:

15 Aug	Hamburg-Geneva	1-2ot
	Berlin-Prague	0-3
16 Aug	Geneva-Stockholm	3-1
	London-Prague	0-2
17 Aug	Stockholm-Hamburg	0-3
	London-Berlin	3-4

Knights' goal scorers: Ahlroos, Kolesar, B Leslie.

18 Aug Playoffs

5th place	London-Stockholm	0-4
3rd place	Berlin-Hamburg	3-2
1st place	Geneva-Prague	2-3

London Knights
Trevor Robins, Dave Trofimenkoff; Ritchie Bronilla, Gerad Adams, Sean Blanchard, Chris Slater, Maurizio Mansi; Kim Ahlroos, Mark Kolesar, Ian McIntyre, Vezio Sacratini, Paul Rushforth, Nate Leslie, Jeff Hoad. *Guests:* Boe Leslie; Chris Snell (Frankfurt); Alexander Barta, Martin Hoffman, Florian Katz (Berlin); Roman Vondracek (Prague).

■ Geneva coach, **Chris McSorley**, was unable to attend the games as he was in Canada acting as best man at the wedding of his brother, **Marty McSorley**.

■ This tournament marked **Trevor Robins'** last appearance. The goalie was forced to pull out with a recurrence of his knee problems which three operations had only succeeded in worsening. 'Robbo', who was once described as the best netminder in Europe, later returned to the States and retired from playing.

■ In the summer of 2003, AEG announced that as part of the 'restructure of their European investments' they would not be organising any further pre-season tournaments.

BT BROADBAND BELFAST ICE CUP

Swedes win Irish trophy

Belfast Giants won only one of their three games - a 2-1 revenge victory over Swedish second league side, Troja Lungby - in their pre-season tournament at the Odyssey Arena. Giants lost to 5-4 to Troja in Sweden at the start of their inaugural season.

Final standings - Södertälje 6 pts, Mulhouse 4 pts, **Giants** 2 pts, Troja Ljungby 0 pts.

Results -

| Fri 30 Aug | Mulhouse-Södertälje | 0-7 |
| | **Giants**-Troja Ljungby | 2-1 |

Sat 31 Aug	**Giants**-Mulhouse	1-3
	Troja Ljungby-Södertälje	1-6
Sun 1 Sep	Mulhouse-Troja Ljungby	3-1
	Södertälje-**Giants**	3-0

ENORDIA CUP, BREMERHAVEN

Bees win first trophy of season

With just 12 regular squad players, **Enio Sacilotto**'s Bracknell Bees upset the odds by winning the Enordia Cup in Bremerhaven, Germany in August 2002. *Results:*

BREMERHAVEN-BEES **7-5**
Bees' goal scorers: Darren Hurley, Ceman 2; Peddle, Arkiomaa, Spring.

ISERLOHN ROOSTERS-BEES **1-1ot**
Dan Ceman scored Bees' goal and Corey Spring had the winning penalty shot.

■ Belfast Giants' coach, **Dave Whistle**, joined Iserlohn as coach at the end of the season.

Overseas visitors

PRINCETON UNIVERSITY

The famous American university, the Alma Mater of Guildford Flames' owner, **John Hepburn**, toured from 15-19 December 2002, losing all three games. Princeton play in Division One of the NCAA, the top level of US college hockey.

PANTHERS-PRINCETON UN **5-2**
Panthers' goal scorers: Hadden, Elders 2; Paek.
On the 18th, Princeton were beaten 4-3 by Flames and a day later were trounced 7-3 by Cardiff Devils.

CANTON UNIVERSITY ALL STARS

The New York team lost all three games against English Premier League sides, including Romford where they played in 2001.

2 Jan **MILTON KEYNES-CANTON UN** **11-0**
Lightning's leading goal scorers: Nick Poole 3; Ross Bowers, Gary Clarke 2.

6 Jan **ROMFORD RAIDERS-CANTON UN** **7-1**
Raiders' leading goal scorer: Jamie Randall 4.

7 Jan **P'BORO' PHANTOMS-CANTON UN** **5-3**
Phantoms' goal scorers: Duncan Cook 2, Doug McEwen, Shaun Yardley and Craig Britton.

We apologise to readers for the absence of our regular Slap Shot column. We hope you agree that there is quite enough punch-ups described elsewhere in this year's Annual without us detailing all the dirty deeds committed on the ice as well.

RINK ATTENDANCES

OVERALL PICTURE	2002-03	ATTENDANCE		2001-02	AVE. DIFF.
	TOTAL	GAMES	AVERAGE	AVERAGE	ON 2001-02
SUPERLEAGUE					
*League	340,944	94	3,627	3,594	No diff.
*Challenge Cup	88,839	24	3,702	4,192	Diff. format
Playoffs	134,937	40	3,373	2,909	Up 16%
Playoff Finals	18,855	3	6,285	7,005	Down 10%
Ahearne Trophy	26,009	10	2,600	2,893	Down 10%
TOTALS	609,584	171	3,565	3,542	No diff.
FINDUS BRITISH NATIONAL LEAGUE					
League	236,924	180	1,316	1,020	Up 29%.
Playoffs	44,492	30	1,483	1,512	Down 1.9%
Findus Cup	64,549	44	1,467	924	Up 58%
TOTALS	345,965	254	1,362	1,049	Up 30%
ENGLISH NATIONAL LEAGUE					
Premier Division	110,734	223	496	430	Up 15%
Playoffs	15,981	26	615	508	Up 21%
TOTALS	126,715	249	509	440	Up 16%
GRAND TOTALS	1,082,264	674	1,606	1,739	Down 7.6%

* Includes games played by Scottish Eagles and Manchester Storm.

THE TOP LEAGUE CROWD-PULLERS			2002-03 LEAGUE	ATTENDANCE Total Average+		2001-02 Average	Notes/ Changes
1	(1)	Belfast Giants	Super	89,705	5,277	6,071	Down 13%
2	(4)	Sheffield Steelers	Super	81,018	4,766	4,038	Up 18%
3	(2)	Nottingham Panthers	Super	79,116	4,654	4,374	Up 6.4%
4	(5)	London Knights	Super	56,056	3,115	3,149	No diff.
5	(7)	Coventry Blaze	BNL	36,783	2,043	1,724	Up 18.5%
6	(-)	Newcastle Vipers	BNL	33,867	1,882	--	New club
7	(8)	Fife Flyers	BNL	29,595	1,644	1,650	No diff.
8	(11)	Guildford Flames	BNL	29,236	1,624	1,558	Up 4.2%
9	(-)	Cardiff Devils	BNL	26,652	1,481	534	2,224 in 00-01.
10	(10)	Dundee Stars	BNL	26,418	1,468	1,607	Down 8.6%
11	(9)	Bracknell Bees	Super	22,098	1,381	1,612	Down 14.3%
12	(12)	Basingstoke Bison	BNL	22,394	1,244	1,130	Up 10%
13	(13	Milton Keynes Kings	EPL	22,941	1,092	1,095	In BNL 01-02.

List includes teams that averaged at least 1,000 fans to league games only (excluding playoffs). Last season's position in brackets.
+ Home games - Superleague teams each played 17, except Bracknell (16) and London (18); British National League (BNL) teams played 18; Milton Keynes (EPL) played 21. Superleague totals include Manchester Storm (3) and Scottish Eagles (2). Storm drew 9,916 fans for an average of 3,305; Eagles attracted 3,035, average 1,518.
Figures are based on the leagues' own media information releases.

NOTES
The crowds following the top 15 clubs dropped below one million (955,549) for the first time since 1991-92. The most successful competition was the *Findus* Cup, the sport's only fully sponsored event, where the fan following swelled by 58 per cent over the previous year.

NEW RINKS NEWS

13 new rinks? - lucky for some

BY THE EDITOR

Much as last year, several large arenas are planned but most of them seem unlikely to come to fruition for a few years yet.

But before I get to them, I'm delighted to record that one new rink actually opened this year, in **SHEFFIELD**. Another one? Just because the sports minister lives up there.

All right, I'm only jealous because my home city of Brighton has no rink at all, while *iceSheffield* has two ice pads (both Olympic size) in a city which already has a arena as well as the Queen's Road rink.

The £15.7m development opened on 21 May 2003 with most of the cost coming from Sports Lottery funding through Sport England. With one rink seating 1,500 and the other 500 and located only a few hundred yards from the *Hallam FM Arena*, it will be Steelers' practice rink as well as home for the Queen's Road Scimitars and junior and women's teams.

For more, go to www.icesheffield.co.uk.

Allan Moore, John Lyttle and **Andy Gibson**, the men behind the BNL's Ice Warriors, have plans for a unique project in the grounds of the King's Hall, **BELFAST**. The trio rented the site in 2003 and intend to import £1 million's worth of refrigeration equipment from the USA.

The unique bit comes from the building which will be a £1 million inflatable air dome previously used by the Royal Ulster Agricultural Society for the annual Balmoral Show. The dome - which will hold up to 1,900 people - will be a permanent erection and the 60 x 30 metres rink will be the first of its kind in Europe.

Warriors appointed former Slough Jet, **Joe Stefan**, as coach and were hoping to play their first BNL games there from October 2003. But though they obtained outline planning permission for the dome there were a number of planning requirements still to be fulfilled and the Ice Warriors' face-off had to be postponed until season 2004-05. Go to www.belfasticewarriors.com for the latest news.

Lambeth Council has granted planning permission for the development of a new ice rink, swimming pool and sports centre in **STREATHAM**, the magazine *Leisure Opportunities* reported in February 2003.

The project, by developers Tesco, also includes a supermarket, homes and community facilities. The scheme allows for the existing ice rink to remain open until the new one, being built on the site of the old Streatham bus garage, is ready for use.

Meanwhile, **Adam Goldstone**, son of the former Redskins' manager, **Alec Goldstone**, has revived the senior team and entered them in the English National League South for 2003-04.

The **CAMBRIDGE** alumni magazine reported in June 2003 that a new £6 million complex with an Olympic-sized rink and curling sheets was being planned for Cambourne, seven miles from Cambridge city centre. Our university correspondent, **Prof. Bill Harris**, told us that the South Cambridge District Council weren't happy with it there so they were working on a site on the northern edge of Cambridge itself which, he said, "almost certainly will get permission".

Regular readers of the *Annual* will recall that £1 million was left in the will of **David Gattiker**, a 1930s Cambridge Blue, specifically for a rink. That was about six years ago. Reminds you of that classic movie about the million-pound note, doesn't it?

Our list of planned arenas keeps growing. To recap, we have the 25,000-seater in **LONDON**'s Millennium Dome, the seven-year-old plans for a Sports Village in **CARDIFF BAY**, and a 5,000-seater in **SOUTHAMPTON**. To this lot, we can now add -

BIRKENHEAD A £300 million project on a 67-acre site on the Wirral includes a 4,000-capacity arena - which has already received backing from *Sony Entertainment* - plus an indoor ski slope, a skating rink and other leisure facilities, possibly including a new ground for Tranmere Rovers football club.

BRIGHTON Fans of a certain age will be going "Yea, yea. Heard it all before." But stay with me, it gets better. I'm one of a group of people who were brought together by the late **Alan Weeks**, the BBC commentator and secretary of Brighton Tigers. We put in a tender to Brighton and Hove City council for a multi-purpose, twin-pad arena on the lines of Nottingham's National Ice Centre to be built on the seafront next to Brighton Marina, at an estimated cost of £45 million.

A NEW HOME FOR BRIGHTON TIGERS?

Yes, we know it's only an artist's impression, sorry, computer-generated image, but this is how the Brighton International Arena could look on the seafront opposite the beautiful old Regency buildings. The inside is modelled on the twin rinks of Nottingham's National Ice Centre.

The group is particularly fortunate to include **Jayne Torvill** and **Robin Cousins**. Both Olympic gold medal winners live in Sussex, Robin actually in Brighton where he takes an active role in the community.

The council were also considering another tender for the same site but it seemed, unofficially, that ours was the favourite. We'd be grateful if you'd cross your fingers for us, but as this is the umpteenth ice rink project in Brighton since Tigers' home, the Sports Stadium, closed in 1965, please don't hold your breath.

BRISTOL The city is planning a £60 million complex on a 14-acre site near Temple Meads station including a 10,000-seat indoor arena for concerts, major shows, exhibitions and sports.

CROYDON Plans to redevelop a 8.6-acre site opposite East Croydon station with a mixed-use scheme have been revived (see *The Ice Hockey Annual 1997-98*) and a planning application was due to be lodged with the local authority in July 2003. Included in the project is a £50 million, 12,500-seat arena.

GREAT BLAKENHAM is in Suffolk where the folk behind Thorpe Park amusement centre are planning to build a vast winter sports complex with everything from ski lodges and a snow dome (whatever that is) to a hotel and golf course.

There will be a twin pad ice rink with one of them seating 5,000 people. The complex is called a Snoasis. No groaning at the back there, please.

HOUNSLOW The West London borough want to redevelop the 34-acre Feltham Arena site. One of the three schemes they are considering includes a 4,000-8,000 capacity indoor arena with an ice pad, a five-a-side football pitch, basketball court and gymnasium.

ISLE OF MAN Provided £1 million can be found to cover various fees, a £40 million redevelopment of the Summerland site, including a 'dual use ice rink and five-a-side football facility' could be completed by 2007.

■ **DUBLIN** Superleague's Dublin Druids never found a home. The proposed multi-million, multi-sports Sports Campus Ireland was ditched by the Irish government a few weeks after they were re-elected in the autumn of 2002.

In August 2003, the *Annual* spoke to Elite League chairman **Eamon Convery**, one of those behind the Druids, but he declined to comment on their plans. The government remains keen on building a national stadium but wants a 'major contribution' from the business sector. It is unclear if Mr Convery and his American partner **Burke McHugh**, a real estate developer who lives in Eire, will invest in the project.

every

kick-off,
facial and put out
every **hail mary**
dunk and **shunt**
every no-look, high sider
and
suicide squeeze
every clutch hit, every cross-check
every **power play**

SEE EVERY PLAY, EVERY DAY - LIVE ON NASN.

NASN is a digital television channel dedicated to North American sports, every minute of every day. You can watch at least 15 live and delayed games every week including the National Hockey League, Major League Baseball, College Football, NASCAR and College Basketball, plus original sports news, highlights and talk shows direct from the USA. The best from over there, now over here.

SUBSCRIBE NOW:
Sky channel 420
08708 50 30 30
ntl:home channel 917
0800 052 2000
(+44 outside the UK)
www.nasn.com

EVERY PLAY, EVERY DAY

NASN
NORTH AMERICAN SPORTS NETWORK

Major Teams 2002~03

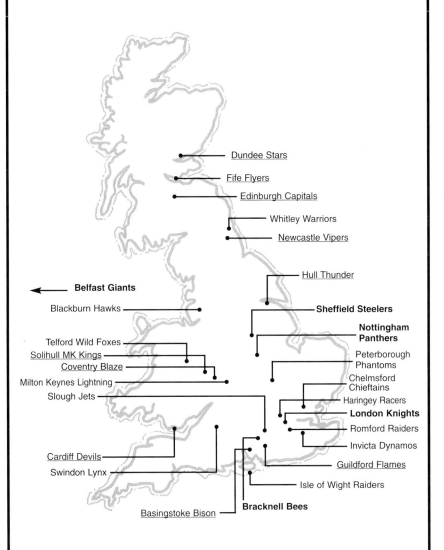

Dundee Stars
Fife Flyers
Edinburgh Capitals
Whitley Warriors
Newcastle Vipers
Hull Thunder
Belfast Giants
Blackburn Hawks
Sheffield Steelers
Nottingham Panthers
Telford Wild Foxes
Solihull MK Kings
Coventry Blaze
Milton Keynes Lightning
Peterborough Phantoms
Chelmsford Chieftains
Haringey Racers
London Knights
Romford Raiders
Slough Jets
Invicta Dynamos
Cardiff Devils
Swindon Lynx
Guildford Flames
Isle of Wight Raiders
Bracknell Bees
Basingstoke Bison

Superleague   <u>British National League</u>   English/Scottish Leagues

BASINGSTOKE BISON

PLAYER	ALL COMPETITIONS					FINDUS BRITISH NATIONAL LEAGUE					PLAYOFFS				
Scorers	GP	G	A	Pts	Pim	GP	G	A	Pts	Pim	GP	G	A	Pts	Pim
Peter Campbell (I)	49	29	33	62	90	35	24	27	51	62	6	3	2	5	8
Mike Ellis	49	33	27	60	60	35	23	22	45	54	6	4	1	5	2
Chris Crombie	50	21	34	55	94	36	16	26	42	74	6	0	4	4	6
Steve Moria	38	25	23	48	26	31	23	20	43	18	6	2	2	4	6
Daryl Lavoie (I)	42	8	38	46	162	28	4	26	30	118	6	2	4	6	18
Neil Liddiard	47	4	27	31	86	33	3	20	23	54	6	0	4	4	4
Paul Berrington	39	10	20	30	80	29	7	11	18	64	2	0	0	0	6
Nick Cross	48	8	20	28	50	34	7	14	21	34	6	0	2	2	4
Marc Levers	50	12	7	19	34	36	6	6	12	20	6	2	0	2	6
Matt Cote	49	2	14	16	50	35	2	12	14	42	6	0	2	2	0
Dwight Parrish (WP) 1	31	5	10	15	38	25	5	8	13	30	6	0	2	2	8
AJ Kelham	14	8	5	13	4	6	2	0	2	2					
Ryan Aldridge	48	3	10	13	44	36	3	8	11	28	4	0	0	0	0
Benoit Cotnoir (WP)	17	0	9	9	36	11	0	6	6	30					
Joe Greener	45	4	2	6	18	31	3	2	5	14	6	1	0	1	0
Peter Nyman	5	0	2	2	0	5	0	2	2	0					
Scott Hay (N) (I)	49	0	2	2	36	36	0	2	2	10	5	0	0	0	2
Bench Penalties					8					6					2
TEAM TOTALS	50	172	283	455	916	36	128	212	340	660	6	14	23	37	72
Netminders	GPI	Mins	SOG	GA	Sv%	GPI	Mins	SOG	GA	Sv%	GPI	Mins	SOG	GA	Sv%
David Ryde	1	12	13	1	92.3						1	12	13	1	92.3
Scott Hay	49	2912	1564	154	90.2	36	2136	1112	112	89.9	5	300	155	16	89.7
Dean Skinns	4	112	71	12	83.1	2	60	32	7	78.1	1	48	37	5	86.5
Empty Net Goals			1	1									1	1	
TEAM TOTALS	50	3036	1649	168	89.8	36	2196	1144	119	89.6	6	360	206	23	88.8

Also appeared: Ashley Skinns 40; Nicky Watts 15; David McGill 7; Mark Richardson, Luke Piggot, James Hutchinson 1.

Also played for: 1 Manchester Storm

All Competitions = league, playoffs and Findus Cup

BASINGSTOKE BISON *left to right, back row:* Glen Wells (medic), Tony Skinns (equipment), Ashley Skinns, Peter Campbell, Joe Greener, Peter Nyman, Chris Crombie, Nick Cross, Dwight Parrish, Marc Levers, Alan Parrott (equipment), Charlie Colon (director of hockey); *front row:* Scott Hay, Neil Liddiard, Steve Moria (player-coach), Ryan Aldridge, Mike Ellis, Matt Cote, Daryl Lavoie, Paul Berrington, Dean Skinns.
Photo: David Taylor

'Mo' rides Herd (and the exercise bike)

GRAHAM MERRY

Steve (Mo) Moria's rookie season as *Wella* Bison's coach was a mixed one with his team repeating their credible fourth place in the British National League but missing out on the Playoffs and the later stages of the *Findus* Cup.

The former GB international forward took on the coaching challenge when he joined the club from Superleague's Nottingham Panthers after **Charlie Colon** moved up to become *Planet Ice*'s director of ice hockey. (Mo's previous coaching experience was in 1993-94 with the Blackburn Hawks.) He didn't give up the playing side, though, as he only turned 42 during the season and, anyway, he didn't want to put the local gym out of business.

As it turned out, the physio went on to overtime soon after the season started. In the opening *Findus* Cup game against Guildford Flames Moria suffered a knee injury after a check from **David Clarke** forced him out of the competition and the first three league games.

BURNT BY THE BLAZE

While **A J Kelham** and assistant coach **Peter Nyman** covered for him on the ice, the Herd made an early exit from the Cup for the first time in years. After a slow start in the league, Mo strengthened his defence by bringing in out-of-work Superleague defenceman **Dwight Parrish** from Manchester Storm and releasing new import **Benoit Cotnoir**.

January brought plenty of excitement. The most thrilling game of the season came on the 4th when high-riding Coventry Blaze came to *Planet Ice* only for Bison to lose a heart-breaker 2-1 in overtime. And on the 26th, defenceman **Neil Liddiard** set a club record of seven assists in the 13-3 humbling of Thunder in Hull.

The next month Moria, again, and defenceman **Daryl Lavoie** were injured in a challenge game against nearby Superleague side, Bracknell Bees. With another blueliner, **Scott Campbell**, out sick the Herd crashed at home to Guildford, ruining their chances of third spot. But they bounced back to win their last three league games, including their first defeat of the Stars in Dundee, and clinched fourth.

Yet another injury, this time to **Ryan Aldridge**, the release of GB forward **Paul Berrington**, and a punishing schedule of four games in the first eight days, brought their early dismissal from the Playoffs with just one win.

PLAYER AWARDS

Players' Player	**Mike Ellis**
Coach's Player	**Joe Greener**
Captain's Player	**Ryan Aldridge**
Supporters Club Player	**Matt Cote**
Most Improved British Player	**Joe Greener**
Basingstoke Gazette's Player	**Joe Greener**

LEADING PLAYERS

Peter Campbell *born 7 September 1979*
The club's top points scorer from Gloucester, Ontario showed a great work ethic and never lost his motivation even when the team was losing.

Joe Greener *born 2 February 1987*
The England under-16 captain made an unexpected impact, earning regular shifts on the team's all-British forward line and standing up to the league's big boys.

Daryl Lavoie *born 10 January 1974*
One of the league's best offensive defencemen was a joy to watch with his silky smooth skills and no-nonsense approach. A vital link to the forwards, he was a key member of the powerplay unit.

FACT FILE 2002-03

British National League:	Fourth
Playoffs:	Third in qr-final group
***Findus* Cup:**	Third in qr-final group

HISTORY

Founded 1988 as Beavers. Name changed to Bison in May 1995.

Leagues British National League 1998-2003; Superleague 1996-98; British League, Premier Div 1993-96; British League, Div One 1990-93; English League 1988-90.

Honours: British League, Div One & playoffs 1992-93; English League (promotion) playoffs 1989-90. *Benson and Hedges* Plate 1999-2000 & 2000-01.

I'M A HOCKEY PLAYER, GET ME OUTTA OF HERE!
Belfast Giants' fast and fearless forward **STEVE THORNTON** finds the downside of 'crashing the net' as he has to be helped back into play by London Knights' goalie **Ake Lilljebjorn** during the final of the Superleague Playoff Championship. *Photo*: Tony Boot

BELFAST GIANTS

PLAYER	ALL COMPETITIONS					SUPERLEAGUE					PLAYOFFS				
Scorers	GP	G	A	Pts	Pim	GP	G	A	Pts	Pim	GP	G	A	Pts	Pim
Kory Karlander (WP)	56	24	30	54	87	29	9	13	22	47	18	12	12	24	24
Kevin Riehl (WP)	57	14	39	53	10	31	11	17	28	4	18	3	14	17	4
Robby Sandrock (WP)	59	11	38	49	100	32	6	24	30	24	18	3	12	15	52
Paxton Schulte (WP)	51	21	23	44	163	26	13	11	24	107	18	7	9	16	48
Ryan Kuwabara (WP)	42	20	21	41	28	19	4	11	15	13	18	13	8	21	15
Rod Stevens	58	21	16	37	16	32	11	6	17	12	18	9	8	17	2
Rob Stewart	59	8	28	36	38	32	5	17	22	20	18	3	10	13	10
Paul Kruse	51	9	26	35	165	25	5	13	18	92	18	3	9	12	53
Dave Matsos	56	15	18	33	14	32	11	11	22	12	18	4	6	10	0
Colin Ward	59	14	17	31	30	32	7	10	17	22	18	4	6	10	6
Steve Thornton	33	9	20	29	10	15	5	6	11	6	18	4	14	18	4
Doug Macdonald	46	14	13	27	72	32	11	10	21	30	5	1	0	1	12
Lee Sorochan (WP)	52	3	19	22	190	31	2	12	14	99	12	1	2	3	49
Shane Johnson (WP)	57	8	12	20	100	32	3	10	13	51	16	2	2	4	37
Todd Kelman	57	5	13	18	72	32	2	5	7	32	16	0	6	6	16
Curtis Bowen	39	8	8	16	86	26	6	7	13	66	6	2	0	2	4
Colin Ryder (N)	14	0	2	2	0	8	0	1	1	0	3	0	0	0	0
Ryan Bach (N)	45	0	2	2	20	24	0	1	1	14	15	0	1	1	6
Mark Cavallin (N) 1	1	0	0	0	0	1	0	0	0	0					
Bench Penalties					16					12					0
TEAM TOTALS	59	204	345	549	1217	32	111	185	296	663	18		71	119	190	342

Netminders	GPI	Min	SOG	GA	Sv%	GPI	Min	SOG	GA	Sv%	GPI	Min	SOG	GA	Sv%
Mark Cavallin 1	1	60	42	1	97.6	1	60	42	1	97.6					
Ryan Bach	45	2720	1404	101	92.8	24	1436	717	57	92.1	15	913	503	30	94.0
Colin Ryder	14	819	414	34	91.8	8	459	243	19	92.2	3	180	86	8	90.7
Empty Net Goals			2	2				1	1				1	1	
TEAM TOTALS	59	3599	1862	138	92.6	32	1955	1003	78	92.2	18	1093	590	39	93.4

Also played for: 1 Scottish Eagles

Shutouts: Bach (3) - cup: 19 Sept at Manchester Storm (32 saves)

league: 22 Jan v Nottingham Panthers (28)

playoff semi-final: 5 Apr v Sheffield Steelers (at Nottingham) (31)

All Competitions = league, playoffs, Challenge Cup and Ahearne Trophy

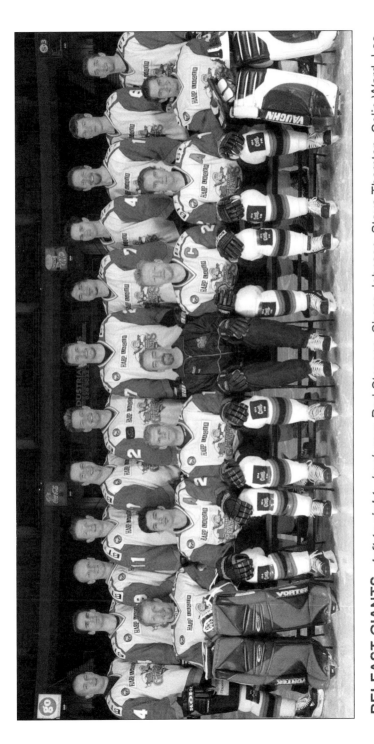

BELFAST GIANTS *left to right, back row:* Rod Stevens, Shane Johnson, Steve Thornton, Colin Ward, Lee Sorochan, Curtis Bowen, Paxton Schulte, Ryan Kuwabara, Todd Kelman, Kory Karlander, Robby Sandrock, Kevin Riehl; *front row:* Ryan Bach, Dave Matsos, Rob Stewart, Dave Whistle (coach), Paul Kruse, Doug Macdonald, Colin Ryder.

Photo: Michael Cooper.

Giants step up

STUART McKINLEY

Belfast Giants' 2002-03 season mirrored that of Superleague itself - an expectant start followed by a winter of discontent, culminating in an exciting end which brought some success.

Much was expected from coach **Dave Whistle**'s side after they had run away with the league title in 2002. He added experience in **Ryan Bach**, **Lee Sorochan**, **Doug MacDonald** and 400-game NHL veteran **Paul Kruse**, who was snapped up after he had led Sheffield Steelers to the 2002 Playoff title. Fans' favourite **Kory Karlander** returned after a season's break.

The defence of their league title started inconsistently with their record winning score - 11-3 in Bracknell - being followed by a four-game losing streak, including a 4-2 defeat by London Knights, the first loss at the Odyssey in almost a year.

On 24 October Manchester Storm played their last ever game in Belfast and, as the league began to crumble so, too, did Belfast as injuries hit hard. But their form was reversed in the Continental Cup semi-final round at the Odyssey as they swept into the Super Final unbeaten.

The roller-coaster went on a downswing again as Giants failed to qualify for the Challenge Cup final afer being able to muster only 12 fit skaters for the semi against Nottingham Panthers.

Whatever Whistle bought his players for Christmas - apart from a new team-mate in GB international forward, **Steve Thornton**, previously at London and Cardiff - it paid dividends. Two defeats by Panthers were the only post-festive league games that failed to go Giants' way as they pushed Steelers all the way to the wire only to lose out by a point.

Although they lost two of their three games in the Continental Cup Super Final in Lugano, Switzerland, they still came a creditable sixth. The experience stood them in good stead as they lost only four games out of 31 after returning from Switzerland. The run ensured that Giants qualified comfortably for the Playoff finals where they saw off Sheffield in a shoot-out before beating Knights in the final for the second trophy in their short history.

By losing their league title by only one point, claiming the Playoff Championship and reaching the last eight in the Continental Cup, Giants' season was arguably more successful than the previous one.

At the end of the season - sadly - Whistle, the unquestioned architect of Giants' productive campaigns, announced that he would be joining a German Elite League (DEL) team.

PLAYERS AWARDS

Most Valuable Player	**Rob Sandrock**
Players' Player	**David Matsos**
Coach's Player	**Rob Stewart**

LEADING PLAYERS

Ryan Bach *born 21 October 1973*

The void left by **Mike Bales** was always going to be hard to fill but he managed it capably. From his debut in the Belfast Ice Cup to his match-winning displays during the Playoff finals weekend, he was outstanding.

Rob Sandrock *born 10 March 1978*

A great find by coach Whistle, the defenceman won over the fans with his shoot-on-sight policy when moving up from the blueline. The Sandrock Slapshot became a well-known ploy as he ripped long distance shots into the net and finished as the club's third highest scorer.

Paxton Schulte *born 16 July 1972*

The team's leading league goal scorer, winning a place on the Writers' second All-Star team, the winger proved once again to be more than just the goon some have labelled him.

FACT FILE 2002-03

Superleague:	Runners-up
Playoffs:	Champions
Challenge Cup:	Semi-Finalists

HISTORY

Founded: 2000.
Leagues: Superleague 2000-03.
Honours: Playoff Champions 2002-03; Superleague 2001-02.

BLACKBURN HAWKS

PLAYER	ALL COMPETITIONS					ENGLISH NATIONAL LEAGUE				
Scorers	GP	G	A	Pts	Pim	GP	G	A	Pts	Pim
Bobby Haig	30	37	39	76	24	18	27	29	56	10
Christopher Black	25	13	30	43	150	15	10	18	28	105
Gordon Whyte	28	12	29	41	36	18	6	20	26	34
David Sheffield	30	20	16	36	20	18	9	14	23	8
Craig Sharman	21	21	11	32	50	14	15	11	26	34
Michael Brunton	27	16	13	29	22	17	15	12	27	16
Neal Haworth	29	7	20	27	108	18	5	13	18	92
Jamie Thomson	21	4	13	17	128	14	4	10	14	95
Wesley Barrett	18	3	13	16	89	11	3	11	14	61
Wayne Slater	14	6	8	14	28	9	5	7	12	22
Eddie Cooper	24	6	4	10	20	17	6	3	9	12
Adam Leaver	18	3	5	8	4	11	1	4	5	2
Peter Tapp	23	4	2	6	64	15	4	2	6	30
Colin Downie (N)	27	0	6	6	18	17	0	4	4	8
Adam Fuller	19	3	1	4	6	12	3	0	3	0
Peter Norgate	27	2	2	4	8	17	2	1	3	4
Scott Barnett	21	1	3	4	26	14	1	1	2	18
Andrew Sheffield	27	1	2	3	20	15	1	1	2	8
Lance Derbyshire	19	2	0	2	24	12	2	0	2	22
Jason Fitton	17	1	1	2	10	11	0	1	1	10
Craig Anscough	2	1	0	1	2	1	0	0	0	2
Mark Arnone	1	0	1	1	0					
Anthony Kinder	2	0	1	1	6	1	0	1	1	4
David Williams	3	0	0	0	4	1	0	0	0	4
Bench Penalties					4					4
TEAM TOTALS	30	163	220	383	871	18	119	163	282	605
Netminders	GPI	Mins	SOG	GA	Sv%	GPI	Mins	SOG	GA	Sv%
Colin Downie	26	1450	923	134	85.5	16	922	568	77	86.4
Robbie Smith	9	330	212	33	84.4	4	158	52	4	92.3
Nick Howard	1	20	19	0	100.0	0	0	0	0	0.0
TEAM TOTALS	30	1800	1154	167	85.5	18	1080	620	81	86.9

Also appeared: Ricci Hulme 5; Daniel Fearon, Matt Southall 2; Chris Kelly,
Danny Armstrong, Steve Hetherington 1.

All Competitions = league, Premier Cup and Northern Cup

The young ones

JIM GILDA

Blackburn Hawks' steady improvement continued when they only narrowly failed to clinch a playoff slot in the English National League North.

Their positive play attracted many new spectators with bigger crowds watching the Hawks than many higher league teams.

Player-coach **Bobby Haig** made one new signing, **Chris Black**, a hard hitting forward who had previously iced for Birmingham Rockets, Nottingham Lions and Dumfries. Haig, Black, **Michael Brunton**, 19-year-old rookie **David Sheffield** and **Craig Sharman** provided most of the side's goal scoring.

Defencemen **Gordon Whyte** and **Neal Haworth** chipped in a few from the blue line, while sharing their defensive duties with **Eddie Cooper**, David's twin **Andy Sheffield** and **Peter Tapp**.

A lack of consistency, particularly away from home, was one of the main reasons for Hawks' missing out on the playoffs. The trend started in their first league game when they were 5-4 up with two minutes to play at Kingston Jets but let it slip to lose 6-5.

A home victory over Whitley was followed by consecutive home defeats to the league's two best sides, Sheffield Scimitars and Altrincham Aces, but they were Hawks' only lapses in their own arena.

All changed with the Northern Cup game at home to Sheffield, when Hawks became the first team to dent Scimitars' 100 per cent record. The 6-6 draw, with Hawks remarkably coming from behind five times, was just reward for their efforts. The fighting spirit and enthusiasm of their youngsters rubbed off on the senior players and galvanised the team back in league competition where five consecutive victories brought them to the brink of playoff qualification.

In the Premier Cup game against Whitley Warriors, the youngsters' commitment was again evident as Hawks took a three-goal lead by the end of the first period. Warriors fought back to 6-6 in the third only for Whyte to fire in the winner with two seconds left on the clock.

Eventually, however, defeat at Billingham Bombers sealed Hawks' playoff chances.

Haig continued to be pleased with the club's junior development programme which is starting to pay off. **Neal Haworth, Wes Barnett** and **Wayne Slater** became regulars in 2001-02 and this year **Scott Barnett, Lance Derbyshire, Adam Fuller, Adam Leaver, Peter Tapp** and the Sheffield twins all forced their way into the side from the under-19 team.

PLAYER AWARDS

Player of the Year	Colin Downie
Players' Player	David Sheffield
Most Improved Player	David Sheffield

LEADING PLAYERS

Colin Downie born 16 May 1973
The goal-stopping talents of this experienced ex-Fife Flyers, Trafford Metros and Manchester Storm netminder were almost over-shadowed by his four assists, a personal record.

David Sheffield born 10 July 1983
In his first full season for the Hawks, he was a major force in the goal scoring charts, despite his youth. Never afraid to take his share of punishment in front of the net, he had a goal or an assist in all but six of Hawks' games.

Gordon Whyte born 29 August 1970
The Dundee-born captain always gave 100 per cent and continued to improve with age. While positional play and stick handling have always been the defenceman's strengths, this year he also scored some key goals.

FACT FILE 2002-03

English National League:	5th in North
Playoffs	Did not qualify
Premier Cup:	Group runners-up
Northern Cup	4th

CLUB HISTORY

Founded 1990 as Blackhawks. Name changed in 1992. Blackburn Phoenix played in 1997-98.

Leagues (Black)Hawks: English National League (North) 1999-2003; English Premier League 1998-99; British League, Div One 1993-96, 1991-92; English League 1992-93, 1990-91. Phoenix: English National League (North) 1997-98.

BLACKBURN HAWKS *left to right, standing at back:* David Sheffield, Neal Haworth, Craig Sharman, Peter Tapp, Jamie Thomson, Scott Barnett, Andy Sheffield; *middle row:* Russ Ginn (equipment), Bobby Haig (player-coach), Wayne Slater, Peter Norgate, Adam Leaver, Adam Fuller, Michael Brunton, Jason Fitton, Lance Derbyshire, Peter Sheffield (manager); *front row:* Colin Downie, Chris Black, Eddie Cooper, Gordon Whyte, Wes Barnett, Robbie Smith.

BRACKNELL BEES

PLAYER	ALL COMPETITIONS					SUPERLEAGUE					PLAYOFFS				
Scorers	GP	G	A	Pts	Pim	GP	G	A	Pts	Pim	GP	G	A	Pts	Pim
Dan Ceman (WP)	56	28	30	58	44	32	16	12	28	22	16	8	14	22	18
Scott Kirton (WP)	56	17	28	45	78	32	8	16	24	37	16	4	10	14	6
Jonathan Delisle (WP)	55	12	18	30	159	32	8	11	19	57	15	2	5	7	65
Brad Peddle (WP)	55	13	14	27	91	31	5	7	12	18	16	6	5	11	16
Tero Arkiomaa	55	12	14	26	32	32	7	9	16	22	15	2	1	3	6
Mike McBain (WP)	56	4	16	20	46	32	3	10	13	38	16	1	2	3	2
Joe Ciccarello	52	13	6	19	20	29	8	4	12	14	16	4	1	5	6
Dino Bauba 1	34	8	10	18	52	17	0	2	2	12	15	8	7	15	8
Darren Hurley	52	5	13	18	137	32	4	9	13	62	14	0	1	1	19
David Struch (WP)	49	5	11	16	26	28	4	6	10	20	16	0	3	3	4
Steve O'Rourke	47	2	11	13	44	25	0	8	8	14	16	1	2	3	12
Corey Spring	49	8	4	12	36	26	3	3	6	16	16	4	1	5	12
Trevor Burgess	27	1	9	10	22	26	1	9	10	20					
Chad Nelson	18	1	5	6	39	2	0	0	0	0	16	1	5	6	39
Mark Matier	50	0	4	4	128	26	0	2	2	67	16	0	2	2	22
Greg Owen	23	2	1	3	2	18	2	1	3	2	5	0	0	0	0
Christian Gosselin (WP)	19	1	2	3	92	12	1	1	2	61					
Jason Rushton 3	3	1	1	2	10	3	1	1	2	10					
James Morgan 2	10	0	1	1	2	5	0	0	0	2					
Brian Greer (N)	38	0	1	1	12	18	0	0	0	4	14	0	1	1	4
Mark McCoy	7	0	0	0	2	3	0	0	0	0	1	0	0	0	0
* Joe Watkins (N)	25	0	0	0	0	19	0	0	0	0	4	0	0	0	0
Bench Penalties					20					10					4
TEAM TOTALS	56	133	199	332	1094	32	71	111	182	508	16	41	60	101	243

Netminders	GPI	Min	SOG	GA	Sv%	GPI	Min	SOG	GA	Sv%	GPI	Min	SOG	GA	Sv%
Brian Greer	38	2066	1308	129	90.1	18	926	608	58	90.5	14	778	488	54	88.9
* Joe Watkins	25	1341	815	95	88.3	19	1024	595	72	87.9	4	187	129	18	86.0
Empty Net Goals			1	1				0	0				0	0	
TEAM TOTALS	56	3407	2124	225	89.4	32	1950	1203	130	89.2	16	965	617	72	88.3

Also played for: 1 Scottish Eagles; 2 Nottingham Panthers, Solihull MK Kings

3 Scottish Eagles, Cardiff Devils, Romford Raiders

Shutouts: Watkins - league: 3 Oct v London Knights (35 saves)

Greer - league: 16 Jan v Sheffield Steelers (37)

All Competitions = league, playoffs, Challenge Cup and Ahearne Trophy

BRACKNELL BEES *left to right, back row:* Chad Nelson, Scott Kirton, Corey Spring, Greg Owen; *middle row:* Mark Matier, Steve O'Rourke, Joe Ciccarello, David Kelly (trainer), Brian Miller (equipment), Jonathan Delisle, Dino Bauba, Tero Arkiomaa; *front row:* Joe Watkins, Brad Peddle, Darren Hurley, Mike McBain, Dan Ceman, David Struch, Brian Greer; *behind front row (middle):* Alex Barker, Stephen Reed, Danny House (stick boys).

No buzz

ALAN MANICOM

Bracknell Bees found to their cost that bigger does not necessarily mean better. Coach **Enio Sacilotto** was instructed to sacrifice speed for size in a bid to halt a decline in fortunes that had begun in the latter half of the previous season.

Out went **Mark Cadotte, Doug Stienstra, Mark Turner, Sam Ftorek, Blake Knox** and **Blair Scott** and in came **Corey Spring, Scott Kirton, Tero Arkiomaa** and **Christian Gosselin** - all of whom were over 6ft 3ins - as well as **Jonathan Delisle** and **David Struch.**

A pre-season triumph in Bremerhaven, Germany gave cause for optimism but it was short-lived as defeat at home to London Knights in the Challenge Cup was followed by a draw at British National Club, Coventry Blaze.

Although Bees scraped an overtime win against Nottingham Panthers, the alarm bells began ringing with another defeat at London, this time in their opening Superleague game. And in their first league outing on home ice, they were booed off by their own fans after crashing 11-3 to Belfast Giants.

There was little for supporters to cheer for the rest of the season, either, as they slumped to the bottom of the table in November and stayed there. Perversely, the only side Bees beat in the last four months of the regular season were winners Sheffield Steelers - three times in all!

Their game at the Hive in October was notable, though, for all the wrong reasons as it was abandoned with just over ten minutes of regular time left, due to a large rut in the ice. The 1-1 scoreline stood for three weeks when Steelers grabbed the bonus point for scoring in an overtime which was bizarrely played out before the clubs' next encounter in Bracknell.

Bees suffered the unexpected departure of rising young British defenceman **James Morgan** to the United States and an elbow injury robbed them of defenceman Gosselin, their biggest physical presence.

Faced with dwindling crowds and poor results in a league that had been reduced to just five teams, owner **John Nike** announced that the club would be dropping down next season to compete in the British National League.

Further drastic action was taken before the start of the Playoffs when Sacilotto was relieved of his duties. Bees took five points from their first three games but old habits returned, and caretaker player-coaches **Mike McBain** and **David Struch** presided over 12 defeats and just one win as Bees finished bottom of the Playoff table, too.

PLAYER AWARDS

Player of the Year	Jonathan Delisle
Players' Player	Jonathan Delisle
Best Forward	Dan Ceman
Best Defenceman	Brad Peddle
Coach's Award	Darren Hurley/Mark Matier

LEADING PLAYERS

Dan Ceman *born July 25 1973*
Despite playing in a side that finished bottom of the table, he finished as the league's top goal scorer with 16 goals from 32 games. His bustling all-action style and exceptional work-rate could always be relied upon.

Jonathan Delisle *born June 30 1977*
One of the few players to improve as the season progressed. Unlike many of his team-mates, he never gave up. His commitment was recognised by team-mates and fans alike when he collected the two top honours at the club's end-of-season awards.

Christian Gosselin *born August 21 1976*
Bees desperately missed the physical presence of their 6ft 5in defenceman, known as 'Goose'. An elbow injury forced him out of the last three-quarters of the season and was a major factor behind a campaign that went from bad to worse.

FACT FILE 2002-03

Superleague:	Fifth
Playoffs:	Fifth
Challenge Cup:	3rd in qr-final group

HISTORY

Founded: 1987.

Leagues: Superleague 1996-2003; British League, Premier Div. 1991-95; British League, Div. One 1995-96, 1990-91; English League 1987-90.

Honours: Superleague 1999-2000, Promotion Playoffs 1991-92, English League 1989-90.

CARDIFF DEVILS

PLAYER	ALL COMPETITIONS					FINDUS BRITISH NATIONAL LEAGUE					PLAYOFFS				
Scorers	GP	G	A	Pts	Pim	GP	G	A	Pts	Pim	GP	G	A	Pts	Pim
Russ Romaniuk (I)	53	36	36	72	98	36	23	29	52	48	10	7	5	12	22
Ivan Matulik (WP) 2	39	16	29	45	89	29	13	22	35	56	10	3	7	10	33
Mike Ware (I)	48	16	27	43	247	30	12	20	32	96	10	3	5	8	43
Jeff Burgoyne (I)	52	13	30	43	119	36	10	24	34	89	10	2	4	6	20
Kurt Walsh (I)	52	27	13	40	92	34	21	8	29	60	10	3	0	3	20
Blake Knox (I)	49	14	21	35	131	31	7	17	24	56	10	4	3	7	16
Blair Scott	53	9	23	32	153	36	9	14	23	86	9	0	7	7	10
Jonathan Phillips	50	10	17	27	62	32	6	12	18	36	10	2	5	7	4
Jim Brown (I)	15	5	17	22	44	7	3	6	9	18					
Henrich Beutel (I)	13	6	6	12	4	12	6	6	12	2	1	0	0	0	2
Jason Rushton (I) 3	10	6	5	11	28	10	6	5	11	28					
Mike Bishop 1	22	3	8	11	22	12	1	8	9	10	10	2	0	2	12
Matt Myers	44	5	5	10	32	30	5	4	9	22	10	0	0	0	10
Jason Stone	40	1	9	10	20	22	1	3	4	8	10	0	3	3	8
Phil Hill	36	4	3	7	20	20	3	3	6	14	10	1	0	1	2
Warren Tait	52	4	3	7	20	34	4	3	7	12	10	0	0	0	4
Lee Cowmeadow	30	2	3	5	8	22	1	3	4	4					
Chris Bailey	46	1	2	3	58	28	1	2	3	28	10	0	0	0	20
David James	13	1	1	2	0	8	1	1	2	0	5	0	0	0	0
Brian Leitza (N) (I)	14	1	0	1	6	6	0	0	0	2					
Phil Manny	14	0	1	1	2	7	0	1	1	2	7	0	0	0	0
Stevie Lyle (N) 2	39	0	1	1	16	29	0	1	1	10	10	0	0	0	6
Mark Hazelhurst	22	0	0	0	50	16	0	0	0	38					
Bench Penalties					20					18					2
TEAM TOTALS	54	180	260	440	1351	36	133	192	325	743	10	27	39	66	234
Netminders	GPI	Min	SOG	GA	Sv%	GPI	Min	SOG	GA	Sv%	GPI	Min	SOG	GA	Sv%
Dan Wood	1	6	5	0	100.0	1	6	5	0	100.0					
Jason Wood	1	32	5	0	100.0	1	32	5	0	100.0					
Nathan Craze	1	28	10	0	100.0	1	28	10	0	100.0					
Stevie Lyle 2	39	2336	1228	103	91.6	29	1735	928	82	91.2	10	601	300	21	93.0
Brian Leitza (I)	14	840	431	44	89.8	6	360	165	21	87.3					
Mike Brabon	1	7	4	1	75.0	1	7	4	1	75.0					
Empty Net Goals		0	0				0	0							
TEAM TOTALS	54	3249	1683	148	91.2	36	2168	1117	104	90.7	10	601	300	21	93.0

Shutouts: Lyle (4) - league: 18 Jan at Solihull MK Kings (30 saves),
1 Feb at Newcastle Vipers (20), 9 Feb v Fife Flyers (26),
playoffs: 15 Mar at Newcastle Vipers (16)
Leitza - cup: 22 Sept at Coventry Blaze (33)
Craze (10 saves), Wood (5 saves) - league: 2 Feb v Hull Thunder.

Also appeared: Chris Deacon 13; Simon Keating 7; Rory O'Neill (4), Rhodri Evans (4) 6.
Also played for: 1 Hull Thunder, Fife Flyers; 2 Manchester Storm; 3 Scottish Eagles,
Romford Raiders, Bracknell Bees; 4 Edinburgh Capitals..

All Competitions = league, playoffs and Findus Cup

Two owners and one hand on a trophy

TERRY PHILLIPS, *South Wales Echo*

Controversy surrounded the *Coca-Cola* Cardiff Devils from the start when **Chris McSorley** helped to save the club, until the end when they swept into the British National League's Playoff finals on an astonishing golden goal.

Devils needed a big start after the disastrous 'ice wars' of the previous campaign when hundreds of fans refused to watch matches and formed picket lines outside the Wales National Ice Rink.

But McSorley's 'together forever' stand when he took over the Devils didn't last as he handed over to Wisbech businessman and former Peterborough owner, **Paul McMillan**. The GB coach found it impossible to maintain his interest from his base in Switzerland where he was coaching 'A' League club, Geneva Eagles, though he retained an interest throughout the season.

On the ice, new coach **Glenn Mulvenna** and his team achieved an amazing change of direction but they took time to settle. They crashed out of the *Findus* Cup and then lost ten of their first 12 league games. Things looked bleak and McMillan had to ask the players to take a pay cut to save the club.

They responded magnificently, accepting lower wages and standing tall for the Devils. Out went imports **Jim Brown** and goalie **Brian Leitza**, and in came Cardiff-born **Stevie Lyle** in goal plus his ex-Manchester Storm team-mates **Ivan Matulik** and **Russ Romaniuk**.

The transformation was complete and Devils charged up the table - after slumping to second from bottom - and comfortably qualified for the Playoffs.

They swept into the semi-finals and defeated Dundee Stars, who were furious when Matulik scored an overtime winner from Romaniuk's pass. Matulik had earlier been thrown out and Romaniuk handed a 10-minute penalty, but league officials surprisingly wiped the slate clean at the start of overtime and Devils produced a winner in the first shift.

Cardiff's eventual defeat by Coventry Blaze over two legs in the final could not spoil a season which finished on a high - the Devils had proved they were back.

"It was a remarkable year," said Mulvenna. "Even when things weren't going well the players stuck together. We knew we had the talent to succeed and they showed massive character by reaching the playoff finals."

PLAYER AWARDS

Player of the Year	**Jeff Burgoyne**
Players' Player	**Jeff Burgoyne**
*Best British Player	
	Matt Myers/Jonathan Phillips
Most Improved Player	**Chris Bailey**
Travelling Supporters Player	**Jeff Burgoyne**

* Norman Watkins Memorial Award.

LEADING PLAYERS

Jeff Burgoyne: *born 26 February 1977*
The fit and fast former Cornell University defenceman was an instant hit in his first season in this country after three seasons in the East Coast Hockey League.

Matt Myers *born 6 November 1984*
The skill and composure of the Cardiff-born centreman shone through the team. A product of Devils' youth development programme, he played for the England under-18 and under-20 teams before earning his first Devils' call-up in 2001.

Russ Romaniuk *born 9 June 1970*
The former NHLer came in from defunct Manchester and admirably fulfilled his role as a team leader as well as topping the club's scoring.

Steve Moria's No 19 shirt was retired before Devils' game against Basingstoke Bison on 8 September 2002. Moria was in his first season as Bison's coach.

FACT FILE 2002-03

British National League:	5th
Playoffs:	Finalists
***Findus* Cup:**	4th in group

HISTORY

Founded 1986.

Leagues British National League 2001-03; Superleague 1996-2001; British League, Premier Div. 1989-96; British League, Div. One 1987-89; British League, Div. Two 1986-87.

Honours Superleague Playoff Champions 1999; British League and Championship winners 1993-94, 1992-93, 1989-90; British League winners 1996-97; *Benson and Hedges* Cup winners 1992.

CARDIFF DEVILS *left to right, back row:* Lee Cowmeadow, Matt Myers, Jeff Burgoyne, Jonathan Phillips; *middle row:* Warren Tait, Jason Rushton, Kurt Walsh, Chris Bailey, Ivan Matulik, Blair Scott; *front row:* Stevie Lyle, Russ Romaniuk, Blake Knox, (mascot), Mike Ware, Glen Mulvenna (coach), Mike Brabon.

Photo: Jason Digby

CHELMSFORD CHIEFTAINS

PLAYER	ALL COMPETITIONS					ENGLISH PREMIER LEAGUE					PLAYOFFS				
Scorers	GP	G	A	Pts	Pim	GP	G	A	Pts	Pim	GP	G	A	Pts	Pim
Kyle Amyotte (I)	44	76	59	135	34	38	65	48	113	30	6	11	11	22	4
Andrew Power (I)	38	50	72	122	293	32	41	64	105	267	6	9	8	17	26
Andy Hannah	42	26	41	67	167	37	25	39	64	145	5	1	2	3	22
Jon Beckett	42	29	36	65	116	37	25	34	59	102	5	4	2	6	14
Steve Birch (I)	44	18	36	54	50	38	16	32	48	42	6	2	4	6	8
Daniel Cabby	39	13	27	40	40	34	11	25	36	38	5	2	2	4	2
Richard Whiting	47	8	15	23	65	41	7	9	16	57	6	1	6	7	8
Shaun Wallis	45	12	10	22	61	39	11	9	20	53	6	1	1	2	8
Ross Jones	47	8	12	20	18	41	7	10	17	16	6	1	2	3	2
Daniel Wright	45	7	11	18	16	39	7	10	17	16	6	0	1	1	0
Richard Tomalin	34	7	11	18	76	29	6	11	17	64	5	1	0	1	12
Russell Bishop	36	4	14	18	38	30	4	14	18	38	6	0	0	0	0
Anthony Leone	15	7	8	15	4	10	6	6	12	4	5	1	2	3	0
Andrew Clements	43	7	5	12	4	37	6	5	11	4	6	1	0	1	0
Tyrone Miller 1	31	2	6	8	113	25	1	4	5	64	6	1	2	3	49
Daniel Hughes	15	5	2	7	0	15	5	2	7	0	0	0	0	0	0
Glen Moorhouse	35	0	5	5	36	30	0	4	4	32	5	0	1	1	4
Ricky Mills	28	1	3	4	0	24	1	3	4	0	4	0	0	0	0
Grant Taylor	14	0	4	4	2	14	0	4	4	2	0	0	0	0	0
Tom Long	7	1	1	2	0	3	1	1	2	0	4	0	0	0	0
Lachlan Coombe	12	0	2	2	12	12	0	2	2	12	0	0	0	0	0
Darren Botha 1	13	0	2	2	20	13	0	2	2	20	0	0	0	0	0
Chris Douglas (N)	47	0	2	2	12	41	0	0	0	12	6	0	2	2	0
Roy Keily	15	0	1	1	8	15	0	1	1	8	0	0	0	0	0
Liam Doyle	7	0	0	0	2	2	0	0	0	2	5	0	0	0	0
Bench Penalties					20					20					
TEAM TOTALS	47	281	385	666	1207	41	245	339	584	1048	6	36	46	82	159
Netminders	GPI	Mins	SOG	GA	Sv%	GPI	Mins	SOG	GA	Sv%	GPI	Mins	SOG	GA	Sv%
Chris Douglas	46	2503	1541	182	88.2	40	2164	1349	151	88.8	6	339	192	31	83.9
Alan Blyth	10	256	136	22	83.8	9	236	120	16	86.7	1	20	16	6	62.5
Paul Wilcock	3	60	34	3	91.2	3	60	34	3	91.2					
Empty Net Goals			1	1	1								1	1	1
TEAM TOTALS	47	2820	1712	208	87.8	41	2460	1503	170	88.7	6	360	209	38	81.8

Also appeared: Reece Covington 7; Ben Clements 4.

Also played for: 1 Romford Raiders

All Competitions = league and playoffs

CHELMSFORD CHIEFTAINS *left to right, back row:* Darren Botha, Kyle Amyotte, Daniel Cabby, Ross Jones, Danny Wright, Andy Hannah, Richard Whiting, Alan Blyth, Richard Tomalin, Jonathan Beckett, Steve Birch, Russell Bishop; *front row:* Shaun Wallis, Mascot, Andy Clements, Danny Hughes, Andrew Power, Glen Moorhouse, Chris Douglas.

We got the Power

IVOR HOBSON

After a season out of the top flight, Chieftains returned to the English Premier League where they challenged for top spot in the Playoffs.

Their return was thanks to an influx of sponsorship revenue which also enabled them to sign **Erskine Douglas**, the coach from their treble-winning 1999-2000 season. His experience, in partnership with his new assistant **Dean Birrell**, paid dividends for the Tribe.

Of the 20 players icing in the opening contest at Romford, nine were making their debuts. Among them were three ex-Raiders - **Dan Cabby**, **Richard Tomalin** and goalie **Chris Douglas**, all of whom made an impact on their new team.

Popular import **Andy Hannah** returned from Invicta and up front **Kyle Amyotte** from the Isle of Wight and new Canadian signing **Andrew Power** added a scoring punch sadly missing in the preceding season. This trio were complemented by a third Canadian, defenceman **Steve Birch**, and a growing band of local talent including **Shaun Wallis** and **Danny Wright** who had made great progress in the league's southern conference during 2001-02.

In a promising start, Chelmsford lost only once in their opening ten contests. But they hit a bad patch from mid-October and their nine-game winless streak was only snapped on 17 November when hat-tricks from Power and Amyotte led them to an impressive 10-6 home victory over league champs, Peterborough.

That they could only manage fifth place was due to a porous defence which conceded 170 goals, combined with a poor penalty record of 26 minutes per game (the third worst). And their poor form against the top four sides produced just three wins and nine points from 16 games.

Despite the low finish, Chieftains had two of the league's leading eight scorers in Amyotte and Power who tallied over 100 points apiece. Hannah's fourth point of the season was his 500th for the Tribe and he ended the year in fourth place on the club's all-time scoring list.

The league season had closed on a six-game winning streak and this sparkling form continued into the Playoffs with opening victories over Swindon and Romford. This set up a showdown with Phantoms, but Chieftains' hopes were dashed when they were crushed 15-2 at Peterborough and 6-5 at the Riverside.

Though this meant they could only make runners-up spot in their group, Amyotte was the competition's top scorer with 11 goals and 22 points.

PLAYER AWARDS

Player of the Year	**Steve Birch**
Player's Player	**Steve Birch**
Coach's Player	**Dan Cabby**
Most Improved Player	**Ross Jones**

LEADING PLAYERS

Kyle Amyotte *born 24 February 1979*

An inspired signing as the Canadian was a one-man scoring machine, improving as the season went on. Finished as sixth leading scorer in the regular season, and upped the pace when it mattered to top all Playoff scorers with a hat-trick in the final game.

Steve Birch *born 9 August 1977*

Voted the club's best player by both supporters and team-mates, he averaged over a point a game while proving a valuable member of the blueline corps. The Chieftain was previously a Chief at Chilliwack.

Andrew Power *born 19 January 1976*

The ex-Shreveport Mudbug forward came up trumps with an impressive goal tally despite spending too long in the sin-bin. Three points plus a stand-up fight with Raider **Jason Rushton** in his first game certainly endeared him to the Chelmsford faithful!

FACT FILE 2002-03

English Premier League:	Fifth.
Playoffs:	Group runners-up
Premier Cup:	Did not enter

CLUB HISTORY

Founded: 1987.

Leagues: English Premier League 2002-03, 1998-2001; English (National) League 2001-02, 1996-98 and 1988-93; British League, Div One 1993-96; British League, Div Two 1987-88.

Honours: League winners, Playoff champions and *DataVision* Millennium Cup winners 1999-2000.

COVENTRY BLAZE

PLAYER	ALL COMPETITIONS					FINDUS BRITISH NATIONAL LEAGUE					PLAYOFFS				
Scorers	GP	G	A	Pts	Pim	GP	G	A	Pts	Pim	GP	G	A	Pts	Pim
Ashley Tait	56	41	45	86	38	36	30	31	61	22	10	4	4	8	8
Hilton Ruggles	56	28	43	71	106	36	18	29	47	48	10	5	8	13	16
Steve Chartrand	56	34	30	64	70	36	24	19	43	40	10	7	6	13	24
Steve Carpenter (I)	56	19	37	56	168	36	14	24	38	106	10	2	7	9	14
Joel Poirier (WP)	56	23	28	51	82	36	16	21	37	36	10	3	2	5	26
Shaun Johnson	52	15	32	47	6	34	11	25	36	4	10	0	5	5	2
Andreas Moborg (I)	56	16	30	46	133	36	13	21	34	115	10	1	4	5	8
Michael Tasker	53	20	24	44	116	36	14	19	33	94	7	4	2	6	4
Ron Shudra	56	15	28	43	30	36	10	22	32	20	10	1	3	4	4
Tom Watkins	54	13	20	33	24	34	9	16	25	12	10	2	3	5	8
Mathias Soderstrom (I)	45	6	15	21	56	28	5	12	17	42	10	1	1	2	0
Russell Cowley	49	5	8	13	10	29	5	5	10	6	10	0	2	2	4
Kurt Irvine	55	2	7	9	205	35	1	6	7	141	10	1	0	1	6
James Pease	48	0	6	6	12	28	0	5	5	4	10	0	1	1	2
Lee Richardson	50	2	3	5	6	30	2	3	5	4	10	0	0	0	2
Gareth Owen	52	2	2	4	39	32	1	1	2	35	10	1	0	1	0
Jody Lehman (N) (WP)	56	0	2	2	28	36	0	1	1	8	10	0	0	0	6
Alan Levers (N)	42	0	1	1	0	30	0	1	1	0	10	0	0	0	0
Adam Radmall	51	0	1	1	6	31	0	1	1	6	10	0	0	0	0
Bench Penalties					10					4					4
TEAM TOTALS	56	241	362	603	1145	36	173	262	435	747	10	32	48	80	138
Netminders	GPI	Mins	SOG	GA	Sv%	GPI	Mins	SOG	GA	Sv%	GPI	Mins	SOG	GA	Sv%
Alan Levers	3	105	64	1	98.4	2	45	18	0	100.0	1	60	46	1	97.8
Jody Lehman (WP)	55	3267	1213	106	91.26	36	2127	780	68	91.3	9	540	203	11	94.6
Empty Net Goals			2	2				1	1						
TEAM TOTALS	56	3372	1279	109	91.5	36	2172	799	69	91.4	10	600	249	12	95.2

Shutouts: Lehman (7) - cup: 14 Sept at Solihull MK Kings (20 saves), .
                        league: 27 Oct at Cardiff Devils (32), 3 Nov v Fife Flyers (20),
                                17 Nov v Solihull MK Kings (16), 1 Feb at Hull Thunder (1) *
                        playoffs: 7 Mar at Newcastle Vipers (21), 9 Mar at Cardiff Devils (22).
                Levers (1) - league: 1 Feb at Hull Thunder (16) *   *shared

Also appeared: Netminders: Dan Burgess, Greg Rockman 3.
All Competitions = league, playoffs and Findus Cup

New Stars Blaze

ANTONY HOPKER

Eyebrows were raised when the Blaze announced that they were going to start the season playing with the big boys in Superleague's Challenge Cup, but the experience was a good one.

Two draws on home ice were credible performances against the import-heavy sides and gave Blaze the conditioning and morale boost needed to bring the first British National League and Playoff trophies to the Skydome.

In **Jody Lehman** Blaze had their best goalie yet, while **Ron Shudra** and **Andreas Moborg** added guile and skill to the blue line. Up front, **Joel Poirier** and **Ashley Tait** forged an alliance with **Shaun Johnson** to send the goal lights flashing.

Blaze's path through their *Findus* Cup group was a little shaky, with perhaps the most memorable moment coming when defenceman **Stephen Cooper**'s no. 55 shirt was retired.

The tone of the season was set with November's game against team-to-beat Dundee Stars when Blaze took a 4-1 lead before eventually winning 6-5 in overtime. They continued this form in the Cup semi-final where they overcame Stars again to reach their second straight final, only to collapse 3-0 to a physical Newcastle Vipers.

The talk was of bridesmaids, as Blaze finished second in a fourth successive tournament, but coach **Paul Thompson** described it as "the making of our season. It made us a team and gave us that hunger."

Coventry went on a long winning streak that took them to the top of table as their rivals faltered. Points were salvaged where they would have been lost before. Christmas smiled with a third victory over the Stars in a third different rink, this time in Dundee. The 6-4 win after being 4-1 down in the third gave the squad another huge psychological boost.

Fittingly, the trophy was secured in the home of the defending champions, a week before the Stars gave Blaze their only spanking of the season, a 5-0 embarrassment at the Skydome on the night of the league cup presentation.

Great three-line hockey had characterised Blaze's triumphs, with veterans **Steve Chartrand** and **Hilton Ruggles** and four GB under-20s all playing their part.

Lehman, voted the league's MVP, produced his best form in the Playoffs, as Blaze cruised through to the semis. After outplaying Guildford, they had two tight, hectic games with Cardiff before completing the double.

PLAYER AWARDS

Player of the Year	**Joel Poirier**
Players' Player	**Ashley Tait**
Best Forward	**Ashley Tait**
Best Defenceman	**Andreas Moborg**
British Player of the Year	**Ashley Tait**
Coach's Player	**Michael Tasker**
Most Improved Player:	**Russell Cowley**

LEADING PLAYERS

Steve Carpenter *born 30 March 1971*
His huge hitting made a big contribution to a miserly defence, and his calm judgement in his forays up ice often led to goals in important games.

Ron Shudra, defence 28/11/67
Now 36, the one-time Edmonton Oiler can still fire the slapshot that earned him the nickname, Rocket Ron. Using more brain than brawn, he shepherded and poke-checked when others would have lunged. Happy to pass on his wide knowledge to the younger players.

Ashley Tait *born 9 August 1975*
Quiet right-winger was the club's leading scorer as his speed and skill combined well with the work-rate of fellow ex-Panther **Joel Poirier**. Marginalised in Superleague, he relished the responsibility conferred on him in the BNL.

FACT FILE 2002-03

British National League:	Winners
Playoffs:	Champions
***Findus* Cup:**	Finalists

HISTORY

Founded: 2000, after club moved from Solihull.
Leagues: *Findus* British National League 2000-03.

COVENTRY BLAZE *left to right, back row:* Steve Small (manager), Tom Watkins, Russ Cowley, Michael Tasker, Ashley Tait, Joel Poirier, Ron Shudra, James Pease, Andreas Moborg, Gareth Owen, Lee Richardson, Adam Radmall, Phil Hadley (Equipment), John Crook (Equipment); *front row:* Gregg Rockman, Steve Carpenter, Hilton Ruggles, Steve Chartrand, Paul Thompson (coach), Kurt Irvine, Mathias Soderstrom, Shaun Johnson, Jody Lehman.

DUNDEE STARS

PLAYER	ALL COMPETITIONS					FINDUS BRITISH NATIONAL LEAGUE					PLAYOFFS				
Scorers	GP	G	A	Pts	Pim	GP	G	A	Pts	Pim	GP	G	A	Pts	Pim
Ken Priestlay	51	48	60	108	38	33	31	40	71	28	8	5	4	9	0
Teeder Wynne (WP)	50	37	67	104	26	36	29	50	79	16	4	1	1	2	0
Tony Hand	46	29	73	102	105	36	22	58	80	99					
Patric Lochi (I)	53	43	38	81	48	35	25	24	49	28	8	9	8	17	10
Johan Boman (I)	53	45	35	80	58	35	34	20	54	36	8	4	6	10	14
Martin Wiita (I)	52	22	49	71	20	34	14	38	52	14	8	5	6	11	0
Jan Mikel (WP)	48	17	39	56	117	31	10	21	31	70	8	1	8	9	8
Scott Young 1	17	12	22	34	44	9	6	13	19	24	8	6	9	15	20
Dan Ratushny (WP) 3	24	8	24	32	14	19	8	23	31	12	5	0	1	1	2
Marty Hughes (WP)	50	10	19	29	64	33	6	8	14	36	7	1	4	5	8
Gary Wishart	53	4	12	16	22	35	1	8	9	10	8	1	2	3	6
Dominic Hopkins	52	4	7	11	34	34	3	5	8	12	8	1	1	2	16
Paul Sample	52	5	5	10	24	34	4	4	8	20	8	1	0	1	0
Laurie Dunbar	50	1	8	9	10	35	1	6	7	10	8	0	0	0	0
Chris Conaboy	49	1	5	6	100	33	1	5	6	92	8	0	0	0	0
Mike Harding 3	1	0	2	2	0	1	0	2	2	0					
Stephen Murphy (N)	54	0	2	2	4	36	0	2	2	4	8	0	0	0	0
John Dolan	3	1	0	1	0	1	1	0	1	0	2	0	0	0	0
Scott Campbell (I) 2	5	0	1	1	16	3	0	1	1	12					
Bench Penalties					14					8					4
TEAM TOTALS	54	287	468	755	758	36	196	328	524	531	8	35	50	85	88
Netminders	GPI	Mins	SOG	GA	Sv%	GPI	Mins	SOG	GA	Sv%	GPI	Mins	SOG	GA	Sv%
Stephen Murphy	52	3094	1646	147	91.1	34	2048	1090	96	91.2	8	481	264	22	91.7
Stewart Rugg	3	155	54	11	79.6	2	120	38	9	76.3					
Empty Net Goals		4	4				4	4							
TEAM TOTALS	54	3249	1704	162	90.5	36	2168	1132	109	90.4	8	481	264	22	91.7

Shutouts: Murphy (4) - league: 26 Oct at Cardiff Devils (39 saves),
29 Jan at Newcastle Vipers (26); 1 Feb v Solihull MK Kings (31);
15 Feb v Coventry Blaze (39).

Also appeared: Craig Phillips 4; Murray Johnstone 3; Dan Clarkson, John Robertson,
Chris Babbage, Lewis Christie, Billy Baxter, Craig Johnstone 1.

Also played for: 1 Hull Thunder; 2 Fife Flyers, Newcastle Vipers, Scottish Eagles;
3 Scottish Eagles.

All Competitions = league, playoffs and Findus Cup

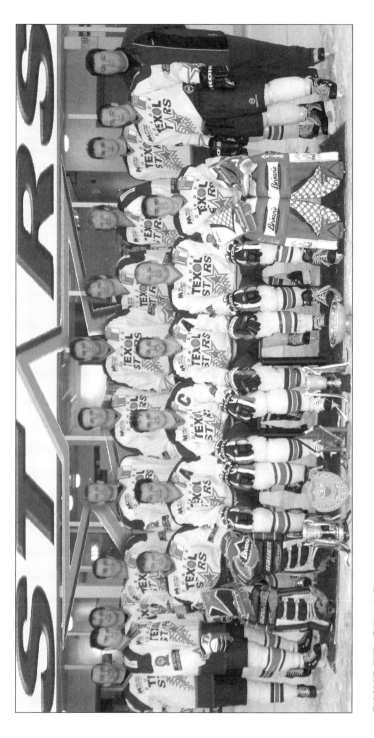

DUNDEE STARS *left to right, back row:* Tony Hand, Marty Hughes, Laurie Dunbar, Patric Lochi, Dan Ratushny, Chris Conaboy, Dominic Hopkins, Johan Boman, Scott Young, Gary Wishart, Paul Sample, Roger Hunt (bench coach); *front row:* Stewart Rugg, Ken Priestlay, Jan Mikel, Teeder Wynne, Martin Wiita, Stephen Murphy.

Photo: Godfrey Mordente

Look, no Hand

This was always going to be a tough season for the *Texol* Stars. The reigning British National League and Playoff champions were the team that every other side would be gunning for.

Sadly, the season ended without a trophy, a messy defeat in the Playoff semis, and the shocking loss of their founding coach and British ice hockey icon, **Tony Hand**.

In the summer, Hand surprised everyone by adding his former Sheffield Steelers' linemate and twice Stanley Cup winner, **Ken Priestlay**, to the roster. Ken had been away from these shores for four years and had not been expected to return. With some key players like **Paul Berrington** and **Craig Nelson** departing, he also signed Fife and GB forward **Gary Wishart**, powerful Swedish forward, **Johan Boman**, and New Yorker **Marty Hughes**.

Starting the season where they left off, Stars finished top of their *Findus* Cup group, thus qualifying for the finals weekend in Newcastle. But they could only manage third place after defeat by Coventry Blaze in the semi-final was followed by a consolation victory over Guildford Flames in the playoff.

FOUR STRAIGHT LOSSES

The league campaign opened with the squad in blistering form and they were heading the table until December when they lost four home games on the run, something unheard of in the previous season.

The turning point came at the Dundee Ice Arena on 29 December when, after finishing the second period with a 4-1 lead against fellow challengers Coventry, they conceded five unanswered third period goals. After a similar let-down in February's return match, the Scots had to settle for the runners-up spot.

Then just as they recovered and were putting together some good performances in the Playoffs, Hand left the club. It rattled the players, especially Priestlay, his old friend. "It was a difficult time," he said. "But we battled through and deserved to get into the final."

That they failed to make it was due not to any lack of effort on their part but to an organisational cock-up which gave Cardiff the overtime winner in the semis. (See BNL section elsewhere in the *Annual*). "That left a sour taste," said Priestlay.

However, season 2002-03 was not entirely unsuccessful as the club added the Capital Cup (against Edinburgh Capitals) and the Meningitis Shield (against Guildford Flames) to their trophy cabinet.

PLAYER AWARDS

Player of the Year	**Martin Wiita**
Players' Player	**Martin Wiita**
Most Improved Player	**Dominic Hopkins**
Website Player	**Marty Hughes**
Top Goal Scorer	**Johan Boman**
Top Points Scorer	**Teeder Wynne**

LEADING PLAYERS

Johan Boman *born 6 July 1973*
Joining this season from Sweden via French club, Mulhouse Les Scorpions, he finished as the league's top goal scorer. A big power forward, he was a nuisance around the crease and was quick to sniff out a goal chance.

Martin Wiita *born 7 February 1973*
In his second season with the club after arriving from Sweden as an unknown, he was honoured by the fans and his fellow professionals. One of the league's real finds, his style is reliable rather than headline-stealing but he gives one hundred per cent in every game.

Teeder Wynne *born 6 December 1973*
The Canadian sniper joined two seasons ago and this year linked up with his old Sheffield team-mates, **Tony Hand** and **Ken Priestlay**, to form the league's most prolific scoring line. Was runner-up in league scoring.

FACT FILE 2002-03

British National League:	Runners-up
Playoffs:	Semi-finalists
***Findus* Cup:**	Third
Caledonian Cup:	Finalists.

HISTORY

Founded: 2001.
Leagues: *Findus* British National League 2001-03.
Honours: *Findus* British National League 2001-02; *Findus* Playoffs 2001-02; Caledonian Cup 2002.

EDINBURGH CAPITALS

PLAYER	ALL COMPETITIONS					FINDUS BRITISH NATIONAL LEAGUE					PLAYOFFS				
Scorers	GP	G	A	Pts	Pim	GP	G	A	Pts	Pim	GP	G	A	Pts	Pim
Peter Konder (WP)	50	21	44	65	144	36	16	37	53	98	6	1	3	4	36
Adrian Saul (I)	47	30	32	62	56	36	26	24	50	38	3	1	3	4	0
Steve Kaye (I)	46	31	29	60	80	33	22	25	47	52	5	3	1	4	6
Jan Krajicek (WP)	48	15	39	54	128	34	10	33	43	89	6	0	1	1	6
Martin Cingel (WP)	31	18	19	37	60	17	11	12	23	30	6	3	3	6	14
Steven Lynch	43	11	17	28	55	29	6	8	14	47	6	2	0	2	4
Vladimir Holik (WP)	41	3	25	28	18	35	2	24	26	18	6	1	1	2	0
Iain Robertson	31	11	8	19	26	24	11	6	17	24	6	0	2	2	2
John Downes 3	28	7	6	13	6	18	2	2	4	4	4	2	1	3	2
Craig Wilson	44	3	8	11	46	30	2	5	7	24	6	1	0	1	14
Alan Hough	31	1	8	9	48	29	1	8	9	48	2	0	0	0	0
Paddy Ward 3	40	0	7	7	34	29	0	3	3	32	6	0	1	1	2
Neil Hay	28	2	4	6	2	19	2	2	4	0	4	0	2	2	0
Stuart Lonsdale	37	2	4	6	2	23	1	3	4	2	6	0	0	0	0
Paul Howes (I)	30	2	2	4	74	18	2	2	4	52	6	0	0	0	0
Ross Hay	31	3	0	3	4	22	3	0	3	0	4	0	0	0	0
Dino Bauba (I) 3	2	1	1	2	2	2	1	1	2	2					
Daniel McIntyre	24	1	0	1	0	15	1	0	1	0	3	0	0	0	0
David Beatson	19	0	0	0	37	16	0	0	0	37	3	0	0	0	0
Ladislav Kudrna (N)(WP)	46	0	0	0	4	36	0	0	0	2	6	0	0	0	0
Bench Penalties					20					14					2
TEAM TOTALS	50	162	253	415	846	36	119	195	314	613	6	14	18	32	88
Netminders	GPI	Mins	SOG	GA	Sv%	GPI	Mins	SOG	GA	Sv%	GPI	Mins	SOG	GA	Sv%
Fraser Croall	1	27	12	1	91.7										
Ladislav Kudrna (WP)	46	2753	1721	158	90.8	36	2173	1409	123	91.3	6	360	199	22	88.9
Grant Pollock	1	60	39	8	79.5										
Ryan Ford	6	138	77	16	79.2	2	5	4	0	100.0					
Alistair Flockhart	1	40	29	10	65.5										
Empty Net Goals			3	3				2	2				1	1	
TEAM TOTALS	50	3018	1881	196	89.6	36	2178	1415	125	91.2	6	360	200	23	88.5

Shutouts: Kudrna (3) - cup: 8 Oct v Newcastle Vipers (31 saves);
league: 1 Dec v Solihull MK Kings (25); 9 Feb v Newcastle Vipers (42)

Also appeared: Chris Jeavons (I) 10; Ian MacFarlane 2; Sean Lamb, David James, Ian Beattie,
Phil Manny, Murray Ren, Chris Blackburn, Rory O'Neill (2), Rhodri Evans (2),
Neil Abel (1), Les Millie (1) 1.

Also played for: 1 Newcastle Vipers, 2 Cardiff Devils, 3 Scottish Eagles.

All Competitions = league, playoffs and Findus Cup

Stars from the East

MARK EASTON

With an influx of east Europeans and a couple of American college kids, the Capitals produced their best season so far as well as increasing their crowds. Only some unfortunate setbacks in the final weekend prevented them from finishing higher than sixth place in the British National League.

Scott Neil used his hockey knowledge to bring in eight 'unknown' imports to feature along with the returning Brits. Many people doubted the GM's selections, but he had the last laugh.

While captain **Steven Lynch**, **John Downes**, **Paddy Ward** and **Craig Wilson** stayed loyal to the Caps it was the new imports who grabbed the headlines.   Canadian duo **Adrian Saul** and **Steven Kaye** brought speed, skill and a wealth of experience from Elmira College in the States. What they lacked in height, they made up for in determination.

But it was the five east Europeans whose performances earned most respect - and surprise - from opponents around the league. Top scorer, **Peter Konder**, 31, came with the best pedigree as he was with the Slovakian Extraleague champions, Hkm Zvolen, in 2001-02.

CAPS CATCH FIRE

Another forward **Martin Cingel**, 27, also played in the Slovakian version of Superleague with MHC Martin as did giant defenceman **Jan Krajicek**, 31, from HK 36 Skalica.   Only a serious mid-season injury prevented Cingel from finishing in the club's top three scorers as he had done in his home country.   From the Czech Republic were the superb netminder **Ladislav Kudrna** and skilful defenceman **Vladimir Holik**.

Canadian **Paul Howes** took the eighth import spot, playing a utility role, and veteran former GB international **Iain Robertson** returned after two seasons with Caps' deadly rivals, Fife Flyers.

After a distinctly forgettable *Findus* Cup campaign, Capitals caught fire in the league and were in fourth place as late as the very last weekend when they returned empty-handed from a double-header in the south.

The Playoffs were always going to be difficult as they were drawn in a group with Flyers, defending champs Dundee Stars and southern powerhouse, Guildford Flames. Upsetting the Fifers home and away wasn't enough to take Caps to the semis but it wasn't a bad end to a season in which skilful recruiting and team work proved that loads-a-money isn't everything.

PLAYER AWARDS

Player of the Year	Jan Krajicek
Players' Player	Jan Krajicek
Best British Player	Steven Lynch

LEADING PLAYERS

Jan Krajicek *born 8 November 1971*

Skilful and quick, the Czech was voted the BNL's Defenceman of the Year and an All-Star by the league and the Writers Association. Club owner **Scott Neil** lost no time in re-signing him at the end of the season.

Ladislav Kudrna *born 10 January 1977*

'Ladi' was one of the league's most impressive goalies.   Unknown on these shores in September, by March all knew the Czech stopper whose save percentage was right up there with the league's best - on a sixth-place team.

Adrian Saul *born 15 March 1976*

The former USA college forward played with great heart and scored some big goals, ending as runner-up in the club's scoring.   He also brought out the best in his team-mates.

At the end of the season, the fans presented club owner and manager, **Scott Neil**, with a cheque for £1,000 to help kick-start the new season. Neil, a long-time Edinburgh forward and former GB international, also received an award for making the greatest contribution to the team in 2002-03.

FACT FILE 2002-03

British National League:	Sixth
Playoffs:	3rd in qr-final group
Findus Cup:	5th in group

HISTORY

Founded: 1998. Known as Murrayfield Royals 1995-98 and 1952-66, Edinburgh Racers 1994-95 and Murrayfield Racers 1966-94.

Leagues: Capitals - *Findus* British National Lge 1998-2003; Royals - British National Lge 1997-98, Northern Premier Lge 1996-97, British Lge, Div One 1995-96, British Lge 1954-55, Scottish National Lge 1952-54; Racers - British Lge, Premier Div 1982-95, Northern Lge 1966-82.

Past Honours: Racers - See *The Ice Hockey Annual 1998-99*.

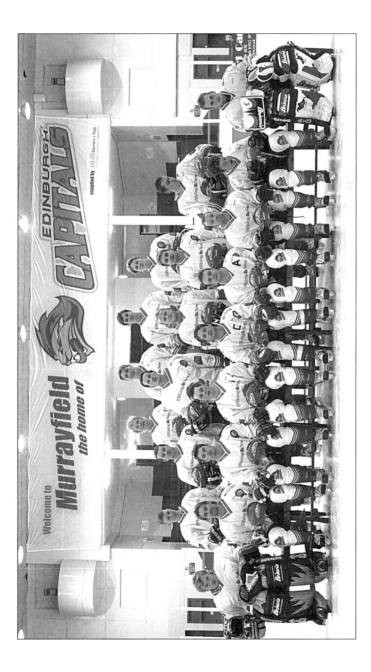

EDINBURGH CAPITALS *left to right, back row:* Ross Hay, David Beatson, Paul Howes, Chris Jeavons; *middle row:* Neil Hay, Peter Konder, Jan Krajicek, Stuart Lonsdale, Martin Cingel, Vladimir Holik; *front row:* Ladislav Kudrna, Adrian Saul, Steven Kaye, John Downes, Steven Lynch, Craig Wilson, Iain Robertson, Daniel McIntyre, Alistair Flockhart.

Photo: Jan Orkisz.

FIFE FLYERS

PLAYER	ALL COMPETITIONS					FINDUS BRITISH NATIONAL LEAGUE					PLAYOFFS				
Scorers	GP	G	A	Pts	Pim	GP	G	A	Pts	Pim	GP	G	A	Pts	Pim
Todd Dutiaume (I)	50	33	35	68	60	36	27	20	47	44	6	1	7	8	2
John Haig	50	21	38	59	56	36	12	29	41	36	6	3	4	7	0
Karry Biette (I)	40	25	24	49	98	27	15	18	33	72	6	4	2	6	16
Steven King	44	14	30	44	30	31	9	19	28	14	6	2	3	5	4
Jason Dailey (WP)	50	13	23	36	76	36	9	17	26	48	6	1	3	4	4
Mark Morrison (I)	48	9	25	34	71	34	6	15	21	61	6	2	3	5	6
David Smith	45	7	23	30	24	34	4	18	22	18	3	0	0	0	0
Jonathan Weaver 1	16	9	13	22	6	11	7	12	19	4	5	2	1	3	2
Steve Roberts (I)	17	7	10	17	28	9	5	5	10	14					
Frank Evans (I)	27	4	13	17	64	21	4	10	14	60	6	0	3	3	4
Frank Morris	27	5	8	13	49	20	4	4	8	39					
Kyle Horne	46	4	8	12	32	32	4	5	9	22	6	0	1	1	0
Derek King	46	3	7	10	108	32	2	4	6	66	6	0	0	0	32
Andy Finlay	47	1	5	6	22	33	0	4	4	10	6	1	0	1	2
Daryl Venters	50	2	3	5	4	36	2	2	4	4	6	0	0	0	0
Scott Campbell (I) 2	3	3	0	3	2	3	3	0	3	2					
Jeff Trembecky (WP) 3	4	0	3	3	4	4	0	3	3	4					
Mike Bishop 4	2	0	2	2	4	2	0	2	2	4					
Adam Walker	23	0	1	1	0	9	0	0	0	0	6	0	1	1	0
Steve Briere (N) (WP)	50	0	1	1	26	36	0	1	1	12	6	0	0	0	6
Bench Penalties					14					12					2
TEAM TOTALS	50	160	272	432	778	36	113	188	301	546	6	16	28	44	80
Netminders	GPI	Mins	SOG	GA	Sv%	GPI	Mins	SOG	GA	Sv%	GPI	Mins	SOG	GA	Sv%
Steve Briere (WP)	50	2986	1824	186	89.8	36	2149	1269	119	90.6	6	357	246	30	87.8
Colin Grubb	2	23	22	4	81.8	1	20	18	3	83.3	1	3	4	1	75.0
Empty Net Goals			6	6				5	5						
TEAM TOTALS	50	3009	1852	196	89.4	36	2169	1292	127	90.2	6	360	250	31	87.6

Shutouts: Briere (3) - league: 21 Dec v Cardiff Devils (37 saves); 4 Jan v Solihull MK Kings (30), 25 Jan v Edinburgh Capitals (25).

Also appeared: Chad Reekie 21; Thomas Muir 5; Gavin Holmes, Euan Forsyth 4; Ewan Heeles 3; David Robb 2; Scott McAndrews 1.

Also played for: 1 Hull Thunder, Scottish Eagles; 2 Dundee Stars, Newcastle Vipers, Scottish Eagles; 3 Newcastle Vipers, Solihull MK Kings; 4 Cardiff Devils, Hull Thunder.

All Competitions = league, playoffs and Findus Cup

Fife floppers

ALLAN CROW

Fife Flyers kept up their record of silverware every season since 1996, but the capture of just the Caledonian Cup couldn't put a shine on a disappointing season.

Injuries to key players shackled the team and left players, officials and fans frustrated as the main prizes went elsewhere.

Mark Morrison returned for his tenth straight season and he brought back forwards **John Haig** and **David Smith** from Guildford, and added another former Flame in the shape of defenceman **Jason Dailey. Andy Finlay** returned from Dundee with forward **Gary Wishart** making the move in the opposite direction. **Karry Biette** and **Todd Dutiaume** re-signed but the import berths remained fluid as **Mike Bishop, Jeff Trembecky** and **Scott Campbell** all passed through the dressing-room at various points. **Frank Evans** came on board late to shore up the blueline.

While many grafted and did what they could to drive the team forward, it wasn't to be Fife's season. Hopes of a bright start crumbled on the very first night when rivals Dundee crushed a home team than looked less than fully prepared.

Within weeks the *Findus* Cup had been prised from their grasp, and, out of the title race, Flyers found themselves stuck in mid-table. Attendances remained static and the lack of buzz on match nights did little to raise spirits - there were no post-season club awards save for the traditional Mirror of Merit.

It wasn't all doom and gloom, however.

Morrison hit his landmark 1,000th point in UK hockey, **Jonathan Weaver** signed late in the season to add some much needed offensive power, and then there was **Steve Briere**, many fans' choice as goalie of the year. He produced displays and saves which simply took your breath away - his stunning 65-shot stoning of Dundee on the road was one of the highlights of the season.

The campaign did at least end on a high note in April as 1,700 fans watched **Frank Morris** take his final bow in a testimonial game. The career of 'Captain Fantastic' had been ended through injury in a midweek game in Newcastle, and Fife missed his drive, his heart and his presence.

At his game he led a line which featured former Fifers, **Ted Russell** and **Russ Monteith**, leaving fans to guess how Flyers might have fared with them in the dressing-room in 2002-03.

PLAYER AWARD

Mirror of Merit   **Steve Briere**

LEADING PLAYERS

Steve Briere *born 25 March 1977*

Blitzed by shots, left exposed by a struggling defence, the netminder from the ECHL's Toledo Storm may have coughed up the odd bad goal but he still saved Fife's bacon on many a night. Virtually dominated the man of the match awards all season.

Frank Morris *born 22 March 1963*

After 16 seasons spanning 774 games, 871 goals, 820 assists, and 1,605 penalty minutes, an eye injury forced the defenceman to call time, although most agreed with his view that he could have skated on for several seasons yet. An intense competitor who was badly missed on the ice and in the locker room.

Jonathan Weaver (F) 20/1/77

A late signing out of the ashes of Superleague's Scottish Eagles, he came as close as any to turning Fife's season round. He linked superbly with Morrison and Haig on a potent second line only for that promise to be halted as the GB international was hit by a nagging injury. Scored a memorably sublime goal against Dundee.

FACT FILE 2002-03

British National League:	Seventh
Playoffs:	4th in qr-final group
***Findus* Cup**	3rd in group
Caledonian Cup:	Winners

HISTORY

Founded: 1938.

Leagues: (*Findus*) British National League (BNL) 1997-2003; Northern Premier League (NPL) 1996-97; British League 1982-96, 1954-55; Northern League (NL) 1966-82; Scottish National League (SNL) 1981-82, 1946-54, 1938-40.

Major Honours:

British Champions 1985. *Leagues*: BNL 1999-2000; NPL 1997-98, 1996-97; British Lge, Div. One 1991-92; NL 1976-78; SNL 1951-52, 1939-40. *Playoffs*: BNL 1999-2000, 1998-99.

Findus Challenge Cup: 2001-02; *Autumn Cup*: 1978, 1976, 1975; Scottish - 1950, 1948.

Scottish Cup: 2001, 2000, 1999, 1998, 1995, 1994.

GUILDFORD FLAMES

PLAYER	ALL COMPETITIONS					FINDUS BRITISH NATIONAL LEAGUE					PLAYOFFS				
Scorers	GP	G	A	Pts	Pim	GP	G	A	Pts	Pim	GP	G	A	Pts	Pim
Jason Lafreniere (WP)	54	26	50	76	166	36	19	37	56	67	8	4	5	9	89
Derek DeCosty (I)	53	34	37	71	16	36	26	27	53	8	7	3	5	8	2
David Clarke	47	35	24	59	124	33	27	17	44	77	8	5	5	10	6
Corey Lyons	54	26	29	55	71	36	22	19	41	18	8	2	5	7	2
Tony Redmond	54	21	30	51	42	36	16	24	40	30	8	3	2	5	8
Nicky Chinn	50	18	27	45	187	32	7	23	30	75	8	6	0	6	18
Craig Lyons (I)	31	15	25	40	34	21	10	18	28	24					
Jeff White (I)	54	10	28	38	100	36	8	21	29	86	8	1	2	3	2
Marc West (I) 1	20	9	22	31	16	12	6	15	21	8	8	3	7	10	8
Paul Dixon	53	8	23	31	34	35	7	14	21	22	8	0	6	6	4
Rick Plant	51	10	15	25	52	33	6	10	16	28	8	1	3	4	4
Ian Herbers (WP)	54	3	20	23	92	36	1	18	19	54	8	0	1	1	6
Mark Galazzi	51	9	11	20	44	33	8	10	18	32	8	0	1	1	0
Jason Bowen (WP) 3	35	4	15	19	110	25	3	12	15	86	8	0	2	2	14
Stan Marple	22	1	5	6	82	13	0	2	2	37	1	0	0	0	0
Mike Torchia (N) 4	34	0	5	5	14	24	0	4	4	14	8	0	0	0	0
Rick Skene	52	0	4	4	18	34	0	3	3	12	8	0	0	0	0
Jamie Hepburn	1	1	2	3	0	1	1	2	3	0					
Anthony Payne 1	1	0	2	2	0	1	0	2	2	0					
Danny Lorenz (N) (I) 2	20	0	2	2	6	12	0	2	2	6					
Mike Timms	1	1	0	1	0	1	1	0	1	0					
Greg Randall	1	0	1	1	0	1	0	1	1	0					
Bench Penalties					10					8					0
TEAM TOTALS	54	231	377	608	1218	36	168	281	449	692	8	28	44	72	163
Netminders	GPI	Mins	SOG	GA	Sv%	GPI	Mins	SOG	GA	Sv%	GPI	Mins	SOG	GA	Sv%
Danny Lorenz (I) 2	20	1196	594	67	88.7	12	716	342	46	86.5					
Mike Torchia (I) 4	34	1974	934	109	88.3	24	1369	655	78	88.1	8	480	234	23	90.2
Grant King	2	20	15	3	80.0	2	20	15	3	80.0					
Dave Hurst	2	72	17	4	76.5	2	72	17	4	76.5					
Empty Net Goals			3	3				2	2				1	1	
TEAM TOTALS		3262	1563	186	88.1	36	2177	1031	133	87.1	8	480	235	24	89.8

Shutouts: Lorenz - cup: 8 Sept v Solihull MK Kings (16 saves)

Also appeared: Oliver Bronniman, Kurt Reynolds 3; Chris Wiggins 2.

Also played for: 1 Hull Thunder, 2 Newcastle Vipers, 3 Scottish Eagles, 4 Manchester Storm.

All Competitions = league, playoffs and Findus Cup

GUILDFORD FLAMES *left to right, back row:* Ricky Skene, Tony Redmond, Mark Galazzi, Nicky Chinn, Ian Herbers, David Clarke, Stan Marple (player-coach), Mike Urquhart (asst coach), Adrian Jenkinson (trainer); *front row:* Grant King, Ricky Plant, Jason Lafreniere, Paul Dixon, Malcolm Norman (managing director), Corey Lyons, Jeff White, Derek DeCosty, Danny Lorenz.

Talent but no trophies

KIRK HUMPHREYS

After a year away from the silverware, Flames' coach **Stan Marple** worked tirelessly over the summer months putting together a squad of boundless talent. So third place in the league and semi-final berths in the playoffs and the *Findus* Cup left the club wanting more.

Marple's biggest signings were former NHLers **Ian Herbers**, **Danny Lorenz** and **Jason Lafreniere**, **Jeff White** from the defunct Paisley Pirates and British star **David Clarke** from London Knights/Milton Keynes Kings. With returnees of the calibre of **Paul Dixon**, **Nicky Chinn** and **Derek DeCosty**, this should have put Flames in a position to challenge for the awards. The *Findus* Cup was the first test and the results were good after an opening road loss to Basingstoke Bison. Flames won six of the next seven, topped their group and secured a place at the Finals weekend in Newcastle.

Their semi-final against the local Vipers was close but not close enough with Flames losing out on their first chance for hardware with a heartbreaking defeat on penalty shots.

Out with the *Findus* Cup and in with the league campaign - the British National League season was one of highs and lows. A difficult start brought two defeats during a doubleheader trip to Scotland but they recovered with four straight wins in October to move off the foot of the table.

But with just one win from nine tries, combined with the consistency of the Coventry Blaze meant that Flames' chance of capturing the league title was in doubt even before the Christmas lights were switched on.

Marple moved swiftly, releasing his disappointing netminder **Danny Lorenz** and replacing him with **Mike Torchia**, fresh from the insolvent Manchester Storm. Another Superleague club collapse enabled Flames to capture defenceman **Jason Bowen** from the Scottish Eagles.

The club bounced back and gave the supporters some Christmas cheer with eight consecutive wins which hoisted them up to around third or fourth place. The ride continued into February with Flames finally landing in third and looking forward to the playoff rounds and their last chance of hardware.

All went to plan as they secured a semi-final berth after only the second weekend, including a defeat of defending champs, Dundee Stars. But consecutive losses of 4-2 and 5-1 against the newly crowned league winners dashed their hopes once more.

PLAYER AWARDS

*Player of the Year	**David Clarke**
Players' Player	**Paul Dixon**
*British Player of the Year	**David Clarke**
British Player of the Year	**David Clarke**
Most Sportsmanlike Player	**Mark Galazzi**
Top Points Scorer	**Jason Lafreniere**

* selected by the Supporters Club. Other awards made by the club.

LEADING PLAYERS

David Clarke *born 5 August 1981*
Speed and a great shot served him well as he finished third among the team's league scorers. Selected several times to the GB national team.

Paul Dixon *born 4 August 1973*
Captaining the club once again, the defender produced his usual high standard of consistent play and 'team first' attitude. Giving 100 per cent in both ends of the rink night in and night out earned him the honour of being selected as Player of the Year by his teammates for the third time in four years.

Jason Lafreniere *born 6 December 1966*
Being the oldest member of the team did not stop Jason from leading the club in scoring and finishing in the league's top ten point getters. With a good work ethic to boot, he earned the respect of team-mates and supporters alike.

FACT FILE 2002-03

British National League:	Third
Playoffs:	Semi-finalists
Findus **Cup**	Semi-finalists

HISTORY
Founded: 1992.
Leagues: (*Findus*) British National League (BNL) 1997-2003; Premier League (PL) 1996-97; British League, Div. One 1993-96; English League 1992-93.
Honours: BNL and Playoffs 2000-01, 1997-98; *ntl* Cup 2000-01; *B&H* Plate 1998-99.

HARINGEY RACERS

PLAYER	ENGLISH PREMIER LEAGUE				
Scorers	GP	G	A	Pts	Pims
Petteri Pitko (I)	35	18	22	40	26
Danny Farren	27	15	21	36	44
Nick Burton	23	12	10	22	21
Gary Dodds	32	9	12	21	8
Rob Cole 2	10	7	5	12	78
Austin Speni (I)	17	4	6	10	76
Cody Mayoh (I)	12	3	7	10	26
Ricky Rutherford	32	4	5	9	10
David Carr	21	5	3	8	10
David Richards	34	3	5	8	61
Tim Collins 1	18	5	2	7	12
Jan Bestic	31	3	4	7	10
Mark Thomas	22	2	5	7	63
Brian McLaughlin (I)	7	2	5	7	20
Tom Boney	13	3	3	6	2
Kwabina Oppong-Addai	15	1	5	6	48
Ian Clark	37	1	3	4	80
Andrew (Smillie) Sillitoe	14	1	2	3	12
Barry Skene 3	20	0	2	2	4
Roger Black	8	0	2	2	31
Brian Clark	14	1	0	1	209
Paul Brown	17	0	1	1	2
Milton Freeman	11	0	1	1	14
Simon Kears	9	0	1	1	6
John Colley	6	0	1	1	16
Harry Bishop	5	0	1	1	0
Pavel Pojdl (I)	5	0	1	1	66
Dave Leverenz (I)	6	0	0	0	26
Tim Poulter	8	0	0	0	4
Liam Doyle	13	0	0	0	4
Tom Wills (N)	35	0	0	0	10
Bench Penalties					18
TEAM TOTALS	38	99	135	234	1017
Netminders	GPI	Mins	SOG	GA	Sv%
Aaron Mallet	1	20	12	1	91.7
Tom Wills	33	1879	1597	232	85.5
Dave Hurst 3	5	183	185	39	78.9
Geoff Butterfield	10	198	162	48	70.4
TEAM TOTALS	38	2280	1956	320	83.6

Also appeared: Dan Prachar (1) 1.
Also played for: 1 Swindon Lynx; .
2 Romford Raiders
3 Slough Jets

Out of their depth

MARTIN BENTLEY

At the start of the season, the Haringey club relaunched under the historic name of Haringey Racers, in honour of the first (professional) team to play in north London in the 1930s.

Unfortunately, their attempt to run a wholly amateur team in the largely semi-professional English Premier League once again met with little success as they finished 11th out of 12.

Team owner and coach **Roger Black** recruited **Nick Lovell** and **David Richards** to share the coaching duties, and augmented returning imports, Finn **Nick Burton** and Canadian goalie **Tom Wills**, with another Finn, winger **Petteri Pitko**, and giant American defenceman, **Austin Speni**. Haringey stalwarts **Gary Dodds**, **Jan Bestic** and the **Clark** brothers, **Ian** and **Brian**, also returned while the talented **Danny Farren** was appointed captain following the retirement of **Steve Fullan**.

After honourable defeats at Slough and Telford, on 15 September the club recorded their first win for over a year at home to Nottingham Lions, and went on to run up double figures with a 10-2 thumping of the England under-20s.

CAN'T GET THE PLAYERS

But the bigger teams in the league were still a bridge too far, while injuries and players' availability also hampered their attempts to compete. On a couple of occasions the roster of 25 was reduced to a piffling 10 or 11 for games.

Despite Wills' heroics in the net, a series of heavy defeats was inevitable until Black steadied the ship with some canny signings in ex-Swindon defenceman **Tim Collins** and former Greyhound **David Carr**. The untimely loss of the impressive Speni was partly offset by the arrival of another college forward, Canadian **Cody Mayoh**.

With ex-Romford and Chelmsford blueliner **Brian McLaughlin** joining the party later, Racers were at least able to be competitive against most of their opponents. There was, however, one gloriously unexpected crumb of comfort for their long-suffering supporters.

No one was expecting anything from a routine late-season match with Romford Raiders but Haringey stunned both sets of fans with a 2-1 victory. **Tom Boney**, just back from a broken wrist, scored the game-winner in the third period.

The result was meaningless and admittedly freakish but it was a glorious high point for the Racers in a difficult season.

PLAYER AWARDS

Player of the Year	**Ian Clark**
Players' Player	**Danny Farren**
Most Improved Player	**Dave Richards**

LEADING PLAYERS

Tim Collins *born 2 January 1979*
With a good hockey brain and a powerful slapshot, he brought some much needed stability to the blue line in mid-season.

Gary Dodds *born 5 August 1971*
With players coming and going around him, the ex-Medway and Lee Valley forward turned up week after week and skated his right wing, contributing his share of important points and taking only a minimal number of penalties. The perfect team man.

Dave Richards *born 19 January 1983*
The ex-Haringey junior improved with every game and by the end of the season was contributing vital points as an established member of the second line.

FACT FILE 2002-03

English Premier League:	11th
Playoffs:	Did not qualify
Premier Cup:	Did not enter

HISTORY

Founded: Various clubs have been run at the Alexandra Palace rink since it opened in 1990. **Roger Black** took over the current club during the 2001-02 season. Previous senior teams were known as Greyhounds in 1992-2002 and Racers in 1990-92.

Leagues: English (Premier) League 1994-2003; English Conference 1991-94; English Div. Three 1990-91.

HARINGEY RACERS *left to right, back row: (standing)* Mark Justice (chairman), 'Muckle' (equipment), 'Wally' (equipment), Jo Ackerman (supporters club), Dave Richards jr, John Colley, Tim Collins, Tim Poulter, Roger Black (player-coach), Mark Thomas, Cody Mayoh, Nick Burton, Petteri Pitko, Dave Richards sr (asst coach), driver and unknown; *front row:* Barry Skene, Geoff Butterfield, Simon Kears, Ian Clark, Jan Bestic, Ricky Rutherford, Paul Brown, Tom Wills; *laying down in front:* Danny Farren, Gary Dodds, mascots.

HULL THUNDER

PLAYER	ALL COMPETITIONS					FINDUS BRITISH NATIONAL LEAGUE				
Scorers	GP	G	A	Pts	Pim	GP	G	A	Pts	Pim
Marc West (I) 2	32	17	34	51	74	24	11	24	35	42
Paul Ferone (I) 3	32	25	17	42	103	24	20	13	33	87
Scott Young 4	32	14	27	41	160	24	11	20	31	114
Dominic Parlatore (I) 1	25	11	24	35	59	25	11	24	35	59
Eric Lavigne (WP)	32	7	16	23	145	24	5	12	17	113
Mike Morin (I)	30	8	14	22	80	22	7	10	17	50
Mark Florence	41	7	13	20	8	33	6	11	17	8
Dan Currie (WP)	13	7	12	19	14	5	1	4	5	2
Jonathan Weaver 5	11	8	10	18	2	11	8	10	18	2
Ryan Lake	38	8	6	14	47	30	7	6	13	43
Anthony Payne 2	25	4	10	14	16	25	4	10	14	16
Paul Wallace	41	6	5	11	26	34	6	5	11	24
Mike Bishop 6	30	3	7	10	99	22	1	5	6	42
Stephen Johnson	10	3	6	9	2	10	3	6	9	2
Steve Smillie (I)	8	2	4	6	18					
Andy Munroe	44	1	4	5	14	36	1	4	5	14
Ben Milhench	23	2	1	3	0	20	2	1	3	0
Jarkko Savijoki	2	1	2	3	0	2	1	2	3	0
Chris Hobson	12	1	2	3	4	12	1	2	3	4
Nathan Hunt	27	1	2	3	12	25	1	2	3	12
Kevin Phillips	20	0	3	3	16	19	0	3	3	16
Keith Leyland 7	19	1	1	2	0	16	1	1	2	0
Andy Winn	11	0	2	2	4	11	0	2	2	4
Marko Kivenmaki (I)	1	1	0	1	0	1	1	0	1	0
David Pyatt	6	1	0	1	0	6	1	0	1	0
Mark Bultje 8	2	0	1	1	0	2	0	1	1	0
Eoin McInerney (N) 9	4	0	1	1	4	4	0	1	1	4
Steven Winn	5	0	1	1	0	5	0	1	1	0
Karl Hopper	41	0	1	1	20	33	0	1	1	16
Neil Hardy	1	0	0	0	2					
Chris Butler	3	0	0	0	2	3	0	0	0	2
Rob Chamberlain	3	0	0	0	2	3	0	0	0	2
James Day	9	0	0	0	10	9	0	0	0	10
Stephen Foster (N)	41	0	0	0	2	33	0	0	0	0
Bench Penalties					10					10
TEAM TOTALS	44	139	226	365	955	36	110	181	291	698
Netminders	GPI	Mins	SOG	GA	Sv%	GPI	Mins	SOG	GA	Sv%
Eoin McInerney	4	245	115	9	92.2	4	245	115	9	92.2
Stephen Foster	37	2116	1291	197	84.7	29	1636	1044	165	84.2
Tristan Rodgers	1	6	5	1	80.0	1	6	5	1	80.0
Sam Roberts	8	279	265	59	77.7	8	279	265	59	77.7
Empty Net Goals			5	5				2	2	
TEAM TOTALS	44	2646	1681	271	83.9	36	2166	1431	236	83.5

Also appeared: Ben O'Connor 6; Lewis Day 5; Milton Freeman 2; David Phillips, Glenn Young, Chris Markham, Chris Shephardson 1.

Also played for: 1 Solihull MK Kings; 2 Guildford Flames; 3 Newcastle Vipers; 4 Dundee Stars; 5 Fife Flyers, Scottish Eagles; 6 Cardiff Devils, Fife Flyers; 7 Sheffield Steelers; 8 Manchester Storm, 9 Scottish Eagles

All Competitions = league and Findus *Cup*

HULL THUNDER *left to right, back row:* Karl Hopper, Chris Hobson, Nathan Hunt, Chris Butler, Dave Pyatt, Kevin Phillips, Andy Winn, James Day, Keith Leyland, Ben Milhench, Stephen Johnson; *front row:* Mark Florence, Sam Roberts, Steven Winn, Anthony Payne, Andy Munroe, Ryan Lake, Paul Wallace, Stephen Foster.

Photo: Arthur Foster.

Thunder lighten owner's pocket

CATHY WIGHAM

Picture the scene: the learned judge, and the defendants, Hull's senior ice hockey team - ."What have you got to say for yourselves this season, Thunder?"

"Well, your honour, we made a real dog's dinner of it. We built an expensive, under-achieving team and then the owner decided not to spend any more money, so we axed the coach, four other players and three more left in January.

"We completed the season with a fully British squad and lost 16 matches on the trot. Oh yes, and to start the next campaign we need a new owner, a new coach, a new name and new money."

"This a repeated offence in Hull, is it not? In the last seven seasons you've had seven coaches, four owners and three names."

"Yes, your honour, but we'll do better next time."

Thunder's campaign started brightly, there was talk of silverware, stability and a team on paper that could compete with the best. With **Mike Bishop** at the helm, the team oozed top-class signings like Canadians **Marc West**, **Dan Currie**, **Domenic Parlatore** and **Scott Young**. Add in former Manchester Storm pair **Mike Morin** and **Paul Ferone** and owner **Martin Jenkinson's** cash and everything looked rosy.

The bright start soon petered out, prompting Thunder to change imports like most people change their socks. At one stage there were ten on the roster, with **Steve Smillie** leaving, Parlatore arriving and three - **Marko Kivenmaki**, **Jarkko Savijoki** and then **Mark Bultje** - on trial.

After six months' hard work, the expensively assembled squad was dismantled in a fortnight. Trundling along in ninth, with a string of one or two goal defeats, was not what Jenkinson had in mind. He had better things to spend his cash on and he halted his investment.

In one drastic January night out went Bishop, Young, Ferone, Morin and **Jon Weaver**. Another two weeks and West, Parlatore and **Eric Lavigne** had all quit. With director O'Connor staying put, **Sid Butt** underwriting the costs, and **Peter Johnson** as coach on a voluntary basis, Thunder limped along to the end of the season. Defeats were a foregone conclusion, but once more Hull unearthed more young British talent just waiting to be given the chance like defensive duo **Nathan Hunt** and **Kevin Phillips**.

It'll all be different next season, your honour, the future's British, the future's prudent.

Honest, m'lud.

PLAYER AWARDS

Player of the Year	**Ryan Lake**
Forward of the Year	**Ryan Lake**
Defenceman of the Year	**Andy Munroe**
Most Improved Player	**Sam Roberts**
Spirit of the Game:	**Anthony Payne**

LEADING PLAYERS

Paul Ferone *born 12 April 1976*
A 110 per cent effort forward with excellent finishing skills. Looked mild-mannered, he was billed as an enforcer but hardly ever dropped his gloves. Perhaps his reputation from Superleague meant he didn't have to.

Ryan Lake *born 31 August 1983*
Turbo-wheeled, bustling, bone-crunching local lad, built like a stick insect. The GB under-20 international was sometimes too quick for his own good, but with the right coaching - and plenty of ice time - can develop into a real talent.

Andy Munroe *born 2 August 1982*
Another under-20 international, the quiet, rock-solid, rapidly improving, stand-out defenceman benefited from playing alongside **Eric Lavigne**. Particularly outstanding late season, after the cost-cutting cull of his more experienced defensive team-mates.

FACT FILE 2002-03

British National League:	9th
Playoffs:	Did not qualify
***Findus* Cup:**	4th in group

HISTORY

Founded: February 1999. The first club in Hull was Humberside Seahawks 1988-96 (known as Humberside Hawks 1993-96). Second club was Kingston Hawks 1996-99 (briefly Hull City Hawks 1998-99).
Leagues: Hull - British National League 1999-2003; *Kingston* - British National Lge 1997-99, Premier Lge 1996-97; *Humberside* - British Lge, Premier Div. 1991-96, British Lge, Div. One 1989-91, English Lge 1988-89.
Honours: British League, Div. One 1990-91; English League 1988-89.

INVICTA DYNAMOS

PLAYER	ALL COMPETITIONS					ENGLISH PREMIER LEAGUE					PLAYOFFS				
Scorers	GP	G	A	Pts	Pim	GP	G	A	Pts	Pim	GP	G	A	Pts	Pim
Matt Beveridge (I)	53	54	77	131	42	38	46	59	105	34	6	4	9	13	2
Duane Ward (I)	50	57	54	111	58	37	43	45	88	40	4	6	3	9	2
Elliot Andrews	53	28	47	75	63	39	24	43	67	30	5	2	2	4	0
Carl Greenhous	49	18	25	43	60	34	13	19	32	40	6	2	4	6	8
Michael Wales	53	17	23	40	206	39	13	19	32	144	6	3	2	5	34
Sean Clement	46	3	32	35	64	31	3	22	25	52	6	0	2	2	4
Phil Chard	51	11	22	33	42	36	9	17	26	32	6	0	4	4	6
Jake French	53	9	17	26	46	38	7	15	22	22	6	2	1	3	4
Stuart Low 1	38	12	11	23	30	24	10	7	17	18	6	1	3	4	6
Peter Korff	54	9	10	19	22	39	6	6	12	22	6	2	2	4	0
Paul Hume	33	4	15	19	14	31	2	15	17	14					
Greg Hales	54	5	6	11	14	39	5	4	9	10	6	0	1	1	0
Ari Samuli Mykkanen (I) 1	6	6	4	10	12	6	6	4	10	12					
Dan Fudger	32	3	3	6	14	18	1	3	4	14	6	0	0	0	0
Adam Smith	10	2	4	6	2	4	1	3	4	2	2	1	0	1	0
Garrett Gaetz-Bruce	14	3	0	3	25	10	3	0	3	25					
Kevin Parrish	14	0	1	1	8	13	0	1	1	8					
Carl Ambler (N)	40	0	1	1	2	26	0	1	1	2	6	0	0	0	0
Matt van der Velden (N)	53	0	1	1	0	38	0	1	1	0	6	0	0	0	0
Jonathan Gray	29	0	0	0	14	24	0	0	0	14					
Bench Penalties					12					8					0
TEAM TOTALS	54	241	353	594	750	39	192	284	476	543	6	23	33	56	66
Netminders	GPI	Mins	SOG	GA	Sv%	GPI	Mins	SOG	GA	Sv%	GPI	Mins	SOG	GA	Sv%
Matt van der Velden	46	2699	1817	206	88.7	32	1886	1203	140	88.4	6	333	268	31	88.4
Carl Ambler	11	541	338	46	86.4	9	454	243	28	88.5	1	27	34	9	73.5
TEAM TOTALS	54	3240	2155	252	88.3	39	2340	1446	168	88.4	6	360	302	40	86.7

Shutout: van der Velden - league: 29 Sept v Haringey Racers (28 saves)
Also appeared: Adam Noctor, Joe White 3.
Also played for: 1 Romford Raiders.
All Competitions = league, playoffs and Premier Cup

Sportsmen, except Wales

ANDY BRADLEY

Winning the English Premier League's Sportsmanship Trophy was all Dynamos had to show for their efforts at the end of a disappointing campaign.

After collecting the league championship and reaching the Cup final in 2001-02, they were hopeful of doing the same or even better. But, quite literally, they were not the same team.

Various factors, including a reduction in the number of imports, contributed. For a start two of the team's most influential players, hard-hitting **Andy Hannah** and **Mikko Skinnari**, moved away during the summer and the 'big gun' brought into replace them fired too many blanks.

Hannah returned to Chelmsford and Skinnari, after four productive years at the Ice Bowl, was allowed to join Milton Keynes. With the benefit of hindsight, Invicta wrongly pinned their hopes on burly Finnish forward **Sammi Mykkanen**. Unfortunately, though scoring a goal a game, he wasn't reckoned up to scratch, and was shipped out after making only half-a-dozen appearances.

To make matters worse, leading British forward **Mike Kindred** announced his decision to quit on the eve of the new campaign. It was a blow from which the Dynamos never really recovered.

As a result new coach **Carl Greenhous**, who iced regularly once Mykkanen had departed, faced an uphill struggle. A 5-2 opening day home defeat by Milton Keynes gave an indication of what to expect. Nearly every time a good result was achieved, a setback followed and the team hovered around mid-table.

Several mainly third-line players decided to call it a day at different stages and this, coupled with the usual spate of injuries, led to the bench becoming ever shorter.

"It was a truly frustrating season," confessed long-serving skipper and players' player, **Phil Chard**. "We took points off all the teams above us and could match anybody on our day. But there were too many occasions when we weren't at our best and at our worst we were awful."

Although new arrivals, **Michael Wales** and **Stuart Low** (from Romford), both made an impact, Dynamos lacked the strength in depth needed to match the leading title contenders.

After months spent seeking a top import forward and two more quality British players to boost the roster, all hope was abandoned and instead emerging youngsters like **Garrett Bruce**, **Daniel Fudger** and **Adam Smith** were thrown in at the deep end. All three underlined their potential by doing well and scoring points.

PLAYER AWARDS

Player of the Year	**Michael Wales**
Players' Player	**Phil Chard**
Best Forward	**Matt Beveridge**
Best Defenceman	**Jake French**
Best British Player	**Matt van der Velden**

LEADING PLAYERS

Matt Beveridge *born 18 March 1975*
Top scorer again in his third season with the club, taking his aggregate tally to nearly 300 points. Previously with Paisley, Peterborough and Whitley, he soon became a favourite among supporters through his creative skills and finishing ability.

Matt van der Velden *born 21 August 1979*
Signed from Romford three years ago, he is still among the best young British netminders in the Premier League. Some of the saves he pulled off were remarkable and he made few mistakes in a busy season.

Michael Wales *born 22 August 1982*
Emerged through Invicta's junior ranks and returned to the club via Solihull. Settled in quickly and was a big hit in more ways than one, picking up most penalty minutes (by more than two hours!) and being voted player of the year by the supporters.

FACT FILE 2002-03

English Premier League:	7th
Playoffs:	4th in group
Premier Cup:	6th in group

HISTORY

Founded: 1997. Previous club was Medway Bears 1984-97.

Leagues: English (Premier) League 1997-2003, 1991-92 & 1984-86; Premier League 1996-97; British League, Div. One 1992-96 and 1986-91.

Honours: English Premier League and playoffs 2001-02; English League & (promotion) playoffs 1991-92; British League, Div. Two 1985-86.

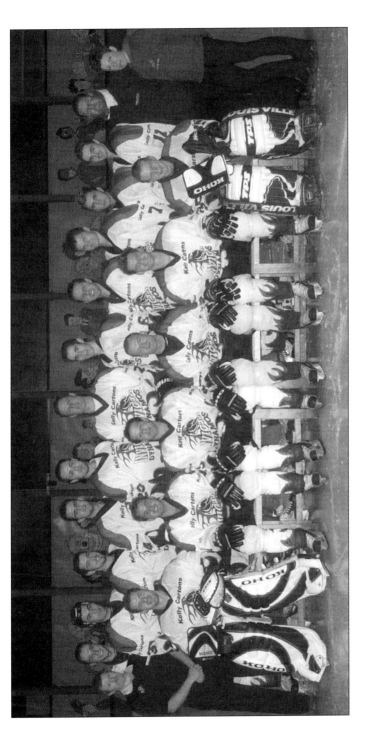

INVICTA DYNAMOS *left to right, back row:* Alf Halford (equipment), Peter Korff, Kevin Parrish, Greg Hales, Jake French, Duane Ward, Sean Clement, Michael Wales, Matt Beveridge, Paul Hume, Garrett Bruce, Jonathan Grey, Andy Mason (manager), Julia Keeley (physio); *front row:* Matt van der Velden, Stuart Low, Phil Chard, Carl Greenhous (player-coach), Elliot Andrews, Carl Ambler.

ISLE OF WIGHT RAIDERS

PLAYER	ALL COMPETITIONS					ENGLISH PREMIER LEAGUE					PLAYOFFS				
Scorers	GP	G	A	Pts	Pim	GP	G	A	Pts	Pim	GP	G	A	Pts	Pim
David Kozier (I)	53	97	82	179	60	37	70	64	134	44	6	5	4	9	2
Jason Coles	50	57	50	107	144	34	39	38	77	77	6	4	1	5	31
Brad Kenny (I)	28	52	43	95	26	27	50	41	91	24	0	0	0	0	0
Adam Carr	38	20	51	71	16	24	11	36	47	14	6	3	5	8	0
Richard Hargreaves	52	16	48	64	193	36	10	33	43	143	6	3	6	9	12
Andy Pickles	43	9	38	47	76	27	7	26	33	56	6	1	5	6	6
Scott Carter	53	11	25	36	48	37	7	17	24	40	6	3	4	7	4
Tony Blaize	40	12	21	33	55	32	12	16	28	53	6	0	2	2	0
Joe Baird	54	6	21	27	144	38	5	15	20	118	6	0	3	3	2
Rob Lamey 1	16	11	12	23	2	3	3	1	4	2	6	5	5	10	0
James Hutchinson	49	4	17	21	40	35	3	13	16	26	5	0	0	0	8
Steve Gannaway	51	2	18	20	88	36	2	12	14	66	6	0	3	3	10
Michael Hargreaves	54	8	11	19	36	38	7	9	16	30	6	1	0	1	6
Neil Leary	54	2	13	15	28	38	2	12	14	22	6	0	0	0	2
Paul Sanderson	40	4	6	10	26	28	3	4	7	22	6	1	1	2	0
Daniel Giden	51	1	4	5	28	37	1	3	4	22	4	0	1	1	0
Damon Larter	40	0	5	5	2	26	0	4	4	0	6	0	0	0	0
Stephen Larter	14	2	2	4	28	13	0	0	0	28	0	0	0	0	0
Andy Moffat (N)	52	0	2	2	12	36	0	2	2	6	6	0	0	0	2
Michael Palin	2	0	0	0	2	2	0	0	0	2	0	0	0	0	0
Bench Penalties					12					10					0
TEAM TOTALS	54	314	469	783	1066	38	232	346	578	805	6	26	40	66	85
Netminders	GPI	Mins	SOG	GA	Sv%	GPI	Mins	SOG	GA	Sv%	GPI	Mins	SOG	GA	Sv%
Andy Moffat	46	2708	1747	180	89.7	32	1869	1203	132	89.0	5	300	211	21	90.0
Toby Cooley	11	530	275	29	89.5	9	410	201	18	91.0	1	60	38	9	76.3
Empty Net Goals		2	3	3			1	2	2						
TEAM TOTALS	54	3240	2025	212	89.5	38	2280	1406	152	89.2	6	360	249	30	87.9

Shutouts: Moffat - league: 2 Nov v Haringey Racers (27 saves)

                Cooley - league: 21 Dec v Haringey Racers (18)

Also played for: 1 Swindon Lynx

All Competitions = league, playoffs and Premier Cup

ISLE OF WIGHT RAIDERS *left to right, back row:* Neil Leary, Mike Hargreaves, Adam Carr, Damon Larter, Tony Blaize; *middle row:* Michael Palin, Richard Hargreaves, Brad Kenny, Daniel Giden, Paul Sanderson, James Hutchinson, David Kozier; *front row:* Toby Cooley, Joe Baird, Jason Coles (co-coach), Scott Carter, Andy Pickles (co-coach), Steve Gannaway, Andy Moffat.

Cosy with Kozier

CLARE WALL

New player-coaches **Jason Coles** and **Andy Pickles** did well in their attempt to rebuild the Raiders after the departure of **Luc Chabot** as the **Steve Porter**-sponsored team finished in mid-table in the English Premier League.

The star of the new-look side was their impressive new import forward, **David Kozier** from Cornell University, the American college which has produced such talented imports as Bracknell's **Doug Stienstra** and Cardiff's **Jeff Burgoyne**.

Kozier, 24, was runner-up in the league scoring and his tremendous ability almost made the fans forget Chabot who joined Peterborough Phantoms, another Planet Ice club, after three seasons on the Island.

The rivalry with the teams in the other Planet Ice rinks was fierce throughout the season. Though Raiders never got the better of their old boss's new club, who emerged as champions, their games against Milton Keynes Lightning were often appropriately electrifying. Their best result was a 5-5 draw at home in November.

PROUD HOME RECORD

In fact, Raiders had a home record to be proud of, losing only five league games, including the two to the title-winning Phantoms.

The Premier Cup was their best competition as they came into the final stages needing only a draw at Milton Keynes or a win in Romford next day to reach the final. Sadly, they lost both contests by two goals.

While Raiders were naturally delighted to qualify for the Playoffs, the bad news was being drawn into a group which included runners-up Lightning and third place Slough Jets. Again it was the games with Lightning which were the most dramatic. After a torturous 6-0 whitewash in the Midlands, Raiders put on one of their best performances of the season and edged them 5-4 in a thrilling return.

Indeed, it would be fair to say that had Raiders played every week the same way they did against Milton Keynes, they would have come away with a trophy.

With crowds around the 500-mark still down on previous seasons, Raiders and their supporters worked hard to attract a new generation of followers. Their charity work for the local community, especially the 'Goals for Cancer' campaign, was a big success and could be copied in other rinks around the league.

PLAYER AWARDS

Player of the Year	David Kozier
Players' Player	David Kozier
Forward of the Year	David Kozier
Defenceman of the Year	Steve Gannaway
Best Newcomer	Adam Carr
Most Improved Player	Damon Larter

LEADING PLAYERS

Steve Gannaway born 20 September 1973

Raiders' fans describe the veteran as like a fine wine - he just gets better with age. The Southampton-born defenceman isn't a point scorer but one his team-mates can trust with the puck. Dedicated to the team and happy to play when and where they need him.

David Kozier born 8 April 1978

Out-pointing his team-mates by almost two to one, he was the best player to have put on a Raiders shirt. His skill even astonished Basingstoke fans when he guested in Bison's *Wella* Cup game and scored a hat-trick against Superleague's Bracknell Bees. A joy to watch.

Damon Larter born 7 May 1986

The precocious 16-year-old played on the first line and often showed seasoned veterans how to play defence. Was benched during the Playoffs, but is definitely one to watch.

FACT FILE 2002-03

English Premier League:	6th
Playoffs:	3rd in group
Premier Cup:	2nd in group

HISTORY

Founded: 1999. The first club on the Island in 1991 was Solent Vikings. The team was known as *Wightlink* Raiders 1992-99.

Leagues: English (Premier) League 1991-2003.

Honours: English Premier Cup 2001; English League 1993-97.

LONDON KNIGHTS

PLAYER	ALL COMPETITIONS					SUPERLEAGUE					PLAYOFFS				
Scorers	GP	G	A	Pts	Pim	GP	G	A	Pts	Pim	GP	G	A	Pts	Pim
Mark Kolesar	56	22	29	51	40	29	10	12	22	10	18	7	13	20	16
Dennis Maxwell (WP)	57	23	23	46	169	30	9	7	16	110	18	10	9	19	33
Vezio Sacratini	52	15	28	43	50	28	9	16	25	16	16	4	10	14	12
Ian McIntyre (WP)	59	18	24	42	60	32	10	9	19	38	18	6	8	14	14
Sean Blanchard (WP)	59	15	24	39	42	32	5	12	17	24	18	8	6	14	6
Jeff Hoad	57	14	25	39	58	32	8	11	19	38	18	4	11	15	18
Rich Bronilla (WP)	59	16	19	35	28	32	10	11	21	14	18	5	4	9	8
Kim Ahlroos	40	12	21	33	16	27	6	19	25	12	4	0	1	1	0
Steve Aronson (WP)	41	12	13	25	16	24	4	9	13	10	14	5	3	8	4
Maurizio Mansi	55	8	16	24	44	29	5	5	10	16	17	2	8	10	20
Gerad Adams	55	4	18	22	126	28	2	7	9	84	18	2	8	10	26
Ed Patterson	24	8	13	21	56	4	1	2	3	2	18	6	10	16	46
Greg Burke	57	6	8	14	129	32	4	6	10	57	18	2	1	3	58
Chris Slater (WP)	59	2	9	11	219	32	1	6	7	135	18	0	2	2	58
Paul Rushforth	46	4	6	10	190	25	2	5	7	144	14	0	1	1	26
Nathan Leslie	50	1	5	6	61	24	0	3	3	27	18	1	0	1	0
AJ Kelham	15	3	2	5	4	9	1	1	2	2	2	0	0	0	0
Dave Trofimenkoff (N)	36	0	1	1	2	24	0	1	1	0	5	0	0	0	0
Ake Lilljebjorn (N)	25	0	0	0	0	9	0	0	0	0	14	0	0	0	0
Bench Penalties					18					16					0
TEAM TOTALS	59	183	284	467	1328	32	87	142	229	755	18	62	95	157	345

Netminders	GPI	Min	SOG	GA	Sv%	GPI	Min	SOG	GA	Sv%	GPI	Min	SOG	GA	Sv%
Dave Trofimenkoff	36	2125	1061	95	91.0	24	1446	752	65	91.4	5	254	147	12	91.8
Ake Lilljebjorn	25	1483	682	64	90.6	9	515	249	23	90.8	14	846	388	37	90.5
EN Goals/GW Shots			4	4				2	2				1	1	
TEAM TOTALS	59	3608	1747	163	90.7	32	1961	1003	90	91.0	18	1100	536	50	90.7

Shutouts: Lilljebjorn (2) - playoffs: 12 Mar at Bracknell Bees (21 saves)

26 Mar v Bracknell Bees (30)

All Competitions = league, playoffs, Challenge Cup and Ahearne Trophy

Jim fixes it

SIMON CROSSE

A late change of coach helped Knights to go out on a high as Swede **Jim Brithen** led them to the final of the Superleague Playoffs for the third time in their five seasons. Sadly, it was to be the club's last hoorah.

Having sold their London Docklands home arena to concentrate on redeveloping the Millennium Dome in nearby Greenwich, the Anschutz Entertainment Group folded the franchise with no date set for a return.

The fans were finally relieved from months of uncertainty when AEG snuck out a brief statement late one evening in April admitting what the fans had feared all along - AEG had failed in their search for a suitable alternative venue.

Coach **Bob Leslie** began his second season in charge by fulfilling his promise to the fans to keep a large core of familiar faces. While long term injuries to forward **Steve Thornton** and goalie **Trevor Robins** continued to frustrate him, the likeable Canadian put out a team able to challenge on most fronts, a lack of scoring from the forwards being the major deficiency.

> Two will always be the magic number for Knights. They've always shown a flair for the dramatic during the Playoffs; winning in sudden-death overtime in 2000 and with 14 seconds remaining in 2001.
>
> But **Dennis Maxwell**'s marker with 00.02 seconds left in the semi-final win over Nottingham Panthers in 2003 overshadowed them all.

New signings **Dennis Maxwell** and **Chris Slater** quickly became fan favourites while **Jeff Hoad**'s quiet return from Belfast gave Knights greater depth at centre-ice. **Mark Kolesar** remained the outstanding contributor, ably assisted by **Vezio Sacratini** and **Kim Ahlroos** who led the way in points along with **Sean Blanchard** and **Rich Bronilla**, defencemen who stepped up and went on lengthy scoring streaks at the turn of the year.

The loss of Sacratini and Ahlroos for the Playoffs was decisive in Knights' final loss to Giants, in spite of the efforts of **Steve Aronson**, London's unlikely scoring leader at the NIC.

When Leslie left the club for family reasons early in the New Year, Brithen took the team to another level. By the end of the season Knights were not only an attractive team to watch but also winning matches while the players, Maxwell in particular, seemed to improve under the smart Swede's guidance.

PLAYER AWARDS

Most Valuable Player	**Rich Bronilla**
Players' Player	**Ian McIntyre**
Best Forward	**Dennis Maxwell**
Best Defenceman	**Sean Blanchard**
Coach's Award	**Greg Burke**
Sportsmanship Award	**Ian McIntyre**

LEADING PLAYERS

Sean Blanchard born 29 March 1978

One of the league's most elegant and hard working defencemen, he contributed on all fronts in his first full term as a Knight. A cousin of former Knight **Neal Martin**, he was second in club scoring during the Playoffs and was voted MVP by the fans.

Mark Kolesar born 23 January 1973

The former Toronto Maple Leaf was Mr Reliable never failing to put in a gritty, team leading performance. Outstanding on the penalty kill.

Dennis Maxwell born 4 June 1974

Revitalising his career in London, the physical winger ensured legendary status among the Knights' faithful with his last second semi-final winner against Panthers. A favourite of Swedish coach **Jim Brithen**, he exploded in the Playoffs, more than doubling his total points output for the regular season and leading the club with ten playoff goals.

FACT FILE 2002-03

Superleague:	4th
Playoffs:	Finalists
Challenge Cup:	Semi-finalists

HISTORY

Founded: 1998.
League: Superleague 1998-2003.
Honours: Superleague Playoffs 1999-2000.

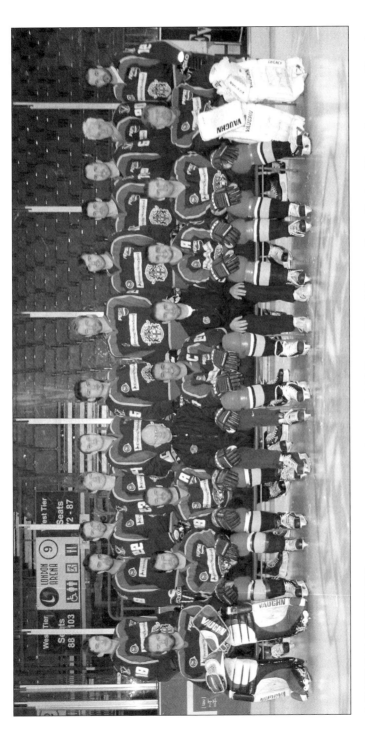

LONDON KNIGHTS *left to right, back row:* AJ Kelham, Kim Ahlroos, Greg Burke, Steve Aronson, Dennis Maxwell, Ritchie Bronilla, Ed Patterson, Nate Leslie, Sean Blanchard, Gerad Adams, Chris Slater, Maurizio Mansi; *front row:* Dave Trofimenkoff, Vezio Sacratini, Jeff Hoad, Jim Brithen (coach) Ian McIntyre, Jason Ellery (equipment); Mark Kolesar, Paul Rushforth, Ake Lilljebjorn.

Photo: Diane Davey

MILTON KEYNES LIGHTNING

PLAYER	ALL COMPETITIONS					ENGLISH PREMIER LEAGUE					PLAYOFFS				
Scorers	GP	G	A	Pts	Pim	GP	G	A	Pts	Pim	GP	G	A	Pts	Pim
Gary Clarke	60	110	73	183	84	41	86	56	142	60	8	14	5	19	10
Nick Poole	61	46	112	158	36	41	35	92	127	24	8	4	12	16	6
Mikko Skinnari (I)	61	40	67	107	40	41	27	52	79	36	8	5	6	11	4
Greg Randall	53	37	58	95	26	34	24	40	64	16	8	4	11	15	4
Greg Owen	53	50	35	85	42	36	40	23	63	30	6	6	4	10	0
Dean Campbell	58	20	37	57	34	38	13	25	38	24	8	3	6	9	4
Dwayne Newman (I)	58	10	33	43	93	40	6	26	32	83	7	2	3	5	0
Claude Dumas	20	20	17	37	41	4	4	0	4	6	8	7	10	17	6
Michael Knights	54	2	26	28	139	35	0	20	20	113	8	1	2	3	10
Simon Howard	55	9	18	27	90	35	7	9	16	78	8	0	4	4	8
Mark Krater	56	9	13	22	24	38	7	13	20	20	7	0	0	0	2
Leigh Jamieson	47	5	16	21	62	33	3	14	17	34	4	1	1	2	22
Phil Wooderson	58	6	10	16	18	40	4	9	13	18	8	0	1	1	0
Geoff O'Hara	52	5	6	11	56	33	4	6	10	52	8	0	0	0	0
Mark Conway	26	3	8	11	20	19	3	7	10	20	3	0	0	0	0
Chris McEwen 2	36	1	7	8	8	16	1	4	5	6	8	0	1	1	0
Keiron Goody	28	2	2	4	8	25	2	2	4	6					
Mark Hazlehurst 1	16	3	0	3	87	3	2	0	2	12	7	1	0	1	59
Richard Munnelly	7	0	3	3	0	7	0	3	3	0					
Barry Hollyhead (N)	59	0	3	3	28	39	0	2	2	28	8	0	0	0	0
Tom Ledgard	1	1	0	1	0	1	1	0	1	0					
Paul Jamieson	5	0	0	0	2	5	0	0	0	2					
Paul Gore	7	0	0	0	2	7	0	0	0	2					
Allen Sutton (N)	61	0	0	0	2	41	0	0	0	2	8	0	0	0	0
Bench Penalties					22					14					2
TEAM TOTALS	61	379	544	923	964	41	269	403	672	686	8	48	66	114	137

Netminders	GPI	Mins	SOG	GA	Sv%	GPI	Mins	SOG	GA	Sv%	GPI	Mins	SOG	GA	Sv%
Barry Hollyhead	42	2488	1364	119	91.3	27	1619	891	83	90.7	7	420	232	14	94.0
Allen Sutton	20	1171	448	45	90.0	14	840	314	29	90.8	1	60	37	5	86.5
Empty Net Goals		1	1	1			1	1	1						
TEAM TOTALS	61	3660	1813	165	90.9	41	2460	1206	113	90.6	8	480	269	19	92.9

Shutouts: Sutton - league: 14 Sept v Nottingham Lions (17 saves);
9 Nov v Nottingham Lions (20).

Also appeared: Bobby Jinks, Russ Bowers 2; Mark Woolf 1.

Also played for: 1 Cardiff Devils, Telford Wild Foxes; 2 Nottingham Lions.

All Competitions = league, playoffs and Premier Cup

MILTON KEYNES LIGHTNING *left to right, back row:* Dwayne Newman, Greg Randall, Nick Poole, Phil Wooderson, Mikko Skinnari, Gary Clarke, Leigh Jamieson, Dean Campbell, Mark Hazlehurst, Chris McEwen; *middle row:* Peter Nolan (physio), Geoff O'Hara, Simon Howard, Allen Sutton, Michael Knights, Liam Nolan (physio); *front row:* Mark Krater, Vito Rausa (manager), Barry Hollyhead, Harry Howton (chairman), Jevon Burness (asst manager), Claude Dumas. *Inset:* Greg Owen

Photo: Keith Perry Sports Photography

Newman, new name

PAUL BROOKMAN

It was a case of all change but no change in Milton Keynes as the Lightning replaced the Kings for the 2002-03 season.

The name may have been new but many of the faces were familiar with no less than 11 of Lightning's roster having iced for Kings. Coach **Nick Poole** was joined by assistant **Simon Howard** - both ex-Kings - and the first signings they made, **Gary Clarke** and **Greg Randall**, were also ex-Kings. The icing on the cake was the acquisition of influential captain, **Dwayne Newman**.

The squad looked more than strong enough for the English Premier League but Lightning had fears about the number of fans who would follow the old Kings to their new home in Solihull.

They needn't have worried as 1,190 turned out for Lightning's first league game against Romford Raiders. The result, a 7-7 draw, was one of only three points dropped at home all season. Had this form been repeated away, Lightning would have won the league.

Early on the defence looked weak leading some fans to call for the side to tighten up but Poole said: "We are not going to play boring defensive hockey. We aim to entertain with attacking hockey." And they did.

From late October they embarked on a 25-game unbeaten streak that was only ended by the Isle of Wight Raiders three months later. Their target of finishing in the top four proved too modest as they headed the league for all but the final weeks - although rivals Peterborough Phantoms had games in hand.

Poole was justifiably proud of the fact that not one player left or was axed during the season. In fact he strengthened the club in November with the signing of fast skating defenceman, **Chris McEwen**, from Nottingham Lions.

And as the regular season entered its final month he staged a coup by persuading goal scoring legend **Claude Dumas** to come out of retirement. This, plus the signing of **Mark Hazlehurst** to add muscle, was decisive even though the league title slipped away.

Lightning reached the final of the Premier Cup only to suffer the agony of losing out 7-6 on aggregate to Peterborough. But the following week when they faced Phantoms yet again in the playoff finals, they at last turned over their rivals. A 10-0 defeat in the home leg - Peterborough's heaviest loss of the season - was followed next day with a 6-4 win in Cambridgeshire.

PLAYER AWARDS

Player of the Year	Dwayne Newman
Players' Player	Dwayne Newman
Top Points Scorer	Gary Clarke
Best Defenceman	Dwayne Newman
Coach's Award:	Dwayne Newman
Best Home-grown Player	Gary Clarke
Most Improved Player	Barry Hollyhead
Most Promising Player	Leigh Jamieson
Clubman	Dean Campbell

LEADING PLAYERS

Gary Clarke *born 7 December 1978*

The Telford-born forward came of age, terrorising defences with his sharp-shooting to finish as the league's top scorer – the only Brit in the top ten – with 86 goals and 56 assists in the regular season.

Dwayne Newman *born 27 May 1971*

The Winnipeg-born defenceman, nicknamed 'The Dog', was one of the best signings of the year and a leader on and off the ice. As Poole remarked: "He made my job so easy."

Nick Poole *born 11 July 1973*

The coach led by example with his best season yet in Milton Keynes, being the provider for most of Clarke's goals. His aim to make hockey fun rubbed off on the other players.

FACT FILE 2002-03

English Premier League	Runners-up
Playoffs	Winners
Premier Cup	Finalists

HISTORY

Founded: 2002. Original club founded 1990 as Kings. Rink closed 1996-98.

Leagues: *Lightning* - English Premier League 2002-03; *Kings* - *Findus* British National League 1999-2002; English League (Premier Div) 1998-99, 1990-91; British League, Premier Div 1994-96; British League, Div One 1991-94.

NEWCASTLE VIPERS

PLAYER	ALL COMPETITIONS					FINDUS BRITISH NATIONAL LEAGUE					PLAYOFFS				
Scorers	GP	G	A	Pts	Pim	GP	G	A	Pts	Pim	GP	G	A	Pts	Pim
Mikko Koivunoro (I)	50	31	46	77	60	34	20	33	53	32	6	4	0	4	16
Joel Irwin (WP)	48	25	31	56	72	32	20	25	45	60	6	0	1	1	4
Mike Lankshear (I)	52	15	25	40	99	36	9	17	26	65	6	0	3	3	28
Simon Leach	46	17	22	39	76	31	11	14	25	48	6	3	1	4	12
David Longstaff 6	19	14	22	36	20	17	13	20	33	20					
Rob Wilson 6	36	9	22	31	76	29	8	21	29	60	5	0	1	1	8
Rob Trumbley (WP)	39	9	20	29	176	27	3	15	18	134	2	0	0	0	0
Stephen Wallace	47	8	19	27	20	31	5	11	16	4	6	1	0	1	2
Stuart Potts	52	2	11	13	10	36	2	10	12	8	6	0	0	0	0
Anthony Johnson	21	0	13	13	18	15	0	10	10	12	6	0	3	3	6
Paul Ferone 1	17	6	6	12	77	11	6	3	9	49	6	0	3	3	28
Karl Culley	48	5	7	12	8	32	5	5	10	8	6	0	2	2	0
Michael Bowman	42	5	4	9	14	36	4	4	8	8	6	1	0	1	6
Martin Lapointe (WP)	17	2	6	8	18	17	2	6	8	18					
Ian Defty	35	1	6	7	62	32	1	5	6	62	3	0	1	1	0
Jeff Trembecky (WP) 2	6	4	2	6	10	6	4	2	6	10					
Scott Campbell 3	19	1	4	5	82	14	1	4	5	52	5	0	0	0	30
Les Millie 4	6	1	3	4	2	4	1	3	4	2					
Martin King	13	0	2	2	56	8	0	2	2	28	5	0	0	0	28
Andre Malo	6	0	1	1	4	6	0	1	1	4					
Richie Thornton	39	0	1	1	16	33	0	1	1	14	6	0	0	0	2
Paul Matthews	2	0	0	0	2										
Danny Lorenz (N) 5	22	0	0	0	10	16	0	0	0	0	6	0	0	0	10
Bench Penalties					22					12					2
TEAM TOTALS	52	155	273	428	1010	36	115	212	327	710	6	9	15	24	182
Netminders	GPI	Mins	SOG	GA	Sv%	GPI	Mins	SOG	GA	Sv%	GPI	Mins	SOG	GA	Sv%
Pasi Raitanen (I)	27	1645	876	90	89.7	17	1040	573	65	88.7					
Danny Lorenz (I) 5	22	1260	708	84	88.1	16	900	495	64	87.1	6	360	213	20	90.6
Stephen Wall	6	240	129	23	82.2	6	240	129	23	82.2					
Empty Net Goals			3	3				3	3						
TEAM TOTALS	52	3145	1716	200	88.3	36	2180	1200	155	87.1	6	360	213	20	90.6

Shutouts: Raitanen - league: 27 Oct at Edinburgh Capitals (38 saves),
15 Dec v Basingstoke Bison (26); cup 25 Nov v Coventry Blaze (28) (at Newcastle)

Also appeared: Michael Allison 7; Adam Carr 6; Neil Abel (4) 4; Kevin Bucas 1;

Also played for: 1 Hull Thunder; 2 Fife Flyers, Solihull MK Kings; 3 Dundee Stars, Fife Flyers,
Scottish Eagles; 4 Edinburgh Capitals; 5 Guildford Flames; 6 Manchester Storm.

All Competitions = league, playoffs and Findus *Cup*

No sting in the tail

PETER ADAMS

After the debacle of the Jesters' season that never was, Vipers gave the long suffering Newcastle fans something to smile about by capturing the *Findus* Cup at their first attempt.

The fledgling club had looked on course for at least a mid-table finish in the British National League but ended in the last playoff position after being adversely affected by personnel changes, injuries and the inability of the team to train together frequently.

As owner **Darryl Illingworth** said, it was "a roller-coaster of a season."

The squad put together by **Alex Dampier** and **Clyde Tuyl** looked better equipped to attack than to defend, and a lot depended on the team's import players because Vipers' ethos was, commendably, to bring on young British talent.

They certainly succeeded in that aim as **Ian Defty**, **Simon Leach**, **Richie Thornton** and **Stephen Wallace** were all included in the GB squads during the season.

Vipers profited from the demise of Manchester Storm by snapping up two of the Superleague players in early November: **David Longstaff** returned to his native north-east quickly followed by his close friend, the experienced blueliner **Rob Wilson**. They were joined by veterans **Neil Abel** and **Les Millie** who guested for the team as they prepared for the *Findus* Cup finals on their home ice at the *Telewest* Arena.

The Cup victory was a special night for Vipers and their fans, the majority of whom had endured much over the years, watching the Cobras, Riverkings and Jesters. "It was pay back time for the fans," said their delighted captain, **Rob Trumbley**.

The team started breaking up soon afterwards, though. Impressive defenceman **Martin Lapointe** decided to return to the East Coast League in mid-December with **Scott Campbell** coming in as his replacement. Longstaff quit amicably in January when the GB captain joined Swiss side, Sierre, after signing off with a four-goal blast in Hull. Forward **Paul Ferone** came north from the troubled Hull Thunder and later additions were Brits **Anthony Johnson** and **Martin King**, whose combative cameo roles earned them cult followings.

Cup winning goalie hero, **Pasi Raitanen**, was sidelined by a knee injury but his replacement, **Danny Lorenz**, was as disappointing as he had been in Guildford. In January, Trumbley's horrific hand injury deprived the team of their inspirational captain. Without him the Vipers lost their venom.

PLAYER AWARDS

Forward of the Year	Mikko Koivunoro
Defenceman of the Year	Ian Defty
Top Points Scorer	Mikko Koivunoro
Players' Player	Ian Defty
Rookie of the Year	Stephen Wallace
Most Sociable Player	Rob Wilson
Unsung Hero	Tim Blake
Correspondents' Cup	Joel Irwin

LEADING PLAYERS

Mikko Koivunoro *born 12 November 1971*
The creative Finn is a smooth playmaker and he racked up the assists, reminding fans of his days as a Riverking. Top scorer in all Vipers' competitions.

Pasi Raitanen *born 13 May 1971*
The goalie was Vipers' Cup hero with a shutout in the final. Joined from Peterborough Pirates and was a rock at the back until an old knee injury flared up again.

Rob Wilson *born 18 July 1968*
The GB international defenceman seemed to be constantly on the ice and was a model of consistency and professionalism.

FACT FILE 2002-03

British National League	8th
Playoffs	4th in qr-final group
***Findus* Cup**	Winners

CLUB HISTORY

Founded

Summer 2002 by speedway promoter **Darryl Illingworth** and former GB and Riverkings coach **Alex Dampier**.

Previous Clubs at the *Telewest* Arena -

Jesters - Superleague 2000-01; *Riverkings* - Superleague 1998-2000; *Cobras* - Superleague 1996-98; *Warriors* - British League, Premier Div 1995-96.

Honours

Vipers Findus Cup 2002; *Jesters* Benson and Hedges Cup finalists 2000; *Riverkings* Superleague Playoff finalists 1999-2000.

NEWCASTLE VIPERS *left to right, back row:* Joel Irwin, Martin King, Stephen Wallace, Karl Culley, Ian Defty, Michael Bowman, Stuart Potts; *middle row:* Alex Dampier (manager), Paul Ferone, Scott Campbell, Mike Lankshear, Rob Wilson, Richard Thornton, Mikko Koivunoro, Tim Blake (equipment), Clyde Tuyl (coach); *front row:* Darryl Illingworth (owner), Rob Trumbley, Stephen Wall, Simon Leach, Bill Flower (marketing).

Photo: Touch The Sky Photography

NOTTINGHAM PANTHERS

PLAYERS	ALL COMPETITIONS					SUPERLEAGUE					PLAYOFFS				
Scorers	GP	G	A	Pts	Pim	GP	G	A	Pts	Pim	GP	G	A	Pts	Pim
Lee Jinman	56	25	50	75	38	32	12	24	36	18	15	4	19	23	6
Mark Cadotte (WP)	55	21	33	54	33	31	11	18	29	18	17	8	10	18	11
Greg Hadden	55	20	26	46	52	32	12	18	30	34	14	5	4	9	6
Jason Elders	54	23	21	44	36	28	8	7	15	24	17	10	10	20	8
Jason Clarke	56	19	21	40	240	32	11	12	23	108	15	6	7	13	74
John Purves (WP)	52	21	18	39	100	27	9	11	20	82	17	8	5	13	6
Scott Allison	52	9	20	29	150	31	5	11	16	68	16	4	8	12	64
Barry Nieckar (WP)	43	13	14	27	222	20	3	4	7	150	15	4	8	12	32
Jim Paek (WP)	58	2	22	24	34	32	1	10	11	10	17	0	4	4	18
Marc Hussey (WP)	56	10	13	23	48	32	6	6	12	24	17	3	5	8	6
Darin (Dody) Wood (WP)	52	5	18	23	249	27	2	8	10	105	16	2	3	5	98
Briane Thompson (WP)	49	8	14	22	153	29	5	9	14	136	11	0	3	3	11
Eric Charron (WP)	54	3	10	13	118	32	2	7	9	80	15	0	2	2	16
Kristian Taubert	56	3	7	10	91	30	2	4	6	45	17	1	2	3	26
Todd Wetzel	17	4	4	8	8	8	3	3	6	6	9	1	1	2	2
* James Morgan 1	22	2	2	4	17	12	0	0	0	8	9	1	0	1	7
Mika Pietila (N)	48	0	3	3	20	26	0	0	0	12	16	0	1	1	8
* Paul Moran	18	1	1	2	2	5	0	0	0	0	11	1	1	2	2
Petter Sandstrom (N)	18	0	0	0	6	10	0	0	0	4	3	0	0	0	0
Bench Penalties					38					30					8
TEAM TOTALS	58	189	297	486	1655	32	92	152	244	962	17	58	93	151	409

Netminders	GPI	Min	SOG	GA	Sv%	GPI	Min	SOG	GA	Sv%	GPI	Min	SOG	GA	Sv%
Mika Pietila	48	2648	1406	108	92.3	26	1437	772	61	92.1	16	916	477	34	92.9
Petter Sandstrom	18	865	469	43	90.8	10	504	287	25	91.3	3	109	69	10	85.5
Empty Net Goals				8	8				6	6				2	2
TEAM TOTALS	58	3513	1883	159	91.6	32	1941	1065	92	91.4	17	1025	548	46	91.6

Also played for: 1 Bracknell Bees, Solihull MK Kings.

Shutouts: Pietila (6) - league: 5 Oct v Bracknell Bees (32 saves), 1 Dec v Belfast Giants (35),
playoffs: 27 Feb at London Knights (27), 1 Mar at Sheffield Steelers (19)
8 Mar at Sheffield Steelers (25), 29 Mar at Sheffield Steelers (29)

All Competitions = league, playoffs, Challenge Cup and Ahearne Trophy

NOTTINGHAM PANTHERS *left to right, back row:* Vince Haywood (physio), Jason Elders, Jason Clarke, Eric Charron, Briane Thompson, Scott Allison, Paws the mascot, Marc Hussey, Jim Paek, Dody Wood, Paul Moran, Adam Goodrich (equipment). *front row:* Petter Sandstrom, Kristian Taubert, Greg Hadden, John Purves, Andy Worth (sponsor), Paul Adey (coach), Gary Moran (general manager), Barry Nieckar, Lee Jinman, Mark Cadotte, Mika Pietila.

New Panthers, old fate

MICK HOLLAND Nottingham Evening Post

A changed squad and glowing references from many pundits, claiming they had the best line-up in the league, didn't change Panthers' fortunes. Their dramatic defeat by London Knights in the Playoff semi-final on their own ice epitomised their season - almost but not quite.

And they rarely seemed to have that extra edge in the big games. In the Challenge Cup final against old rivals Sheffield Steelers, for instance, they dominated for much of the game but a soft mistake by goalie **Mika Pietila** at one end and a one-man show by **Joel Laing** at the other proved decisive as Steelers won 3-2.

In that Superleague Playoff, Panthers were leading 2-0 but went to pieces when Knights pulled one back. Although **Dennis Maxwell's** winner 0.2 seconds from the final hooter was particularly cruel, London's 4-3 win was no more than they deserved. Panthers' coach, **Paul Adey**, said it all afterwards: "We had so many players struggling with injuries, we wouldn't have done ourselves justice in the final." That comment could have been repeated for the entire league season.

Taking the reins for the first time on a solo basis, Adey certainly rang the changes during the summer, with new arrivals **Scott Allison** (from Steelers) and **Dody Wood** (Eagles) the main talking points because of their past records against Panthers. There were two Scandinavian netminders - Finn Pietila and Swede **Petter Sandstrom** as back-up - and a new look defence, with **Jim Paek** and ex-London man **Marc Hussey** the only familiar faces.

NHL round one draft pick **Eric Charron**, **Briane Thompson** who boasted a rocket shot, and hard-hitting Finn, **Kristian Taubert**, gave a very solid look to the D. The problem was that they didn't get much help from the wingers at key times and too many goals were leaked. Up front, they had three of the league's leading scorers - **Mark Cadotte** from Bracknell and returning duo **Greg Hadden**, playing his final season, and the irrepressible **Lee Jinman**.

Other new faces included **Jason Clarke**, a renowned scrapper, described by a North American newspaper as "a brawl on skates". With Allison, Wood and the returning **Barry Nieckar**, one wondered why Panthers needed another tough guy.

But at least Clarke could find the net on a regular basis. The output of Allison (5 goals), Nieckar (3) and Wood (2) was another reason why Panthers, though entertaining, again failed to win a trophy.

PLAYER AWARDS

Players' Player:	Eric Charron
Most Valuable Player:	Lee Jinman
Most Consistent Player:	Eric Charron
Supporters' Player:	Lee Jinman
Sponsors' Player:	Briane Thompson
Most Entertaining Player:	Jason Clarke
Team Spirit (Gary Rippingale Memorial Award):	
	Marc Hussey

LEADING PLAYERS

Mark Cadotte born 11 March 1977
A former East Coast League team-mate of **Lee Jinman** while with Arkansas, he was snapped up from Bracknell and coach Adey was quick to pair them together again. The duo terrorised the league, particularly when **John Purves** was providing the passes.

Eric Charron born 14 January 1970
Montreal's first round draft pick in 1988, the defenceman will be the first to admit his NHL career didn't pan out as he would have hoped. But there was no denying his class and technique at this level and it was a surprise that he missed out on the All Star teams.

Lee Jinman born 10 January 1976
The league's top scorer and a real handful for any defence. His electrifying speed and skills made him a great favourite throughout the league and it was hardly surprising he picked up the glut of Panthers' awards.

Greg Hadden (11) and Paul Adey (22) had their shirt numbers retired by the club

FACT FILE 2002-03

Superleague	Third
Playoffs	Semi-Finalists
Challenge Cup	Finalists

HISTORY

Founded 1946. Re-formed 1980. Club suspended operations 1960-80. Purchased by Aladdin Sports Management in 1997. Moved into the National Ice Centre in August 2000.
Leagues Superleague 1996-2002; British Lge (BL) (Premier Div) 1982-96 and 1954-60; English Nat Lge (ENL) 1981-82 and 1946-54; Inter-City Lge 1980-82.
Honours: British Champions 1989; League - BL 1955-56, ENL 1953-54 and 1950-51; Autumn Cup winners 1998, 1996 & 1994 *(B&H)*, 1991, 1986, 1955; Ahearne Trophy 1956.

PETERBOROUGH PHANTOMS

PLAYER	ALL COMPETITIONS					ENGLISH PREMIER LEAGUE					PLAYOFFS				
Scorers	GP	G	A	Pts	Pim	GP	G	A	Pts	Pim	GP	G	A	Pts	Pim
Duncan Cook (l)	56	79	83	162	118	40	59	61	120	90	8	6	11	17	14
Doug McEwen	55	34	80	114	42	39	26	61	87	32	8	6	9	15	10
Darren Cotton	51	50	43	93	84	36	33	31	64	74	8	9	6	15	6
Jon Cotton	56	42	50	92	68	40	31	34	65	56	8	5	4	9	12
Luc Chabot 3	32	36	42	78	28	26	27	29	56	26	0	0	0	0	0
Jesse Hammill	52	23	37	60	233	38	15	29	44	197	8	5	2	7	10
Lewis Buckman	49	33	25	58	34	35	21	17	38	24	8	7	4	11	4
Shaun Yardley	55	21	33	54	78	39	15	21	36	64	8	1	5	6	8
Jake Armstrong 1	34	20	33	53	68	23	14	24	38	50	8	5	7	12	16
Craig Button	56	12	34	46	104	40	10	28	38	84	8	0	3	3	10
Jason Buckman	56	15	9	24	50	40	12	5	17	48	8	1	1	2	2
Russell Coleman	53	12	12	24	28	38	7	8	15	16	8	0	1	1	8
Antti Kohvakka 1	21	6	17	23	81	11	4	8	12	30	8	2	9	11	45
Grant Hendry	45	3	9	12	70	29	2	6	8	54	8	0	1	1	2
Peter Morley	12	6	5	11	26	11	3	5	8	26					
James Ellwood	34	2	7	9	14	24	1	3	4	6	6	0	1	1	6
Stuart Coleman	35	2	6	8	30	28	2	6	8	26	4	0	0	0	4
Jon Fone	38	1	6	7	8	27	0	5	5	4	7	0	0	0	2
David Whitwell (N)	54	0	6	6	10	38	0	5	5	8	8	0	1	1	0
Steve Duncombe 2	19	0	4	4	4	9	0	3	3	2	8	0	1	1	2
Jason Porter	10	1	2	3	6	4	1	1	2	6	4	0	1	1	0
James Moore (N)	50	0	3	3	4	34	0	1	1	4	8	0	0	0	0
Bernie Bradford	34	0	3	3	4	25	0	3	3	2	4	0	0	0	2
David Micheli	2	1	0	1	2										
Bench Penalties					6					4					2
TEAM TOTALS	56	399	549	948	1200	40	283	394	677	933	8	47	67	114	165

Netminders	GPI	Mins	SOG	GA	Sv%	GPI	Mins	SOG	GA	Sv%	GPI	Mins	SOG	GA	Sv%
David Whitwell	43	2326	1130	129	88.6	33	1794	895	95	89.4	7	382	172	28	83.7
James Moore	23	1034	501	65	87.0	15	606	324	41	87.3	2	98	52	9	82.7
TEAM TOTALS	56	3360	1631	194	88.1	40	2400	1219	136	88.8	8	480	224	37	83.5

Shutouts: Whitwell - 15 Dec v Ch'ford Chieftains (32 saves), 1 Mar v Nottingham Lions (10)

Also appeared: Robert Amos 6; Terry South 3; Clint Herring, John Cranston, Julian Smith1.

Also played for: 1 Solihull MK Kings, 2 Sheffield Steelers, 3 Romford Raiders.

All Competitions = league, playoffs and Premier Cup

Two crowns for King

STEVE JUDGE

Phantoms rose from the ashes of the much missed Pirates and, thanks to a solid base of home-grown talent, swept to an English Premier League and cup double.

All the Peterborough-based players who had starred for Pirates in recent seasons signed on for new coach **Luc Chabot.** The former Isle of Wight boss attracted Solihull's Canadian forward **Duncan Cook,** the leading EPL scorer in 2001-02, to replace **Nick Poole** who had been snapped up by Milton Keynes.

The ever-popular **Doug McEwen** and **Jesse Hammill** returned but it was **Darren Cotton** who made the headlines early on, despite being overlooked by Great Britain. His goals and performances helped Phantoms to a winning start, including a crucial 6-4 victory over fellow contenders Milton Keynes. Phantoms had lost only once before defenceman **Pete Morley** - a goal scorer in that game - departed for a tour of Australia in October.

Then, incredibly, back-to-back home defeats by Slough and Milton Keynes cost Chabot his job. Unrest in the locker room was blamed for his shock departure after Christmas as Phantoms had lost only three of their 29 games.

GB under-20 coach **Kevin King** was brought in and he made an instant impact by avenging their two home defeats by Slough with victory in Berkshire. But as hard as he tried, he could not put one over the old adversaries, Milton Keynes.

Phantoms were brushed aside 8-2 in the last league clash with **Nick Poole**'s team, but King had the last laugh as he guided his squad through the choppy waters of a tricky run-in to lift the title.

That left a fortnight of double-headers with MK, their rivals in both the cup finals and the Playoff championship. On a storming Sunday evening in April, Phantoms overcame a two-goal deficit from the first leg in Milton Keynes to claim the cup by just one goal. But the Playoff title and a remarkable treble was a bridge too far, especially after Milton Keynes had recorded a crushing 10-0 victory in the first leg.

Still, nothing could wipe away the pride shining on the faces of the coach and his new side as King paraded their two trophies in front of their fans - while Milton Keynes were being presented with their only piece of silverware for the season.

PLAYER AWARDS

Player of the Year	Doug McEwen
Players' Player	David Whitwell
Best Forward	Duncan Cook
Best Defenceman	Antti Kohvakka
Most Improved Player	Jason Buckman
Young Player of the Year	Lewis Buckman
Maggie MacFarlane Award	David Whitwell

Darren Cotton *born 21 February 1978*
A real match winner on his day, he fired Phantoms to cup victory with a second leg hat-trick in the final. But he mysteriously lost his form in mid-season and coach Kevin King ordered him to take a three-week rest. The move worked as he returned to near his best form for the Playoffs.

Doug McEwen *born 2 October 1963*
Now pushing 40, he can still come up with the goods when needed, like the goal he scored in Telford when he lobbed the puck over the netminder from the neutral zone, while his coast-to-coast efforts brightened up every game he played. Opponents realised that the key to beating Phantoms was to shut him down but not many managed to stop the former Cardiff Devil and GB international.

David Whitwell *born 7 April 1982*
Returned to Peterborough after a season in Solihull with many fans questioning his ability between the pipes. But he produced several match-winning performances to emerge with the league's third best save percentage.

FACT FILE 2002-03
English Premier League: Winners
Playoffs: Finalists
Premier Cup: Champions

HISTORY
Founded: 1982.

Leagues: English Premier Lge 2002-03; British National Lge 1997-2002; Premier Lge 1996-97; British Lge, Div One 1995-96, 1986-87, 1982-85; British Lge, Premier Div 1987-95, 1985-86.

Honours: English Premier Lge & Cup 2002-03; (*Heineken*) British Championship finalists 1991; Christmas Cup 1999; British Lge, Div. One playoffs 1987-88; British Lge, Div. One 1986-87, 1984-85.

ROMFORD RAIDERS

PLAYER	ALL COMPETITIONS					ENGLISH PREMIER LEAGUE					PLAYOFFS				
Scorers	GP	G	A	Pts	Pim	GP	G	A	Pts	Pim	GP	G	A	Pts	Pim
Rob Douglas (I)	55	45	79	124	52	39	39	56	95	34	6	2	9	11	12
Danny Marshall	50	36	63	99	86	36	30	54	84	64	5	1	5	6	6
Noel Burkitt (I)	36	44	42	86	112	23	34	35	69	54	5	3	2	5	16
Jamie Randall	55	25	41	66	12	39	21	33	54	8	6	2	4	6	2
Anthony Child	51	29	30	59	158	37	23	25	48	132	5	0	1	1	6
Adam Collins (I)	52	17	32	49	6	36	11	26	37	2	6	2	1	3	2
Luc Chabot 1	19	17	11	28	6	5	6	4	10	2	6	6	3	9	2
Jason Rushton (I) 2	7	11	14	25	70	7	11	14	25	70					
Rob Cole 5	39	9	13	22	47	24	8	11	19	16	6	1	0	1	2
Phil Lee	49	3	13	16	105	33	2	7	9	40	6	0	0	0	28
Greg Oddy (I)	14	6	9	15	14	13	6	9	15	14					
Timo Kauhanen (I)	13	5	8	13	4	11	3	8	11	4	1	2	0	2	0
Ben Pitchley	52	2	11	13	118	37	2	10	12	84	5	0	0	0	8
Darren Botha 6	34	1	10	11	40	20	1	9	10	28	6	0	1	1	6
Ari-Samuli Mykkanen (I) 3	7	5	5	10	20	6	5	5	10	8					
Grant Taylor	35	5	4	9	77	21	3	3	6	45	5	1	1	2	12
Mark Williams	52	2	7	9	156	37	2	5	7	105	6	0	2	2	12
Kelvin Solari (I)	11	3	4	7	152	11	3	4	7	152					
Ian Robinson	45	2	3	5	16	35	2	3	5	16	1	0	0	0	0
Robert Jenner	35	3	1	4	4	25	3	1	4	4	2	0	0	0	0
Tom Looker	22	0	4	4	39	8	0	4	4	31	6	0	0	0	0
Stuart Low 3	6	1	2	3	4	6	1	2	3	4					
Keiron Lowe	10	0	2	2	2	2	0	2	2	2	5	0	0	0	0
Scott Beeson	8	1	0	1	0	2	1	0	1	0	5	0	0	0	0
Tyrone Miller 6	14	1	0	1	28	14	1	0	1	28					
Chris Jackson	10	0	1	1	0	2	0	1	1	0	5	0	0	0	0
Thomas Spinks	39	0	1	1	2	28	0	1	1	2	5	0	0	0	0
Bench Penalties					20					18					0
TEAM TOTALS	55	273	410	683	1350	39	218	332	550	967	6	20	29	49	114
Netminders	GPI	Mins	SOG	GA	Sv%	GPI	Mins	SOG	GA	Sv%	GPI	Mins	SOG	GA	Sv%
Mathieu Davidge	34	1719	1120	155	86.2	25	1367	879	114	87.0	1	12	5	3	40.0
Alec Field	23	1228	743	105	85.9	11	620	344	45	86.9	6	348	244	36	85.2
Simon Smith 4	7	353	214	40	81.3	7	353	214	40	81.3					
TEAM TOTALS	55	3300	957	145	84.8	39	2340	1437	199	86.1	6	360	249	39	85.2

Also appeared: Carl Ambler (N) (3), Liem Le Huen, Daniel Kruse 2; Anthony Laird 1.

Also played for: 1 Peterborough Phantoms; 2 Bracknell Bees, Scottish Eagles, Cardiff Devils; 3 Invicta Dynamos; 4 Slough Jets; 5 Haringey Racers; 6 Chelmsford Chieftains

All Competitions = league, playoffs and Premier Cup

'Fads' shops for imports

VINCE SWEENEY

For the first time in three seasons, Romford failed to put silverware into their trophy cabinet after an unstable campaign that sometimes threatened to fall apart completely.

Raiders' supporters are used to turmoil but even long-time fans were bewildered by the player merry-go-round that blighted the opening months. Even before the first puck had been dropped, NHL draftee **Heath Gordon** reneged on his contract and the American was quickly replaced by Saskatoon centre **Rob Douglas**, who proved to be one of the club's most effective signings.

A tie at title favourites Milton Keynes in the opening fixture, though only after a late powerplay equaliser from the Lightning, augured well. But an embarrassing home defeat the following night, against neighbours Chelmsford of all teams, made Raiders' followers wince.

A week later, after an even heavier road defeat by the Chieftains, coach **Shaun McFadyen** quit, citing personal reasons. Many thought at least one of those reasons was a simmering feud with star forward **Jason Rushton**. With a bitter dressing room and players leaving wholesale, Raiders' management decided to cut their losses and release the hugely talented but self-destructive Canadian. That was just the start of Rushton's troubles!

Poor research overlooked **Kelvin Solari**'s *Meccano* limbs and suspect attitude and he was soon out after racking up 152 penalty minutes in just 11 games. 'Fads' was back in the fold by Christmas but even he could do nothing to turn the tide. Apart from skipper **Danny Marshall** who seemingly broke points records on a weekly basis, evergreen **Phil Lee** and the industrious **Jamie Randall**, there were few player successes.

As ever, consistency was the biggest problem. Raiders took something from every team bar Peterborough but could never be relied upon to finish the job. A home double over Milton Keynes and defeat at lowly Haringey; victories at Swindon, Slough and the Isle of Wight but home defeats by all of those teams...and there was worse to come.

Raiders led in half of their Playoff games yet contrived to lose all but one, and that a 5-5 tie against Swindon after leading 5-1 with 15 minutes to go. The season closer, a Playoff fixture against Chelmsford, pretty much summed up the season. Three up after 20 minutes, Romford eventually went down 7-4 against a team stuffed with ex-Raiders. Ouch!

PLAYER AWARDS

Player of the Year	**Mark Williams**
Players' Player	**Rob Douglas**
Forward of the Year	**Rob Douglas**
Defenceman of the Year	**Adam Collins**
Coach's Player	**Jamie Randall**
Rookie of the Year	**Robert Jenner**

LEADING PLAYERS

Phil Lee *born 22 December 1965*
The veteran Durham-born blueliner was a surprise signing but oozed class and proved a loyal and committed team member.

Danny Marshall *born 14 May 1977*
A long overdue GB senior cap and 100 points in all games gave the Londoner, dubbed 'Super-Dan', a season to remember.

Jamie Randall *born 5 February 1975*
The Doncaster-born winger continued his Iron Man record, bagged over 60 points and was again named player of the year by his coach.

FACT FILE 2002-03

English Premier League:	8th
Playoffs:	4th in group
Premier Cup:	5th in group

HISTORY

Founded: 1987. (Withdrew from Div One midway through 1994-95 for financial reasons.)
Leagues: English (Premier) League 1995-2003, 1989-90; British League, Div One 1990-94 and 1988-89; British League, Div Two 1987-88.
Honours: English Premier Cup 2001-02; English National League, Premier Div playoffs 2000-01; British League, Div Two 1987-88.

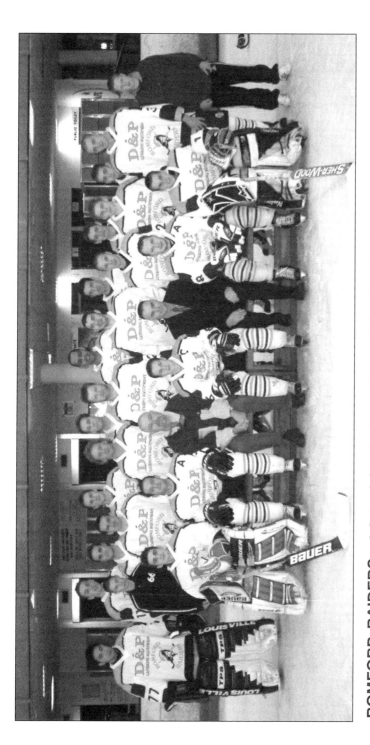

ROMFORD RAIDERS *left to right, back row:* Darren Botha, Tom Looker, Greg Oddy, Rob Cole, Mark Williams, Phil Lee, Ian Robinson, Danny Kruse; *middle row:* Liem Le Huen, Dan Simpson (equipment), Jamie Randall, Noel Burkitt, Adam Collins, Ben Pitchley, Timo Kauhanen, Thomas Spinks, Robert Jenner, Chris Beck (equipment); *front row:* Mathieu Davidge, Anthony Child, Mick Cahill (manager), Danny Marshall, Derek Bartlett (sponsor), Rob Douglas, Alec Field.

Photo: Alan White

SHEFFIELD STEELERS

PLAYER	ALL COMPETITIONS					SUPERLEAGUE					PLAYOFFS				
Scorers	GP	G	A	Pts	Pim	GP	G	A	Pts	Pim	GP	G	A	Pts	Pim
Kent Simpson (WP)	59	16	28	44	41	32	9	17	26	28	17	4	8	12	9
Jason Sessa (WP)	58	15	27	42	146	32	8	11	19	122	16	1	7	8	22
Mark Dutiaume	50	16	23	39	40	29	9	14	23	26	12	3	5	8	8
Warren Norris (WP)	55	17	22	39	48	32	11	13	24	32	13	2	5	7	12
Scott Levins	47	19	15	34	95	25	12	10	22	73	14	3	3	6	8
Rhett Gordon (WP)	33	16	15	31	36	25	10	12	22	22	1	0	0	0	0
Rick Brebant	47	8	21	29	113	23	6	9	15	24	17	1	7	8	46
Chris Szysky (WP)	29	7	15	22	46	18	2	12	14	24	5	2	1	3	7
Calle Carlsson	59	7	14	21	26	32	3	8	11	14	17	2	2	4	4
Jeff Brown	58	4	15	19	75	32	2	9	11	34	16	2	3	5	20
Dion Darling	55	8	8	16	153	28	5	4	9	95	17	3	1	4	40
Brent Bobyck	53	5	11	16	28	27	1	6	7	20	17	3	1	4	4
Marc Laniel (WP)	57	5	10	15	64	31	4	3	7	26	17	0	2	2	20
Mike Morin	29	3	3	6	12	10	0	1	1	4	17	1	2	3	6
Iain Fraser	8	2	4	6	2	3	1	2	3	2	4	1	0	1	0
Timo Willman	59	3	2	5	192	32	3	0	3	107	17	0	2	2	77
Wes Dorey	27	1	4	5	16	7	0	1	1	2	17	0	1	1	10
Boe Leslie	13	0	2	2	2	11	0	1	1	0					
Joel Laing (N) (WP)	52	0	2	2	10	28	0	2	2	2	17	0	0	0	6
Trevor Prior (N)	9	0	1	1	4	4	0	0	0	0	1	0	0	0	0
* Simon Butterworth	2	0	0	0	0										
* Stevie Weeks	4	0	0	0	0						2	0	0	0	0
* Keith Leyland 1	7	0	0	0	0	5	0	0	0	0	1	0	0	0	0
* Steve Duncombe 2	11	0	0	0	0	9	0	0	0	0	2	0	0	0	0
Bench Penalties					32					18					12
TEAM TOTALS	59	152	242	394	1181	32	86	135	221	675	17	28	50	78	311
Netminders	GPI	Min	SOG	GA	Sv%	GPI	Min	SOG	GA	Sv%	GPI	Min	SOG	GA	Sv%
Joel Laing	52	3080	1436	101	93.0	28	1710	756	44	94.2	17	985	500	45	91.0
Trevor Prior	9	517	235	29	87.7	4	245	109	12	89.0	1	52	22	5	77.3
EN Goals/GW Shots			4	4				1	1				3	3	
TEAM TOTALS	59	3597	1675	134	92.0	32	1955	866	57	93.4	17	1037	525	53	89.9

Shutouts: Laing (10) - cup: 8 Sept v Belfast Giants (25 saves)

league: 27 Sept v Scottish Eagles (13) *, 29 Sept v London Knights (27), 6 Oct v Belfast Giants (22), 12 Oct v Nottingham Panthers (27), 28 Nov at London Knights (28), 30 Nov v Belfast Giants (25), 15 Feb v Bracknell Bees (13).

playoffs: 16 Mar v Bracknell Bees (25), 5 Apr v Belfast Giants (32) (at Notts)

* result expunged

Also played for: 1 Hull Thunder, 2 Peterborough Phantoms.

All Competitions = league, playoffs, Challenge Cup and Ahearne Trophy

SHEFFIELD STEELERS *left to right, back row:* Iain Fraser, Rhett Gordon, Mark Dutiaume, Wes Dorey, Calle Carlsson, Jason Sessa, Dion Darling, Jeff Brown, Timo Willman, Mike Morin, Brent Bobyck, Andy Ackers (equipment); *front row:* Rick Brebant, Joel Laing, Kent Simpson, Mike Blaisdell (coach), Marc Laniel, Norton Lea (owner), Scott Levins, Trevor Prior, Chris Szysky.

Photo: Joanne Vaughan

Laing may he play

DAVE HAWKINS

Even with two trophies, Sheffield Steelers undoubtedly felt that their 2002-03 Superleague campaign was incomplete. When the season ended at the Playoff weekend, the team fell just short of what would have been a second Grand Slam in three seasons.

Their achievement in winning the league's shortened campaign and the Challenge Cup was another impressive demonstration of coach **Mike Blaisdell**'s ability to coax blood and thunder from a team with limited finesse. With slender financial resources, he built the squad around a resolute blue line and the awe-inspiring goaltending of Canadian **Joel Laing**.

The diminutive but self-assured shot-stopper had only an East Coast Hockey League pedigree but his seven league shutouts - ten in all - broke **Trevor Robins**' record.

Offensively the team were no match for their rivals. **Rhett Gordon** aside, no Steeler hit the back of the net with regularity and players like **Jason Sessa** were no match for the departed **Chris Lipsett**. The soldiering **Rick Brebant** played two-thirds of his last season with an injury that should have ended his campaign early, but he still played a key role.

Steelers' make-up was characterised by the non-stop skating of **Brent Bobyck**, **Warren Norris** and **Kent Simpson** and an outstanding penalty kill. Bobyck may rarely have looked like scoring but his presence in the face of opposing defencemen created as many turnovers as a bakery. **Mark Dutiaume** was impressive without being flashy and **Dion Darling** starred on the blue-line.

After securing the league title, to the delight of the club's fans on Nottingham ice, Steelers were simply terrible in the Playoff qualification round. They played as if they knew that a place in the semi-finals was assured simply because of the ineptitude of the Bracknell Bees.

After sealing a semi-final spot by the narrowest of margins following just two wins in 16 Playoff games, it would have been a travesty had Sheffield eliminated Belfast Giants in the first game at Nottingham.

As it was, penalty shots pitted the league's two best goalies against each other with Belfast's **Ryan Bach** eventually eliminating his team of last year at the expense of Laing, the league's undoubted MVP.

☑ Steelers retired **Ken Priestlay**'s no. 9 shirt and **Tony Hand**'s no. 16 before a challenge game against Dundee Stars on 21 January 2003.

PLAYER AWARDS

Player of the Year	**Joel Laing**
Players' Player:	**Joel Laing**
Coach's Player	**Mark Dutiaume**
Away Travel Player of the Year	**Joel Laing**
Kids of Steel Player of the Year:	**Joel Laing**

LEADING PLAYERS

Joel Laing born 3 November 1975
His figures may have been exaggerated by the 'defence first' team philosophy but there is no doubt that he was the star of the team and one of the best to have played in the ISL era. His understudy **Trevor Prior** got just seven games all year.

Warren Norris born 19 September 1974
The reverse of Laing in that he's a better player than his figures suggest. His potential was hidden by a dearth of snipers but when a big goal was needed he was often the scorer.

Kent Simpson born 20 July 1975
In his two seasons in Sheffield (split by a year in Germany) the Canadian has won five trophies and it's no coincidence. Like Norris, had he played alongside more gifted offensive players he would have challenged the league leaders for points. Scored more short-handed goals than anyone else in the league, a fine penalty killer and team leader.

FACT FILE 2002-03

Superleague	Winners
Playoffs	Semi-finalists
Challenge Cup	Winners

HISTORY

Founded: 1991. Franchise purchased in August 2001 by **Norton Lea**. In May 2002, Lea set up a company, South Yorkshire Franchise Ice Hockey Club Ltd, to own both the team and the franchise.

Leagues: Superleague 1996-2003; British League, Premier Div 1993-96; British League, Div One 1992-93; English League 1991-92.

Honours: Superleague Playoff Champions 2001-02, 2000-01 & 1996-97; Superleague 2002-03, 2000-01; Challenge Cup 2002-03, 2000-01, 1999-2000 & 1998-99; British League and Championship 1995-96 & 1994-95; B&H Autumn Cup 2000-01, 1995-96.

SLOUGH JETS

PLAYER	ALL COMPETITIONS					ENGLISH PREMIER LEAGUE					PLAYOFFS				
Scorers	GP	G	A	Pts	Pim	GP	G	A	Pts	Pim	GP	G	A	Pts	Pim
Marc Long (I)	52	60	48	108	140	40	47	36	83	114	6	3	7	10	4
Matt Sirman (I)	51	41	42	83	32	39	36	34	70	32	6	2	3	5	0
Rob Coutts	49	27	45	72	68	37	20	37	57	60	6	4	2	6	0
Norman Pinnington	49	29	39	68	236	36	24	31	55	151	5	0	4	4	40
Adam Bicknell	50	17	47	64	95	36	13	28	41	83	6	1	8	9	10
David Heath	54	14	43	57	59	41	12	36	48	30	6	0	4	4	2
Matthew Foord	54	28	23	51	119	40	19	14	33	101	6	4	4	8	10
Jason Reilly	42	11	24	35	70	31	8	19	27	50	6	2	1	3	10
Warren Rost	48	11	20	31	159	37	8	17	25	141	3	1	0	1	14
Scott Moody	49	4	26	30	72	37	2	18	20	66	6	2	1	3	0
Jan Hoest (I)	40	5	10	15	30	30	5	7	12	28	3	0	1	1	2
Matt Towalski	41	8	4	12	40	29	6	3	9	34	6	1	0	1	4
Michael Plenty	50	5	7	12	30	37	4	6	10	26	6	0	0	0	2
Adam Greener	48	5	6	11	203	35	3	5	8	170	6	2	0	2	0
Simon Greaves	25	2	8	10	14	24	2	8	10	14					
Chris Babbage	40	4	3	7	8	30	2	3	5	6	6	0	0	0	0
Stuart Tait	54	1	6	7	91	41	1	4	5	63	6	0	0	0	2
Terry Miles	28	0	4	4	6	20	0	2	2	4	6	0	2	2	2
John Denovan	33	1	2	3	2	32	1	2	3	2					
Carl Graham	35	0	2	2	2	29	0	2	2	2	2	0	0	0	0
Barry Skene	24	0	2	2	2	24	0	2	2	2					
Simon Smith (N) 1	48	0	0	0	34	34	0	0	0	32	6	0	0	0	0
Awarded Goals (Cup)		10		10											
Bench Penalties					38					36					0
TEAM TOTALS	55	283	411	694	1550	41	213	314	527	1247	6	22	37	59	102
Netminders	GPI	Mins	SOG	GA	Sv%	GPI	Mins	SOG	GA	Sv%	GPI	Mins	SOG	GA	Sv%
Tommy Brooks	4	168	50	5	90.0	4	168	50	5	90.0					
Simon Smith 1	43	2486	1347	143	89.4	29	1649	899	96	89.3	6	359	199	18	91.0
Adam Dobson	6	253	119	15	87.4	6	253	119	15	87.4					
Dave Hurst 2	7	389	167	24	85.6	7	389	167	24	85.6					
Empty Net Goals		4	1	1			1	0	0			1	0	0	
TEAM TOTALS	55	3132	1634	183	88.8	41	2292	1185	135	88.7	6	360	199	18	91.0

Shutouts: Smith - league: 12 Oct v Telford Wild Foxes (22 saves); playoffs: 22 Mar v Invicta Dynamos (14)

Also appeared: Tom Smith 2.

Also played for: 1 Romford Raiders; 2 Haringey Racers.

All Competitions = league, playoffs and Premier Cup

New-look Jets fly into third

DICK BELLAMY

Third place in the highly competitive English Premier League was an achievement for Jets as finances continued to handicap the amateur team when some of their fans couldn't accept the team dropping out of the British National League.

After tax problems forced the disbanding of the old club, supporter **Scott Parsons** and his accountant son, **Matthew**, set up a new company, Teal & White, and appointed veteran Jet **Warren Rost** as coach in place of the departed **Joe Stefan**. This was the first season without a Stefan in the Jets' line-up.

Rost assembled the largest squad with which Slough had ever started a season and they were regularly able to ice 17 players - despite injuries or clashes with junior games - which helped them to gain several vital points.

They were led by their only returning import, **Marc Long**, and captain **Rob Coutts** who were joined by new overseas signings, **Matt Sirman** from Niagara Falls and Dane **Jan Hoest**. Rost also recruited **Michael Plenty** (Guildford) and **Simon Greaves** (Nottingham and Hull) and brought up **Barry Skene**, **Jon Denovan** and **Stewart Tait** from Slough's ENL team.

But perhaps the most important signing was netminder **Simon Smith** from EPL side, Romford, who replaced **Dave Hurst** three weeks into the campaign.

The high point of the year was their second victory at league winners, Peterborough Phantoms, on 5 January. Their first trip, on the late September night when Smith made his debut, had been a little lucky, but Jets outplayed their hosts the second time for a 6-5 win.

The lows included a 3-3 draw at Telford, Swindon Lynx ending a run of eight consecutive wins in front of the *Sky* cameras in the Hangar [see *Review of the Year*], and a 7-0 drubbing by the Phantoms in February.

The Isle of Wight proved to be a 'bogey' team with the Jets taking only five points from their six encounters, and Rost and his lads had major problems with a referee in one November game which culminated in him taking the entire team off the ice in Gillingham before the final whistle.

Adam Bicknell, **Scott Moody** and Coutts received national recognition when they played for GB during the year, with Moody going on to score against the host nation in the World Championships in Croatia. **Matt Towalski** and Plenty played in the World under-20 games.

Coutts and **David Heath** decided to retire and Heath, who spent almost his entire career in Slough, was recognised with a testimonial match.

PLAYER AWARDS

Player of the Year	**Rob Coutts**
Players' Player	**Rob Coutts**
British Player of the Year	
	Scott Moody/Matt Towalski
Coach's Award	**Terry Miles/Matt Towalski**

LEADING PLAYERS

Adam Bicknell *born 10 April 1980*

Though a full-time PE teacher, he has improved to the point where he is regarded as a senior player. His talent attracted the attention of the GB coaches who called him up for a Euro Challenge series. Once turned down a chance to play soccer for Chelsea's juniors to stick with ice hockey.

Scott Moody *born 6 September 1979*

One of the country's best home-grown defencemen, he was called up by Britain for the Euro Challenges and made sufficient impression to play in the World Championships. Always reliable, he can come up with the goals when it matters.

Matt Towalski *born 6 March 1984*

A bright future is predicted for this 19-year-old who earned a first team place with Jets, being preferred over import **Jan Hoest** during the playoffs. He scored seven points (two goals) for GB in the under-20 World Championships. Also competed for Slough's under-19 Comets.

FACT FILE 2002-03

English Premier League	3rd
Playoffs:	Runners-up in group
Premier Cup	3rd in group

HISTORY

Founded: 1986.

Leagues: English Premier Lge 2002-03; British National Lge 1997-2002; Premier Lge 1996-97; British Lge, Premier Div 1995-96; British Lge, Div One 1986-95.

Honours: British National League 1998-99; *Benson and Hedges* Plate 1997-98; British League, Div One 1994-95 (and Playoffs), 1993-94 (south), 1989-90.

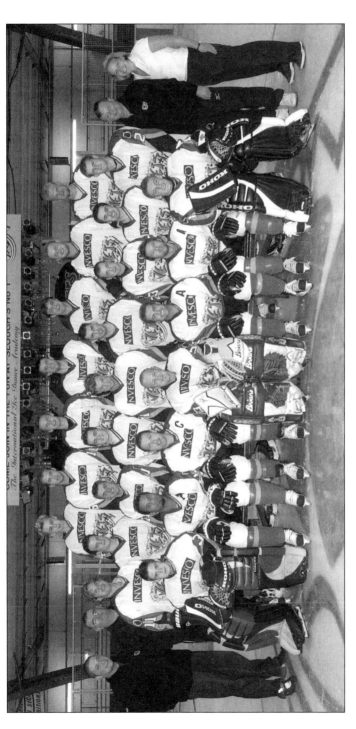

SLOUGH JETS *left to right, back row:* Chris Babbage, Carl Graham, Adam Bicknell, Scott Moody, Warren Rost (player-coach), Adam Greener, Jan Hoest; *middle row:* Paul Johnson (sticks), Alan Champion (equipment), Matt Sirman, Matt Towalski, Terry Miles, Barry Skene, Marc Long, Matt Foord, Stewart Tait, John Denovan, Michael Plenty, Joe Gibson (equipment), Helen (physio); *front row:* Adam Dobson, Norman Pinnington, Rob Coutts, Simon Smith, David Heath, Jason Reilly, Tommy Brooks.

SOLIHULL MK KINGS

PLAYER	ALL COMPETITIONS					FINDUS BRITISH NATIONAL LEAGUE				
Scorers	GP	G	A	Pts	Pim	GP	G	A	Pts	Pim
Todd Wetzel (I)	35	15	16	31	65	35	15	16	31	65
Slava Koulikov	44	9	19	28	48	36	8	17	25	44
Janne Ronkainen (I)	37	15	6	21	30	29	11	5	16	16
Brent Pope	40	6	14	20	126	32	5	13	18	100
Rick Strachan	44	3	17	20	20	36	3	14	17	16
Mike Shewan	26	10	7	17	24	18	5	6	11	6
Jeff Daniels (I)	30	1	15	16	41	22	1	8	9	37
Jeff Trembecky (WP) 1	25	7	7	14	42	25	7	7	14	42
Danny Meyers	38	3	10	13	38	30	3	9	12	34
Paul Moran	34	4	7	11	38	26	2	6	8	20
Dominic Parlatore 2	12	5	3	8	12	12	5	3	8	12
Antti Kohvakka (I) 4	24	2	5	7	28	16	1	3	4	18
Neil Adams	11	4	0	4	2	7	1	0	1	2
Andy Howarth	42	2	2	4	45	34	2	0	2	16
Pavel Gomenyuk (WP)	10	1	3	4	8	10	1	3	4	8
Rob Eley	24	1	1	2	10	24	1	1	2	10
Johan Erikkson (I)	9	0	2	2	4	1	0	0	0	0
James Morgan 3	1	1	0	1	2	1	1	0	1	2
Jake Armstrong 4	19	0	1	1	8	11	0	0	0	2
Rhys McWilliams	35	0	1	1	4	32	0	1	1	4
Domenic DeGiorgio (I) (N)	44	0	0	0	12	36	0	0	0	10
Bench Penalties					4					4
TEAM TOTALS	44	89	136	225	611	36	72	112	184	468
Netminders	GPI	Mins	SOG	GA	Sv%	GPI	Mins	SOG	GA	Sv%
Domenic DeGiorgio (I)	44	2665	1675	180	89.3	36	2185	1361	143	89.5
Empty Net Goals			7	7				7	7	
TEAM TOTALS	44	2665	1682	187	88.9	36	2185	1368	150	89.0

Shutouts: DeGiorgio - league: 20 Oct v Fife Flyers (30)

Also appeared: *Netminders*: Tom Ayers 24, Dan Page 7, Elliot Foley 6, Dale Albutt 5, Brian Albutt 2; Phil Knight 3.

Also played for: 1 Newcastle Vipers, Fife Flyers; 2 Hull Thunder.
3 Bracknell Bees, Nottingham Panthers
4 Peterborough Phantoms

All Competitions = league and Findus Cup

SOLIHULL MK KINGS *left to right, back row:* Jeff Daniels, Slava Koulikov, Rick Strachan, (player-coach) Paul Moran, Rhys McWilliams; *middle row:* Jake Armstrong, Jeff Trembecky, Todd Wetzel, Matt Darnell, Mike Shewan, Andy Howarth; *front row:* Domenic DeGiorgio, Danny Meyers, Brent Pope, Janne Ronkainen, Tom Ayers.

Unforgettable

PHIL PRINCE

Milton Keynes Kings' coach **Rick Strachan** and many of his players relocated to Solihull in the close-season taking with them the heart of the Kings' supporters. The team, renamed Solihull MK Kings, had new owners in husband and wife pair, **Mike** and **Sue Pack**, and a new logo.

Among the fans' favourites who moved to Solihull to play for Strachan again was their skilful and entertaining goalie, **Domenic DeGiorgio**. His second season provided many heart-stopping moments and great saves.

Rick looked to Europe to complete his line-up with recruits from Finland and Sweden. Some of them took a while to adjust to playing without plexi, but the nets certainly added to the match night atmosphere.

The opening *Findus* Cup game against Cardiff produced a win but it was one of the very few to come Kings' way. Though they gave many fine performances against strong opposition and were good value, Strachan's options were severely restricted by a small budget.

A few games into the season he made the first of several changes in an endeavour to find a winning formula. **Todd Wetzel's** arrival to replace the struggling **Johan Eriksson** lifted the entire team as his speed and manoeuvrability added a new dimension to the offence. However, one change was not enough to turn around the fortunes of his small squad and he snapped up **Jeff Trembecky** after the Canadian's forward's release from Newcastle.

Then during the Christmas break the team unexpectedly lost the services of **Mike Shewan**. The search for his replacement ended in the Ukraine where Rick found **Pavel Gomenyuk** who added strength and control to the D. He became a firm favourite, but his season was cut short at Basingstoke when he sustained a broken ankle after using it to stop a shot.

The final throw of the dice brought in **Dominic Parlatore** to replace **Jeff Daniels** as the Kings fought for a Playoff spot. Sadly that goal was not achieved as Kings ended the season at the bottom of the table.

Calls to the GB squads for various players, including captain **Brent Pope**, as well as Strachan who doubled as the national side's assistant coach, left the team short of key players for 17 games during the season, a particular problem given the already short bench.

From an outsider's point of view the season was not a success, but for the Kings' organisation, not to mention their extraordinarily loyal fans, this was an unforgettable year.

PLAYER AWARDS

Player of the Year	**Domenic DeGiorgio**
Players' Player	**Brent Pope**
Most Valuable Player	**Domenic DeGiorgio**
Most Improved Player	**Rhys McWilliams**
Coach's Award	**Matt Darnell**
Junior Supporters' Player	**Paul Moran**
KingsTalk *MVP*	**Danny Meyers**

LEADING PLAYERS

Domenic DeGiorgio *born 9 Nov 1977*

The only goalie to ice in every league game, the 'Dominator' faced an abundance of shots and again proved that his unusual style was both entertaining and effective, if at times a little scary.

Pavel Gomenyuk *born 21 April 1978*

During the Ukrainian's first stint in this country he showed all the qualities you would expect from an Eastern European-trained player. A first-class blueliner, he left a lasting impression on the fans.

Rhys McWilliams born 29 Nov 1985

The 16-year-old Solihull-trained forward made the tough decision to step up from the u19s, but he improved from game to game and proved to be a player with character who showed no fear on the ice.

FACT FILE 2002-03

British National League:	10th
Playoffs:	Did not qualify
Findus **Cup**:	5th in group

HISTORY

Founded: 2002. The original Solihull team were the Barons who were formed in 1965, disbanded in 1996, reformed in 2000 and disbanded again in 2002. The Blaze played in Solihull from 1996 before moving to Coventry in 2000.

Leagues: *MK Kings* - British National League 2002-03; *Barons* - English Premier League 2000-02, British Lge, Div. One/Two 1993-96 & 1982-86; English Lge 1991-93; British Lge, Premier Div. 1986-91; Inter-City Lge 1978-82; Southern Lge 1972-78; *Blaze* - Premier League 1996-97, British National League 1999-2000, English League 1997-99.

Honours: *Blaze* - English Lge, Premier Div 1998-99, 1997-98; *Barons* - English League 1992-93, British Lge, Div One 1985-86, Div Two 1983-84, Southern League 1977-78.

SWINDON LYNX

PLAYER	ALL COMPETITIONS					ENGLISH PREMIER LEAGUE					PLAYOFFS				
Scorers	GP	G	A	Pts	Pim	GP	G	A	Pts	Pim	GP	G	A	Pts	Pim
Merv Priest	53	80	72	152	60	40	66	59	125	42	6	7	7	14	12
Ken Forshee (I)	53	41	53	94	78	40	33	38	71	62	6	4	8	12	12
Robin Davison	31	21	46	67	100	29	19	44	63	100	0	0	0	0	0
Rob Lamey 1	33	25	33	58	66	31	25	31	56	62	0	0	0	0	0
Mark McCoy	33	15	31	46	50	31	14	31	45	50	0	0	0	0	0
Dan Pracher 2	43	15	25	40	26	31	11	21	32	22	6	2	3	5	2
Mark Richardson	38	18	20	38	6	29	15	17	32	6	3	2	0	2	0
Wayne Fiddes	52	7	30	37	63	39	5	28	33	47	6	1	1	2	8
Gareth Endicott	47	23	12	35	135	34	17	10	27	107	6	4	2	6	8
Grant Bailey	51	12	15	27	98	38	10	10	20	92	6	1	2	3	2
Lee Braithwaite	35	5	16	21	76	24	2	9	11	56	6	2	4	6	12
John Dewar	31	3	15	18	36	23	2	11	13	18	4	0	1	1	10
Rob Johnston	39	4	6	10	36	29	1	4	5	28	6	1	1	2	6
Dan Madge	40	2	8	10	30	31	1	7	8	20	2	0	0	0	4
Andrew Shurmer	35	2	6	8	22	23	2	5	7	18	6	0	0	0	2
Shane Moore	18	0	7	7	26	10	0	3	3	14	4	0	1	1	12
Matt Myers	6	5	1	6	16	5	5	0	5	14					
Shaun Littlewood	20	2	3	5	2	11	2	3	5	2	6	0	0	0	0
Sean Tarr (I)	7	3	1	4	22	3	1	0	1	4	3	2	1	3	16
Tim Collins 2	16	0	3	3	31	16	0	3	3	31					
Niall Quinn	3	1	1	2	0	3	1	1	2	0					
Harry Lenton	1	1	0	1	0	1	1	0	1	0					
Nick Eden	19	1	0	1	4	16	1	0	1	4					
Drew Chapman	2	0	1	1	0	2	0	1	1	0					
Jamie Thompson (N)	19	0	1	1	2	18	0	1	1	2					
Greg Rockman (N)	36	0	0	0	8	24	0	0	0	8	6	0	0	0	0
Dan Shea (N)	44	0	0	0	10	32	0	0	0	10	6	0	0	0	0
Bench Penalties					20					14					4
TEAM TOTALS	53	286	406	692	1025	40	234	337	571	835	6	26	31	57	110
Netminders	GPI	Mins	SOG	GA	Sv%	GPI	Mins	SOG	GA	Sv%	GPI	Mins	SOG	GA	Sv%
Greg Rockman	33	1949	1257	149	88.1	21	1247	775	88	88.6	6	342	245	25	89.8
Dan Shea	12	525	238	29	87.8	11	507	225	26	88.4	1	18	13	3	76.9
Jamie Thompson	13	705	368	56	84.8	12	645	331	47	85.8					
Empty Net Goals		1	1	1			1	1	1						
Forfeit Goals (Cup)				10											
TEAM TOTALS	53	1231	607	96	86.8	40	1153	557	74	87.8	6	18	13	3	89.1

Shutouts: Shea - league: 5 Oct v Haringey Racers (21 saves).

Also appeared: Joe Dickens, James Skaife 4; Greg Martin 1.

Also played for: 1 Isle of Wight Raiders; 2 Haringey Racers

All Competitions = league, playoffs and Premier Cup

Some Lynx missing

DAVE EATON

The 2002-03 season will certainly not go down as one of the most memorable in Swindon's ice hockey history book. The campaign was fraught with problems on and off the ice and it was remarkable that the *Innogy* Lynx managed to survive to the end of the season.

That they did was a tribute to a group of volunteer match-day helpers who banded together to keep the show on the road after Christmas, and to a set of players who stuck to their job even when their patience was taxed to the hilt.

Despite everything Lynx still finished fourth in the league, topped only by Peterborough, Milton Keynes and Slough, all of whom had stepped down from the previous year's British National League. And they were denied a possible chance of third spot only by an EIHA ruling.

Everything in the garden had looked rosy at the beginning of the campaign. Lynx director **Phil Jefferies** had secured local company *Innogy* for a second season as team sponsors, and appointed **Merv Priest** as player-coach to succeed the retired **Bryan Larkin**.

Priest brought on board imports **Mark McCoy** and **Dan Prachar**, and signed new British players **Matt Myers** and **Dan Madge** from Cardiff plus GB international **Rob Lamey** from Basingstoke. **Jamie Thompson** returned in goal after a lay-off from the sport. But there were soon changes to the roster as **Greg Rockman** was signed from Coventry to replace Thompson as number one netminder and Myers disappeared back to Cardiff.

Results were mostly encouraging although Peterborough and Milton Keynes proved impregnable. But the crowds at the Link Centre were very disappointing until Christmas and there were rumbles of cash-flow problems and players' wages not being paid.

Director Jefferies was hospitalised for a week after the Isle of Wight game at the end of December and from then on took a back seat although he was still responsible for the team. Things came to a head for the Haringey match on 11 January when it was confirmed that wages were owed but a players' walkout was averted and a skeleton squad travelled to Invicta.

Priest praised his team's loyalty. "It was a frustrating season. But they're a committed bunch of guys and we wouldn't have got through it all without them," he said.

PLAYER AWARDS

Player of the Year	Merv Priest
Players' Player	Lee Brathwaite
Best Forward	Merv Priest
Best Defenceman	Lee Brathwaite
Most Improved Player	Mark Richardson
Best Newcomer	Shane Moore

LEADING PLAYERS

Lee Brathwaite *born 17 July 1978*
The club captain and born leader, he learned to play in Swindon. A tough GB junior international defenceman, he was sorely missed by his club when he was sidelined with a troublesome back and groin injury. Works full-time as a fire fighter.

Merv Priest *born 3 August 1973*
Canadian player-coach had a big influence on the team as both playmaker and goal scorer. When he clicked so did the Lynx. Scored over 150 points in all competitions and always gave 100 per cent.

Mark Richardson *born 3 October 1986*
A great prospect who made the switch from junior to senior hockey with ease. Impressed the GB selectors who picked him for their tournament in the Ukraine. When he iced against Belarus on 13 December 13 2002 he became the youngest GB senior international at 16 years and 72 days old.

FACT FILE 2002-03
English Premier League: Fourth
Playoffs: 3rd in group
Premier Cup: 4th in group

HISTORY
Founded: 2000 as Phoenix. Name changed to Lynx in 2001. The town's team was the Chill in 1997-2000, IceLords in 1996-97 and Wildcats in 1986-96.
Leagues: Lynx and Phoenix - English (Premier) League 2000-03; Chill - English League 1997-2000; IceLords - Premier League 1996-97; Wildcats - British League, Div One 1986-96.

SWINDON LYNX *left to right, back row:* Shane Moore, Dan Madge, Mark Richardson, Nick Eden, John Dewar; *middle row:* Phil Jefferies (manager), Hannah Boardman (physio), Dan Prachar, Rob Lamey, Grant Bailey, Wayne Fiddes, Rob Johnston, Ian Smith (equipment), Jim Dobson (equipment); *front row:* Jamie Thompson, Ken Forshee, Merv Priest (player-coach), Lee Brathwaite, Gareth Endicott, Dan Shea.

TELFORD WILD FOXES

PLAYER	ENGLISH PREMIER LEAGUE				
Scorers	GP	G	A	Pts	Pims
Danny Mackriel	39	43	25	68	34
Jared Owen	38	20	30	50	120
Keith Mitchell (I)	36	19	20	39	91
Adam Brittle	32	11	19	30	6
Marc Lovell	33	14	12	26	34
Ashley Stanton	37	4	14	18	78
Jason Parry	30	6	5	11	68
Tom Carlon	24	5	6	11	20
Johan Gille (I)	14	8	2	10	18
Mike Rodger	18	1	9	10	28
Graham Oldham	26	2	7	9	49
Dave Fielder	11	2	7	9	73
Mike Roden	25	0	8	8	92
Dillan Leslie-Rowe	7	3	4	7	4
James Clarke	28	4	2	6	32
Mark Hazlehurst 1	3	1	4	5	8
Ryan Stanton	29	2	1	3	24
Daniel Karlsson (I)	7	1	2	3	6
Simon James	28	0	3	3	22
Perry Richardson	1	1	1	2	0
Daniel Croft	18	0	2	2	113
Daniel Heslop (N)	37	0	2	2	36
Matthew Drake	1	0	1	1	0
Matt Jones	2	0	1	1	4
Daniel Brittle (N)	35	0	1	1	8
Marc Smith	9	0	0	0	2
Bench Penalties					18
TEAM TOTALS	40	147	188	335	988
Netminders	GPI	Mins	SOG	GA	Sv%
Daniel Heslop	28	1523	1244	175	85.9
Daniel Brittle	20	877	757	156	79.4
TEAM TOTALS	40	2400	2001	331	83.4

Also appeared: Mark Smith 5; David Price,
Stuart Bates 2; Aaron Crisford,
Andrew Martin 1.

Also played for: 1 Cardiff Devils,
Milton Keynes Lightning

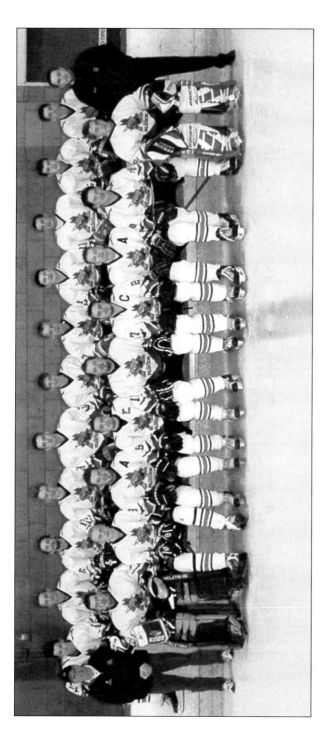

TELFORD WILD FOXES *left to right, back row:* Keith Mitchell, Tom Carlon, James Clarke, Matt Jones, Mike Rodger, Gareth Bates, Adam Brittle, Jason Parry, Johan Gille, Marc Lovell, Ryan Stanton; *front row:* Dave Fielder sr (manager-coach), Daniel Heslop, Mike Roden, Jared Owen, Danny Mackriel, Dave Fielder jr, Daniel Croft, Ashley Stanton, Graham Oldham, Daniel Brittle, Rich Clarke.

Wild ride for amateur Foxes

TOM NOTMAN

For the first time since the heyday of **Chuck Taylor**'s Tigers, a team from Telford moved up to play with the 'big boys' in the English Premier League.

The ambitious move was "tough but worth it" according to Wild Foxes' manager-coach, **Dave Fielder**. "As an amateur team with such a young side we were always going to find it hard going. But our club is about development."

The EPL, with its paid imports, was indeed a difficult competition for a 'development' team and the squad, though studded with teenage GB or England internationals, were left struggling near the bottom of the 12-strong league, ahead of their fellow amateurs, Nottingham Lions and Haringey Racers, but 25 points behind eighth-placed Romford.

Their cause wasn't helped by an unfortunate mid-season fracas with Racers, which led to lengthy bans to Fielder and popular bad boy **Daniel Croft**.

Nevertheless, they took some satisfaction from the season as they made the likes of Romford, Chelmsford and Invicta all work harder than they expected, tied Slough Jets at home, and won all but one of their seven games against Lions and Racers.

But they endured the usual headache of amateurs. "Our biggest problem was consistency," said Fielder, a former GB under-20 player. "We suffered too much from second period blues, much to everyone's frustration." Foxes were especially disappointed not to reach the Playoffs.

Top scorer **Danny Mackriel,** a former GB under-18 international, hit the back of the net at over a goal-a-game clip, twice as many as his best team-mates, who included Canadian teenage import, **Keith Mitchell**.

Their most internationally honoured player was **Adam Brittle**, their fourth highest scorer. The England under-17 skipper was selected for the GB under-20 squad and was later top scorer with the GB under-18s, which he also captained.

Foxes missed goalie **Dillan Leslie-Rowe** who took a year off to travel round the world, though they were fortunate that **Dan Heslop** agreed to stay and help his old team.

Apart from Mitchell, Foxes' other overseas players had only a few games. The unluckiest of them had to be Swedish forward, **Johan Gille**, who broke his collar bone at Swindon in a collision with Lynx **Robin Davison** - twice! Once in the first game of the season and again in November's return.

PLAYER AWARDS

Player of the Year	Marc Lovell
Players' Player	Marc Lovell
Supporters' Player	Danny Mackriel
Most Valuable Player	Jason Parry
Top Points Scorer	Danny Mackriel
Clubman of the Year	Daniel Croft
Most Improved Player	Tom Carlon

LEADING PLAYERS

Marc Lovell born 2 June 1982
Forward with an eye for goal and endless energy who won plaudits from fans and teammates alike. In his second season with the team after joining from Flintshire.

Danny Mackriel born 16 July 1980
His 43 goals put him among the league's leading goal scorers. Born and bred in Telford, 'Budzie' first skated at the town's rink at the age of six and was on the junior team that won the club's first trophy in 1990. Has also played in Blackburn and Solihull.

Jason Parry born 20 May 1976
High work rate and ability to play in any out position made him a natural for the club's MVP award. Previously with Altrincham Aces.

FACT FILE 2002-03
English Premier League: 9th
Playoffs: Did not qualify
Premier Cup: Did not enter

HISTORY
Founded: 2001. Previous teams in Telford were Royals 1997-2001 and Tigers 1985-97. The Timberwolves played six *B&H* Cup games in September 1999.
Leagues: *Wild Foxes*: English Premier League 2002-03, English National League South 2001-02; *Royals*: English (National) League 1997-2001; *Tigers*: Premier League 1996-97, British League, Div One 1985-96.
Honours: None.

WHITLEY WARRIORS

PLAYER	ALL COMPETITIONS					ENGLISH NATIONAL LEAGUE				
Scorers	GP	G	A	Pts	Pim	GP	G	A	Pts	Pim
Paul Graham	34	44	37	81	24	16	29	19	48	14
Andrew Tindale	31	25	51	76	34	15	15	31	46	8
Lee Baxter	28	35	38	73	40	16	22	29	51	24
Andrew Carter	23	31	33	64	147	13	20	23	43	93
Bryan Dunn	33	23	22	45	157	17	16	13	29	80
Kevin Bucas	30	15	27	42	119	18	11	21	32	63
Bobby Bradley	24	10	25	35	75	12	8	20	28	47
Daniel Good	27	15	12	27	20	14	6	8	14	4
Paul Matthews	14	5	16	21	41	10	5	13	18	12
Darren Taylor	14	10	10	20	18	10	9	8	17	2
Stephen Winn	28	5	12	17	193	15	2	7	9	30
Ian Emmerson	29	6	8	14	0	16	4	6	10	0
Andrew Robinson	32	1	12	13	61	15	0	7	7	18
Dale Howey	31	4	7	11	81	17	1	5	6	24
Gary Dowd	13	2	8	10	35	6	2	5	7	10
Paul McGinnety	10	2	5	7	14	7	2	5	7	10
Robert Cairns	20	3	3	6	34	10	2	1	3	14
Robert Wilson	31	1	5	6	68	18	1	2	3	44
Anthony Markham (N)	21	0	5	5	14	11	0	4	4	12
Simon McGinnety	4	1	0	1	8	2	0	0	0	6
Shaun Kippin	5	1	0	1	0	1	0	0	0	0
John Shreeve	3	0	1	1	0					
Ben Campbell	5	0	1	1	0	2	0	0	0	0
Ryan Sample	5	0	1	1	2	2	0	1	1	0
Richard Horkan	14	0	1	1	6	9	0	1	1	6
David Barrett	30	0	0	0	119	16	0	0	0	84
Bench Penalties					30					26
TEAM TOTALS	36	239	340	579	1352	18	155	229	384	637
Netminders	GPI	Mins	SOG	GA	Sv%	GPI	Mins	SOG	GA	Sv%
Anthony Markham	21	1143	743	95	87.2	11	640	366	39	89.3
Stephen Hoult	19	806	574	77	86.6	8	373	227	29	87.2
Chris McKay	7	204	169	24	85.8	2	60	23	4	82.6
Neil Secombe	1	6	3	0	100.0	1	6	3	0	100.0
Empty Net Goals		1	1	1			1	1	1	
TEAM TOTALS	36	2160	1490	197	86.8	18	1080	620	73	88.2

Also appeared: Richard Dunne 5; Ricky Box, Shaun Croft, Simon Day 2; Brad Brooks, Gareth Hughes, Nick Rowe, Peter Winn 1.

All Competitions = league, Premier Cup and Northern Cup

No Winn situation

DAVID HALL

The seeds of the Warriors' disappointing 2002-03 campaign were sown when the club failed in its summer bid to bring English Premier League ice hockey to the Hillheads Road rink.

This resulted in coach **Peter Winn** losing several key players, including inspirational skipper **Karl Culley** and the hard-working **Stuart Lonsdale**. The talents of the players in maroon and gold had become well known after Warriors' Grand Slam success of the previous season.

"To be honest the desire was missing from my squad this year," confessed Winn. "We achieved all we set out to achieve last term and everyone was looking forward a new challenge in the Premier League. So when that didn't happen, everyone was very flat and we never really got going."

Some supporters had complained that games were too easy in the Grand Slam season, but even though the quality on some nights in this campaign was of a good nature, the home side still invariably ended up on the wrong end of the score line.

A prime example was when Whitley led Sheffield Scimitars 5-2 in December only to see the eventual champions claw back the deficit and come away with a 6-5 victory.

Though never in contention for the league or Northern Cup, Warriors ended the regular season well enough to contest the playoffs. But following an incident involving the spectators in the last league game at Bradford, Winn took his side off the ice in a game they were winning 8-5 with just under five minutes remaining.

Though the EIHA allowed the result to stand, the subsequent suspensions of the coach, along with two of his leading players, **Andrew Carter** and **Kevin Bucas**, effectively ended Warriors' bid to land the playoff championship for a fourth consecutive season.

With only a young side left, they finished with six consecutive defeats, the last a 14-0 mauling at Sheffield with a side that had only keeper **Chris McKay** over the age of 20. However, they did manage a club record when they opened February with a 34-3 home win over Grimsby. Carter, **Bryan Dunn** and **Paul Graham** each scored seven.

As the season closed, Winn decided that after five years his tenure as coach should end and that he would concentrate on Whitley's youth development programme. After bringing six trophies to Hillheads in that time, he could leave with his head high.

PLAYER AWARDS

Supporters' Player of the Year   **Lee Baxter**
Hillheads Player of the Year   **Paul Graham**

LEADING PLAYERS

Lee Baxter *born 22 October 1980*
After being nominated as one of the *Annual's* players to watch a couple of years ago, he was back to his best despite a 12 months' layoff. He led the second forward line and scored some of the team's best goals.

Kevin Bucas *born 16 May 1980*
Defenceman took over the captaincy following the departure of Culley to Newcastle and proved to be an inspirational leader under difficult circumstances. He restrained his overly aggressive instincts and still managed some big hits.

Paul Graham *born 19 May 1983*
A speedy winger with an eye for goal, he led the team's scoring for the first time and could be the next Whitley player to find a place at a higher league team.

FACT FILE 2002-03

English National League: 3rd in North
Playoffs: 4th in group
Premier Cup: 3rd in group
Northern Cup   3rd

HISTORY

Founded: 1956. Known as Newcastle Warriors in 1995-96, playing part of the season in Newcastle's *Telewest* Arena.

Leagues: English (National) League 1997-2003; Northern Premier League 1996-97; British League, Premier Division 1982-96; Northern League 1966-82.

Honours: English National League playoff champions 2000-02; English National League North and English Cup 2001-02; English League, Div One playoffs 1999-2000; Scottish Cup 1992; Northern League 1973-75; Icy Smith Cup 1972-73 & 1973-74.

LEAGUE ORGANISATION

Organised ice hockey in Britain in 2002-03 was divided into three independent leagues.

Superleague was a commercial organisation run under the auspices of a limited liability company, Ice Hockey Superleague Ltd (ISL), with each member club having a director on the ISL Board.

The players were professionals recruited worldwide but mostly from North America. There was a £400,000 limit per club on players' salaries and team rosters were limited to 20 skaters including two netminders.

Players requiring work permits, i.e. non-EU passport holders, were not to exceed one-third of a team's roster. North Americans had to have played in a league at East Coast Hockey League (ECHL) level or above; Europeans had to have played on a team from a country which competed in the World Championships (A Pool) the previous season.

The **British National Ice Hockey League** Ltd (BNL), also a limited liability company, comprised ten teams. The clubs agreed that at least 50 per cent of each team's players on the ice should be British trained and eligible to play for the GB national team. Teams could sign as many non-Brits as they liked.

The league imposed a wages' ceiling of £4,500 a week per club (over 26 weeks this amounted to £117,000), though this could be increased up to £6,750 (£202,500) provided the club paid a 20 per cent 'luxury tax' to the league. This 'tax' is designed to help support and promote the smaller fan-based clubs and help them build upwards.

The **English Leagues**, which are run by the English Ice Hockey Association (EIHA), comprise a wide range of clubs from the virtually amateur to those with budgets as large as the smaller BNL clubs. The teams with the most ice time and largest budgets competed in the Premier League and the remainder played in one of the National League's two regional conferences.

Each Premier League team could dress only four non-British trained players per game and had to ice at all times at least three British trained players - defined as one who completed two years playing at under-19 level. National League teams were allowed one non-British trained player or player-coach.

Players' wages are limited only by what a club can afford.

STEELERS WIN LAST SUPERLEAGUE TROPHY
Sheffield Steelers' captain **MARC LANIEL** with the Monteith Bowl. Flanking him are Steelers' chairman **Norton Lea** and league administrator **Brian Storey**.   *Photo*: Diane Davey

SUPERLEAGUE

FINAL STANDINGS

	GP	W	L	D	OL	GF	GA	Pts	Pct.
(1-3) **Sheffield Steelers** SHE	32	18	8	5	1	86	57	42	65.6
Home	16	12	2	2	0	55	26	26	81.3
Away	16	6	7	3	1	31	31	16	50.0
(6-1) **Belfast Giants** BEL	32	17	8	6	1	111	78	41	64.1
Home	16	10	3	3	1	55	35	24	75.0
Away	16	7	6	3	0	56	43	17	53.1
(8-4) **Nottingham Panthers** NOT	32	15	13	4	0	92	92	34	53.1
Home	16	10	5	1	0	43	33	21	65.6
Away	16	5	8	3	0	49	59	13	40.6
(4-6) **London Knights** LON	32	11	12	8	1	87	90	31	48.4
Home	16	7	4	5	0	56	45	19	59.4
Away	16	4	9	3	1	31	45	12	37.5
(3-5) **Bracknell Bees** BRK	32	5	20	5	2	71	130	17	26.6
Home	16	4	9	3	1	40	59	12	37.5
Away	16	1	13	2	1	31	71	5	15.6

Pct. = *percentage of points gained to points available*
Figures in brackets are the last two seasons' league positions (2000-01/2001-02)
Scoring system: *two points for a win in regulation (W), one point for a draw (D) or overtime loss (OL), no points for a loss (L).*

LEADING SCORERS

excluding playoffs	GP	G	A	Pts	Pim
Lee Jinman NOT	32	12	24	36	18
Greg Hadden NOT	32	12	18	30	34
Robby Sandrock BEL	32	6	24	30	24
Mark Cadotte NOT	31	11	18	29	18
Dan Ceman BRK	32	16	12	28	22
Kevin Riehl BEL	31	11	17	28	4
Kent Simpson SHE	32	9	17	26	28
Vezio Sacratini LON	28	9	16	25	16
Kim Ahlroos LON	27	6	19	25	12
Paxton Schulte BEL	26	13	11	24	107

SIN-BIN

Most Penalised Players	GP	Pim	Ave
Barry Nieckar NOT	20	150	7.50
Paul Rushforth LON	25	144	5.76
Briane Thompson NOT	29	136	4.69
Chris Slater LON	32	135	4.22
Jason Sessa SHE	32	122	3.81

LEADING NETMINDERS

excluding playoffs	GPI	Mins	SoG	GA	Sav%
Joel Laing SHE	28	1710	756	44	94.2
Ryan Bach BEL	24	1436	717	57	92.1
Mika Pietila NOT	26	1437	772	61	92.1
Dave Trofimenkoff LON	24	1446	752	65	91.4
Brian Greer BRK	18	926	608	58	90.5

Qualification: 640 minutes

FAIR PLAY

Team Penalties	GP	Pim	Ave
Bracknell Bees	32	508	15.9
Belfast Giants	32	663	20.7
Sheffield Steelers	32	675	21.1
London Knights	32	755	23.6
Nottingham Panthers	32	962	30.1
LEAGUE TOTALS	160	3563	22.3

POWERPLAY

Powerplay percentages	Adv.	PPG	Pct.
Belfast Giants	118	19	16.1
London Knights	137	18	13.1
Sheffield Steelers	200	26	13.0
Nottingham Panthers	143	17	11.9
Bracknell Bees	139	14	10.1
LEAGUE TOTALS	737	94	12.8

Adv. - Times with man advantage
PPG - powerplay goals scored
Pct. - percentage of goals scored to powerplays.

TOP POWERPLAY GOAL SCORERS
Scott Levins SHE 6, Kevin Riehl BEL 5, Lee Jinman NOT 4.

PENALTY KILLING

Penalty killing percentages	TSH	PGA	Pct.
Sheffield Steelers	137	10	92.7
London Knights	167	21	87.4
Nottingham Panthers	157	21	86.6
Belfast Giants	133	20	85.0
Bracknell Bees	143	22	84.6
LEAGUE TOTALS	737	94	87.2

TSH - times short-handed
PGA - powerplay goals against

TOP SHORT-HANDED GOAL SCORERS
Kent Simpson SHE 3; Jonathan Delisle BRK, Dennis Maxwell LON 2.

Tight budget, tight defence
Sheffield Steelers won their second Superleague title in three years - the only side to win the league twice - and their first unsullied by accusations of breaking the wage cap.

On the contrary, **Mike Blaisdell**, who won the coach of the year award, was restricted by a tight budget. He built his squad around goalie, **Joel Laing**, whose seven shutouts broke the league record, and the opposition found it as difficult to score as the coach did to coax funds out of the club's owner, **Norton Lea**.

Even with only five teams, the league's last season was competitive. Steelers led from start to finish but it took a goal from **Chris Szysky** 2.52 from the end of their final game at rivals Nottingham before they clinched first place.

Dave Whistle's Belfast Giants chased Steelers for most of the year but Sheffield won all but two of the head-to-heads which made a crucial difference.

OVERTIME RECORDS

	OT	W	L	D	Pts
Sheffield Steelers	9	3	1	5	12
Belfast Giants	8	1	1	6	9
London Knights	9	0	1	8	9
Bracknell Bees	7	0	2	5	7
Nottingham Panthers	5	1	0	4	6

"There's a certain section of players who do not appear to be putting in the effort while others are busting a gut. The problem is that there are too many not doing it to tell them all to sit and not play."
Martin Weddell, the exasperated GM of Bracknell Bees. *Evening Post, Reading*

PAST LEAGUE WINNERS
2001-02	Belfast Giants
2000-01	* Sheffield Steelers
1999-2000	Bracknell Bees
1998-99	Manchester Storm
1997-98	Ayr Scottish Eagles
1996-97	Cardiff Devils

* Exceeded £450,000 wage cap

PAST SCORING CHAMPIONS
2001-02	Kevin Riehl BEL
2000-01	Greg Bullock MAN
1999-2000	Ed Courtenay SHE
1998-99	Paul Adey NOT
1997-98	Tony Hand SHE
1996-97	Dale Junkin BRK

Nottingham Panthers were a big disappointment as they failed yet again to win a league title in the sport's modern era. Coach **Paul Adey** signed three of the league's highest scorers in **Lee Jinman, Greg Hadden** and **Mark Cadotte** but the critics complained that he employed too many 'goons': two Panthers were among the league's most penalised players.

London Knights' Swedish coach, **Jim Brithen**, arrived too late to retrieve Knights' fourth place after poor recruiting by his Canadian predecessor **Bob Leslie**. The club also missed leading netminder, **Trevor Robins**, who was forced into retirement by injury, and lost top forward, **Steve Thornton**, to Giants when he returned after a lengthy spell on the sidelines.

Perhaps it's best to draw a veil over **Bracknell Bees'** 'annus horribilis'. Recruiting problems also dogged coach **Enio Sacilotto** who was lucky to survive as long as the end of the league season after Bees won only five games.

RESULTS CHART

	BEL	BRK	LON	MAN	NOT	SCO	SHE
BELFAST Giants	** ** ** **	3-2 18/10 3-3ot 6/12 5-2 28/12 5-2 24/1	2-4 11/10 7-2 3/1 2-2ot 17/1 4-2 4/2	7-2 24/10	5-2 25/9 3-2 26/10 2-3 29/12 2-0 22/1	4-1 20/9 2-4 30/10	2-3ot (2) 8/11 4-1 13/12 2-2ot 30/1 4-3ot (3) 31/1
BRACKNELL Bees	3-11 22/9 2-6 3/11 3-3ot 28/11 1-4 16/2	** ** ** **	2-0 3/10 4-1 27/10 3-4 30/11 1-1ot 11/1		4-7 29/9 3-6 21/11 1-5 5/1 4-6 19/1	6-3 24/10	2-1ot (1) 20/10 & 10/11- see note below 2-2ot 10/11 3-1 22/12 3-0 16/1
LONDON Knights	4-5 1/11 3-3ot 5/1 1-5 26/1 4-6 2/2	5-2 19/9 4-4ot 14/11 8-1 15/12 5-4 26/12	** ** ** **	2-3 6/10	1-1ot 17/11 4-4ot 13/12 3-1 20/12 8-3 31/1	3-2 26/9	1-1ot 8/10 3-2 3/11 0-2 28/11 2-1 12/1
M'CHESTER Storm	2-0 13/10 played last	game on	5-4 17/10 24.10.02	** **			1-6 22/9
NOTT'HAM Panthers	3-3 9/11 2-0 1/12 5-3 18/1 1-4 11/2	5-0 5/10 7-2 16/11 4-1 18/12 2-1 12/1	3-1 19/10 1-4 12/11 3-1 28/12 3-2ot (4) 25/1		** ** ** **	7-3 3/11	0-3 12/10 2-1 23/11 1-4 4/1 1-3 16/2
SCOTTISH Eagles	 played last	game on	6-4 13/10 3.11.02		1-3 2/10	** **	
SHEFFIELD Steelers	1-0 6/10 3-2 16/10 1-0 30/11 6-1 15/12	3-4 6/11 3-2ot (5) 18/1 4-1 25/1 5-0 15/2	2-0 29/9 2-2ot 24/10 5-2 29/12 1-3 11/1	5-2 5/10	7-2 21/9 5-2 2/11 3-3ot 26/12 4-2 9/1	5-0 27/9	** ** ** **
	BEL	**BRK**	**LON**	**MAN**	**NOT**	**SCO**	**SHE**

Second figure is date of game

Manchester Storm's and Scottish Eagles' results shown for reference only - results were officially expunged.

* Game abandoned at 49.56 as ice unplayable with score at 1-1. Sheffield won in overtime on 10 November under the following ISL ruling: 'The 20 October match was treated as completed in relation to regulation time and each team was awarded one point. On 10 November, the teams completed the required period of five minutes (4 on 4) sudden-death overtime in an effort to win an extra point. All player stats from the original game stood and the goalkeepers' times were recorded as playing 60 minutes. All players eligible to play at the time of the 10 November match and who did not play in the original match were added to the game record sheet as if they played in the whole game.'

OVERTIME WINNERS

Key to above:

(1)	SHE	Dutiaume (Gordon, Darling)	60.34
(2)	SHE	Gordon (Darling, Szysky)	64.18
(3)	BEL	Riehl (Kelman)	61.11
(4)	NOT	Thompson (Purves, Hadden) pp	60.57
(5)	SHE	Norris	63.40

Above Two of Belfast Giants' leading players, All-Stars **ROBBY SANDROCK** *left* probably Superleague's best defenceman, and forward **PAXTON SCHULTE** in crease menace mode in the final of the Superleague Playoff Championship; *below* Bracknell Bees' **DAN CEMAN** *left* the league's top goal scorer, and **DENNIS MAXWELL** putting London Knights into the Superleague Playoff final with a goal 0.02 seconds from the end of their semi against Nottingham Panthers.

Photos: Tony Boot, Diane Davey, Dave Page

PLAYOFFS

QUALIFYING ROUND

	GP	W	L	D	OL	GF	GA	Pts
Belfast Giants	16	12	2	1	1	65	36	26
London Knights	16	10	4	2	0	55	42	22
Nott'ham Panthers	16	10	5	1	0	55	42	21
Sheffield Steelers	16	2	10	1	3	28	52	8
Bracknell Bees	16	3	12	1	0	41	72	7

RESULTS

	BEL	BRK	LON	NOT	SHE
Belfast	**	3-2 8-4	1-1ot 3-4ot (4)	6-3 3-1	3-1 3-1
Br'cknell	3-1 3-6	**	0-3 6-3	1-4 3-4	5-2 4-5
London	2-6 4-2	7-3 6-0	**	0-3 6-3	3-2ot (1) 3-2ot (3)
Nott'ham	1-3 2-7	6-3 10-3	4-4ot 2-1	**	1-0 8-2
Sheffield	5-2 2-5	1-1ot 3-0	2-4 2-3ot (2)	0-2 0-1	**

Overtime winning goals
(1) McIntyre (Sacratini) LON 60.56
(2) Blanchard LON 61.43
(3) Blanchard (Slater) LON 63.48
(4) Kolesar (Maxwell, Bronilla) LON 62.53

SEMI-FINALS

at the Nottingham Ice Centre
5 April   Belfast-Sheffield   0-0ot
       Giants won 1-0 after penalty shots
       London-Nottingham   4-3

FINAL

at the Nottingham Ice Centre
6 April   **Belfast-London**   5-3

BELFAST GIANTS win Superleague Playoff Championship

Giants leap for Whistle

As someone nearly said: "Never have so few laboured so long to eliminate even fewer."

All five Superleague teams took part in the longest Playoff campaign in the league's (and probably Britain's) history - six weeks - before Bracknell Bees, who had staggered through the league season, predictably failed to reach the Final Four in Nottingham.

But not before league champs, Sheffield Steelers, had given them a run for their money. **Mike Blaisdell's** team suffered an almost complete collapse. They were saved partly by their knack of dragging three games into overtime before losing them.

Though Nottingham Panthers' fans again had little to cheer, they roared as **Paul Adey's** men made a clean sweep of their four games against the old enemy, with Finnish goalie **Mika Pietila** twice shutting out Sheffield in the Steel House and once more in the NIC.

Blaisdell was so upset at his team's performances that he threatened to bench half of them for the semi-final. "A lot of the same players have made the same mistakes over and over in the last few weeks," he thundered to the local *Star*. "I will only play the guys who I think can do the job in the semi."

Bracknell's coach, **Enio Sacilotto**, didn't have any Playoff worries. He was sacked before the first game, though the club's press release described it as 'taking some time out'.

Forward **Dave Struch** and captain **Mike McBain** took over the bench duties - while continuing to play - and, surprise, Bees thumped old rivals Belfast Giants 3-1 at home. The win was no fluke, either, as Bees drew 1-1 in overtime at Sheffield two days later and then whacked Steelers 5-2 in the Hive. But the streak ended there as Bees crumbled 7-3 in Docklands against a Knights' side revitalised by Swedish Elite League coach, **Jim Brithen**.

The Playoff honours belonged to Belfast Giants who rarely stumbled after that early loss in Bracknell. Indeed, **Dave Whistle's** squad avenged the defeat in style with an 8-4 trouncing of Bees in the Odyssey to clinch a semi-final berth with two weeks to spare.

The Irish fans' delight at going to Nottingham for the first time in the club's history was tinged with sadness at Giants' last home game of the season on 28 March. After the team had secured first place the night before, beating Steelers 3-1, a sell-out crowd of 6,500 turned up for the expected encore against London Knights.

Not only did Knights win in overtime - their fourth Playoff OT victory - but Whistle announced he was leaving to join a German DEL club. But he had one more UK honour to come...

PLAYOFF SEMI-FINALS

Nottingham Arena

Saturday 5 April 2003

BELFAST GIANTS	0	(0-0-0-0)
SHEFFIELD STEELERS	0	(0-0-0-0)

Giants won 1-0 after overtime and penalties

First Period
No scoring.
Penalty minutes: Giants 2, Steelers 2.
Second Period
No scoring.
Penalty minutes: Giants 2, Steelers 2.
Third Period
No scoring.
Penalty minutes: Giants 4, Steelers 8.
Overtime Period
No scoring.
Penalty minutes: None.
Penalty Shots
Scorers: BEL - Karlander, Riehl GWPS; SHE - Levins.
Shots on Goal
Bach BEL   8- 8-10-5 31
Laing SHE   8-10-11-3 32
Men of Match: Bach BEL, Laing SHE.
Referee: Andy Carson.   Attendance: 6,285
Linesmen: Michael Hicks, Lee Young.

LONDON KNIGHTS	4	(1-1-2)
NOTTINGHAM PANTHERS	3	(2-0-1)

First Period
0-1 NOT Wood   7.54
0-2 NOT Elders (Thompson, Taubert)   13.15
1-2 LON Blanchard (Maxwell, Mansi)   17.46
Penalty minutes: None.
Second Period
2-2 LON Aronson (Hoad, Kolesar) pp   34.54
Penalty minutes: Knights 4, Panthers 4.
Third Period
2-3 NOT Purves sh   49.26
3-3 LON Aronson (Kolesar, Hoad) pp   49.48
4-3 LON Maxwell (Bronilla)   59.59
Penalty minutes: Knights 4, Panthers 8.
Shots on Goal
Lilljebjorn LON   10-9- 9 28   save percent 89.3
Pietila NOT   14-7-15 34   save percent 88.2
Men of Match: Patterson LON, Purves NOT.
Referee: Moray Hanson.   Attendance: 6,285
Linesmen: Alan Craig, Gordon Pirry.

PLAYOFF FINAL

Nottingham Arena

Sunday 6 April 2003

BELFAST GIANTS	5	(1-1-3)
LONDON KNIGHTS	3	(0-1-2)

First Period
1-0 BEL Karlander (Kelman)   0.47
Penalty minutes: Giants 8, Knights 8.
Second Period
1-1 LON Bronilla   23.28
2-1 BEL Johnson (Stevens, Sorochan)   39.15
Penalty minutes: Giants 14, Knights 8.
Third Period
3-1 BEL Johnson (Karlander, Kruse)   43.41
3-2 LON Aronson (Hoad)   48.49
4-2 BEL Kuwabara (Stevens, Thornton) pp   51.19
4-3 LON Patterson (Hoad)   54.28
5-3 BEL Matsos en   59.13
Penalty minutes: Giants 4, Knights 6.
Shots on Goal
Bach BEL   7-5-8 20   save percent 85.0
Lilljebjorn LON   10-6-6 22   save percent 77.3
Men of Match: Johnson BEL, Aronson LON.
Referee: Simon Kirkham.   Attendance: 6,285
Linesmen: Marco Coenen, Paul Staniforth.

LEADING PLAYOFF SCORERS

	GP	G	A	Pts	Pim
Kory Karlander BEL	18	12	12	24	24
Lee Jinman NOT	15	4	19	23	6
Dan Ceman BRK	16	8	14	22	18
Ryan Kuwabara BEL	18	13	8	21	15
Jason Elders NOT	17	10	10	20	8

LEADING PLAYOFF NETMINDERS

	GPI	Mins	SoG	GA	Sv%
Ryan Bach BEL	15	913	503	30	94.0
Mika Pietila NOT	16	916	477	34	92.9
Joel Laing SHE	17	985	500	45	91.0

Qualification: 320 minutes

SIN-BIN

Players' penalties	GP	Pims	Ave
Dody Wood NOT	16	98	6.12
Jason Clarke NOT	15	74	4.93
Timo Willman SHE	17	77	4.53

THE FINAL FOUR

BELFAST GIANTS

Ryan Bach, Colin Ryder; Shane Johnson, Robby Sandrock, Lee Sorochan, Rob Stewart, Todd Kelman; Kory Karlander, Colin Ward, Doug MacDonald, Kevin Riehl, Steve Thornton, David Matsos, Curt Bowen, Rod Stevens, Paxton Schulte, Paul Kruse capt, Ryan Kuwabara.
Head coach: Dave Whistle.
Assistant coach: Rob Stewart.

LONDON KNIGHTS

Ake Lilljebjorn, Dave Trofimenkoff; Gerad Adams, Maurizio Mansi, Chris Slater, Rich Bronilla, Sean Blanchard; Nate Leslie, Mark Kolesar, AJ Kelham, Jeff Hoad, Ian McIntyre capt, Greg Burke, Steve Aronson, Ed Patterson, Paul Rushforth, Dennis Maxwell.
Head coach: Jim Brithen.
Assistant coach: Paul Rushforth.

NOTTINGHAM PANTHERS

Mika Pietila, Petter Sandstrom; Jim Paek, Marc Hussey, Eric Charron, Briane Thompson, Kristian Taubert; Greg Hadden, Dody Wood, Jason Elders, Scott Allison, Mark Cadotte, John Purves capt, Paul Moran, Barry Nieckar, Jason Clarke, Lee Jinman.
Coach: Paul Adey.   *Manager*: Gary Moran.

SHEFFIELD STEELERS

Joel Laing, Trevor Prior; Jeff Brown, Marc Laniel, Dion Darling, Timo Willman, Calle Carlsson; Rhett Gordon, Wes Dorey, Mark Dutiaume, Mike Morin, Chris Szysky, Kent Simpson, Scott Levins, Marc Laniel capt, Rick Brebant, Brent Bobyck, Jason Sessa.
Head coach: Mike Blaisdell.
Assistant coach: Rick Brebant.

PAST PLAYOFF FINALISTS

2002 **Sheffield Steelers** beat Manchester Storm 4-3 (after penalties) at Nottingham Arena.

2001 **Sheffield Steelers** beat London Knights 2-1 at Nottingham Arena.

2000 **London Knights** beat Newcastle Riverkings 7-3 at the *MEN* Arena, Manchester.

1999 **Cardiff Devils** beat Nottingham Panthers 2-1 at the *MEN* Arena, Manchester.

1998 **Ayr Scottish Eagles** beat Cardiff Devils 3-2 at the *Nynex* Arena, Manchester.

1997 **Sheffield Steelers** beat Nottingham Panthers 3-1 at the *Nynex* Arena, Manchester.

Luck of the Irish

It could be argued that Belfast Giants only reached the Superleague Playoff Championship final thanks to the luck of the Irish. But then the same would have to be said of their defeated opponents, London Knights.

Kevin Riehl put Giants into the league's last ever game by beating Sheffield Steelers' keeper, **Joel Laing**, with a coolly taken penalty shot. His goal was the only difference between the league's two best teams - and coaches - in Saturday's well played but defensive semi-final.

Laing's shutout was his tenth of the season as the league's player of the year broke **Trevor Robins**' record of nine set in 2000-01.

Steelers' coach, **Mike Blaisdell**, admitted: "We tried to be a bit too physical. It nearly came off but that style doesn't really work against a team like the Giants."

His assistant, **Rick Brebant**, confirmed that this had been his last game. Asked what his plans were for the future, he said: "I'm having a hernia op. on Monday and after that I'm just looking forward to waking up in the morning without pain!"

In the evening's semi, Knights and Nottingham Panthers looked like going into overtime as well, after they split six goals. But London's **Denis Maxwell** - better known in the league for his penalty minutes (110) than his goals (9) - stunned several thousand Panthers' fans with his goal just 0.02 seconds from the final hooter.

It was a just reward for the 28-year-old winger from Manitoba who had apparently beaten **Mika Pietila** two minutes earlier only for it to be disallowed as it went through a hole in the side netting. But it was a bad defeat for Panthers who were 2-0 up early on. "It's hard to protect a two-goal lead," admitted coach **Paul Adey**. "But it was our mistakes which allowed them back in."

Meanwhile, Knights' Swedish coach, **Jim Brithen**, was asked the usual post-semi-final question - how will you do against Giants in the final? "I know how [Mike] Tyson boxes," he replied, "but that doesn't mean I can beat him."

Belfast packed a punch themselves in a hard-hitting and entertaining final. Brithen brought all his many years' experience in Scandinavia to bear but Giants were in unbeatable form, urged on by their huge, flag-waving band of supporters.

Giants' coach **Dave Whistle** commiserated with his opposite number afterwards, pointing out that Knights were missing key players, **Kim Ahlroos** and **Vezio Sacratini**. Brithen was equally sporting. "That was a great game," he said. "Both teams were winners. We're proud of the silver."

CHALLENGE CUP

The Superleague teams were joined by Findus British National League side, Coventry Blaze, in the qualifying round and the teams played a round-robin in two four-team, geographically divided groups during September and October.

The leading two teams in each group qualified for the semi-finals at Sheffield Arena where the first placed team in one group faced the runner-up in the other.

The Cup's destination was decided in a one-game final at Manchester's MEN Arena.

QUALIFYING ROUND STANDINGS

Group A	GP	W	L	D	OTL	GF	GA	Pts
Sheffffield Steelers	6	5	1	0	0	22	12	10
Scottish Eagles	6	3	2	0	1	18	20	7
Belfast Giants	6	2	2	1	1	13	14	6
Manchester Storm	6	1	4	1	0	13	20	3
Group B								
Nottingham Panthers	6	4	0	1	1	23	13	10
London Knights	6	4	2	0	0	19	12	8
Bracknell Bees	6	2	2	0	2	15	18	6
Coventry Blaze	6	0	4	1	1	13	27	2

QUALIFYING ROUND RESULTS

Group A	BEL	MAN	SCO	SHE
Belfast Giants	-	3-2	6-5ot (1)	1-2
Manchester Storm	0-0ot	-	1-3	4-3
Scottish Eagles	4-3ot (3)	3-2	-	2-3
Sheffield Steelers	1-0	8-4	5-1	-
Group B	BRK	COV	LON	NOT
Bracknell Bees	-	6-4	1-4	2-1ot (2)
Coventry Blaze	2-2ot	-	2-3ot (4)	1-6
London Knights	4-1	4-1	-	2-4
Nottingham Panthers	3-3ot	6-3	3-2	-

Overtime Goal Scorers
1) BEL McDonald 62.11
2) BRK Hurley 61.54
3) SCO Williams 63.36 pp
4) LON Maxwell (Slater, Blanchard) 62.18

SEMI-FINALS

8 December 2002 at Sheffield Arena
NOTTINGHAM-BELFAST   **3-2** (1-1,0-1,2-0)
Scoring: NOT Jinman 2g; Hadden 1g; Nieckar, Paek 1a. BEL Kelman, Sandrock 1g; Karlander, MacDonald, Sorochan 1a.
Penalty minutes: Panthers 8, Giants 16 (Bowen 2+10-check/behind)
Shots on Goal: Pietila NOT 33, Ryder BEL 22.
Referee: Nigel Boniface.   *Attendance*: 4,600.

SHEFFIELD-LONDON   **4-4ot** (2-0,1-3,1-1,0-0)
Steelers won 5-4 after penalty shots
Scoring: SHE Norris GWPS; Carlsson, Sessa 1+1; Levins, Simpson 1g; Gordon, Szysky, Dutiaume, Darling 1a. LON Kolesar 2g; Aronson 1+1; Hoad 1g; Maxwell, McIntyre, Blanchard 1a.
Penalty minutes: Steelers 22, Knights 22.
Shots on Goal:
Laing SHE 31, Trofimenkoff LON 25.
Referee: Moray Hanson.   *Attendance*: 5,145.

FINAL

26 January 2003 at MEN Arena, Manchester

SHEFFIELD STEELERS	**3**	**(2-0-1)**
NOTTINGHAM PANTHERS	**2**	**(0-0-2)**

First Period
1-0 SHE Simpson (Sessa) pp   10.56
2-0 SHE Sessa (Simpson, Carlsson)   16.34
Penalty minutes: Steelers 2, Panthers 4.
Second Period
No scoring.
Penalty minutes: Steelers 10, Panthers 6.
Third Period
3-0 SHE Dutiaume (Brown, Simpson) pp 49.54
3-1 NOT Thompson   sh   54.11
3-2 NOT Hadden   56.53
Penalty minutes: Steelers 2, Panthers 26 (Charron 2+10 check/behind).
Shots on Goal:
Laing SHE   10-10-13 33
save percentage   93.9
Pietila/Sandstrom NOT   6- 7- 4 17
save percentage   82.3
Referee: Nigel Boniface.   *Attendance*: 8,766
Linesmen: Folka, Staniforth.

THE WINNING TEAM
SHEFFIELD STEELERS

Joel Laing, Trevor Prior; Jeff Brown, Marc Laniel, Dion Darling, Timo Willman, Calle Carlsson; Jason Sessa, Wes Dorey, Mark Dutiaume, Mike Morin, Kent Simpson, Scott Levins, Warren Norris, Rick Brebant, Brent Bobyck.
Head coach: Mike Blaisdell
Assistant coach: Rick Brebant

.

WE'RE IN THE FINAL!

Sheffield Steeler **WARREN NORRIS** celebrates *inset* after beating London Knights' netminder **Dave Trofimenkoff** for the winning penalty shot in the Challenge Cup semi-final.

Photo: Diane Davey

Fourth Cup for Steelers

Sheffield Steelers won Superleague's first competition of the season, the last in which all seven league sides competed. Scottish Eagles, under coach **Paul Heavey**, actually qualified for the semis but were replaced by Belfast Giants when **Bob Zeller**'s team collapsed.

Coventry Blaze of the British National League accepted the league's invitation to make up an even eight teams and the semi-pro side acquitted themselves well, gaining two home points after drawing with Bracknell Bees and taking London Knights into overtime.

Lee Jinman's two goals, including the winner ten minutes from time, helped to put Nottingham Panthers into their third cup final in five attempts with their one-goal victory over Giants.

Dave **Whistle**'s injury-hit squad could muster only 12 skaters.

In the other semi the same evening, the home town Steelers were surprised by a stubborn London squad who forced a penalty shootout before they succumbed to the league leaders and cup favourites. "It was a tough game," said Sheffield's relieved coach **Mike Blaisdell**. "They were the better team for the last 35 minutes but I thought we were awesome in the first period."

The Sheffield-Nottingham final, which was belatedly moved from London to Manchester to help keep the sport alive there, drew almost 9,000, many of them Panthers' fans eager to see yet another round in the undying rivalry.

But their lads had an off-night, especially their normally reliable Finnish keeper **Mika Pietila** who allowed two goals on six first period shots. When **Mark Dutiaume** made it 3-0 with ten minutes left, Panthers' two replies came too late to stop Steelers skating off with their fourth cup in five years.

PAST FINALISTS

2001-02 Ayr Scottish Eagles beat Belfast Giants 5-0 at the Odyssey Arena, Belfast.

2000-01 Sheffield Steelers beat Ayr Scottish Eagles 4-2 at the Odyssey Arena, Belfast.

1999-00 Sheffield Steelers beat Nottingham Panthers 2-1 at London Arena.

1998-99 Sheffield Steelers beat Nottingham Panthers 4-0 at Sheffield Arena.

*1997-98 Ayr Scottish Eagles beat Bracknell Bees 3-2 at *Telewest* Arena, Newcastle.

* *competition sponsored by* The Express.

HOLD THE BOTTOM OF PAGE 33!

London Knights' head coach **Bob Leslie** hit out at the penalty-shot system after seeing his team lose 5-4 to the Sheffield Steelers in the Challenge Cup semi-final at Sheffield Arena last night.

An angry Leslie said: "I'm not happy. I think shoot-outs are ridiculous."

The entire match report in London's Evening Standard, *Knights' sponsors.*

AHEARNE TROPHY

The Ahearne Trophy was named after **John Francis 'Bunny' Ahearne** (1901-1985), from 1933 the general secretary (and later president) of the British Ice Hockey Association and the post-World War 2 driving force behind the International Ice Hockey Federation, the world governing body.

A member of the British, Canadian and IIHF Halls of Fame, he was the manager of the GB national team in 1936 when they became the first country to win the Triple Crown of Olympic, World and European Championships.

The original trophy was first competed for in 1952 (Nottingham Panthers won it in 1956) and the last winner in 1974 was Djurgardens of Stockholm. The organisers received permission from the Swedish Federation to revive the tournament, with a new trophy being struck for the occasion, hand-crafted by Tyrone Crystal of Northern Ireland.

The competition was organised by Superleague on an invitational basis with the opposition being drawn from an overseas league. This year's opponents came from the Norwegian A League and the ten games were played during one of the IIHF's 'international breaks'. The league whose teams gained most points won the trophy.

With Superleague being reduced to five teams at short notice, Coventry Blaze of the British National League again lined up alongside the Superleague teams.

Germany's Deutsche Elite League (DEL) won the trophy in 2002.

RESULTS

1 Feb	Nottingham-Sarpsborg	11-3
2 Feb	Sheffield-Sarpsborg	3-5
5 Feb	Coventry-Trondheim	6-3
7 Feb	Belfast-Trondheim	3-0
	London-Storhamar	8-4
8 Feb	Belfast-Asker	5-4
	Bracknell-Valerengen	1-3
	Sheffield-Storhamar	5-1
9 Feb	Bracknell-Asker	5-2
	London-Valerengen	3-2

FINAL STANDINGS

	GP	W	L	D	GF	GA	Pts
Superleague	10	8	2	0	50	27	16
Norway A League	10	2	8	0	27	50	4

First win for Superleague

Five Superleague teams and the BNL's Coventry Blaze won the second Ahearne Trophy tournament of the modern era by a decisive margin of eight games to two.

Nottingham Panthers, who were able to host only one of the games due to the unavailability of the National Ice Centre, recorded the biggest victory, 11-3 over Sparta Sarpsborg, sixth place finishers in Norway in 2001-02.

League stragglers Bracknell Bees and, unexpectedly, leaders Sheffield Steelers were the only sides to lose in the ten-games-in-nine-days series against five of Norway's leading clubs. Even Coventry comfortably beat Trondheim.

The only winning Norwegian sides were Sarpsborg who bounced back from their Nottingham embarrassment to beat Sheffield, and league winners Valerengen of Oslo, who conquered the Bees.

The Norwegians were somewhat handicapped by the absence of their national team players as the games were staged during one of the IIHF's 'international breaks'. Their teams comprise mainly home-grown talent.

Crowd support, never at its best for 'friendlies' against overseas opposition, was down ten per cent on last year. (See *Rink Attendances*).

But both leagues professed themselves pleased with the games. "All our teams will take away happy memories of this tournament," said the Norwegian president, **Steinar Froysa.**

Superleague's administrator, **Brian Storey**, declared: "The Ahearne Trophy is now well established as a tournament that attracts the best in entertainment with foreign teams involved."

The trophy was presented on the last night in London Arena by Superleague chairman **Albert Maasland**, the owner of Belfast Giants. Receiving it on the league's behalf was Knights' captain, **Ian McIntyre.**

ALL-TIME SUPERLEAGUE RECORDS

COMPLETE LEAGUE STANDINGS

Seasons 1996-97 to 2002-03	S	GP	W	OW	L	OL	D	GF	GA	Pts	Pct.
Belfast Giants BEL	3	128	65	6	33	10	14	446	356	183	71.5
Cardiff Devils CAR	5	202	113	5	62	13	9	756	590	282	62.4
Sheffield Steelers SHE	7	282	145	5	89	14	29	980	840	373	60.9
Ayr Scottish Eagles AYR	6	250	117	4	95	10	24	865	801	297	54.2
Manchester Storm MAN	6	250	113	6	98	12	21	840	822	286	52.8
Nottingham Panthers NOT	7	282	122	8	119	12	21	893	945	303	49.5
Bracknell Bees BRK	7	282	111	6	120	19	26	973	1053	298	48.7
London Knights LON	5	212	76	7	90	12	27	609	673	223	47.2
Newcastle Cobras/Riverkings/Jesters NEW	5	202	60	3	112	21	6	580	776	165	36.5
Basingstoke Bison BAS	2	70	16	0	38	9	7	232	318	48	27.9

W - 2 pts (except 2000-01 - 3pts), OW - 2pts (2000-01 only), OL & D - 1 pt.

LEADING SCORERS

1996-2003	S	GP	G	A	Pts	Ave
Vezio Sacratini LON/CAR	7	269	111	161	272	1.01
Greg Hadden NOT	7	259	129	121	250	0.97
Ed Courtenay AYR/SHE	5	199	122	126	248	1.25
Rick Brebant SHE/MAN/LON/NEW	7	231	75	152	227	0.98
Tony Hand AYR/SHE	5	191	60	160	220	1.15
Ivan Matulik MAN/CAR	7	250	102	114	216	0.86
Steve Thornton BEL/LON/CAR	7	208	82	133	215	1.03
Steve Moria NOT/CAR	6	244	106	97	203	0.83
Blake Knox BRK/NEW/NOT/BAS	6	243	69	124	193	0.79
Jeff Hoad NOT/AYR/LON/BEL	7	271	85	103	188	0.69

Ave = Points per game

LEADING NETMINDERS

1996-2003	S	GPI	Mins	SoG	GA	Sav%
Joel Laing SHE	1	28	1710	756	44	94.2
Rob Dopson AYR	1	28	1674	885	66	92.5
Jim Hrivnak MAN	1	15	927	515	40	92.2
Mika Pietila NOT	1	26	1437	772	61	92.1
Mike Bales BEL	1	34	1996	965	77	92.0

Qualification: One-third of team's games in a season.

FINDUS BRITISH
NATIONAL LEAGUE

FINAL STANDINGS

P/pos		GP	W	L	D	OL	GF	GA	Pts	Pct
(4-2)	**Coventry Blaze** COV	36	30	4	1	1	173	69	62	86.1
(/-1)	**Dundee Stars** DUN	36	27	8	0	1	196	109	55	76.4
(1-5)	**Guildford Flames** GUI	36	22	14	0	0	168	133	44	61.1
(2-4)	**Basingstoke Bison** BAS	36	20	14	1	1	128	119	42	58.3
(/-12)	**Cardiff Devils** CAR	36	20	15	0	1	133	104	41	56.9
(9-7)	**Edinburgh Capitals** EDI	36	19	15	0	2	119	125	40	55.5
(3-3)	**Fife Flyers** FIF	36	15	18	0	3	113	127	33	45.8
(/-/)	**Newcastle Vipers** NEW	36	12	22	2	0	115	155	26	36.1
(6-6)	**Hull Thunder** HUL	36	8	28	0	0	110	236	16	22.2
(/-/)	**Solihull MK Kings** SOL	36	4	27	2	3	72	150	13	18.1

Scoring system

Games tied after the regulation 60 minutes gained one point each and played ten minutes of sudden-death overtime. The winning team in overtime gained an extra point (W) but if they were still tied at the end of overtime, the teams shared the points (D). The losing team kept one point (OL).
P/pos *- league position in each of last two seasons, 2000-01 and 2001-02. First year of competition for Newcastle Vipers and Solihull MK Kings.*

LEADING SCORERS

	GP	G	A	Pts	Pim
Tony Hand DUN	36	22	58	80	99
Teeder Wynne DUN	36	29	50	79	16
Ken Priestlay DUN	33	31	40	71	28
Ashley Tait COV	36	30	31	61	22
Jason Lafreniere GUI	36	19	37	56	67
Marc West HUL/GUI	36	17	39	56	50
Johan Boman DUN	35	34	20	54	36
Derek DeCosty GUI	36	26	27	53	8
Mikko Koivunoro NEW	34	20	33	53	32
Peter Konder EDI	36	16	37	53	98
Russ Romaniuk CAR	36	23	29	52	48

LEADING NETMINDERS

	GPl	Mins	SoG	GA	Sv%
Stevie Lyle CAR	29	1735	928	82	91.5
Jody Lehman COV	36	2127	780	68	91.3
Ladislav Kudrna EDI	36	2173	1409	123	91.3
Stephen Murphy DUN	34	2048	1090	96	91.2
Steve Briere FIF	36	2149	1269	119	90.6

Qualification: 720 mins

SIN-BIN

Players' Penalties	GP	Pim	Ave
Rob Trumbley NEW	27	134	4.96
Eric Lavigne HUL	24	113	4.71
Daryl Lavoie BAS	28	118	4.21

OFFICIAL *FINDUS* BNL WEBSITE
www.britnatleague.co.uk

RESULTS CHART

	BAS	CAR	COV	DUN	EDI	FIF	GUI	HUL	NEW	SOL
BAS	**	5-4 16/11	1-3 7/12	1-5 19/10	2-4 9/11	5-4 2/11	2-4 1/2	5-7 12/10	3-3ot 21/9	1-2 25/1
	**	3-1 14/12	1-2ot (5) 4/1	5-3 18/1	5-2 22/2	5-3 1/12	4-6 15/2	4-1 21/12	4-1 13/10	4-1 9/2
CAR	2-3 3/11	**	0-4 7/10	2-3 28/9	2-5 5/10	4-1 15/12	6-3 17/11	4-2 19/10	6-3 30/11	4-2 7/12
	2-3ot (6) 19/1	**	7-4 11/1	0-5 26/10	4-1 4/1	7-0 9/2	8-3 5/1	12-0 2/2	4-2 22/2	5-2 29/12
COV	4-2 22/12	6-2 8/12	**	5-4ot (3) 2/11	8-1 28/12	4-0 3/11	5-2 30/11	12-1 10/11	6-1 25/1	6-0 17/11
	9-1 5/1	6-4 12/1	**	0-5 15/2	2-1 8/2	5-3 19/1	4-3 26/1	5-4 15/12	10-2 2/2	3-1 23/2
DUN	10-5 27/10	2-3 22/12	4-6 29/12	**	7-1 16/11	7-1 10/11	3-2 29/9	4-3 1/12	4-3 9/11	4-3 5/1
	4-6 23/2	4-1 25/1	1-3 9/2	**	2-4 8/12	5-4 2/2	5-7 15/12	13-5 19/1	8-1 12/1	7-0 1/2
EDI	4-5 17/11	4-2 10/11	2-1 20/10	1-5 7/12	**	3-2 10/12	2-5 14/12	6-4 3/11	0-5 27/10	3-0 1/12
	4-2 12/1	2-1 26/1	2-1ot (8) 16/2	5-7 21/12	**	4-2 5/1	2-3ot (7) 19/1	6-3 29/12	8-0 9/2	5-2 2/2
FIF	2-1 26/10	4-1 9/11	2-4 19/10	1-4 28/12	6-0 25/1	**	4-2 28/9	5-3 5/10	6-2 16/11	3-0 4/1
	2-3ot 11/1	2-0 21/12	1-2 14/12	5-8 22/2	5-3 1/2	**	5-4 18/1	5-4 7/12	5-4 16/2	9-3 15/2
GUI	1-5 10/11	4-1 1/12	2-9 16/11	3-5 3/11	5-4ot (1) 19/10	5-2 8/12	**	6-2 4/1	5-1 7/12	5-2 27/10
	5-1 2/2	6-7 16/2	1-4 2/1	5-9 8/2	4-2 23/2	6-4 29/12	**	15-3 25/1	6-4 21/12	6-2 12/1
HUL	2-3 20/10	4-5 28/12	1-7 9/11	3-1 17/11	6-2 30/11	4-3ot (2) 27/10	3-5 2/11	**	4-5 8/12	4-3 13/10
	3-13 26/1	1-6 23/2	0-7 1/2	4-17 16/2	2-7 18/1	1-6 12/1	2-12 9/2	**	3-6 5/1	6-3 22/12
NEW	2-0 15/12*	2-6 20/10	2-8 1/12	2-4 4/1	8-4 22/12	2-3 20/11	3-5 30/10	12-3 11/1	**	4-1 22/9
	3-8 29/12	0-2 1/2	2-1 18/1	0-5 29/1	3-5 15/2	5-1 23/2	6-4 7/11	6-3 8/2	**	4-1 10/11
SOL	3-5 8/12	0-4 18/1	1-1ot 21/12	4-5 12/10	1-4 15/12	3-0 20/10	1-6 9/11	3-6 26/10	5-5ot 3/11	**
	1-2ot (9) 16/2	3-4 8/2	1-5 22/2	4-6 26/1	3-6 11/1	4-2 30/11	1-2ot (4) 28/12	2-3ot (3) 16/11	4-1 19/1	**
	BAS	CAR	COV	DUN	EDI	FIF	GUI	HUL	NEW	SOL

Second figure is date of game

* postponed from 29 September when police took over the Telewest Arena to investigate the death of a teenager during a 'Rave' the night before the game.

OVERTIME WINNERS

Key to above:

(1)	GUI	Lafreniere (DeCosty, Chinn)	68.29
(2)	HUL	Ferone (West, Young)	60.19
(3)	HUL	Weaver (West, Munroe)	64.57
(4)	GUI	Clarke (Dixon, Torchia)	60.59
(5)	COV	Chartrand (Carpenter, Ruggles)	63.53
(6)	BAS	Campbell (Ellis, Parrish)	68.46
(7)	GUI	Clarke	65.46

LEAGUE AWARDS

INDIVIDUAL

Player of the Year	Jody Lehman COV
Best Netminder	Jody Lehman COV
Best Defenceman	Jan Krajicek EDI
Best British Player	Tony Hand DUN
Coach of the Year	Paul Thompson COV

ALL-STARS

Goal	Jody Lehman COV
Defence	Jan Krajicek EDI
	Steve Carpenter COV
Forwards	Ashley Tait COV
	Tony Hand DUN
	Russ Romaniuk CAR

BRITISH ALL STARS

Goal	Stephen Murphy DUN
Defence	Paul Dixon GUI
	Neil Liddiard BAS
Forwards	Ashley Tait COV
	Tony Hand DUN
	David Clarke GUI

Selections made by the team coaches, excluding their own team.

FAIR PLAY

Team Penalties	GP	Pim	Ave
Solihull MK Kings	36	468	13.0
Dundee Stars	36	531	14.7
Fife Flyers	36	548	15.2
Edinburgh Capitals	36	613	17.0
Basingstoke Bison	36	660	18.3
Guildford Flames	36	692	19.2
Hull Thunder	36	698	19.4
Newcastle Vipers	36	710	19.7
Cardiff Devils	36	743	20.6
Coventry Blaze	36	747	20.7
LEAGUE TOTALS	360	6410	17.8

PAST WINNERS

2001-02		Dundee Stars
2000-01		Guildford Flames
1999-2000		Fife Flyers
1998-99		Slough Jets
1997-98		Guildford Flames
1996-97	Premier Lge	Swindon IceLords
	N Premier Lge	Fife Flyers

Blaze burn up league

Coventry Blaze captured their first major title when they won the British National League by seven points from the holders, Dundee Stars.

Former North American minor league goalie, **Jody Lehman**, led a string of award winning Coventry players who were forged into winners by **Paul Thompson** who was himself voted Coach of the Year.

Dundee Stars failed to recapture the glory of their first year. Perhaps the old chemistry was lost when returning coach **Tony Hand** made several changes to key personnel. Stars were certainly no match for Blaze whom they beat only once in four meetings and then only after the title had been decided.

There was little to choose between the next four sides with only four points separating the highly favoured *Guildford Flames* from the perennially hard-up *Edinburgh Capitals*.

Defence was the big difference between these two with **Stan Marple**'s men being the league's fourth leakiest team while Capitals' owner **Scott Neil** shrewdly signed a Czech goalie **Ladislav Kudrna**, and defenceman **Jan Krajicek**, who were among the BNL's best.

> "Last year went really well, the team was made up of a good group of guys, there were no cliques, and we ended up winning the double."
> *Ron Shudra, Coventry Blaze.*

Basingstoke Bison contended all season under rookie coach **Steve Moria**, and *Cardiff Devils* made a welcome return to their old form. **Glen Mulvenna**'s team was helped by the late addition of home-town goalie, **Stevie Lyle**, who finished with the league's best stats after joining from the defunct Manchester Storm.

Newcastle Vipers struggled in their first year, rather surprisingly given the pedigree of Sheffield Steelers' fomer winning duo, **Alex Dampier** and **Clyde Tuyl**. GB captain **David Longstaff**'s move to Switzerland halfway through the campaign was a big loss.

Hull Thunder again hit financial trouble in mid-season but veteran coach **Peter (Jonker) Johnson**, who replaced **Mike Bishop**, enjoyed a Last of the Summer Wine time in charge of a mostly British squad.

We should perhaps avert our gaze from *Fife Flyers* who had a distinctly off-year despite the belated signing of GB forward **Jonathan Weaver**. And the rescue of *Solihull MK Kings* from ice hockey's version of the knacker's yard was only partially successful.

PLAYOFFS

The top eight BNL teams qualified for the championship playoffs. In the quarter-finals the teams were split into two groups of four with the teams finishing 1st, 4th, 5th and 8th in the league going into group A and the others into group B.

The top two teams in each group qualified for the semi-finals with the winner of one group playing a home-and-away, total points series against the runners-up in the other group.

The winning semi-finalists competed for the title using the same playing format with the choice of playing the first leg on home ice being made by the teams finishing highest in the Playoff group. In the final, the choice of home ice went to the team finishing highest in the league.

Draws were decided by ten minutes' sudden-death overtime. Teams winning in overtime gained two points and the losers none with the points being shared if the teams were still tied. In the second legs of the semi-finals and final where necessary, overtime (and penalty shots, if necessary) was used to decide the result.

QUARTER-FINAL STANDINGS

Group A	GP	W	L	D	GF	GA	Pts
Coventry Blaze	6	6	0	0	18	6	12
Cardiff Devils	6	4	2	0	17	9	8
Basingstoke Bison	6	1	5	0	14	23	2
Newcastle Vipers	6	1	5	0	9	20	2
Group B							
Dundee Stars	6	5	1	0	28	14	10
Guildford Flames	6	4	2	0	25	15	8
Edinburgh Capitals	6	2	4	0	14	23	4
Fife Flyers	6	1	5	0	16	31	2

QUARTER-FINAL RESULTS

Group 1	BAS	CAR	COV	NEW
Basingstoke	-	1-3	1-6	5-3
Cardiff	3-2	-	0-1	5-2
Coventry	5-3	3-1	-	2-1
Newcastle	3-2	0-5	0-1	-
Group 2	DUN	EDI	FIF	GUI
Dundee	-	4-2	9-2	3-1
Edinburgh	1-5	-	3-2	2-8
Fife	4-6	1-4	-	5-4
Guildford	4-1	3-2	5-2	-

SEMI-FINALS

First semi-final
Game One 22 Mar Cardiff-Dundee 5-3
Game Two 23 Mar Dundee-Cardiff 4-2
CARDIFF DEVILS won in overtime.
Second semi-final
Game One 22 Mar Guildford-Coventry 2-4
Game Two 23 Mar Coventry-Guildford 5-1
COVENTRY BLAZE won two games to nil.

CHAMPIONSHIP FINALS

Game One, Thursday 27 March 2003

CARDIFF DEVILS	2	(1-0-1)
COVENTRY BLAZE	3	(0-2-1)

First Period
1-0 CAR Romaniuk (Matulik) sh 11.58
Penalty minutes: Devils 8, Blaze 4.
Second Period
1-1 COV Watkins (Ruggles, Chartrand) 21.19
1-2 COV Ruggles pp 23.17
Penalty minutes: Devils 2, Blaze 0.
Third Period
2-2 CAR Romaniuk (Burgoyne, Ware) pp 43.47
2-3 COV Tait (Carpenter, Poirier) 48.55
Penalty minutes: Devils 4, Blaze 10.
Shots on Goal
Lyle CAR 9-9-10 28 save percent. 89.3
Lehman COV 8-8- 7 23 save percent. 91.3
Referee: Michael Evans. Attendance: 2,516.
Linesmen: Andy Dalton, James Kavanagh.

Game Two, Sunday 30 March 2003

COVENTRY BLAZE	2	(0-2-0)
CARDIFF DEVILS	1	(0-1-0)

First Period
No scoring.
Penalty minutes: Blaze 4, Devils 6.
Second Period
0-1 CAR Hill (Scott) 25.03
1-1 COV Carpenter (Ruggles, Chartrand) pp 28.15
2-1 COV Shudra (Moborg, Tait) 33.53
Penalty minutes: Blaze 4, Devils 14.
Third Period
No scoring.
Penalty minutes: Blaze 10, Devils 10.
Shots on Goal
Lehman COV 5-8-6 19 save percent. 94.7
Lyle CAR 15-4-9 38 save percent. 94.7
Referee: Simon Kirkham. Attendance: 2,750.
Linesmen: Andy Dalton, James Kavanagh.

COVENTRY BLAZE are champions
two games to nil.

THE FINALISTS

CARDIFF DEVILS
Stevie Lyle, Dan Wood; Mike Bishop, Jeff Burgoyne, Blair Scott, Jason Stone, Chris Bailey; Matt Myers, Blake Knox, Russ Romaniuk, Jonathan Phillips, Warren Tait, Ivan Matulik, Phil Hill, Mike Ware, capt, Kurt Walsh, Phil Monny, David James. *Manager-coach*: Glen Mulvenna.

COVENTRY BLAZE
Jody Lehman, Alan Levers; Steve Carpenter, James Pease, Andreas Moborg, Mathias Soderstrom, Ron Shudra, Adam Radmall; Shaun Johnson, Steve Chartrand, capt, Kurt Irvine, Russell Cowley, Tom Watkins, Ashley Tait, Gareth Owen, Joel Poirier, Hilton Ruggles. Lee Richardson.
Coach: Paul Thompson. *Manager*: Steve Small.

LEADING PLAYOFF SCORERS

	GP	G	A	Pts	Pim
Patric Lochi DUN	8	9	8	17	10
Scott Young DUN	8	6	9	15	20
Steve Chartrand COV	10	7	6	13	24
Hilton Ruggles COV	10	5	8	13	16
Russ Romaniuk CAR	10	7	5	12	22
Martin Wiita DUN	8	5	6	11	0
David Clarke GUI	8	5	5	10	6
Johan Boman DUN	8	4	6	10	14
Marc West GUI	8	3	7	10	8
Ivan Matulik CAR	10	3	7	10	33

LEADING PLAYOFF NETMINDERS

	GPI	Mins	SoG	GA	S%
Jody Lehman COV	9	540	203	11	94.6
Stevie Lyle CAR	10	601	300	21	93.0
Stephen Murphy DUN	8	481	264	22	91.7

PAST PLAYOFF FINALISTS
*2002 Dundee Stars beat Coventry Blaze 8-5 on aggregate (7-4a, 1-3h)
*2001 Guildford Flames Basingstoke Bison 12-4 on aggregate (7-2a, 5-2h)
2000 Fife Flyers beat Basingstoke Bison 3-0 in best-of-five games series
1999 Fife Flyers

1998		Guildford Flames
1997	*Premier Lge*	Swindon IceLords
	N Premier Lge	Fife Flyers

* sponsored by *Findus*.

Double for Thommo's men

Coventry Blaze completed a league and championship double with a clean sweep of Cardiff Devils in the BNL's home-and-away Playoff final.

All-Star Brit forward **Ashley Tait** scored the winner in the Wales National Ice Rink and then helped to set up veteran **Ron Shudra**'s clinching goal in front of a capacity crowd in the SkyDome. Devils' keeper **Stevie Lyle** was man of the match in Game Two as the Blaze doubled Cardiff's shot total.

Coventry never dropped a point throughout the Playoffs, a first in the league's six seasons. Coach **Paul Thompson** praised his team. "There's a lot of players who wouldn't like the sort of regime we have here," he told the local *Evening Telegraph*. "I work them pretty hard. To go ten games undefeated in the Playoffs is remarkable."

In the semis, while Blaze were dismissing Guildford Flames with surprising ease, Cardiff's victory in the home of the defending champs, Dundee Stars, made the biggest news of the competition; the league's strange - and late - decision to alter the format of the semis and final (the fourth change in six years) confused players, fans and, critically, both match and league officials.

Fans are accustomed to two-leg, aggregate goals finals so it seemed perverse of the BNL to have what amounted to best-of-two-games affairs - especially when each side won one game and league official-on-the-spot, **Gary Stefan**, was unsure of the tie-break system.

The league's intention was a ten-minute OT extension of Game Two, followed by a penalty shootout if necessary, but 'Stef' told referee **Mike Evans** to treat the extra time as a Game Three. He made his decision after apparently coming under pressure from the Devils who refused to play on unless their two penalised players, **Ivan Matulik** and **Russ Romaniuk**, were allowed back on the ice for the tie-break.

That might not have been so bad but guess who scored Devils' winning goal? That's right: Romaniuk, assisted by Matulik. Angry protests from the Stars, who demanded a replay, were turned down by the league who, naturally, were unwilling to overturn the decision of one of their own officials. There was no time, in any case, for teams from opposite ends of the country to meet again when the first leg of the final had been scheduled just four days later.

FINDUS CUP

QUALIFYING ROUND STANDINGS

South	GP	W	L	D	GF	GA	Pts
Guildford Flames	8	6	2	0	31	21	12
Coventry Blaze	8	5	3	0	30	21	10
Basingstoke Bison	8	4	3	1	30	26	9
Cardiff Devils	8	2	4	2	20	23	6
Solihull MK Kings	8	1	6	1	17	37	3
North							
Dundee Stars	8	5	1	2	48	24	12
Newcastle Vipers	8	5	2	1	30	22	11
Fife Flyers	8	3	4	1	31	38	7
Hull Thunder	8	2	5	1	29	35	5
E'burgh Capitals	8	2	5	1	29	48	5

QUALIFYING ROUND RESULTS

South	BAS	CAR	COV	GUI	SOL
B'stoke	-	4-1	3-6	4-2	7-2
Cardiff	3-3	-	5-3	2-4	3-3
Coventry	6-3	0-2	-	5-2	4-2
Guildford	4-3	2-1	4-2	-	4-0
Solihull	2-3	4-3	0-4	4-9	-
North	DUN	EDI	FIF	HUL	NEW
Dundee	-	16-3	2-2	7-5	5-3
Edinburgh	3-3	-	5-6	5-2	3-0
Fife	2-8	8-5	-	5-4	2-4
Hull	2-4	8-4	4-2	-	3-3
Newcastle	4-3	5-1	6-4	5-1	-

SEMI-FINALS
Telewest Arena, Newcastle
23 November 2002
GUILDFORD-NEWCASTLE   3-3ot
                          (2-2,0-1,1-0,0-0)
Newcastle won 4-3 after penalty shots (1-0)
Scoring: GUI Bowen, DeCosty, Clarke 1g; Lyons, Lafreniere, Bowen, White, Torchia 1a. NEW Koivunoro 2g; Trumbley 1g; Irwin, Leach 1a.
Game Winning Penalty Shot: Longstaff.
Penalty minutes: Flames 20, Vipers 18.
Shots on Goal:
Torchia GUI 22, Raitanen NEW 28.
Referee: Matt Thompson.   *Attendance*: 3,008

PAST FINALISTS
2002   **Fife Flyers** beat Coventry Blaze 6-3 at Nottingham Arena.

DUNDEE-COVENTRY   4-6   (1-2,1-1,2-3)
Scoring: DUN Priestlay, Wynne 1+1; Lochi, Mikel 1g; Hand, Wiita 2a; Boman 1a. COV Shudra 2g; Tait, Carpenter, Ruggles 1+1; Watkins 1g; Johnson, Poirier 2a; Moborg 1a.
Penalty minutes: Stars 37 (Mikel 5+game check/behind),   Blaze   26   (Carpenter 10-misc/abuse).
Shots on Goal
Murphy DUN 37, Lehman COV 26.
Referee: Dave Cloutman.   *Attendance*: 3,008

THIRD PLACE PLAYOFF
24 November 2002
GUILDFORD-DUNDEE 1-4   (1-0,0-2,0-2)
Scoring: GUI Bowen 1g; DeCosty, Lyons 1a. DUN Mikel 1+2; Priestlay, Boman 1+1; Lochi 1g; Hand 2a.
Penalty minutes: Flames 37 (Lyons 5+game check/behind), Stars 10.
Shots on Goal: Torchia GUI 23, Murphy DUN 27.
Referee: Matt Thompson.   *Attendance*: 3,620

FINAL
24 November 2002

NEWCASTLE VIPERS	3	(1-2-0)
COVENTRY BLAZE	0	(0-0-0)

First Period
1-0 NEW Lankshear (Longstaff, Koivunoro) 5.35
Penalty minutes: Vipers 14, Blaze 12.
Second Period
2-0 NEW Wilson (Irwin, Longstaff) pp   29.26
3-0 NEW Bowman (Koivunoro, Lapointe)
                                      pp   37.31
Penalty minutes: Vipers 4, Blaze 6.
Third Period
No scoring.
Penalty minutes: Vipers 4, Blaze 2.
Shots on Goal
Raitanen NEW 9- 4-15 28   *save percent.* 100.0
Lehman COV 5-10- 8 23   *save percent.* 86.9
Referee: Dave Cloutman.   *Attendance*: 3,620
Linesmen: Joy Tottman, Andy Dalton.

THE WINNING TEAM
NEWCASTLE VIPERS
Pasi Raitanen, Stephen Wall; Ian Defty, Mike Lankshear, Martin Lapointe, Richie Thornton, Rob Wilson, Andre Malo; Neil Abel, Joel Irwin, Les Millie, David Longstaff, Michael Bowman, Mikko Koivunoro, Karl Culley, Rob Trumbley (capt), Simon Leach, Stuart Potts, Stephen Wallace.
Coach: Clyde Tuyl. *Manager*: Alex Dampier.

BRITISH ALL-STARS

Basingstoke Bison defenceman **NEIL LIDDIARD** *left* and Coventry Blaze forward **ASHLEY TAIT**.

Photos: Chris Valentine, Tony Boot.

LEADING SCORERS

	GP	G	A	Pts	Pim
Ken Priestlay DUN	10	12	16	28	10
Teeder Wynne DUN	10	7	16	23	10
Tony Hand DUN	10	7	15	22	6
Mikko Koivunoro NEW	10	7	13	20	12
Ashley Tait COV	10	7	10	17	8
Johan Boman DUN	10	7	9	16	8
Marc West HUL	8	6	10	16	32
Jan Mikel DUN	9	6	10	16	39
Patric Lochi DUN	10	9	6	15	10
Dan Currie HUL	8	6	8	14	12

LEADING NETMINDERS

	GPI	Mins	SoG	GA	S%
Pasi Raitanen NEW	10	605	303	25	91.8
Danny Lorenz GUI	8	480	252	21	91.7
Brian Leitza CAR	8	480	266	23	91.3

SIN-BIN

Player Penalties	GP	Pim	Ave
Mike Ware CAR	8	108	13.5
Nicky Chinn GUI	10	94	9.4
Blake Knox CAR	8	59	7.4

First time lucky for Vipers

The changing of the BNL guard from Dundee Stars to Coventry Blaze was interrupted by the unexpected success of the first year Newcastle Vipers. Helped by having the *Findus* Cup finals staged in their home arena, Vipers won the Cup in their first season with a shutout victory over the favoured Blaze.

Vipers' Finnish keeper, **Pasi Raitanen**, the cup's leading goalie, frustrated Blaze by turning aside 28 shots and leaving them with their fourth runners-up medal in a row. The Midlands outfit came second in all the 2001-02 competitions.

GB skipper **David Longstaff** put Vipers into the final with the winning penalty shot when their semi against Guildford Flames had been stalemated at 3-3 after overtime. 'Lobby' was a teammate of Flames' goalie **Mike Torchia** on the 2000-01 Steelers' team. "I went high on his glove hand," he grinned. "That's his best move so I never tried that in practice in Sheffield."

Longstaff's was the only shot Vipers needed as the rules called for sudden-death rather than the usual best-of-five. Raitanen saved **Corey Lyon**'s shot for Flames.

Dundee relinquished their hold on the league's trophies (though not on the *Findus* Cup which had been the property of fellow Scots, Fife Flyers) with a lacklustre display against the Blaze. Stars' new Canadian signing, **Ken Priestlay**, said Blaze had better British players than he remembered from his time with Steelers four years ago.

ENGLISH LEAGUES

The English leagues - the Premier and the National - comprise the sport's third tier and are designed for clubs with low budgets whose chief aim is developing local players.

The Premier League was first established in 1997-98 to accommodate the non-Superleague clubs who were unable to afford the increasing cost of competing in the British National League (BNL). The low budget teams now compete in the National League's north and south conferences. There is no automatic promotion to the BNL from the English leagues.

In the Premier League, teams met four times, twice at home and twice away, as did the National League South. The National League North sides played each other twice, once home and once away.

LEADING SCORERS

Premier League	GP	G	A	Pts	Pim
Gary Clarke MIL	41	86	56	142	60
David Kozier IOW	37	70	64	134	44
Nick Poole MIL	41	35	92	127	24
Merv Priest SWI	40	66	59	125	42
Duncan Cook PET	40	59	61	120	90
Kyle Amyotte CHE	38	65	48	113	30
Matt Beveridge INV	38	46	59	105	34
Andrew Power CHE	32	41	64	105	267
Rob Douglas ROM	39	39	56	95	34
Brad Kenny IOW	27	50	41	91	24
National League North					
Greg Allen ALT	18	42	44	86	20
Jason Hewitt ALT	15	35	38	73	84
Billy Price ALT	15	33	29	62	103
Bobby Haig BLA	18	27	29	56	10
John Ross SHE	15	26	30	56	51
National League South					
Ross Mackintosh PET	19	31	17	48	65
Drew Campbell BAS	18	25	23	48	43
Mark Jordan BAS	18	13	23	36	34
Simon Beere BAS	18	21	14	35	12
Tony Dawson PET	19	17	17	34	16

FINAL STANDINGS

Premier League	GP	W	L	D	GF	GA	Pts
P'boro' Phantoms PET	42	34	5	3	283	136	71
MK Lightning MIL	42	30	6	6	269	113	66
Slough Jets SLO	42	24	10	8	213	140	56
Swindon Lynx SWI	42	24	12	6	234	162	54
Ch'ford Chieftains CHE	42	24	12	6	245	170	54
I of Wight Raiders IOW	42	24	14	4	232	152	52
Invicta Dynamos INV	42	20	15	7	192	168	47
Romford Raiders ROM	42	19	17	6	218	199	44
Telford W Foxes TEL	42	9	32	1	147	331	19
Nottingham Lions NOT	42	6	35	1	93	251	13
Haringey Racers HAR	42	4	38	0	99	320	8
England u-20 ENG	22	0	22	0	23	106	0

National Lge North							
Sh'ffield Scimitars SHE	18	16	1	1	162	52	33
Altrincham Aces ALT	18	15	3	0	198	64	30
Whitley Warriors WHI	18	13	5	0	155	73	26
Kingston Jets KIN	18	11	7	0	114	87	22
Blackburn Hawks BLA	18	10	8	0	119	81	20
Bill'ham Bombers BIL	18	10	8	0	101	68	20
Flintshire Freeze FLI	18	6	12	0	81	131	12
Sun'land Chiefs SUN	18	5	13	0	79	143	10
Grimsby Buffaloes GRI	18	3	14	1	71	213	7
Bradford Bulldogs BRD	18	0	18	0	47	215	0

National Lge South							
Bas'stoke Buffalo BAS	20	18	1	1	145	39	37
Bracknell Hornets BRK	20	11	6	3	84	75	25
Invicta Mustangs INV	20	8	8	4	52	55	20
M Keynes Thunder MIL	20	8	10	2	77	76	18
P'boro' Islanders PET	20	3	12	5	87	136	11
Birm'ham Barons BIR	20	4	15	1	71	135	9

Position of teams tied on points decided on the results between them.
England under-20 played one game for double points at each opponent's rink.
National League South - Invicta Mustangs played all games at home for double points.

Above Peterborough Phantom **JESSE HAMMILL** *left* with the English Premier League trophy; Phantoms' top scorer **DUNCAN COOK**; *below* promising teenager **ADAM BRITTLE** *left* of Telford Wild Foxes; **NICK POOLE** who took over in mid-season as coach of Milton Keynes Lightning.

Photos: Dave Page

RESULTS CHART

	CHE	*ENG	HAR	INV	IOW	MIL	NOT	PET	ROM	SLO	SWI	TEL
CHELMSFORD	**	9-3 16/2	7-1 1/12	10-5 22/9	5-2 29/9	2-7 12/1	9-2 5/10	10-6 17/11	8-1 8/9	3-3 27/10	5-8 13/10	17-2 24/11
Chieftains	**	X	11-2 9/2	2-3 19/10	4-3 8/12	5-2 9/3	7-1 28/12	3-5 2/2	5-5 10/11	3-2 26/1	2-7 19/1	15-5 22/2
HARINGEY	3-10 6/10	10-2 13/10	**	2-6 19/1	2-5@ 5/1	4-8 8/9	5-2 15/9	2-9 30/11	2-14 29/12	2-6 22/9	4-9 17/11	5-7@ 9/3
Racers	5-12 8/2	X	**	2-6 2/3	X	2-9 24/11	3-5 12/1	4-10 8/12	2-1 23/2	3-4 3/11	1-7 16/2	X
INVICTA	3-6 15/9	7-1 27/10	7-0 29/9	**	4-2 3/11	2-5 1/9	7-4 10/11	1-5 6/10	4-2 12/10	4-2 8/9	4-1 20/10	14-3 5/1
Dynamos	4-6 29/12	X	11-4 26/1	**	3-4 22/12	4-4 17/11	9-4@ 1/12	3-3@ 9/3	5-5 15/12	4-2# 24/11	5-6 12/1	13-5 16/2
I OF WIGHT	5-5 16/11	10-3 23/11	14-0 2/11	7-6 14/9	**	5-5 10/11	10-4 7/9	2-7 28/9	12-5 21/9	4-5 5/10	5-8 29/12	12-1 18/1
Raiders	7-3 7/12	X	12-0 21/12	8-4 30/11	**	4-2 19/1	10-1 25/1	5-8 13/10	5-6 11/1	6-3 15/12	5-2@ 1/3	10-4 8/2
M KEYNES	9-8 7/9	13-2 25/1	11-1 28/9	8-1 5/10	8-4 19/10	**	6-0 14/9	4-4 21/12	7-3 16/11	5-3 30/11	7-1 23/11	13-2 21/9
Lightning	8-1 12/10	X	11-1 26/10	7-2 11/1	3-2 14/12	**	11-0 9/11	8-2 8/2	7-7 31/8	4-1 2/2	10-3 5/1	10-2 28/12
NOTT'HAM	4-7 5/1	5-2 17/11	5-2@ 15/2	1-4 13/10	1-4@ 24/11	2-6 22/9	**	2-10 3/11	3-8@ 8/12	1-5 20/10	2-14 8/9	4-3 21/12
Lions	3-7 2/3	X	X	X	X	2-7 23/2	**	1-7 19/1	X	1-6 22/12	6-6 6/10	2-4 26/1
PETERBORO'	7-6 20/10	13-1 12/1	12-4 10/11	5-2 25/1	5-3 8/9	6-4 15/9	6-5 23/11	**	11-2 5/10	7-8 29/9	7-6 27/10	12-3 16/11
Phantoms	5-0 15/12	X	10-2 1/2	X	4-2 16/2	3-8 29/12	8-0 1/3	**	6-1 22/12	5-6 5/1	6-2 1/12	17-3 8/3
ROMFORD	1-5 1/9	16-3 9/11	13-2 26/12	3-3 7/9	4-3 6/10	6-4 29/9	9-6 29/9	4-6 7/12	**	8-4 15/9	6-8 22/9	10-5 17/11
Raiders	5-5 3/11	X	16-2 4/1	2-2 28/12	4-8 1/12	2-1 20/10	X	5-7 26/1	**	5-7 13/10	3-4 24/11	5-4 19/1
SLOUGH	3-3 14/9	7-1 7/12	5-3 7/9	6-4 21/9	7-2 26/10	4-3 6/10	5-1 14/12	1-3 18/1	5-4 28/9	**	2-4 19/10	6-0 12/10
Jets	9-3 9/11	X	14-2 25/1	5-5 4/1	4-4 17/11	2-2 2/11	19-1 11/1	0-7 22/2	8-5 23/11	**	4-3 21/12	9-4 8/12
SWINDON	5-5 28/9	11-3 14/12	11-0 5/10	8-1 9/11	5-5 28/12	3-7 7/12	6-3 12/10	3-6 21/9	7-8 14/9	3-3 16/11	**	9-2 7/9
Lynx	4-2 25/1	X	5-2 11/1	6-4 8/2	X	2-2 26/1	7-2 4/1	3-5 26/10	5-2 30/11	4-4 16/2	**	10-6 2/11
TELFORD	4-5 30/11	5-2 6/10	4-3 14/9	4-6 23/11	4-11 22/9	2-5 13/10	6-3 29/9	2-11 14/12	5-6 26/10	3-3 10/11	1-10 1/9	**
Wild Foxes	1-4 22/12	X	9-5 7/12	8-10 15/2	3-10 12/1	1-8 3/11	6-4 29/12	5-7 9/2	3-6 22/2	1-11 2/3	5-8 15/12	**
	CHE	*ENG	HAR	INV	IOW	MIL	NOT	PET	ROM	SLO	SWI	TEL

*Second figure is date of game. * All games played at opponents' rinks for double points.*
X One game played for four points.   @ played for double points.
 # game abandoned at 59.49 when Slough Jets refused to continue playing. Result allowed to stand.

LEADING NETMINDERS

Premier League	GPI	Mins	SoG	GA	Sv%
Allen Sutton MIL	14	840	314	29	90.76
Barry Hollyhead MIL	27	1619	891	83	90.68
David Whitwell PET	33	1794	895	95	89.39
Andy Moffat IOW	32	1869	1203	132	89.03
Chris Douglas CHE	40	2164	1349	151	88.81
National Lge North					
Mike Snook BIL	15	812	469	46	90.19
Anthony Markham WHI	11	640	366	39	89.34
National Lge South					
Craig Astill BAS	14	738	347	26	92.51
Dan Green BRK	13	676	410	36	91.22

Qualification: one-third of team's games (minutes played).

FAIR PLAY

Premier League	GP	Pims	Ave
Invicta Dynamos	39	543	13.9
Nottingham Lions	37	615	16.6
Milton Keynes Lightning	41	686	16.7
England under-20	11	195	17.7
Swindon Lynx	40	835	20.9
Isle of Wight Raiders	38	805	21.2
Peterborough Phantoms	40	933	23.3
Telford Wild Foxes	40	988	24.7
Romford Raiders	39	967	24.8
Chelmsford Chieftains	41	1048	25.6
Haringey Racers	38	1017	26.8
Slough Jets	41	1247	30.4

PAST (PREMIER) LEAGUE WINNERS

2001-02	Invicta Dynamos
2000-01	Swindon Phoenix
1999-00	Chelmsford Chieftains
1998-99	Solihull Blaze
1997-98	Solihull Blaze
1996-97	*Wightlink* Raiders
1995-96	*Wightlink* Raiders
1994-95	*Wightlink* Raiders
1993-94	*Wightlink* Raiders
1992-93	Solihull Barons
1991-92	Medway Bears
1990-91	Oxford City Stars
1989-90	Bracknell Bees
1988-89	Humberside Seahawks
1987-88	Romford Raiders

Phantoms spook league

Peterborough Phantoms won the Premier League in the first season after their untimely 'relegation' from the British National League.

Despite changing coaches in mid-season when former Isle of Wight coach **Luc Chabot** was replaced by **Kevin King** of the GB under-20s, Phantoms beat **Milton Keynes Lightning**, their old BNL rivals, by five points.

They were fortunate in retaining veteran **Doug McEwen**, the hard working former GB and Cardiff forward, who was voted the team's player of the year, while also snapping up Solihull's Canadian **Duncan Cook**, the league's leading scorer in 2001-02.

Lightning's Brit **Gary Clarke**, one of the brightest home-grown talents who has yet to appear for his national team, had the most goals (86) and points (142) in the EPL.

Apart from Clarke and goalie **Allen Sutton** who topped the netminding stats, Lightning's most influential player was their Canadian captain, **Dwayne Newman**, who carried off four of the club's awards. Coach **Nick Poole** assembled a team that worked well together and hardly changed from start to finish.

Warren Rost signed 17 players, the largest squad in **Slough Jets'** history, which proved to be a big factor in their third place finish. Jets, too, were in the BNL last year.

There was little to choose between the middle six teams who were divided by only 12 points.

Carl Greenhous, the new coach of the defending champs, **Invicta Dynamos**, was unable to find the magic formula again. This may have been down to budget restrictions as Dynamos still had difficulty in attracting crowds to the Gillingham rink.

Merv Priest and his **Swindon Lynx** fought through the club's widely publicised financial problems and, against the odds, moved up one place from 2001-02 against stiffer competition.

The wisdom of expanding the EPL by four teams was called into question when the new boys won only 19 games between them. This quartet were pure amateurs who couldn't afford imports like the league's other teams.

The best showing came from **Dave Fielder's** **Telford Wild Foxes** whose many promising young home-grown players included **Adam Brittle**, the top scorer on the GB under-18s.

Nottingham Lions, in their last season, were an exception to this rule as their coach, **Matt Bradbury**, was firmly opposed to using overseas players, anyway.

■ **Basingstoke Buffalo** retained their National League South title, and **Sheffield Scimitars** knocked **Whitley Warriors** off their Northern perch after four seasons at the top.

PREMIER LEAGUE PLAYOFFS

At the end of the league games, the top eight teams in the Premier League qualified for the Playoffs.

The league winner was placed in group A along with the fourth, fifth and eighth placed teams, with the remaining sides going into group B. Each team played the other in their group and the winning team in each group met in a home and away final.

PRELIMINARY ROUND STANDINGS

Group A	GP	W	L	D	GF	GA	Pts
P'boro' Phantoms	6	5	0	1	43	21	11
Chelmsford Chieftains	6	4	2	0	36	37	8
Swindon Lynx	6	1	3	2	26	28	4
Romford Raiders	6	0	5	1	20	39	1
Group B							
M Keynes Lightning	6	4	2	0	32	15	8
Slough Jets	6	3	2	1	22	18	7
Isle of Wight Raiders	6	3	3	0	26	30	6
Invicta Dynamos	6	1	4	1	23	40	3

PRELIMINARY ROUND RESULTS

Group A	CHE	PET	ROM	SWI
Chelmsford Chieftains	-	5-6	9-2	8-7
Peterboro' Phantoms	15-2	-	10-6	4-4
Romford Raiders	4-7	2-3	-	5-5
Swindon Lynx	3-5	2-5	5-1	-
Group B	INV	IOW	MIL	SLO
Invicta Dynamos	-	6-4	1-7	5-5
Isle of Wight Raiders	13-9	-	5-4	1-3
Milton Keynes Lightning	6-2	6-0	-	6-2
Slough Jets	5-0	2-3	5-3	-

FINALS

First leg, 12 April 2003, Planet Ice Milton Keynes

MILTON KEYNES LIGHTNING	10	(2-5-3)
PETERBOROUGH PHANTOMS	0	(0-0-0)

First Period
1-0 MIL Skinnari (Howard, Dumas)   10.31
2-0 MIL Randall (Dumas)   11.09
Penalty minutes: Lightning 8, Phantoms 6.
Second Period
3-0 MIL Skinnari (Newman)   pp   22.31
4-0 MIL Dumas (Campbell, Knights)   29.14
5-0 MIL Clarke (Poole, Jamieson)   32.19
6-0 MIL Clarke (Poole, Newman) sh   34.45

7-0 MIL Dumas (Clarke, Knights)   35.27
Penalty minutes: Lightning 4, Phantoms 6.
Third Period
8-0 MIL Clarke (Poole)   41.03
9-0 MIL Campbell (Dumas, Randall)   43.59
10-0 MIL Knights (Poole, Campbell)   56.38
Penalty minutes: Lightning 10, Phantoms 10.
Shots on Goal
Hollyhead MIL 22-11-13 46 *save percent* 100.0
Whitwell PET 11-11-13 35 *save percent* 71.4
Referee: Matt Thompson.   *Attendance*: 1,692
Linesmen: James Ashton, Dave Goodwin.

Second leg, 13 April 2003, Planet Ice P'boro'

PETERBOROUGH PHANTOMS	4	(0-3-1)
MILTON KEYNES LIGHTNING	6	(2-3-1)

First Period
0-1 MIL Randall (Skinnari)   pp   11.00
0-2 MIL Dumas (Campbell, Randall)   15.52
Penalty minutes: Phantoms 27 (Kohvakka 5+game - rough), Lightning 20 (Jamieson 2+2+10 misc.- rough).
Second Period
0-3 MIL Poole (Clarke, Howard)   21.40
1-3 PET Buckman (Cook)   22.59
1-4 MIL Clarke   30.03
2-4 PET J Cotton (McEwen, D Cotton)   34.59
3-4 PET Buckman (Coleman, Yardley)   36.00
3-5 MIL Campbell (Randall, Dumas)   37.38
Penalty minutes: Phantoms 4, Lightning 4.
Third Period
4-5 PET Armstrong (Cook)   46.11
4-6 MIL Dumas   59.11
Penalty minutes: Phantoms 2, Lightning 0.
Shots on Goal
Whitwell/Moore PET 5-11- 7 23 *save%* 73.9
Hollyhead MIL   19-15-13 47 *save%* 91.5
Referee: Matt Thompson.   *Attendance*: 1,500
Linesmen: Dave Emmerson, Gordon Wilson.

MILTON KEYNES LIGHTNING
are champions *16-4 on aggregate*

THE WINNING TEAM
MILTON KEYNES LIGHTNING
Barry Hollyhead, Allen Sutton; Chris McEwen, Michael Knights, Leigh Jamieson, Phil Wooderson, Mark Krater, Gary Clarke, Mark Conway, Dean Campbell, Geoff O'Hara, Claude Dumas, Dwayne Newman (capt), Mikko Skinnari, Mark Hazelhurst, Greg Randall, Simon Howard, Nick Poole.
Coach: Nick Poole.   *Manager*: Vito Rausa.

LEADING PLAYOFF SCORERS

	GP	G	A	Pts	Pim
Kyle Amyotte CHE	6	11	11	22	4
Gary Clarke MIL	8	14	5	19	10
Andrew Power CHE	6	9	8	17	26
Claude Dumas MIL	8	7	10	17	6
Duncan Cook PET	8	6	11	17	14
Nick Poole MIL	8	4	12	16	6

LEADING PLAYOFF NETMINDERS

	GPI	Mins	SoG	GA	Sv%
Barry Hollyhead MIL	7	420	232	14	93.9
Simon Smith SLO	6	359	199	18	90.9
Andy Moffat IOW	5	300	211	21	90.O

PAST PLAYOFF WINNERS

2001-02	Invicta Dynamos
2000-01	Romford Raiders
1999-00	Chelmsford Chieftains
1998-99	Solihull Blaze
1997-98	Solihull Blaze
1996-97	*Wightlink* Raiders
1995-96	*Wightlink* Raiders
1994-95	*Wightlink* Raiders
1993-94	*Wightlink* Raiders
1992-93	Trafford Metros (A),
	Chelmsford Chieftains (B)
1991-92	Medway Bears (A),
	Sheffield Steelers (B)
1990-91	Milton Keynes Kings (A),
	Lee Valley Lions (B)
1989-90	Basingstoke Beavers
1988-89	Humberside Seahawks

Lightning strike

Milton Keynes Lightning avenged their league defeat by Peterborough Phantoms with a thumping 16-4 aggregate Playoff victory over the league champs.

In one of the most lop-sided and surprising results of the season, Lightning racked up ten goals in the first leg with goalie **Barry Hollyhead** almost standing on his head (sorry) with a 46-shot shutout in front of his home crowd.

Despite their team's dreadful result, there was a sellout crowd in Peterborough the following night when Phantoms went a further three goals down before recovering for a more respectable 6-4 defeat. Hollyhead again saved over 40 shots.

PREMIER CUP

The top eight Premier League teams, except Chelmsford Chieftains, were joined by three sides from the National League North.

In the preliminary round, the ten teams competed in two geographically divided groups, each team playing the other in its own group once at home and once away.

The top team in each group met in the final - also home and away - to decide the cup's destination.

FIRST ROUND STANDINGS

Group A	GP	W	L	D	GF	GA	Pts
Peterborough Phantoms	6	6	0	0	62	15	12
Blackburn Hawks	6	2	3	1	23	49	5
Whitley Warriors	6	2	4	0	38	37	4
Kingston Jets	6	1	4	1	26	48	3
Group B							
Milton Keynes Lightning	10	7	1	2	56	26	16
Isle of Wight Raiders	10	7	2	1	56	30	15
Slough Jets	10	6	4	0	48	30	12
Swindon Lynx	10	3	6	1	26	55	7
Invicta Dynamos	10	1	6	3	25	44	5
Romford Raiders	10	2	7	1	35	62	5

FINAL

First leg, *5 April*
Milton Keynes-Peterborough   **4-2**
Second leg, *6 April*
Peterborough-Milton Keynes   **5-2**
PETERBOROUGH PHANTOMS
win Premier Cup *7-6 on aggregate*

Claude Dumas with four goals and eight points and **Gary Clarke** (four goals, six points) were the top scorers in the finals.

Lightning's victory was all the more surprising as a week earlier, Phantoms had beaten them in the final of the Premier Cup, though only by a one-goal margin this time. The win gave **Kevin King's** squad the league and cup double for the first time since Chelmsford Chieftains captured all three English Premier League trophies in 1999-2000.

The experiment of including National League sides in the first round was repeated but though this gave the fans a greater variety of opposition, Phantoms were too strong for them.

NATIONAL LEAGUE PLAYOFFS

The top four teams in each group of the National League qualified for the Playoffs, in which they met the other teams in their group once at home and once away. The winning team in each group played again, home and away, to decide the Championship.

FIRST ROUND STANDINGS

North	GP	W	L	D	GF	GA	Pts
Altrincham Aces ALT	6	4	1	1	35	23	9
Sh'ffield Scimitars SHE	6	4	2	0	49	27	8
Kingston Jets KIN	6	3	2	1	27	25	7
Whitley Warriors WHI	6	0	6	0	17	53	0
South							
B'stoke Buffalo BAS	6	6	0	0	57	18	12
M Keynes Thunder MIL	6	3	3	0	30	28	6
Bracknell Hornets BRK	6	1	4	1	22	36	3
Invicta Mustangs INV	6	1	4	1	21	48	3

FINALS

First leg, 3 May at Blackburn Arena
ALTRINCHAM-BASINGSTOKE　　　　**5-4**
　　　　　　　　　　　　(1-2,2-0,2-2)
Scorers: **Aces** Hewitt 3g; Price 1+1; Crawley 1g; Allen 3a; Dempsey 2a. **Buffalo** Campbell 1+2; Page 1+1; Beere, Jordan 1g; Elliott, Morgan 1a.
Shots on Goal: Higgin ALT 36, Astill BAS 42.
Penalty minutes: Aces 30 (Richardson 2+10misc. - ch/behind), Buffalo 12.
Referee: Dave Metcalfe.　　　*Attendance*: 324.

Second leg, 4 May at Planet Ice Basingstoke
BASINGSTOKE-ALTRINCHAM　　　　**6-4ot**
　　　　　　　　　　(1-1,2-3,2-0,1-0)
Scorers: **Buffalo** Campbell 2+1; Jordan, Phillimore 1+1; Etheridge, Morgan 1g; Wyatt, Page, Beere, Newberry 1a. **Aces** Allen, Worrall, Hewitt, Richardson 1g; Mills 2a.
Shots on Goal:
Astill BAS 33, Higgin/Verstappen ALT 25.
Penalty minutes: Buffalo 20, Aces 41 (Cassidy 5 x-check+game che/behind).
Referee: Ian Hayden.　　　*Attendance*: 655.

LEADING NETMINDERS

	GPI	Mins	SoG	GA	Sv%
Craig Astill BAS	6	340	189	18	90.5
Karl Holmes KIN	6	354	200	22	89.0
Chris McKay WHI	4	118	129	16	87.6

LEADING SCORERS

	GP	G	A	Pts	Pim
Drew Campbell BAS	8	17	12	29	10
Anthony Page BAS	8	11	12	23	0
John Ross SHE	6	10	10	20	0
Billy Price ALT	8	8	12	20	8
Jason Hewitt ALT	8	10	9	19	8
Greg Allen ALT	8	11	7	18	24
Simon Beere BAS	8	8	8	16	2

THE FINALISTS
ALTRINCHAM ACES
Danny Higgin, Phil Verstappen; Tim Dempsey, Greg Allen, Russ Richardson, Steve Michie, Brian Worrall, Nick Crawley, Jason Hewitt, Simon Mills (capt), Arran Richardson, Stephen Elliott, Billy Price, Kevin Cassidy.
Manager-coach: Paul Bayliss.

BASINGSTOKE BUFFALO
Craig Astill, Vicky Robbins; Andrew Robinson, Oliver Beckwith, James Broadhurst, Dean Phillimore, Nigel Sheppard, Darren Elliott, Anthony Page (capt), Matt Wynn, Mike Leary, Andy Morgan, Simon Beere, Andrew Jordan, Drew Campbell, Rob Etheridge, Mark Jordan, Ryan Cathcart, Steve Kochli, Adam Franks, Leigh Baker, Greg Wyatt, Andy Robinson, Michael Newberry.
Coach: Ed Campbell. *Manager*: Andy Worship.

Aces trumped by Buffalo

After four straight years of domination by the Whitley Warriors, southern club Basingstoke Buffalo snatched the 2003 National League Playoff Championship by one goal from Altrincham Aces.

Both legs of the final were tightly fought with Aces determined to win a trophy in their last ever games and favourites Buffalo keen to complete the league and playoff double.

Even though the Altrincham rink closed after Aces had played their first round games, forcing them to stage their home leg in nearby Blackburn, they took a one-goal lead down south, inspired by a hat-trick from **Jason Hewitt**.

Aces had one hand on the trophy when **Brian Worrall** extended their aggregate lead with an eighth-minute goal at Planet Ice. **Mark Jordan** and **Drew Campbell**, the competition's leading scorer, equalised early in the middle session and with each side adding three more, the game was still deadlocked after 60 minutes.

Andy Morgan gave Buffalo their first championship 5.26 into OT, cruelly ending Aces' dreams.

SCOTTISH COMPETITIONS

CALEDONIAN CUP

The competition was originally designed to bring together all the sport's senior teams in Scotland, but when Superleague's Scottish Eagles folded after playing only two games, they were replaced by the BNL's Newcastle Vipers.

Each team played the others home and away with rosters being restricted to 50 per cent home-grown players in accordance with the guidelines of the British National League.

All four teams qualified for the semi-finals which were one-game affairs while the final was played over two legs, home and away.

FIRST ROUND STANDINGS

	GP	W	L	D	GF	GA	Pts
Dundee Stars	6	4	1	1	36	17	9
Newcastle Vipers	6	4	2	0	34	25	8
Fife Flyers	6	3	2	1	34	34	7
Edinburgh Capitals	6	0	6	0	13	41	0

SEMI-FINALS

18 February 2003 at Dundee Ice Rink
DUNDEE-EDINBURGH   **10-2** (3-1,3-0,4-1)
Goal scorers: **Stars** Wynne 3, Hand, Sample, Dunbar, Mikel, Hopkins, Wiita, Young; **Capitals** Krajicek 2.

19 February 2003 at Telewest Arena, Newcastle
NEWCASTLE-FIFE   **3-4** (1-2,2-2,0-0)
Goal scorers: **Vipers** Ferone 2, Irwin; **Flyers** Weaver, Dutiaume, S King, Morrison.

FINALS

First leg, 25 February 2003 at Fife Ice Arena
FIFE-DUNDEE   **5-3** (3-0,2-2,0-1)
Goal scorers: **Flyers** Biette 2, Haig, Morrison, Finlay; **Stars** Hand, Boman, Wiita.

Second leg, 26 Feb 2003 at Dundee Ice Rink
DUNDEE-FIFE   **4-4** (2-2,1-1,1-1)
Goal scorers: **Stars** Mikel 2, Priestlay, Lochi; **Flyers** Dutiaume 2, Biette, Walker.

FIFE FLYERS win Caledonian Cup
9-7 on aggregate

Flyers blot out Stars

Backstopped by the superb **Steve Briere**, Fife Flyers wrested the second Caledonian Cup from the holders, Dundee Stars, *writes* **Ronnie Nichol**.

Flyers, who were finalists last year, dominated for most of the first leg at home, leading 4-0 and 5-1 until a late Stars' comeback. But any hopes **Tony Hand**'s team might have had of retaining the cup at home were dashed by early strikes from **Todd Dutiaume** and teenage Brit **Adam Walker**, and Stars could never get on terms.

Dundee fired 43 shots on Briere in each game but he held them to seven goals, and Hand failed to register even a point.

EAGLES' LAST GAME

Scottish Eagles played their last game on 5 November 2002, a 3-3 draw with Edinburgh Capitals. The only point that **Scott Neil**'s side gained in the cup, it was erased after Eagles were forced to pull out.

Eagles, who iced a scratch team, scored through **Jason Bowen**, **Jeff Johnstone** and **Bob Quinnell**. The coach was **Peter Russell** who was imported from the Paisley juniors. Eagles' regular coach, **Paul Heavey**, refused to continue as he and his players had not been paid after their Continental Cup games in Rouen.

SCOTTISH NATIONAL LEAGUE

Edinburgh Capitals, icing an all-Scottish squad, retained their Scottish National League title, winning 15 of their 16 games in the nine-team circuit.

Coach **Jock Hay** told the *Edinburgh Evening News:* "Everybody wants to beat the champions but my lads went about their task in a professional manner." Perhaps too professional for some of the smaller Scottish outfits. Capitals walloped last placed Inverness 21-1 in their penultimate game.

Final placings: **1 Edinburgh Capitals**, 2 Camperdown (Dundee) Stars, 3 Kirkcaldy Kestrels, 4 Paisley Pirates, 5 Kilmarnock Avalanche, 6 Solway (Dumfries) Sharks, 7 Dundee Tigers, 8 Moray (Elgin) Tornados, 9 Moray Firth (Inverness) Senators.

YOUTH INTERNATIONALS

Players born 1 January 1984 or later
Nottingham Arena, 6 April 2003

ENGLAND UNDER-19	8	(1-5-2)
SCOTLAND UNDER-19	4	(0-3-1)

Scorers: **England** - Wallace 2g; Carr 1+2; M Richardson, Towalski !+1; Hutchinson, Miles, Radmall 1g; Meyers 4a; Thomas, Duncombe 1a. **Scotland** - Walker 3g; Murray 1g; McCaig, Hannah 1a.
Shots on Goal Levers/Shea ENG 33, Arthur/Johnstone SCO 39.
Penalty minutes: England 39 (Day 5+game - slashing), Scotland 12. *Referee*: Tom Darnell.

Sassenachs again

Newcastle's rookie of the year **Stephen Wallace**, who was the top scorer for the GB under-20s in the World Championships, chipped in two goals for England to help them retain the under-19 title against the auld enemy.

Fife's **Adam Walker** scored a hat-trick for the Scots in front of an estimated 3,000 fans who saw the game before the Superleague final.

THE TEAMS
ENGLAND UNDER-19
Dan Shea, Alan Levers COV; Dave Thomas BIL, Rhodri Evans CAR, Adam Radmall COV, James Day HUL, James Hutchinson IOW, Steve Duncombe SHE, Dale Howey WHI; Joe Greener BAS, Matt Myers CAR capt, Keith Leyland HUL, Adam Carr IOW, Stephen Wallace NEW, Chris Colegate NOT, Terry Miles, Matt Towalski (both SLO), John Dewar, Mark Richardson (both SWI), Adam Brittle TEL, Dan (DJ) Good WHI.
Coach: Mick Mishener.
Manager: Barry Knock.

SCOTLAND UNDER-19
Craig Johnstone DUN, Craig Arthur FIF; Alan Crane DUM, Andrew Hannah DUN, Paddy Ward EDI capt, Euan Forsyth, Chad Reekie (both FIF); Scott Welsh DUM, David Robb, Marc McAndrew, Scott McAndrew, Scott McKenzie, Adam Walker (all FIF), Neil Hay, Dan McIntyre (both MUR), Stuart McCaig PAI, George Murray (Znojmo, CZE).
Coach: Kevin King PET.
Manager: Graham Grubb FIF.

Players born 1 January 1986 or later
Hull Ice Arena, 4 May 2003

ENGLAND UNDER-17	2	(1-0-1)
SCOTLAND UNDER-17	1	(0-0-1)

Scorers: **England** - Dewar 1+1; Richardson 1g; Greener 1a. **Scotland** - Walker 1g; Mitchell 1a.
Shots on Goal: Craze ENG 14, Findley SCO 45.
Penalty minutes: England 37 (Parsons 5+game - tripping), Scotland 12.
Referee: Andrew Dalton.

Mark's late winner

A 43-save performance from Scots goalie **Darryl Findley** kept his side in the game which wasn't decided until 56.57 when GB under-18 international **Mark Richardson** put the winner past him on a powerplay. This was the second successive one-goal win for the English.

THE TEAMS
ENGLAND UNDER-17
Nathan Craze CAR, Dan Brittle TEL; Joe Greener, Nicky Watt (both BAS), Steven Pritchard BIL, Luke Boothroyd BRD, James Parsons CAR, Rob Chamberlain, Lewis Day, Kevin Phillips (all HUL), Stuart Bliss, James Cooke (both NOT), Simon Butterworth, Greg Wood (both SHE), Shaun Thompson SLO, John Dewar, Shane Moore, Mark Richardson, capt (all SWI) , Rob Wilson WHI.
Coaches: Martin Etheridge NOT, Terry Flett BIL. *Managers*: Sue Aldridge SWI, Jeremy Griffiths BIL.

SCOTLAND UNDER-17
Stuart Grubb FIF, Darryl Findley KIL; Alan Crane DUM, Tommy Muir, Chad Reekie capt, Ross McDonald (all FIF), Chris Blackburn MUR, Jamie Carruth (North Ayr), Ryan McNeill PAI; Chris Linton, Scott McAndrew, Scott McKenzie, Lee Mitchell, Adam Walker (all FIF), Ian Crockett, Allan Mailand (both KIL), Ian Beattie MUR, Alan Campbell PAI, George Murray (Znojmo, CZE).
Coaches: Martin Grubb FIF, Peter Russell PAI.
Manager: Graham Grubb FIF.

Players born 1 January 1987 or later

RIVERSIDE MIDGET TOURNAMENT

Windsor, Ontario, 27-30 December 2002

ENGLAND UNDER-16 RESULTS

27 Dec **England-Windsor** **4-1** (0-0,2-0,2-1)
England scoring: Thompson 2g;
Greener, Moore 1g; Day, Carlon, Potter,
Wood.

28 Dec **England-Tecumseh** **4-1** (0-0,1-0,3-1)
England scoring: Day, Thompson,
Carlon 1g; Wood 1+1; Greener, Dewar,
Phillips 1a.

29 Dec *Semi-Final*
England-South Point 2-1 (1-0,1-0,0-1)
England scoring: Day, O'Connor 1g;
Greener 1a.

30 Dec *Final*
England-Riverside **4-3** (2-0,2-1,2-1)
England scoring: Ferrara, Greener,
Carlon, Phillips 1g; Peacock, Day, Moore
1a.

Our kids are the best

If proof were needed that this country possesses some of the world's best young players, the results on this page and the next will provide it.

While some senior clubs complained about 'the lack of junior development', British teams at under-16, under-14 and under-13 levels were going abroad and winning major tournaments.

First with a gold medal were **Warren Rost's** under-16s who swept the board in Canada's prestigious Riverside Tournament in Windsor, Ontario against stiff competition from four North American sides. What's more coach Rost from

ENGLAND UNDER-16

Ben Clements CHE, Joe Dollin GUI; Steven Pritchard BIL, Luke Boothroyd BRD, David Phillips HUL, Ben Morgan, Ben O'Connor SHE, Shane Moore SWI, Stuart Bates TEL; David Meikle ALT, Joe Greener BAS capt, Liam Telfer BIL, Lewis Day HUL, Curtis Potter INV, James Ferrara PET, Craig Peacock PET, Shaun Thompson SLO, Greg Wood SHE, John Dewar SWI, Tom Carlon TEL. *Head coach*: Warren Rost SLO. *Manager*: Bob Wilkinson.

CHRIS VERWIJST TOURNAMENT

Tilburg, Netherlands, 21-23 March 2003

ENGLAND UNDER-16 RESULTS

21 Mar **England-Netherlands** **6-1** (1-0,3-0,2-1)
England scoring: Day 2g; Wood 1+1;
Thompson, Pritchard, Dewar 1g;
Greener, Potter 2a.
England-Slovenia **2-1** (0-0,2-0,0-1)
England scoring: Dewar, Greener 1g;
Day 1+1; Moore 1a.

22 Mar **England-Switzerland** **4-3** (1-1,2-2,1-0)
England scoring: Carlon 3g; Dewar 1g;
Moore, Potter, Day 1a.

23 Mar *Semi-Final*
England-Austria **2-0** (1-0,1-0,0-0)
England scoring: Carlon, Day 1g; Wood,
Greener 1a.
Final
England-France **2-4** (0-2,1-1,1-1)
England scoring: Thompson, Carlon 1g;
Meikle, O'Connor 1a.

Slough Jets and one of his Slough protégés, 15-year-old forward **Shaun Thompson**, were honoured with the top awards in the competition in which 24 teams from Europe and North America took part.

The old established tournament, which was first played in 1961, is followed closely by NHL scouts and **Joel Quenneville**, head coach of St Louis Blues, was among the talent spotters.

Quenneville was one of over 2,000 spectators in the Riverside Arena - which sits on the one bank of the Detroit River across from the Motor City - as England upset the home team (then the Ontario League leaders) 4-3 in the final. **Tom Carlon** of Telford Wild Foxes scored the winner at 35.12 and Hull junior **David Phillips** iced the game seven minutes later.

The result almost overshadowed England's silver medal in the Dutch junior tournament, the Chris Verwijst, though they had no reason to be disappointed as this long running event featured some of Europe's leading nations.

In the final, England were down 2-0 to France after only two-and-a-half minutes until Thompson pulled one back near the end of the second. But two more French markers made Carlon's backhand shot in the third rather a formality.

■ **Ashley Tait** was the last English player to be voted MVP of the Riverside Tournament in 1990.

Brett Perlini 13, of Guildford, winner of *The Ice Hockey Annual* award as MVP of the Junior Inter-Conference Championship in Hull.

Players born 1 January 1989 or later

FÜSSEN UNDER-15 TOURNAMENT
Füssen Ice Arena, Germany, March 2003

ENGLAND UNDER-14 RESULTS

Salzburg Red Bulls (Austria)-**England**	**0-2**

England's goal scorers: Tonks, Falsetta. *Shutout:* Clarkson.

KEV Hanover (Germany)-**England**	**0-6**

England's goal scorers: Parton 2; Wood, Tonks, Thompson, Murdy. *Shutout:* Jaszczyk.

England- German Women's under-20	**2-1**

England's goal scorers: Falsetta, Wood.

England-Lukko Rauma (Finland)	**1-3**

England's goal scorer: Tonks.
Semi-Final

WSV Sterzing (Italy)-**England**	**3-0**

3rd/4th place playoff

PK83 Parkano-England	**2-3**

England's goal scorers: Parton, Wood, Falsetta.

CHALLENGE GAMES

England-HC Latemar (Italy)	**10-1**
PK83 Parkano (Finland)-**England**	**4-3**

Britain's youngsters, some of them only 13, won a bronze medal in these games held in the Bavarian home of the German national team.

Danny Wood of Sheffield was England's top scorer with seven goals and 12 points.

ENGLAND UNDER-14
Andrew Jaszczyk SHE, Martin Clarkson CAR; Danny Hammond CHE, Steven Lee HUL, Joe Graham NOT, Lloyd Gibson, Mike Holland, Danny McAleese SHE; Jason Falsetta GUI, Dean Tonks, Danny Wood SHE, Adam Holton, Carl Thompson SLO, Kevin Parton TEL, Dan Murdy SUN, Mark Nicholson, Nathan Taylor WHI.
Coach: David Graham.
Manager: Kevin Thompson.

Players born 1 January 1990 or later

The England under-13s made their 11th trip to Quebec, Canada to take part in the unofficial world pee-wee championship and, for the first time, came back as the winners in their class.

INTERNATIONAL PEE-WEE TOURNAMENT
Colisée Pepsi, Quebec, February 2003

14 Feb	**England-Hudson Bay Inuits**	**15-0**
17 Feb	**England-Mission Honeybake**	**7-1**
18 Feb	**England-Chaudiere Ouest**	**5-2**
21 Feb	*Quarter-Final*	
	England-Bellechasse	**7-0**
22 Feb	*Semi-final*	
	England-St Georges de Bouce	**8-1**
23 Feb	**England-Centre Maurice**	**2-1ot**

ENGLAND UNDER-13
Jonathan Tindall SHE, Mark Thurman SUN; Richard Bentham BLA, Danny House BRK, Tom Duggan, James Francis GUI, Stephen Lee HUL capt, Joe Graham NOT, Ryan Handisides SHE; Danny Moore BLA, Joe Wiggell CAR, Brett Perlini GUI, Matthew Davies HUL, Robert Farmer, Robert Lachowitz, James Neil NOT, Tom Squires SHE, Jamie Milton SLO, Aaron Nell SWI.
Coach: Marty Parfitt. *Manager:* John Ramsden.

Pee-wees' overtime victory

England were the first European team to win this top-rated Canadian pee-wee tournament and moreover they did it by winning all five of their games, also believed to be a first for the team.

NHL stars, **Wayne Gretzky** and **Mario Lemieux**, are on the roll of former players in this 26-team event in which the final day's games were shown on Canadian TV and watched by almost 8,000 fans in Quebec's Colisée *Pepsi.*

And the fans had their money's worth as the final between England and a French-Canadian select side went into two overtime periods before Sheffield's **Tom Squires** scored the winner at 1.56 of the second extra session. **Fred Perlini's** son, **Brett Perlini** of Guildford, had forced the game into sudden-death by scoring with just 1.6 seconds left in regulation time.

■ **Marty Parfitt's** side were originally selected from a School of Excellence held in Hull in the summer of 2002. A squad of 25 was given eight hours training before a second cut was made reducing the roster to 19 players. These lads underwent more training and played five games in England (4-0-1) before leaving for Canada where they played four local teams in friendlies, beating three of them.

WOMEN'S ICE HOCKEY

PREMIER LEAGUE STANDINGS

	GP	W	L	D	GF	GA	Pts
Cardiff Comets CAR	16	13	2	1	68	22	27
Sund'land Scorpions SUN	16	12	2	2	85	36	26
Guildford Lightning GUI	16	9	4	3	48	28	21
Sheffield Shadows SHE	16	8	8	0	61	46	16
Slough Jets SLO	16	7	7	2	58	46	16
Brack'll Queen Bees BRK	16	7	8	1	55	50	15
Kingston Diamonds KIN	16	6	8	2	33	44	14
Swindon Top Cats SWI	16	3	13	0	39	71	6
B'stoke Lady Bison BAS	16	1	14	1	18	122	3

LEADING SCORERS

	GP	G	A	Pts	Pim
Louise Wheeler SLO	16	28	13	41	40
Nicola Bicknell SLO	16	16	22	38	6
Teresa Lewis SUN	15	21	13	34	12
Sarah Warren CAR	12	21	11	32	22
Lynsey Emmerson SUN	15	18	13	31	6
Emily Turner SHE	16	19	10	29	4
Fiona King GUI	16	17	8	25	2
Claire Oldfield SUN	14	11	14	25	4

LEADING NETMINDERS

	GPI	Mins	SoG	GA	Sv%
Emma Hayman CAR	16	915	353	22	93.8
Verity Boome SLO	15	701	467	36	92.3
Laura Saunders GUI	16	810	329	28	91.5

CHAMPIONSHIP PLAYOFFS

Premier League
Final	**CARDIFF**-Sunderland	**4-4ot**
	Comets won after penalty shootout	
3rd place	Sheffield-Guildford	0-3
Semi-finals	Cardiff-Sheffield	5-4
	Sunderland-Guildford	3-2ot
	Scorpions won after penalty shootout	

Division One
Final	Flintshire-**SOLIHULL**	**0-1**
3rd place	Milton Keynes-Blackburn	3-0
Semi-finals	Flintshire-Milton Keynes	7-4
	Solihull-Blackburn	12-0

Double for Comets

Cardiff Comets pulled off the Premier League and championship double in only their third season at the top level. Both triumphs were achieved by the narrowest of margins. They beat Sunderland Scorpions, twice league winners, by only point in the league, and it took **Sarah Warren**'s winning penalty shot before they knocked out Scorpions in the championship final.

In Division One, Solihull Vixens won the South section and Flintshire Furies the North. Furies were voted into the Premier League for the coming season.

Comets had only one player (defender **Ami Merrick**) on the national team for Britain's fourth World Championships entry since 1999. Disappointingly, Britain gained only one point - over runners-up Denmark - and were relegated. Paisley's **Angela Taylor** was GB's top goal (4) and points (5) scorer

WORLD WOMEN'S CHAMPIONSHIP
Div II, Lecco, Italy, 31 March-6 April 2003

	GP	W	L	D	GF	GA	Pts
Norway	5	4	0	1	24	9	9
Denmark	5	3	1	1	16	13	7
Slovakia	5	2	1	2	23	7	6
Italy	5	2	3	0	13	21	4
Netherlands	5	1	3	1	8	18	3
Britain	5	0	4	1	12	28	1

BRITAIN'S RESULTS
31 Mar	Britain-Slovakia	1-8 (0-5,0-3,1-0)
1 Apr	Norway-Britain	8-3 (1-0,5-1,2-2)
3 Apr	Britain-Denmark	4-4 (1-0,1-2,2-2)
4 Apr	Netherlands-Britain	4-2 (2-0,1-2,1-0)
6 Apr	Italy-Britain	4-2 (0-0,4-0,0-2)

BRITAIN
Vicky Robbins BAS, Verity Boome SLO; Vicky Burton BRK, Ami Merrick CAR, Alex von Hasselberg GUI, Kirstin Beattie MUR, Gillian Wyatt SHE, Nicola Bicknell SLO; Heather Brunning BRK, Fiona King, Hannah Young GUI, Eleanor Maitland KIL, Angela Taylor, Gemma Watt PAI, Zoe Bayne, Laura Burke, Emily Turner SHE, Lynsey Emmerson, Teresa Lewis, Clare Oldfield SUN. *Manager:* Ian Turner. *Head coach:* Tony Hall.

FIRST GAME

The only building to open its doors to ice hockey for the first time during 2002-03 was *Glasgow's Braehead Arena*.

Holding 4,000 spectators, the arena itself first opened in September 1999 for the World Curling Championships. The rink is part of a £285 million leisure and retail complex in the Glasgow suburb, located next to the M8 motorway in central west Scotland.

The state-of-the-art venue has a 60-by-30 metres main ice pad, a circular leisure pad, and a 50-by-35 metres curling pad on the first floor overlooking the River Clyde.

Braehead itself is in Renfrewshire, 30 miles north of Scottish Eagles' former home, Centrum in Ayr-Prestwick, and only five miles or so from Paisley's Lagoon Centre, the home of the Scottish National League's Pirates. Eagles' first game - a friendly against BNL champions, Dundee Stars - was played in the Lagoon.

Eagles Hockey Ltd was set up by Belfast Giants' Canadian partners, **Bob Zeller** (who owned 75 per cent) and **Albert Maasland** (25 per cent) to run and market the team. Maasland, 43, a retired merchant banker and former University of Toronto goalie, spent most of his time with the Giants after Bob Zeller moved to Glasgow.

The club was still owned by Ayr-based **Bill Barr**, a Scottish construction magnate, through one of his companies, Ice Hockey Services Ltd, and had the support and sponsorship of his main company, Barr Holdings Ltd.

Much of Barr Holdings' business is in the building of football stadiums and when the bottom fell out of that market, Bill Barr was forced to cut back on his sports interests which included Ayr United and well as the Eagles.

That's when he asked Zeller and Maasland to run the club for him, with the sweetener that they could buy Eagles at a later date. It was agreed that the team should play at Braehead rather than Centrum as the Glasgow arena has a larger capacity.

The franchise arrangements with Superleague were completed only seven weeks before their first game. This gave Bob Zeller and his small staff too little time to market the sport in the football-crazy area and the club was forced into liquidation after playing only five home games.

For more on the Eagles, see *Collapse of the Superleague*.

First game - and nearly the last

29 September 2002, Challenge Cup, Braehead Arena, Glasgow

EAGLES-MANCHESTER STORM	3-2

Eagles made a triumphant home-coming, winning their first home game after five successive defeats on the road.

Their historic first goal was scored by Swede **Johan Astrom** on a powerplay to level the score at one apiece. The honour of scoring the first ever goal in the Braehead Arena went to Manchester's **Geoff Peters**.

> Manchester Storm, Eagles' first opponents in Braehead, went out of business within days of Eagles. Spooky, eh?

Scoring summary
0-1 MAN Peters (Matulik, Cardarelli) 0.41
1-1 SCO Astrom (Quinnell, Harding) pp 13.52
2-1 SCO Bowen (Majic, Johnstone) 39.35
3-1 SCO Selmser (Bowen, Majic) sh 48.26
3-2 MAN Pepperall (Longstaff, Allard) pp 53.27
Shots on Goal
Cavallin SCO 11- 9-8 28
Torchia MAN 12-16-5 33
Penalty minutes Eagles 30, Storm 18.
Referee: Moray Hanson.
Linesmen: Pirry, Cowan. *Attendance*: 2,466
SCOTTISH EAGLES
Mark Cavallin, Eoin McInerney; Evan Marble, Bob Quinnell, Stefan Bergqvist, Paddy Ward; Xavier Majic, Jeff Johnstone, Jonathan Weaver, Jeff Williams, Johan Astrom, Mike Harding, Dan Ratushny, Jonni Vauhkonen, Jason Bowen, Sean Selmser capt, Dino Bauba.
Manager-coach: Paul Heavey.
MANCHESTER STORM
Mike Torchia, Stevie Lyle; Rob Wilson, Dan Preston, Shawn Maltby, Geoff Peters, Mike Perna, Pasi Nielikainen, Dwight Parrish, Mark Bultje, Ivan Matulik, Pierre Allard, David Longstaff, Ryan Stewart, Joe Cardarelli, Dan Hodge. *Manager-coach*: Daryl Lipsey.

EAGLES' GAMES IN BRAEHEAD

Date	Comp	Visitors	Score	Att.
29 Sept	CC	Manchester Storm	3-2	2466
2 Oct	ISL	Nottingham Panthers	1-3	984
5 Oct	CC	Belfast Giants	4-3ot	1381
13 Oct	ISL	London Knights	6-4	2051
26 Oct	CC	Sheffield Steelers	2-3	2429

HALL OF FAME

STEPHEN COOPER

During **Stephen Cooper's** long and distinguished career he was the outstanding British-born defenceman and an impeccable role model.

On the ice at left defence, his 12-and-a-half-stone (178 lbs) of pure muscle on a 5ft 10in frame, helped him and his teams to a remarkable tally of titles throughout the heyday of the *Heineken* British League and beyond into the tougher Superleague era.

.He assisted Durham Wasps and Cardiff Devils to five consecutive league and championship doubles, including two Grand Slams, and made 61 appearances for Britain where he featured in their quick-fire World Championship climb from Pool D to Pool A.

The British Ice Hockey Writers Association awarded him their Alan Weeks Trophy as the Best British Defenceman a record nine times.

Along with his younger brother Ian - already a Hall of Fame member - Stephen was the epitome of professionalism. It was arguably the impact that these brothers, and the likes of their Scottish contemporary **Tony Hand**, which laid the foundations for the boom of the 1980s.

Stephen Cooper was born on 11 November 1966 at Peterlee, Co Durham. While skating at Durham's Riverside rink, he and Ian saw a poster advertising a testimonial game for legendary Wasp forward **Kenny Matthews** and duly went to their first game. A few weeks later, armed with old sticks, the boys went to their first training session. Actually, much of Stephen's early training took place at the Crowtree rink in nearby Sunderland and between the ages of 9 and 14, he played predominantly as a forward.

He moved back to Durham when he was 13 and played for both the junior Mosquitoes and the B team, Hornets. He estimates that he laced up his skates around six times a week.

He made his debut for the senior Wasps in the 1980-81 season and by 1982-83 he had already won silverware as Wasps topped the tougher of the two English sections in the British League. In the following five seasons, his reputation grew and by the time Cardiff Devils made a move on him in the summer of 1988 he had added two *Heineken* Premier Division and two British Championship titles to his collection.

His presence in a team was now considered to be the equivalent of any import. The opportunities offered by his move to the Division One club meant that he could afford to quit the day job and become a full-time player. It was a gamble on both sides, but his game scaled new heights and he was the rock on which Devils built their assault on the sport's upper echelons.

Blessed with great strength and stamina, he played a hard-hitting, energy-sapping brand of hockey and regularly clocked up 45-50 minutes a match. He became a leader by example. Devils lifted the division title, won the promotion play-offs to gain entry to the Premier Division, and captured the Autumn Trophy. His selection as an All-Star was a formality.

Back in the top flight, Cardiff overturned odds of 500-1 to clinch the Premier Division title in 1989-90. This was followed by perhaps the most dramatic British Championship final ever in front of a packed Wembley Arena. Pitched against arch-rivals Murrayfield Racers, Devils never led. Then 95 seconds from the end of regulation, Cooper charged up ice, connected with a pass from brother Ian and snatched the tying goal.

The subsequent marathon shootout went to 24 shots before the outcome went Cardiff's way.

That summer, realising the mistake they had made, Durham offered both Coopers professional wages. The call of home proved too strong and their return was decisive in transforming Wasps' fortunes. They raced to a Grand Slam of *Heineken* Premier Division, Championship and *Norwich Union* Cup titles with Stephen racking up 118 points.

After helping Wasps to retain the league and championship titles he returned to Cardiff in 1992 and during the next four years Devils and Cooper added two league titles, two championships and an Autumn Cup.

In the summer of 1996, he left Cardiff for the last time to join Devils' manager **John Lawless** at Manchester Storm for the start of Superleague. The new circuit, dominated by

Canadian imports, produced a higher quality game but his defensive talents, such as the difficult-to-pull-off centre-ice hit, were no longer in vogue as the game lost much of its free-flowing nature.

He completed two years with Storm before playing a season each with Superleague sides at Newcastle and Nottingham. In all, he played 974 major competitive games with Wasps, Devils, Storm, Panthers and Newcastle Riverkings before ending his career in the British National League with Hull Thunder and Coventry Blaze.

Always a big game player, he scored some crucial goals in his last season and was a key factor in Blaze's success in reaching the 2002 BNL playoff finals. Above all, perhaps, Stephen Cooper demonstrated how to play a hard, physical game uncompromisingly but in a sporting manner. His penalty totals were modest throughout his long career.

- Anthony Beer, research by Gordon Wade

FREDERICK MEREDITH

As president of the British Ice Hockey Association, **Frederick William Louis Meredith** was one of the greatest influences on the sport during his term of office from 1982 to 1998.

This was the time that has rightly been described as a Golden Era in British ice hockey. With the help of the Sports Council who provided the impetus for over two-dozen new ice rinks in the Eighties, the public's awareness of the game has arguably never been higher.

The major commercial achievements of his 18-year reign were acquiring three blue-chip sponsors - *Heineken, Benson and Hedges* and *Norwich Union Insurance* - and a contract with BBC TV. Through their marketing agents, the Wight Company, *Heineken* produced the Wembley Weekend; the showpiece *Heineken* Championships were held for ten years in the capital's world famous arena.

And a nation-wide game of the month was shown on BBC for many years, augmented by the annual live transmission of the Wembley finals on *Grandstand*.

When tobacco company, Gallagher, lit up the Autumn Cup with £2 million over nine years through their *Benson and Hedges* brand name, they also tied up a two-year deal with *Sky Sports* for weekly live games.

On the playing front Frederick was an ardent advocate for limiting the number of overseas skaters. His eagerness for the sport's success to be recognised internationally ensured that the GB senior team returned to the world stage in 1989 after a gap of eight years. Remarkably, after only another five years Britain were playing alongside Canada in the elite A Pool.

Frederick Meredith was born in 1937 in Montreal where he naturally learned to skate at an early age. His talent for standing in the way of an object rather than knocking it around soon became apparent at his school, Bishops College, and led to him converting to netminding. Having a British father, he also took to cricket as a wicket keeper.

At 18, he was awarded a place at Trinity College, Cambridge - his father's old college - where he was welcomed into the Light Blues ice hockey team. His goaltending debut ended in an embarrassing 11-1 defeat but the perennial losers to their great rivals in Oxford were about to undergo a change of fortune.

In 1958, his third year, Frederick added the coaching duties and guided the team to a 6-1 victory, their first for six years. After graduating with degrees in law and economics, he enjoyed more success: in the five Varsity Matches played between 1958 and 1962, Cambridge lost just once.

Meanwhile, he had become the university's representative on the British Ice Hockey Association's ruling council. His ability must have impressed the council as in 1960 he was elected a 'personal' member - effectively a directorship - of the sport's then governing body.

Two years later he travelled to the USA with Britain's World Championship squad as the BIHA's representative and was the governing body's secretary for a brief spell in 1971-73.

His day job as a management consultant with IBM curtailed his ice hockey activities, unfortunately at precisely the time of its grass roots' revival in Britain. However, he retained his place on the BIHA and upon the retirement of long-time president and secretary, **John F (Bunny) Ahearne**, Meredith took over.

In 1988, he moved into the upper echelons of the world governing body, the IIHF, and eventually became a member of their governing council. He currently chairs their influential legal and rules committees.

- Stewart Roberts, research by Martin C Harris.

TRIBUTES

Joe Baird

Winger **George Baird**, who was always known as Joe, played for 14 different clubs during a long career in Scotland.

A protégé of legendary Canadian coach **George McNeil**, in 1971 he played for Scotland against England, and for The Rest against Britain when he scored two goals.

In those less pressure-filled days, George believed that the spectators needed a bit of light relief. When serving a penalty on one occasion and needing to attract the attention of his coach, he leaned over the announcer, grabbed his mike and bellowed 'Jackson' at the top of his voice.

He didn't really need this sort of distraction to keep the fans happy as he scored at a goal-a-game pace in the first eight seasons of the Northern League. In November 1974 he was listed as 15th overall in all-time NL competitions with 143 goals and 115 assists from 143 matches.

George, who never knew how he acquired the nickname Joe, was born in Falkirk on 9 June 1936. He died of asbestosis in September 2002.

Martin C. Harris

Jimmy Forsyth

James (Jimmy) Forsyth played for Wembley Lions, Birmingham Maple Leafs and Perth Panthers for three years before World War Two.

He was among the first wave of Canadian pros to come to this country, joining Lions in their inaugural season of 1934-35. A memorable season it was, too, as he was part of Lions' sensational 2-0 shutout victory over Winnipeg Monarchs who represented Canada in 1935.

The next winter he helped the short-lived Maple Leafs to the northern section of the English League and playoffs, scoring 16 goals and 50 points in 29 games.

Edmonton-born Jimmy was also a talented pianist and singer, releasing a record of two songs in 1935. He died on 1 September 2001, aged 88.

Martin C Harris

Doug Free

Doug Free, a high scoring winger with the 1947-48 Ayr Raiders, died in February 2003. Hailing from Ontario, he was a member of Sudbury Wolves who won silver when they represented Canada at the 1949 World Championships in Stockholm.

In 60 Scottish National League outings with Raiders, he tallied 62 points, including 47 goals, while serving only 26 penalty minutes. On 28 March 1948 when Raiders entertained the Czechoslovak national side, he netted twice in a respectable 8-5 loss.

Martin C. Harris

Charlie Knott

Cricket commentator, **John Arlott**, once declared that **Charlie Knott** was the finest amateur bowler to play for Hampshire. Many were disappointed that the immensely popular and infuential cricketer declined to turn professional, putting his family's fishmonger's business before his love for the sport.

Charlie, affectionately known as 'CJ', preferred to be regarded as an unpaid professional and often stayed at the same hotels as the pros. He hated the snooty attitudes of the time that led to separate changing rooms for amateurs.

His regard for the amateur sportsman carried over to ice hockey and when he took charge of the Southampton rink, his first team in 1952-53 consisted entirely of home-grown players.

Not Southampton lads, unfortunately, because ice hockey had not been played in the city for a dozen years. The rink had been destroyed in World War Two and was not rebuilt until March 1952. To overcome this handicap, Charlie talked to **Benny Lee**, the boss of the Sports Stadium in Brighton, and agreed to take over the amateur Sussex team which saw little ice time after the professional Tigers had taken their share.

The new Southampton Vikings joined the Southern Intermediate League and were an instant success, drawing capacity crowds and winning the league title in their first season.

Charlie soon elevated the status of the SIL, whose amateur teams had been used to playing late at night in front of a handful of spectators, by advertising games at Southampton as 'the heart of English ice hockey'.

His promotional skills kept the crowds coming throughout his 11 seasons at the helm, with the fans also being treated to visits from England, Scotland, Sweden, the USA and Czechoslovakia as well as foreign club sides. Vikings won Southampton's BIHA Cup five times and the Southern Cup on three occasions.

By 1959 the British Ice Hockey Association had made him an England selector, and he was appointed to the governing body's ruling Council a year later in recognition of his efforts on behalf of native players. By then roughly half the Vikings' roster comprised locally trained lads, in sharp contrast to the British League teams of the time which were dominated by Canadians.

Another honour followed for CJ when he joined the British party as the BIHA's representative at the 1961 World Championships in Switzerland.

Charlie's brief reign in ice hockey ended sadly in the summer of 1963 when the family sold the rink and the adjacent speedway and greyhound stadium to the Rank Organisation. Rank removed or walled-off all the seats in the rink and refused to stage ice hockey.

It took 13 long years before they reluctantly accepted that the sport attracted paying customers and when the Vikings were revived, Charlie returned to head the club's management committee for a season.

Charles James Knott Jr died on 27 February 2003, aged 88. He took 647 wickets for Hampshire between 1938 and 1954, finishing with a highly respectable average of 23.53. He was club chairman for 21 years until his retirement in 1989, and was one of only three life vice-presidents of Hampshire. A housing estate near the old county cricket ground - around the corner from the rink, now demolished - was named Charles Knott Gardens in tribute to both father and son.

He was married with two daughters.

Martin C Harris/Stewart Roberts

Red Kurz

When **Lou Bates**, Wembley Lions' legendary coach of the 1930s and 1940s, returned to England after World War Two with a bunch of players destined for Lions and sister club, Monarchs, they didn't look too impressive - especially one long, gangly redhead of 19 years.

But **Ernest Kurz**, inevitably labelled Red, turned out to be an outstanding defenceman in both England and Scotland. Season after season, he rarely missed a game, 60 to 70 a year. And in the course of a season or two he learned to become more of an offensive threat, doubling his output.

In his third season, 1948-49, when Monarchs won the International Tournament and the Autumn Cup, Red racked up 43 points; the following term he played 70 games, scoring 22 goals and 49 points.

Quietly spoken off the ice, like many a redhead he had a fiery temper which earned him a suspension for the whole of 1950-51. That season of 1949-50 he clocked up 136 minutes in penalties, including four misconducts.

After a spell in the Scottish League where he became a firm favourite as captain and player-coach of Dundee Tigers, the highlight of his career came in 1957 back in England. He was captain of Brighton Tigers when they became the first British team to conquer the Soviet Russian bear, 6-3.

Ice Hockey World said of this match: 'Kurz played like the blazes for those **Benny Lee** Blazers [each player was to be rewarded with one for a victory], and time and again his stickwork and occasional bodycheck saved the situation.'

Kurz played in all 14 seasons of the post-war, mostly Canadian-staffed national leagues. He was voted to the *World*'s All-Star A team five times, and the B team twice, once as coach of Dundee. He scored 180 goals and 552 points.

He married Thelma, a lovely north London girl and settled in his native Winnipeg, although at one time they toyed with the idea of buying a garage business in East Anglia. The couple, who were married for more than 50 years, were visiting their daughter, Tracy, in Vancouver, when Red suffered a massive stroke. He was airlifted back to Winnipeg where he died on 23 October 2002. He was 74.

His great joy in recent years had been watching his grandson, Mason, 14, a centreman who was drafted by an American college after scoring 100 goals for his junior team.

Phil Drackett

Geoff Marsh

Geoff Marsh, who died on 22 April 2003 aged 73, worked tirelessly behind the scenes in support of Great Britain's under-18 and under-20 world championship squads.

A Londoner, he first became involved in the sport as back-up netminder for Streatham Royals of the Southern Intermediate League in the early 1950s. He met his future wife Pat on New Year's Eve 1949 and on an early date took her to see a game at Streatham ice rink, where she first watched the sport that had such an influence on their life together.

While Geoff's career was in the travel industry with *Thomas Cook*, Pat became secretary to **John F (Bunny) Ahearne**, for years the driving force behind the British Ice Hockey Association and the International Ice Hockey Federation.

Geoff spent countless unpaid hours assisting with all the menial but necessary tasks in ensuring a party of 20-plus youngsters left and returned safely. He often put his travel experience at the disposal of the BIHA and was especially keen to support the teams when they travelled abroad.

On such occasions, he was invariably accompanied by Pat to whom he was married for over 50 years. They were one of the best-known couples in British ice hockey. A devoted family man, Geoff also leaves a daughter, Alison, and two grandsons, Nicholas and Christopher.

Martin C Harris

Cecil MacIntosh

A stalwart in maintaining ice hockey at Sheffield's Queens Road rink, died of cancer during 2001.

A Scotsman by birth but a long time resident of Rotherham, Cecil first joined Sheffield's ice hockey club in 1976 as public relations officer to the year-old club. He later served as manager and club secretary of the senior Lancers who played in the Southern League.

Throughout the 1990s he was the chief business partner of the rink's lessee, **Tom Shipstone**, and only a few months before his death, he was still coaching the Saturday morning beginners' sessions at Queens Road.

A fitting tribute to his teaching skills is that two years after his passing, Sheffield's teams won the English Under 12, 14 and 16 Northern 'A' leagues.

Martin C. Harris

Jackson McBride

Jackson McBride, a well-liked and respected player and coach in Scottish ice hockey for over 40 years, died suddenly on 8 July 2003. He was 57.

Born in Paisley on 28 August 1946, he only took up the game in his mid-teens but by the time he was 20, he was an automatic choice with Paisley Mohawks. He credited his quick grasp of the game to Mohawks' legendary player-coach **Billy Brennan**. When Mohawks folded three years later he was snapped up by Ayr Bruins who made him player-coach.

JACK KILPATRICK

Jack Kilpatrick was the youngest player ever to win a gold medal for Britain at a Winter Olympics, according to records recently unearthed by **Joanne Collins**. He was born in Bootle on 7 July 1917 making him 18 years and seven months old when he played right-wing in Britain's amazing Triple Crown triumph at Garmisch-Partenkirchen, Germany in 1936. He died on 18 December 1989.

He gained his first cap for GB in the 1971 World Championships and went on to play 15 times for Britain in three World Championships during the Seventies, scoring four goals and eight points.

He remained with Bruins into the *Heineken* era while their forward trio of **Jimmy Young**, **Joe Baird** and Jackson became famous as the 'J' line. His last full playing season, 1985-86, coincided with the first one in Britain for the high scoring Canadian duo of **Kevin Conway** and **Tim Salmon**.

The following year he was back in Ayr's coaching seat late in the campaign, and he played four games in his final season for the Premier Division club which had then been taken over by **Glenn Henderson**, the local businessman who was later responsible for building Centrum.

Jackson remained close to the sport after his serious playing days were over. He set up the first team to play out of Kilmarnock's Galleon Centre in 1989, assisted with the coaching programmes at several west coast clubs and played recreational hockey with Ayr Jets.

He leaves Aileen, his wife, sons Ryan and Blair, and a daughter, Krysta.

Martin C Harris/Frank Dempster

Brian Millard

Brian Millard, an English born and trained netminder, later a forward, played for Streatham Royals from 1949 to 1962. He helped the amateur team to three cup victories - the Liverpool Tournament in 1951-52, and the Southampton BIHA Cup and Blackpool IceDrome Trophy in 1957-58.

He set a record in the Southern Intermediate League in 1952-53 with eight shutouts, resulting in his call-up to the senior Streatham squad for one game the following February. Unfortunately, Royals were on the wrong end of an 8-6 score.

He achieved the odd distinction of twice coming close to being capped for England at two different positions. In February 1955 he was selected as their back-up netminder against the USA and six years later he just missed the final cut as a forward after scoring an assist for England B in a trial game against England A.

Brian died in late 2002.

Martin C. Harris

Bert Oig

Bert Oig, a Canadian who was equally at home at centre and on defence, played in Scotland and London mostly during the Fifties.

His major stint came with Dundee Tigers in 1953-54 when his powerfully built 5ft, 11in, 198lb frame provided 55 goals and 78 assists in 60 Scottish National League games. His contribution was recognised by his election to the All-Star 'B' team as a centreman.

In a chequered British career he also played 16 games for Wembley Lions in 1948-49, one game for Fife Flyers in 1953-54, another 49 games for Tigers in 1954-55, 59 games with Harringay Racers in 1955-57 and finally, 46 games for Paisley Pirates in 1956-57.

His total statistics for his six seasons were 231-133-169-302 with 358 penalty minutes. He also played in Canada.

He died, aged 74, on 18 September 2002 at Prince George Hospital, British Columbia.

Martin C. Harris

Cliff Ryan

Cliff Ryan was one of the fastest skaters who ever played in Britain - in his native Canada they called him the Comet.

The left-winger played seven seasons here, starting in 1947-48 with Fife Flyers when he finished runner-up in the scoring championship with 49 goals. After a spell back in Canada, he signed for Streatham in 1951 but found it difficult at first in the higher grade English National League. His break came when player-coach **Duke Campbell** offered him a berth with Earls

Court Rangers. When Rangers folded after London's Empress Hall management pulled the plug on hockey, Ryan had shown enough ability to be picked by Wembley Lions, along with his team-mates **Les Anning, Kenny Booth** and **Stan DeQuoy.**

Cliff stayed with Lions until early 1956 when he appeared in the last Nottingham Panthers line-up to win a league title. In all, he played 345 games in Britain, scoring 280 goals and 421 points and spending 362 minutes in the sin-bin. He ended his hockey career as a coach in Sweden with elite league clubs, AIK Stockholm and Gothenburg.

He then took up the Canadian hockey player's time-honoured career as pub landlord, in Cliff's case, the King and Tinker near Enfield, Middlesex. His greatest honour came in 1995 with his induction into the Hall of Fame in his home town of North Bay, Ontario where he was once the youngest player on the local team.

Clifton John Ryan was born on 15 June 1928 and married an English girl, Betty, who survives him. A cousin of the late **Les Costello** (see obituary on page 192), he died, age 75, in Hove, Sussex, two days before Christmas 2002.

Phil Drackett

Paddy Ryan

When he arrived in Britain from his home in Regina, Saskatchewan in 1947, **Paddy Ryan** was hailed by Streatham as 'the defence discovery of the year'. The 23-year-old lived up to this hype, helping his team to win the National Tournament in his first season and ending as the English National League's highest scoring blueliner with 31 goals in 55 games.

Tall and fast skating he was a colourful player as befits one who was raised with a family large enough to form their own team! He and his nine siblings spent their early winters playing hockey in their back yard with Dad in the net.

He was a consistent goal scorer, averaging 25 goals a season during his time with the south Londoners. For a big defender, he had a modest penalty total, his worst record coming in 1948-49 when he collected 41 minutes, including a major. He was twice voted to the All-Star B team.

After three seasons with Streatham during which they won the ENL and the National Tournament a second time, Paddy went to Scotland where he played a couple of seasons with Dunfermline Vikings before they folded. He won the Scottish Cup with them in 1953.

Patrick Thomas Ryan was born on 11 November 1924 and died in 2001.

Phil Drackett/Martin C Harris

Harry Smith

Harry Smith, a much respected referee in the 1960s and 1970s, died in February 2003 at Nottingham. He was in his mid-seventies and had been in poor health for some time.

Hailing from Kilmarnock, he began by handling matches all over Scotland and south of the border at Durham and Whitley Bay. He was the regular official at nearby Ayr for the Rangers matches of the mid-1960s and then the Bruins games, until the Beresford Terrace rink closed in 1972.

Following the retirement of London-based **Ernie Leacock** in the spring of 1965, Harry became regarded as Britain's referee-in-chief. One of his earliest international assignments was the GB Select v Poland encounter at Paisley in December 1965. Further international duties included the England v Scotland fixtures of 1971 at Durham and two years later at Billingham.

Recognition beyond these shores came with two World Championship, Pool C, assignments - to Holland in 1973 and five years later to Las Palmas in the Canaries.

One of his last international calls was to the Four Nations tournament held in the three north-east England rinks in October 1978.

His encouragement and the courses he conducted enabled the next generation of whistlers to take over as the sport boomed in the 1980s.

Martin C Harris

The Hon. George Stanley

The **Hon. George Francis Gillman Stanley**, who suggested the original design for the Canadian flag, was one of the oldest and most respected former members of Oxford University's ice hockey team. He was 95 when he died on 12 September 2002.

He played for the Dark Blues in the southern section of the first British League during 1929-30 and was twice on the winning side in the annual Oxford-Cambridge Varsity Match. During the team's Christmas tours of the Continent, he and his fellow students regularly competed in the prestigious Spengler Cup at Davos, Switzerland, winning it in 1931.

George took up a history professorship on his return to Canada and enjoyed an outstanding academic career, publishing numerous books and serving on countless committees. He was appointed lieutenant-governor of New Brunswick, made an Officer of the Order of Canada in 1976 and promoted to Companion of the Order 19 years later.

The Calgary native had joined Oxford on a Rhodes Scholarship after graduating with a BA from the University of Alberta. At Oxford he joined Keble College where he acquired three further degrees and a Doctorate in Philosophy.

His widow, Ruth, recently donated a box of hockey memorabilia, including his Spengler Cup medals, to the archivist of Oxford's ice hockey club.

Martin C. Harris

Doug Young

Londoner **Doug Young** was one of the colourful characters of English ice hockey in the sport's post-World War Two era.

He is recorded as having played in 186 games in the elite English National League, but he scored only four goals and 12 points while playing in the shadows of the mainly Canadian stars of the Harringay Racers and Greyhounds.

As in the current era, the home-grown lad was good enough to play for his country being selected for the 1952 World Championships in Liege, Belgium. He scored a goal in the 10-0 shutout of the French as Britain won Pool B.

Doug was born in Holloway, north London on 7 October 1923 and his first job was page-boy at his local rink, the 10,000-seat Harringay Arena. Smitten by the sport, he played in their house league in the 1939-40 season but with war having broken out, he was not there long.

After service as a PE instructor in the Royal Fusiliers, he got back into hockey through **Lou Bates**' youth programme on the other side of London at Wembley but soon returned to play his first senior game for Greyhounds.

Over the years at Harringay he filled almost every spot - winger, back-up goalie, even assistant trainer - in addition to his usual position on defence, while boosting morale in the dressing-room with a laugh and a quip.

Away from hockey he starred in ice shows, partnering another English puck-chaser, **Kenny Gardner**, in an adagio act. Eventually, he followed **Ted Hallam**, another English defenceman, to the San Bernadino Valley in the USA and became manager of an ice rink popular with the children of Hollywood stars. Both he and Ted appeared in movies.

Doug died in northern California in December 2002, aged 79.

Martin C Harris/Phil Drackett

*All photos in this section are from the Harris Ice Hockey Archive and reproduced with the kind permission of the curator, **Martin Harris**.*

LES STRONGMAN

The veteran player's thoughts - he's still alive and well - on the current state of the game and his great times in Nottingham as he returned to his native Canada after over 50 years in Britain.

*This interview was given to **Mick Holland** of Nottingham's Evening Post and is reproduced here with their kind permission.*

Les Strongman, one of Nottingham Panthers' all-time greats, has returned to live in Canada - 56 years after playing in the club's first competitive game.

Originally from Winnipeg, Manitoba, the British Ice Hockey Hall of Famer and his wife Margaret sold their home of 30 years at the side of the Trent embankment to live in Edmonton. They flew out in January 2003 to join their son, Mark, who was briefly a Panther, and GB international daughter, Kim, who both now live and work in Canada. He will also be near former Panther, **Randall Weber**, and his family.

Players and officials from Nottingham's ice hockey clubs turned out to pay tribute to him, and **George Land**, chairman of the junior section, presented him with a Trojans shirt.

When Les gave up his job as a policeman in 1946 and sailed over on the good ship Aquitania to join the brand new Panthers in an expanding league, it was very much a trip into the unknown.

Panthers [then as now staffed almost entirely by Canadians] survived until 1960, when soaring wages and fewer teams saw the demise of the sport at the highest level. Ice hockey didn't return to the old Ice Stadium until 20 years later and Les's love of the game was rekindled.

He became coach and subsequently secretary and director and, until a couple of years ago, he continued to coach the youngest of kids. Now a sprightly 76 - and a gentleman in the truest sense of the word - Les has stopped skating in recent years. "I can't tell which way my legs are going to go," he laughed. And he holds similar views on the current British game when once

more, high wages and few teams have put the game at its top level in danger.

"What I can't understand is that the people who are running the majority of teams are businessmen. Yet they still operate at costs beyond what money is coming in," he said. "And that's been allowed to go on for years.

"I don't think the grade of hockey is that important. Around 16-18 years ago, the players were nowhere near as good as they are now, but I enjoyed the hockey as much, or perhaps even more than I currently do."

Strongman was particularly critical of referees and puts much of the blame on them for the excitement going out of the sport because they do not allow skilful players to perform. "When I played, there were chances to score on every shift because the refs penalised all the holding and obstruction.

"I remember the three Czech international players who joined Fife in the late 1980s. They played the game how it should be played. They passed their way up the ice and if they had no one to pass to, they turned around and passed it back to retain possession. It's as easy as that.

"To their credit, that's what the Princeton University team did the other night against Panthers - probably because they don't know any different. Unfortunately, many of the former NHL players we are getting over here have forgotten how to pass and all they seem to do is dump the puck in and chase it - or not, as the case may be."

Despite his strong views on refs and the current state of the game, Les says he will miss Panthers and the people of Nottingham, who took him to their hearts all those years ago.

He starred in the original teams with players like **Chick Zamick** and **Lorne Smith, Rupe Fresher** and **Kenny Westman** - players still revered today by the veteran fans who still talk about the 'good old days'.

"Except for six years when I was in Zurich and then player-coach in Sweden, I've lived in Nottingham all that time and I've met so many good friends," added Les. "There was nothing like the atmosphere and noise at the old Ice Stadium on match nights and it is never going to be reproduced in the bigger National Ice Centre, although the Panthers-Sheffield games run it pretty close.

"I hope Panthers carry on - at whatever level. It would be awful for the people of Nottingham to miss out on the most exciting team sport in the world. My only regret is that Panthers stopped in 1960 and we had to wait 20 years for hockey to start again. All in all, because of ice hockey, I've had a great life in this country and I wouldn't change a thing." Except perhaps referees?

INTERNATIONAL ROUND-UP

No European league

The IIHF's attempt to revive the European Hockey League appears to have been shelved. The first league lasted four seasons in the late 1990s and the world body hoped to announce plans for its return by the end of 2002.

In July of that year the London research institute, SMS, presented the results of their survey into the ice hockey structures of 14 selected European countries. The findings were submitted to an IIHF working group on a CD-Rom - the equivalent of 500 pages - analysing all the answers on the questionnaires.

The *Annual* asked the IIHF in June 2003 what progress had been made since then. "There has been no progress at all," a spokesman told us, admitting: "The research did not come out very well."

The main obstacle is that ice hockey is a regional sport rather than a national one in Europe. IIHF President **René Fasel** expressed his mild annoyance that "many clubs in the highest ranked leagues feel they are on top of the world if they beat their next door neighbour."

With this attitude, it is difficult to persuade TV comapnies, whose coverage is vital for attracting the essential sponsorship, to back a Europe-wide competition.

- The IIHF did manage to reach agreement with the NHL for the Stanley Cup winner to play the European League champion. Until that great day dawns, however, the only time European and NHL club sides meet is during pre-season 'goodwill' games when a willing NHL team or teams play in Europe, as far as possible in the home of the Continental Cup champ.

- The *Annual* learned that **Philip Anschutz**, who once owned six European teams, told his Los Angeles organisation that he is shelving his plans to create a European League.

Anschutz, the owner of Superleague's London Knights, who is sometimes described as 'the wealthiest American you've never heard of', dropped this year from the list of 'hockey's most powerful men' by the influential Toronto-based weekly paper, *The Hockey News*.

IIHF keeps growing

The International Ice Hockey Federation, who moved into new offices in January 2003, have 23 people working in their new headquarters in Zurich, Switzerland. When the world governing body moved from Vienna to their old Zurich building in 1991, they had just four employees.

Longest Game

The world record for the longest game ever played was broken twice during the winter of 2002-03. According to the last report received by the *Annual* (courtesy of *The Hockey News* of Toronto), the record was set on 16 February and stands at three days and eight hours.

The marathon match was played by 40 amateurs on an outdoor rink in Ardrossan, near Sherwood Park in Alberta, Canada. The friends took to the ice in hour-long shifts, taking breaks in a makeshift dressing room in a garage and having hot baths. Split into two teams, they played in full equipment to NHL rules with five attackers and a goalie on each side, keeping physical contact to a minimum. The Blue team won 650-628.

"We're feeling a bit tired, but we could have gone on for another 10 or 20 hours," said organiser, **Brent Saik**.

The game, which raised $40,000 for cancer research, beat the old record, set a month earlier, by 17 hours, 45 minutes. That was staged in a little town called Moosomin (pop. 2,500) in the western province of Saskatchewan. Forty players from the Moosamin Moose split into Blue and White teams with the Blues winning 429-411 when the game ended on 12 January.

Former London Knight, **Kelly Glowa**, scored the winning goal for the Iles-des-Chenes North Stars to give the Manitoba team their first Allan Cup.

Glowa's goal for a 3-2 win over Stony Plain (Alberta) Eagles came in double overtime of the Canadian senior hockey championship game.

This attempt on the record, which was the idea of **Mike Schwean**, the town's recreation director, raised $250,000 towards the town's new hospital. Afterwards, he wasn't so sure it was a good idea. "'Thank God that's over," he said. "I'd never do it again, not for that long."

Nevertheless, the paper reported that the Moosamin men, who broke the previous record of 54 hours set a month earlier in the Bell Centre, Montreal, were planning another attempt to beat Ardrossan's amateurs.

EUROPE'S LONGEST ELITE GAME

The Norwegians set the record for the longest game at European elite level on 8 March 2003.

Swede **Joakim Backlund** scored the winning goal for Vålerengen seven minutes into the seventh period in game two of the best-of-five championship semi-finals against Trondheim.

The goal for a 2-1 win at 127:02 ended the game - which had started at 3 p.m. - after four hours and 31 minutes.

- from www.eurohockey.net

First outdoor NHL game

As the *Annual* went to press, the Edmonton Oilers were planning the first outdoor game in the NHL's 86-year history.

The Oilers were expecting 60,000 at the game - dubbed the Heritage Classic - on 22 November 2003 which was to be held in Edmonton's Commonwealth Stadium as part of Oilers' 25th anniversary celebrations. Montreal Canadiens were lined up as the opposition.

Krefeld Penguins, winners of Germany's DEL in 2002-03, were coached by fomer New York Islander **Butch Goring**.

The German title was Goring's seventh major trophy after four Stanley Cups as an Islanders player, and two Turner Cups as a coach in the International League.

Goring joined Krefeld two weeks into the season. They upset defending champs, Cologne Eagles, for their first championship.

Face-off was scheduled for 5 p.m. Edmonton time with tickets ranging from $35 to $135 Canadian. The NHL was to provide the boards, glass and refrigeration unit and the complete installation was estimated to cost $2 million.

According to the locals, the average temperature in the area during November is between minus 3 and minus 11 Centigrade. "We'll know at five that morning what the weather is going to look like that day," said Oilers' president, **Patrick LaForge**. "If there's a bit of bite in the air, we're going to play it."

If it's too nasty, the plans called for the game to be relocated to Oilers' home arena, the Skyreach Centre, and for around 40,000 tickets to be refunded.

• The biggest crowd to watch an outdoor game was 74,554 in October 2001 at Michigan State Spartans football stadium. (See *The Ice Hockey Annual 2002-03*).

McSorley's Eagles in Swiss A league playoffs

GB coach **Chris McSorley**'s Geneva-Servette Eagles finished sixth in the 12-team Swiss A League, winning 19 of their 44 games. The former coach of London Knights took the team owned by the Anschutz Entertainment Group (AEG) out of the B league only last season.

Eagles qualified for the playoffs with six games to spare, the first A league newcomers to clinch a playoff place since Davos in 1994.

Chris had strengthened the team's defence and signed veteran goalie **Reto Pavoni**. The 35-year-old was rated the league's top netminder. Apart from runners-up, Davos, Eagles conceded fewer goals than any other side - a McSorley trademark, as Knights' fans will know. In the first round of the playoffs, Eagles met third place Bern but with Pavoni out injured, Europe's best supported club knocked out Geneva by four games to two.

In the off-season, the coach signed ex-NHL forward **Oleg Petrov** and re-signed former France international forward, **Philippe Bozon**, another NHLer.

Tikhonov, 73, back with Russia

The most successful coach in the history of international ice hockey returned to the scene of his former triumphs - at the age of 73.

Viktor Tikhonov, the man behind Russia's and the Soviet Union's 'Big Red Machine' teams from 1978 to 1994, was appointed head coach of Russia in June 2003. His three-year contract will enable him to lead the team at the 2006 Winter Olympics. He has already won three Olympic golds, in 1984, 1988 and 1992, as well as eight World Championship titles.

He replaced **Vladimir Plyushchev** who was released after Russia finished a distant sixth in the World Championships.

After Tikhonov retired from the national team in 1994, he coached club side, CSKA Moscow, in the Russian league where he has produced some talented youngsters. **Nikolai Zherdev**, who went fourth overall in the 2003 NHL draft, was the latest in a long line of Tikonov protégés.

Freezers are DEL's hottest team

When Hamburg Freezers moved into the new *Color Line* Arena in Germany's second largest city in November 2002 they sold out the 12,325-seat, 80 million Euros building and turned away over a thousand fans.

This was a pleasant surprise for arena owner, **Harry Harkimo**, as Hamburg is a football city and had never had a German elite league (DEL) team before. The wealthy Finnish businessman, who once owned an interest in Superleague's Newcastle franchise, had budgeted for around 5,000 fans a game.

Even better, Freezers who were dead last in the 14-team DEL before moving from their old 6,000-seater, beat reigning DEL playoff champs, Cologne Sharks, 5-4.

Freezers, who are owned jointly by Harkimo and the Anschutz Entertainment Group, went on to sell out another eight games in their first 20 matches in the arena.

FORMER AYR GOALIE BANNED IN SWEDEN

Joaquin Gage, Djurgarden's Vancouver-born goaltender, was barred from three games after a fight in the Djurgarden game against Leksand (5-1) on Sunday [16 February 2003].

With just 15 seconds to play, Gage was speared in the groin and stomach by Leksand winger **Johan Eneqvist** and retaliated by giving the well-built Leksand player - also suspended for three games - a thorough beating.

Two days later, Gage took a beating of his own and Djurgarden will have to do without one of the best goalies in the Elitserien for the reminder of the regular season. *faceoff.com*

Fasel returns as IIHF Prez

The International Ice Hockey Federation (IIHF) re-elected their president **René Fasel** for a five-year term, 2003-08.

The vote, taken in Marbella, Spain in June 2003, was 'unanimous and by acclamation' by representatives of the 63 national associations who make up the General Congress, the IIHF's highest legislative body.

Fasel, of Fribourg, Switzerland, entered his third term as president after he was initially elected in 1994 and again in 1998. Providing he completes his third term, he will be the second longest serving president in IIHF history with 15 consecutive years. German **Günther Sabetzki** served for almost 20 years prior to Fasel.

.Among the 12 members of the Federation's ruling Council who were also elected was **Frederick Meredith**, the former president of the British Ice Hockey Association .

Jorma (Jerry) Salmi

The former British league forward was inducted into the Finnish Hall of Fame in May 2003.

He iced seven times for Brighton Tigers in 1955-56 and the following season appeared in 11 games for Nottingham Panthers and five for Southampton Vikings.

WORLD CHAMPIONSHIPS

Helsinki, Turku and Tampere, Finland, 26 April-11 May 2003

FINAL
11 May Hartwall Arena, Helsinki
CANADA-SWEDEN   **3-2ot** (1-2,0-0,1-0,1-0)

SEMI-FINALS
9 May Hartwall Arena, Helsinki
CANADA-CZECH REP.   **8-4** (1-0,2-2,5-2)
SLOVAKIA-SWEDEN   **1-4** (0-1,1-1,0-2)

WORLD RANKINGS
1 **CANADA**, *World Champions,*
2 Sweden, 3 Slovakia, 4 Czech Rep., 5 Finland, 6 Russia, 7 Germany, 8 Switzerland, 9 Latvia, 10 Austria, 11 Denmark, 12 Ukraine, 13 USA, 14 Belarus, 15 Slovenia, 16 Japan.
Belarus and Slovenia relegated to Div I in 2004; Japan must compete in the Far East Qualification tournament.

LEADING SCORERS

	GP	G	A	Pts	Pim
Zigmund Palffy SVK	9	7	8	15	18
Jozef Stumpel SVK	9	4	11	15	0
Lubomir Visnovsky SVK	9	4	8	12	2
Teemu Selanne FIN	7	8	3	11	2
Saku Koivu FIN	7	1	10	11	4

LEADING NETMINDERS

	GPI	Mins	SoG	GA	Sv%
Sean Burke CAN	6	329	156	7	95.5
Mikael Tellqvist SWE	7	393	150	9	94.0
Jan Lasak SVK	6	359	168	11	93.4

ALL-STAR TEAM
Goal   **Sean Burke** CAN
Defence   **Lubomir Visnovsky** SVK,
        Jay Bouwmeester CAN.
Forwards   **Dany Heatley** CAN, **Mats Sundin** SWE, **Peter Forsberg** SWE.
Selected by the media.

Canadians win Treble

Canada's men made it a trio of World and Olympic titles when they added the 2003 World Championship to their Olympic gold and the World under-18 Championship.

New York Rangers' right winger **Anson Carter** scored at 13.49 of overtime to give Canada a 3-2 final victory over Sweden. The winning goal was confirmed only after a lengthy video review when the red light failed to go on and the Russian ref, **Vladimir Sindler**, was not in position to make such a close and important call.

This was the 22nd world title for the Canadians who were last champions in 1997, also in Finland. **Andy Murray**'s team dropped only one point in their nine games, a shock 2-2 draw with newly promoted Denmark.

The Danes were the surprise package of the tournament as they beat the USA 5-2 in the opening game and successfully avoided a swift return to Div I. The Americans, on the other hand, iced their weakest line-up since 1982 and were fortunate to stay in the elite group.

DIVISION I
Group A, Budapest, Hungary, 15-21 April
1 **Kazakhstan**, 2 Poland, 3 Hungary, 4 Netherlands, 5 Romania, 6 Lithuania.
*Kazakhstan promoted to World Championship in 2004, **Lithuania** relegated to Div II.*
Group B, Zagreb, Croatia, 13-20 April
See next page.

DIVISION II
Group A, Seoul, South Korea, 5-12 April
1 **Korea**, 2 Yugoslavia, 3 Spain, 4 Australia, 5 South Africa, 6 Mexico.
*(South) **Korea** promoted to Div I in 2004, **Mexico** relegated to Div III.*
Group B, Sofia, Bulgaria, 24-30 March
1 **Belgium**, 2 China, 3 Bulgaria, 4 DPR Korea, 5 Israel, 6 Iceland.
*Belgium promoted to Div I in 2004, **Iceland** relegated to Div III.*

DIVISION III
Auckland, New Zealand, 3-6 April
1 **New Zealand** 2 Luxembourg 3 Turkey.
*New Zealand and **Luxembourg** promoted to Div II in 2004.*

SPOT THE PUCK

Anson Carter's game winner sneaks in between post and pad to give Canada gold in the World Championships.

Photo: BruceJessop/Ice Hockey Archives

DIVISION I

GROUP B
Zagreb, Croatia

FINAL STANDINGS

	GP	W	L	D	GF	GA	Pts
France FRA	5	4	0	1	21	5	9
Norway NOR	5	4	1	0	19	9	8
Estonia EST	5	2	3	0	12	20	4
Italy ITA	5	2	3	0	16	11	4
Britain GB	5	1	3	1	16	14	3
Croatia CRO	5	1	4	0	10	35	2

GB'S WORLD RANKING: 21st

France are promoted to the World Championships in 2003; **Croatia** *are relegated to Division II.*

RESULTS

	FRA	NOR	EST	ITA	CRO
GB	2-2	2-3	3-4	2-4	7-1
FRA		4-2	6-0	1-0	8-1
NOR			3-0	5-2	6-1
EST				3-1	5-7
ITA					9-0

GB's BEST PLAYERS
Steve Thornton
Rob Wilson
Colin Shields
selected by the GB coaching staff
Steve Thornton
selected by the GB Supporters Club

FAIR PLAY CUP

Penalty minutes per team
Italy 82, Norway 92, France 119, Estonia 123, **Britain 161**, Croatia 180.
Britain, Estonia and Croatia disqualified for taking match penalties.

BRITAIN'S SCORING

	GP	G	A	Pts	Pim
Steve Thornton	5	1	8	9	0
David Longstaff	5	3	5	8	2
Jeff Hoad	5	2	3	5	4
Rob Wilson	5	2	3	5	6
Colin Shields	5	4	0	4	2
Jonathan Weaver	5	2	2	4	4
Paul Berrington	5	1	2	3	2
Ashley Tait	5	0	3	3	0
Darren Hurley	5	0	2	2	10
Scott Moody	4	1	0	1	2
Scott Campbell	4	0	1	1	27
Jonathan Phillips	5	0	1	1	6
TEAM TOTALS	5	16	30	46	161

BRITAIN'S NETMINDING

	GPI	Mins	SoG	GA	Sv%
Mark Cavallin	3	178	149	9	93.96
Joe Watkins	2	119	76	5	93.42
TEAM TOTALS	5	297	225	14	93.78

THE BRITISH TEAM

*#Mark Cavallin (Bad Tolz, GER), Joe Watkins (Bracknell), Stephen Murphy (Dundee); #Chris Bailey (Cardiff), #Kyle Horne, Jonathan Weaver (Fife), *Scott Campbell, *Rob Wilson (Newcastle), #Scott Moody (Slough), *Brent Pope (Solihull); *Paul Berrington, *Mike Ellis (Basingstoke), *Steve Thornton (Belfast), *Darren Hurley (Bracknell), #Jonathan Phillips (Cardiff), #Russ Cowley (Coventry), Ashley Tait (Coventry), David Clarke, #Mark Galazzi (Guildford), *Jeff Hoad (London), #Greg Owen (Milton Keynes), David Longstaff, capt (Sierre, SWI), Colin Shields (Maine Un, USA).
Head coach: Chris McSorley (Geneva, Switz.).
Asst coaches: Rick Strachan SOL, Gary Stefan (BNL). *Manager:* Andy French (ISL).
* Dual national (9). # New cap (8)

BRITAIN *left to right, back row:* Russ Cowley, Colin Shields, Scott Moody, Mark Galazzi, Jonathan Weaver, Scott Campbell, Kyle Horne, Brent Pope, Chris Bailey, Darren Hurley, David Clarke, Ashley Tait, Greg Owen, Jonathan Phillips, Paul Berrington, Tom Watkins, Mike Ellis; *front row:* David Longstaff, Rob Wilson, Andy French (manager), Chris McSorley (head coach), Stephen Murphy, Joe Watkins, Mark Cavallin, Gary Stefan (asst coach), Rick Strachan (asst coach), Steve Thornton, Jeff Hoad.

Photo: Diane Davey

BRITAIN'S GAME SUMMARIES

14 April 2003, Dom Sportova, Zagreb

BRITAIN-FRANCE   2-2 (1-0,1-1,0-1)

GB scoring:

Hoad (Thornton, Longstaff)	12.50 pp	(1-0)
Weaver (Thornton)	23.49	(2-0)

Goalies:
Cavallin GB *Shots*: 17-16-20 53 *Save %*: 96.2
Lhenry FRA *Shots*: 10- 9- 3 22 *Save %*: 90.9
Penalty minutes: Britain 16, France 10.
Goals/powerplays: Britain 1/5, France 1/8.
GB Man of Match: Cavallin
Referee: Bertolotti ITA.   *Attendance*: 310

The official shot tally only slightly flatters Cavallin as he performed Olympian feats of acrobatics to keep the French at bay. But this shouldn't have been necessary as France were missing four of their best players, including Geneva's ex-NHLer **Philippe Bozon.**

Hoad's opening goal came on a McSorley master class in gambling. With two Frenchmen in the bin, he pulled 'Cavy' for a six-on-three advantage. After Weaver knocked in a rebound for 2-0, France fought back and when Wilson took a bad penalty with a minute left, Meunier beat a screened 'Cavy' for his second goal.

"I'm glad this isn't basketball, we didn't want a fourth quarter," said a relieved McSorley.

15 April 2003, Dom Sportova, Zagreb

ITALY-BRITAIN   4-2 (1-0,2-2,1-0)

GB scoring:

Wilson (Thornton, Longstaff)	31.49	(3-1)
Shields (Thornton, Wilson)	36.54	(3-2)

Goalies
Rosati ITA *Shots*: 2-17-12 31 *Save %*: 93.5
Watkins GB *Shots*: 18-16-12 46 *Save %*: 91.3
Penalty minutes: Italy 14, GB 12.
Goals/powerplays: Italy 1/5, GB 0/6.
GB Man of Match: Thornton.
Referee: Albers USA.   *Attendance*: 700

Thornton's skill and speed led to assists on both GB's goals, the man of the match award and the accolade of 'world class forward' from his coach. But McSorley was critical of his other top players as Italy, who are going through a rebuilding phase, built a three-goal lead while GB went 10-6 ahead in penalty minutes.

GB played some of their best hockey in the last half and might even have gone 3-2 up if Shields' shot had not hit a post late in the second. Hurley had the puck in the net in the dying moments but it was disallowed and Britain dropped to fifth in the standings.

Fumed McSorley: "We must get out of here with a medal. Anything else is unacceptable."

17 April 2003, Dom Sportova, Zagreb

ESTONIA-BRITAIN   4-3 (1-1,2-0,1-2)

GB scoring:

Longstaff (Hoad, Wilson)	16.20	(1-1)
Shields (Berrington, Tait)	45.01 pp	(4-2)
Shields (Tait)	52.31	(4-3)

Goalies:
Terentjev EST *Shots*: 12- 9-17 38 *Save %*: 92.1
Cavallin GB *Shots*: 10-24-11 45 *Save %*: 91.1
Penalty minutes: Estonia 8, Britain 12.
Goals/powerplays: Estonia 2/5, Britain 1/3
GB Man of Match: Shields.
Referee: Ryhed SWE   *Attendance*: 500.

After 'Lobby' equalised Estonia's opening goal, GB went to sleep and Cavallin had to pull off some big stops in the second to prevent an avalanche. One shot even clipped the underside of the bar before rebounding out.

As against the Italians, GB spotted their opponents three goals before rallying and then Shields' two late efforts were not enough to lift the team into the hoped-for fourth place.

Describing the loss as "heartbreaking", McSorley said: "We didn't get a concerted effort from all 22 guys."

18 April 2003, Dom Sportova, Zagreb

BRITAIN-CROATIA   7-1 (1-1,3-0,3-0)

GB scoring:

Moody (Berrington, Hurley)	.4.42	(1-0)
Thornton (Longstaff, Wilson)	23.12	(2-1)
Longstaff (Thornton, Hoad)	26.25	(3-1)
Shields (Tait, Campbell)	36.41	(4-1)
Wilson (Thornton, Hoad)	42.47	(5-1)
Berrington (Phillips, Hurley)	47.32	(6-1)
Hoad (Longstaff, Weaver)	54.45 pp	(7-1)

Goalies:
Watkins GB *Shots*: 14- 7- 9 30 *Save %*: 96.7
Martinovic CRO
            Shots: 12-15-18 45 *Save %*: 84.4
Penalty minutes: GB 107 (Bailey, Campbell, Galazzi - fighting 5+match, Owen game misc.), Croatia 83 (Kuznar, Mladenovic, Sertic - fighting 5+match).
GB Man of Match: Wilson
Referee: Albers USA   *Attendance*: 4,500.

A win at last but hardly in the best of circumstances as defeat would have doomed GB to relegation. And it took a full period before Britain got on top of the pesky homers and their noisy partisan crowd.

Even then disaster struck in the last three minutes when tiredness (their fourth difficult game in five days) and weak ref'ing (Albers called nothing for the first half of the game) led to a bust-up, with Campbell and Bailey (in a rare shift for the Brit) in the thick of it.

The three match penalties left GB short for their final game of the tournament while McSorley was reduced to complaining yet again about the lack of player development in Britain.

20 April 2003, Dom Sportova, Zagreb

NORWAY-BRITAIN   3-2 (2-2,0-0,1-0)

GB scoring:
Longstaff (Thornton, Weaver)   0.16   (0-1)
Weaver (Longstaff, Thornton)   5.29   (1-2)
Goalies:
Wiberg NOR   *Shots:*   6- 4-11 21   *Save%:* 90.5
Cavallin GB   *Shots:* 15-23-13 51   *Save%:* 94.1
Penalty minutes: Norway 8, GB 14.
Goals/powerplays: Norway 0/6, GB 0-3.
GB Man of Match: Weaver.
Referee: Homola.   *Attendance:* 600.
The players agreed that this last game was their best of the tournament. "We get better as we go on," said McSorley.

With the spectre of relegation no longer hanging over GB, and Norway pressing as they were still in with a chance of gold, even a British win could not be ruled out. They made a great start as 'Lobby' put them on the scoreboard after only 16 seconds and Weaver made it 2-1 after NHLer **Espen Knutsen** equalised. But Knold tied it up again after 16 minutes.

"We weren't ready," admitted Norway's coach. "I had to wake them up for the second."

But even with GB taking four minors in 20 minutes - once allowing a five-on-three for a full minute - Norway couldn't break down GB's defence until Marthinsen capitalised on a loose rebound early in the last session.

Thornton's sweet play

STEWART ROBERTS

Another year, another World Championship, another disappointment. But if not winning promotion means GB and their devoted fans are going to be disappointed, then there will always be a lot of disappointed people.

Even coach **Chris McSorley** is beginning to appreciate the magnitude of the task he has taken on, because British ice hockey is just not geared towards winning world glory, only domestic titles.

Many fans realise this but it doesn't stop them supporting their national side. Around 100 of them travelled to the pleasant city of Zagreb to see their heroes lose perhaps the most difficult tournament they've entered since Pool A in 1994. Hosts Croatia were the only weak nation.

The opposition was so good that only a real optimist had expected GB to top the six-team group. France, Italy and Norway are all fringe A

Pool nations, Estonia are notoriously unpredictable and home teams are under-estimated at your peril.

But most had predicted a good deal better than fifth place (the worst since Slovenia in 1998), especially as McSorley had arranged a week-long training camp in Zagreb when GB twice beat their hosts in friendlies (see later). The low finish was particularly hard to swallow because, as **Mike Ewer** pointed out on his website, www.eurohockey.net -

---

BEST PLAYERS

Fabrice Lhenry, of France, took the title of Goalkeeper of the Tournament. **Espen Knutsen** of Norway, who plays his hockey at Columbus in the NHL, was the best forward and top points scorer.

- GB's **Steve Thornton** was tied with Norway's NHLer **Espen Knutsen** for most points (nine),
- Thornton had the most assists (eight),
- GB's **Colin Shields** tied with 'Shampoo' Knutsen for most goals (four),
- GB were the only nation with two players (Thornton and **David Longstaff**) in the top five points scorers,
- GB's **Rob Wilson** and **Jonathan Weaver** (playing out of his normal position) were the highest scoring defencemen,
- Weaver, Wilson and Longstaff (in that order) were the leading plus/minus players,
- GB goalie **Mark Cavallin** was runner-up in save percentage behind France's **Fabrice Lhenry**.
- GB finished above .500 with a plus-two goal difference in all games.
- GB drew with Division I champs, France.

But, of course, this is a team game and as a team, GB did not play well enough, often enough. This is the World Championships where you have five hard games in seven short days and you have to bring your 'A' game every time. In the British National League, where most GB players ply their trade, games are only played twice a week, at an intensity of at best 70 per cent of a world championship game.

McSorley was forced into drawing attention to the fact that just about every one of the players whom he iced regularly, played or learned the game overseas. A glance at the scoring chart will prove his point. To critics who say he shouldn't have shortened his bench, and should have allowed native Brits more ice-time, that's the job of club coaches in league games, not the national coach in a world championship.

There were two cheering stories, however, one involving Thornton and the other, Weaver. Steve joined Belfast in mid-season after a long battle to recover from a knee injury which nearly ended his career.

-169-

His 30 odd games for Giants were enough to have him really hit his stride in Zagreb where he centred GB's number one line between Longstaff and Shields. His speed, vision and soft hands won him two selections as GB's best player.

The shortage of defencemen, already acute, worsened when **Neil Liddiard** and **James Morgan** both had to pull out because of work commitments. The GB players are amateurs, another reason they struggle in world play.

Fortunately, McSorley unearthed a new defensive talent in Fife's Weaver who was praised by his teammates and coach for his intelligent play. The converted forward, who'd had a difficult season after playing with two troubled clubs, Scottish Eagles and Hull Thunder, took to his new duties like the proverbial duck.

Overcoming a groin injury which he suffered during the training camp, he wasn't fully fit until game four and then surprised himself by how much he enjoyed his new role. "I thought it would be a lot harder than it was," he said.

McSorley worked tirelessly to motivate his players, and was invariably animated not just on the bench but often down by the boards. He was always focused for the full 60 minutes.

Thankfully, he gave no sign of wanting to quit his (unpaid) post but he conceded: "It's going to take longer than I thought to build a team that can qualify for the Olympics."

☐ Friendlies in Zagreb:

9 April - **GB-Croatia 3-1**. *GB scorers*: Pope, Weaver, Clarke. *GB goal*: Cavallin 17 shots.

10 April - **GB-Croatia 4-0**. *GB scorers*: Owen, Berrington, Longstaff, Pope. *GB goal*: Watkins 16 shots.

BRITAIN'S RECORD 1989-2002

2002   **Divison I/B**
Szeskesfehervar and Dunaujvaros, Hungary.
Coach: **Chris McSorley** (Geneva)
Denmark 3-5, Hungary 1-4, Romania 5-2,
China 8-3, Norway 1-2.
World Ranking: 20th. *Group standing*: 4th

2001   **Pool B**, Ljubljana, Slovenia
Coach: **Chris McSorley** (London)
Estonia 6-2, Croatia 10-1, Slovenia 3-3,
China 12-1, Kazakhstan 11-2.
World Ranking: **18th**. *Group Standing*: 2nd.

2000   **Pool B**, Katowice, Poland
Coach: **Peter Woods** (Superleague)
Estonia 5-6, Slovenia 3-3, Netherlands 9-0,
Poland 6-4, Denmark 5-4, Kazakhstan 3-1,
Germany 0-5.
World Ranking: 19th.

1999   **Pool B**, Copenhagen, Denmark
Coach: **Peter Woods** (Superleague)
Slovenia 2-1, Kazakhstan 1-0, Germany 2-3,
Estonia 6-2, Poland 4-3, Hungary 4-2,
Denmark 5-5.
World Ranking: 18th

1998   **Pool B**, Ljubljana/Jesenice, Slovenia.
Coach: Peter Woods (Superleague).
Ukraine 1-6, Denmark 7-1, Estonia 4-5,
Slovenia 3-5,
Poland 4-3, Norway 3-4, Netherlands 10-3.
World Ranking: 22nd

1997   **Pool B**, Katowice/Sosnowiec, Poland
Coach: **Peter Woods** (Basingstoke)
Poland 3-4, Kazakhstan 2-4, Netherlands 8-2,
Denmark 9-1, Austria 2-2, Switzerland 2-3,
Belarus 2-6.
World Ranking: 18th

1996   **Pool B**, Eindhoven, Netherlands
Coach: **Peter Woods** (Basingstoke).
Latvia 5-6, Switzerland 2-7, Poland 4-2,
Netherlands 6-2, Japan 3-3, Denmark 5-1,
Belarus 4-2.
World Ranking: 16th

1995   **Pool B**, Bratislava, Slovakia.
Coach: **George Peternousek** (unatt.)
Slovakia 3-7, Romania 0-2, Netherlands 3-2,
Denmark 2-9, Japan 3-4, Poland 4-3, Latvia 4-8.
World Ranking: 19th

1994   **Pool A** in Bolzano, Italy.
Coach: **Alex Dampier** (Sheffield)
Russia 3-12, .Germany 0-4, Italy 2-10,
Canada 2-8,   Austria 0-10, Norway 2-5.
World Ranking: 12th

1993   **Pool B** in Eindhoven, Netherlands.
Coach: **Alex Dampier** (Sheffield).
Poland 4-3, Denmark 4-0, Japan 5-4,
Bulgaria 10-0,
Netherlands 3-2, Romania 10-4, China 14-0.
World Ranking: 13th

1992   **Pool C** in Hull, England.
Coach: **Alex Dampier** (Nottingham).
Australia 10-2, S Korea 15-0, Belgium 7-3,
N Korea 16-2, Hungary 14-3.
World Ranking: 21st

1991   **Pool C** in Copenhagen, Denmark.
Coach: **Alex Dampier** (Nottingham).
China 5-6, N Korea 7-2, Denmark 2-3,
Belgium 11-0,
Hungary 3-3, Bulgaria 4-5, S Korea 7-1,
Romania 6-5.
World Ranking: 21st

1990   **Pool D** in Cardiff, Wales.
Coach: **Alex Dampier** (Nottingham)
Australia 14-0, 13-3; Spain 13-1, 17-3.
World Ranking: 26th

1989   **Pool D** in Belgium.
Coach: **Terry Matthews** (Whitley Bay).
New Zealand 26-0, Romania 6-6, Belgium 5-6,
Spain 8-4.
World Ranking: 27th

BRITAIN 2002-03

All players listed (51) competed for Britain in the Euro Challenge series, except Scott Campbell. Players and staff shown in bold also participated in the World Championships.

Name (in club order)	Pos	Birth Date	GP	Club/Lge	Birth Place
Joe Watkins	G	**27.10.79**	**7 (10)**	**Bracknell/ISL**	**Durham**
Stephen Murphy	G	**11.12.81**	**3 (3)**	**Dundee/BNL**	**Dundee**
#Ryan Ford	G	2.9.80	0 (3)	Edinburgh/BNL	Edinburgh
#Grant King	G	15.11.77	2 (3)	Guildford/BNL	London, England
#Andy Moffat	G	9.5.82	2 (3)	I of Wight/EPL	Scotland
Barry Hollyhead	G	4.6.75	0 (3)	M Keynes/EPL	England
#*Mark Cavallin	G	20.10.71	6 (7)	**Scot Eagles/ISL**	**Mississauga, Ont.**
Neil Liddiard	D	7.3.78	8	Basingstoke/BNL	Swindon
#Chris Bailey	D	5.1.82	13	Cardiff/BNL	Beverley, Hull
#James Pease	D	10.9.81	9	Coventry/BNL	Torquay
#Chris Conaboy	D	12.6.81	3	Dundee/BNL	Glasgow
Kyle Horne	D	**13.9.82**	**14**	**Fife/BNL**	**Kirkcaldy**
#Karl Hopper	D	21.2.80	6	Hull/BNL	Hull
*Rob Wilson	D	18.7.68	8	Manchester/ISL	Toronto
*Scott Campbell	D	22.1.72	4	Newcastle/BNL	Glasgow
#Ian Defty	D	20.4.79	6	Newcastle/BNL	Durham
#Richard Thornton	D	4.10.82	6	Newcastle/BNL	Hartlepool
#James Morgan	D	2.5.82	3	Nottingham/ISL	P'boro', England
#*Rob Coutts	D	18.3.67	3	Slough/EPL	England
#Scott Moody	D	6.9.79	13	**Slough/EPL**	**England**
*Brent Pope	D	20.2.73	14	**Solihull/BNL**	**Hamilton, Ont**
*Rick Strachan	D	27.3.63	3	Solihull/BNL	Winnipeg
*Paul Berrington	F	24.1.75	17	**Basingstoke/BNL**	**Kitchener, Ontario**
Nick Cross	F	7.4.76	3	Basingstoke/BNL	Coulsden, Surrey
*Mike Ellis	F	21.5.73	8	**Basingstoke/BNL**	**Burlington, Ont**
#Marc Levers	F	30.6.81	3	Basingstoke/BNL	Derby
*Steve Thornton	F	8.3.73	8	**Belfast/ISL**	**Edmonton**
*Darren Hurley	F	14.6.73	8	**Bracknell/ISL**	**Toronto**
#Jonathan Phillips	F	14.7.82	14	**Cardiff/BNL**	**Cardiff**
Rick Plant	F	23.11.77	6	Guildford/BNL	Telford
Warren Tait	F	17.4.81	3	Cardiff/BNL	Nottingham
#Russ Cowley	F	12.8.83	8	**Coventry/BNL**	**Edmonton, Alberta**
#Tom Watkins	F	6.3.78	6	Coventry/BNL	Durham
#Dominic Hopkins	F	3.8.80	3	Dundee/BNL	Reading, Berks
#Paul Sample	F	26.5.82	3	Dundee/BNL	North Shields
Gary Wishart	F	28.8.81	6	Dundee/BNL	Kirkcaldy
Jonathan Weaver	F	**21.1.77**	**8**	**Fife/BNL**	**Sunderland**
David Clarke	F	**5.8.81**	**11**	**Guildford/BNL**	**Peterborough**
#Mark Galazzi	F	15.11.77	10	Guildford/BNL	Camberley, Surrey
Ashley Tait	F	**9.8.75**	**8**	**Guildford/BNL**	**Toronto**
#Mark Florence	F	30.12.79	9	Hull/BNL	Hull
*Jeff Hoad	F	26.1.73	11	**London/ISL**	**Brandon, Man.**
David Longstaff	F	**26.8.74**	**8**	**Manchester/ISL**	**Whitley Bay**
#Greg Owen	F	19.6.81	14	**M Keynes/EPL**	**Northampton, Eng**
#Simon Leach	F	3.8.74	3	Newcastle/BNL	North Shields
#Danny Marshall	F	14.5.77	6	Romford/EPL	England
#Adam Bicknell	F	10.4.80	6	Slough/EPL	England
#Jason Reilly	F	8.1.71	6	Slough/EPL	England
Paul Moran	F	10.9.83	3	Solihull/BNL	Nottingham
Rob Lamey	F	4.9.80	6	Swindon-IOW/EPL	England
#Mark Richardson	F	3.10.86	3	Swindon/EPL	England
Colin Shields	F	**27.1.80**	**5**	**Un of Maine, USA**	**Glasgow**

Head Coach: **Chris McSorley** (Geneva). *Asst coaches:* **Gary Stefan** (BNL), **Rick Strachan** SOL.
Managers: Andy French (ISL), John Bailey (unatt.), Jim Graves BEL, Gill Short (Ice Hockey UK).
Team captains: Paul Berrington BAS; Steve Thornton BEL; **David Longstaff** (Switz.); Brent Pope, Paul Moran SOL.
*# New cap (7/23). * Dual national (9/11).*
GP - Maximum - 5 World, 12 Euro Chall. (For goalies, this is games actually iced in. Games selected for are shown in brackets.)
Note - Paul Berrington is a Canada-born Brit who acquired Canadian nationality in 2001.

EURO CHALLENGE

Twelve of Europe's middle-ranking nations played a series of games among themselves during season 2002-03.

The idea came from the French who believed these countries needed more international competition to help them blood new players.

Britain played six of the other teams: Hungary, four 'Pool A' nations - Austria, Belarus, Slovenia and the Ukraine - and Italy who had been relegated to Division I only in May 2002.

The other sides were Denmark, France, Latvia, Norway and Poland.

Each competing country organised one of the four-nation tournaments, three during each of the IIHF's 'national team breaks' in August/September, November, December and February.

Britain's home games in Nottingham were organised by the National Ice Centre who paid Ice Hockey UK £6,000 for the rights to the tournament. Siemens and Findus were the main sponsors.

The away games were organised by Ice Hockey UK with financial assistance coming from the GB Supporters Club who contributed over £8,000 to the governing body during the season to assist with all the GB teams.

FIRST SERIES
Nottingham Arena, England
FINAL STANDINGS

	GP	W	L	D	GF	GA	Pts
Belarus BEL	3	3	0	0	12	3	6
Slovenia SLO	3	1	1	1	9	9	3
Hungary HUN	3	1	2	0	8	8	2
Britain GB	3	0	2	1	7	16	1

Game One, 30 August 2002

GB-SLOVENIA	4-4ot	(0-1,3-0,1-3,0-0)

GB scorers: Hoad 2g; Tait 1+1; Wishart 1g; Longstaff 3a; Levers, Liddiard 1a.
GB Man of Match: Longstaff.
Shots on Goal: Watkins GB 43, Klemen SLO 24.
Pims: GB 24, Slovenia 16.
Referee: Bervensky BEL. Attendance: 2,500 est.

Game One Notes: A cracking performance from netminder **Joe Watkins**....GB's first line of **Jeff Hoad-David Longstaff-Ashley Tait** really clicked....Coach **Chris McSorley** was impressed with GB's youngsters - "They showed some great intelligence"....The Slovenian coach said his country has only seven rinks and 200 registered players.

Game Two, 31 August 2002

BELARUS-GB	6-0	(3-0,2-0,1-0)

GB Man of Match: Berrington.
Shots on Goal:
Grishukevich BEL 24, Murphy GB 41.
Pims: Belarus 49 (Vinokovrov: match - fighting), GB 41 (Liddiard: match - fighting).
Referee: Arkovics SLO. Attendance: 2,500 est.

Challenge, 29 August 2002
Wales National Ice Rink, Cardiff
CARDIFF DEVILS-GB 2-3 (1-1,1-2, 0-0).
This was a rare example of a man, **Chris McSorley**, coaching one team, GB, against a team he part-owned. But it was Devils' 15-year-old netminder, **Nathan Craze**, who stole the show with a series of great stops in the first half before he was replaced by **Dan Wood**. Over 1,500 fans gave McSorley a warm welcome before Devils' first game under the GB coach's management.

GB scorers: Plant, Watkins, Levers 1g; Pope, Berrington, Clarke 1a. Devils' scorers: Knox, Cowmeadow 1g; Romaniuk, Brown, Phillips, Walsh 1a. Pims: Devils 32, GB 14. Shots on Goal: Craze/Wood CAR 34, Watkins./Murphy 47.
Referee: Gary Plaistow. Attendance: 1,532.

BRITAIN
Joe Watkins BRK, Stephen Murphy DUN; Neil Liddiard BAS, Kyle Horne FIF, Ian Defty, Richard Thornton NEW, Brent Pope, Rick Strachan SOL; David Clarke, Ricky Plant, Mike Ellis BAS, Nick Cross, Paul Berrington, Tom Watkins, Gary Wishart, Mark Florence, Mark Levers. Head coach: Chris McSorley. Manager: John Bailey.

Game Two Notes: GB could consider themselves a tad unlucky to be shutout: Belarus had lost to Hungary the day before and Britain got the backlash....Belarus went on to win the tournament. GB captain **David Longstaff** said: "They play game the way it's meant to be"....This was GB's second consecutive defeat by the former Soviet republic who had regained their 'Pool A' status in April. Britain won the only other game, 4-2 in Eindhoven in 1996....GB weren't as disappointed as Sweden were when Belarus knocked them out of the 2002 Olympics at the quarter-final stage!....Belarus were coached by **Vladimir Safonov** who coached Poland to defeat by Britain in the 1993 World Championship.

GB's Player of the Tournament
PAUL BERRINGTON
Selected by the GB Supporters' Club

Game Three - *1 September 2002*

| HUNGARY-GB | 6-3 | (1-1,2-1,3-1) |

GB scorers: Hoad 1+1; Wilson, Clarke 1g; Ellis, Levers 1a.
GB Man of Match: Cross.
Shots on Goal:
Levente HUN 21, Watkins GB 38.
Pims: Hungary 16, GB 10.
Referee: Dremel SLO. *Attendance:* 2,500 est.
Game Three Notes: McSorley reckoned this was Britain's best game of the three but not everyone agreed as GB ran out of steam in the third and Watkins was below par in goal.....GB were up against Hungary's 'secret weapon' - NHL goalie, **Levente Szuperman**. Against that, however, 'superman' wasn't really tested that much.... Longstaff failed to convert his penalty shot after **Mike Ellis** had been pulled down.... McSorley was upset at the absence of players like **Jonathan Weaver, Tony Hand, Paul Dixon** and **Stevie Lyle**. "They might have lost their privilege [to play for GB]," he hinted darkly.... Assistant coach, **Paul Thompson**, resigned before the games began, citing "the pressures of his full-time commitment to Coventry Blaze and his young family". His place was taken by GB's veteran dual national defender, **Rick Strachan**, who retired from international play after this tournament.

BRITAIN
The team in Nottingham
Joe Watkins BRK, Stephen Murphy DUN; Neil Liddiard BAS, Kyle Horne FIF, *Rob Wilson MAN, #Ian Defty, #Richard Thornton NEW, *Brent Pope, *Rick Strachan SOL; *Paul Berrington, Nick Cross, *Mike Ellis, #Marc Levers BAS, Jonathan Phillips CAR, Ashley Tait, Tom Watkins COV, Gary Wishart FIF, David Clarke, Rick Plant GUI, #Mark Florence HUL, *Jeff Hoad LON, David Longstaff MAN (capt.)
Head coach: Chris McSorley (Geneva).
Manager: John Bailey (unatt.).
* Dual national (6). # New cap (4).

McQUOTE
"Surround the women and children, lock arms and wait for the Indians!"
"We look like David against Europe's Goliath but that contest came out well for the little guy."
The GB coach on his team's chances in the Euro Challenge games.
"I took off all my clothes, lay on the physio's table, adopted the foetal position and sucked my thumb."
Asked what he did in the dressing room after GB went 5-0 behind to Belarus after two periods.

SECOND SERIES
Szekesfehervar, Hungary
FINAL STANDINGS

	GP	W	L	D	GF	GA	Pts
Ukraine UKR	3	3	0	0	14	0	6
Slovenia	3	1	1	1	6	8	3
Britain	3	1	2	0	3	8	2
Hungary	3	0	2	1	2	9	1

Game Four, *8 November 2002*

| GB-SLOVENIA | 1-4 | (0-1,0-1,1-2) |

GB scoring: Berrington (Watkins, Horne) pp 56.28.
GB Man of Match: Berrington.
Shots on Goal: Cavallin GB 29, Glacvic SLO 14
Pims: GB 14, Slovenia 18.
Referee: Urda. *Attendance:* not recorded.
Game Four Notes: GB's first defeat by Slovenia since the 1998 World B Pool in Ljubljana.... Rookie defenceman **James Pease**, 21, was voted man of the match by the GB Supporters Club.

Game Five, 9 November 2002

UKRAINE-GB   4-0   (1-0,2-0,1-0)

GB Man of Match: Cavallin.
Shots on Goal: no record. GB goalie: Cavallin
Seliverstov UKR 12, Cavallin GB 40.
Pims: Ukraine 10, GB 16.
Referee: Trillar.   Attendance: 300.
Game Five Notes: The former Soviet republic
are ranked ninth in the world and iced five NHL
draftees....In only his second game for GB,
Superleague netminder, **Mark Cavallin**, had a 90
per cent save rate and was a key factor in this
far-from-embarrassing result.

GB's Player of the Tournament
MARK CAVALLIN
Selected by the GB Supporters' Club

Game Six, 10 November 2002

HUNGARY-GB   0-2   (0-0,0-2,0-0)

GB scoring:
0-1 Clarke (Pope, Watkins)   pp   27.03
0-2 Watkins (Clarke, Berrington)   31.30
GB Man of Match: Cavallin.
Shots on Goal: Budai HUN 18, Cavallin GB 30.
Pims: Hungary 8, GB 8.
Referee: Urda.   Attendance: not recorded.
Game Six Notes: This turned out to be GB's only
win of the 12-game series. It was achieved in
fine style with a shutout for Cavallin....That said,
Hungary, the host team, were the weakest side
here, even though 15 of their squad played on
the 2002 World Championship team that beat
GB....Then again, Hungary's goalie, **Levente**
(Superman) **Szuper**, was playing in North
America... Coach McSorley said: "Outside of
bringing home the silver medal two years ago,
this has been one of my proudest moments in ice
hockey!"...Former Sheffield Steeler, **Frank
Kovacs**, a veteran of the Hungarian side,
enquired: "Who are these guys? They're better
than the team you sent to the World
Championships."....It was unclear whether it was
their clubs or the players themselves who left GB
without two of their best goalies - Cardiff's **Stevie
Lyle** and Dundee's **Stephen Murphy**....This was
the last tournament for GB's manager, **John
Bailey**, who had been with the team since the
2001 World Championships....The tournament's
best forward, Ukraine's **Dmitri Khristich**, played
811 NHL games between 1990 and 2002 and
played for Ukraine in the Salt Lake City
Olympics....The games were sponsored by
pharmaceutical giants, Astra-Zeneca....The
legend of Hungary being a two-rink nation was

spoiled in December 2002 when a third one,
seating 9,000, opened in the capital, Budapest....
Only five intrepid supporters made their way
back to Szekesfehervar - maybe they were the
only five who could spell it!

BRITAIN
The team in Hungary
Barry Hollyhead MIL, *Mark Cavallin SCO; Chris
Bailey CAR, #James Pease COV, Kyle Horne
FIF, #Karl Hopper HUL, Ian Defty, Richard
Thornton NEW, Scott Moody SLO, *Brent Pope
SOL (capt); *Paul Berrington BAS, Warren Tait
CAR, Tom Watkins COV, Gary Wishart DUN,
David Clarke, Ricky Plant GUI, Mark Florence
HUL, #Greg Owen MIL, #Danny Marshall ROM,
#Adam Bicknell SLO, Paul Moran SOL (capt),
Rob Lamey SWI.
Head Coach: Chris McSorley (Geneva).
Manager: John Bailey (unatt.)
* dual national (3), # new cap (5)
Note Brent Pope was captain in the first two
games and Paul Moran in the last.

THIRD SERIES
Palace of Sport, Kiev, Ukraine
FINAL STANDINGS

	GP	W	L	D	GF	GA	Pts
Belarus	3	3	0	0	23	9	6
Ukraine	3	2	1	0	16	4	4
Hungary	3	1	2	0	9	14	2
Britain	3	0	3	0	5	26	0

Game Seven, 13 December 2002

BELARUS-GB   10-3   (4-0,2-2,4-1)

GB scoring: Liddiard 1+1; Berrington, Cowley 1g;
Horne, Leach 1a.
GB Man of Match: Liddiard.
Shots on Goal:
Mezin/Grishukevich BEL 14, King GB 40.
Pims: Belarus 14, GB 34 (Horne 2+10
check-behind, Berrington 10-misc).
Referee: Incze.   Attendance: 2,300.
Game Seven Notes: GB took the youngest side
ever picked to represent this country at senior
level. The average age was 23....Newcastle
Vipers forward **Simon Leach** was the old man at
28 and Swindon's **Mark Richardson** set a record
with his first appearance for the senior squad at
the tender age of 16 years and two
months....These games were something of a
poisoned chalice for coach **Rick Strachan** who
was standing in for McSorley but he was proud of
his team. "They knew they were in for a pasting
but they kept working hard," he said....Belarus
leads GB 1-3-0 in all-time games.

Game Eight, 14 December 2002

UKRAINE-GB   11-0   (3-0,4-0,4-0)

GB Man of Match: Galazzi.
Shots on Goal: Simchuk UKR 9, Moffat GB 64.
Pims: Ukraine 43 (Klymentyev (5+game - roughing), GB 45 (Conaboy 5+game - roughing).
Referee: Incze.   *Attendance*: 7,000
Game Eight Notes: The third shutout of the tournament for GB....Scots goalie **Andy Moffat** had the misfortune to gain his first cap in Britain's most one-sided defeat since the 1994 World A Pool games in Bolzano....This was GB's third defeat by Ukraine in four internationals. They drew 2-2 in the Olympic qualifier in Sheffield in 1999.

GB's Player of the Tournament
GREG OWEN
Selected by the GB Supporters Club

Game Nine, 15 December 2002

BRITAIN-HUNGARY   2-5   (0-1,1-2,1-2)

GB scoring: Cowley (pp), Liddiard (pp) 1g; Berrington 2a; Horne, Leach 1a.
GB Man of Match: Leach.
Shots on Goal:
Moffat/King GB 27, Budai HUN 16.
Pims: Britain 57 (Conaboy match - fighting, Bailey 2+2+10-misc - roughing), Hungary 47 (Horvath match - fighting).
Referee: Bervensky.   *Attendance*: 3,000
Game Nine Notes: Coventry's **Russ Cowley**, the son of Blaze owner **Mike Cowley**, made an impressive start to his international career, scoring two of Britain's five goals in this tournament....The nations' all-time W-L-T record now stands at 3-2-2 in GB's favour.

BRITAIN
The team in the Ukraine:
#Grant King GUI, #Andy Moffat IOW; Neil Liddiard BAS, Chris Bailey CAR, James Pease COV, #Chris Conaboy DUN, Kyle Horne FIF, Karl Hopper HUL, #Scott Moody SLO; *Paul Berrington BAS (capt), Greg Owen BRK, Jonathan Phillips CAR, #Russ Cowley COV, #Paul Sample DUN, #Mark Galazzi GUI, Mark Florence HUL, #Simon Leach NEW, Danny Marshall ROM, Adam Bicknell SLO, #Mark Richardson SWI.
Coach: Rick Strachan SOL.
Manager: Jim Graves BEL.
* dual national (1). # new cap (9).

FOURTH SERIES
Villach, Austria

	GP	W	L	D	GF	GA	Pts
Austria AUT	3	1	0	2	14	9	4
Italy ITA	3	1	0	2	8	7	4
Slovenia	3	1	1	1	8	7	3
Britain	3	0	2	1	6	13	1

Game Ten, 7 February 2003

SLOVENIA-GB   4-2 (1-0,1-1,2-1)

GB scoring: Morgan, Thornton (sh) 1g.
Shots on Goal: no record. *GB goalie*: Watkins.
Pims: Slovenia 18, GB 30.
Referee: Mair AUT   *Attendance*: 200.
Game Ten Notes: A disappointing start after Superleague regulars **Darren Hurley, Jeff Hoad** and **Joe Watkins** had been added to the squad along with newly fit **Steve Thornton** and Fife's **Jonathan Weaver**...But Slovenia had a strong squad and GB were jaded after a five-hour bus journey from Vienna airport....The third forward line of Greg Owen-Mark Galazzi-Rob Lamey were a revelation but the performances of some of the more talented players were patchy....The nations' all-time W-L-T record now stands at 3-3-3.

GB's Player of the Tournament
JOE WATKINS
Selected by the GB Supporters' Club

Game Eleven, 8 February 2003

GB-ITALY   1-1 (0-0,0-1,1-0,0-0)

GB scoring: Weaver (Morgan) 41.58 pp.
Shots on Goal: Watkins GB 56, Carpano ITA 39.
Pims: GB 16, Italy 16.
Referee: Popovic SLO   *Attendance*: 250
Game Eleven Notes: An excellent result against this former 'Pool A' nation and a good omen for the forthcoming World Championships where the two countries will meet again....The Italians were icing a similar squad to the one they were expected to take to Zagreb....The last time the teams met - in the 1994 A Pool - Italy won 10-2....Britain's goal was scored in unusual circumstances, in a six-on-three situation after coach McSorley, typically, pulled Watkins after two Italians had been penalised....All-time W-L-T record now 3-4-1 to Italy.

Game Twelve, 9 February 2003

AUSTRIA-GB   8-3 (2-1,6-2,0-0)

GB scoring: Galazzi (pp), Owen (pp), Reilly 1g;
Lamey, Pope 2a.
Shots on Goal:
Prohaska AUT 24, Watkins GB 42.
Pims: Austria 41 (Pfeffer 5+game - roughing),
GB 35 (Hurley 5+game - roughing).
Referee: Popovic SLO.   *Attendance*: 600
Game Twelve Notes: Britain just didn't turn up
for the second period against the world's 12th
ranked nation who poured a demoralising six
goals past Watkins in just over 11 minutes....The
loss wasn't the Bracknell 'tender's fault. He
played some of his best international hockey in
this series.

GB FOR THE BRITS

"In ice hockey, I reckon if you can't make your own
national team then you shouldn't play international
hockey." *Mark Florence of Hull Thunder with his
thoughts on the use of dual nationals in the GB
team.*   Hull Daily Mail.

BRITAIN

The team in Austria:
Joe Watkins BRK, #Ryan Ford EDI; Neil Liddiard
BAS, Chris Bailey CAR, James Pease COV,
James Morgan NOT, #*Rob Coutts, Scott Moody
SLO, *Brent Pope SOL; *Paul Berrington BAS
(capt), *Steve Thornton BEL, *Darren Hurley
BRK, Jonathan Phillips CAR, #Dominic Hopkins
DUN, Jonathan Weaver FIF, Mark Galazzi GUI,
Rob Lamey IOW, *Jeff Hoad LON, Greg Owen
MIL, #Jason Reilly SLO.
Head Coach: Chris McSorley (Geneva).
Manager: Gill Short (Ice Hockey UK).
* dual national (6)   # new cap (4)
Selected but did not travel: defence - *Scott
Campbell, *Rob Wilson NEW; forwards - David
Clarke GUI, Danny Meyers SOL.
Note Steve Thornton was captain in the game
against Italy.

FINAL STANDINGS

GB games only	GP	W	L	D	GF	GA	Pts
Britain	**12**	**1**	**9**	**2**	**21**	**63**	**4**
Ukraine	2	2	0	0	15	0	4
Belarus	2	2	0	0	16	3	4
Hungary	3	2	1	0	11	7	4
Slovenia	3	2	0	1	12	7	3
Austria	1	1	0	0	8	3	2
Italy	1	0	0	1	1	1	1

COMPLETE BRITISH SCORING

All series	GP	G	A	Pts	Pim
Paul Berrington	12	2	3	5	28
Jeff Hoad	6	3	1	4	2
Neil Liddiard	8	2	2	4	43
David Clarke	6	2	1	3	18
Tom Watkins	6	1	2	3	0
David Longstaff	3	0	3	3	4
Brent Pope	9	0	3	3	16
Kyle Horne	9	0	3	3	18
Russ Cowley	3	2	0	2	2
Ashley Tait	3	1	1	2	2
James Morgan	3	1	1	2	8
Marc Levers	3	0	2	2	2
Simon Leach	3	0	2	2	6
Rob Lamey	6	0	2	2	4
Jonathan Weaver	3	1	0	1	2
Rob Wilson	3	1	0	1	2
Jason Reilly	3	1	0	1	4
Steve Thornton	3	1	0	1	4
Gary Wishart	6	1	0	1	2
Mark Galazzi	6	1	0	1	8
Greg Owen	9	1	0	1	2
Mike Ellis	3	0	1	1	2
TEAM TOTALS	**12**	**21**	**27**	**48**	**330**

Giving youth a chance

GB won only one of their 12 games in the newly
established Euro Challenge series. But winning
wans't really the name of the game. The idea
was to give prospective young players a run-out
with the national squad and exactly 50 players
enjoyed the privilege.

The very nature of the tournament meant that
GB never had a settled squad and was not the
ideal preparation for the World Championships.

But the Geneva-based McSorley was able to run
the rule over the youngsters - who mostly
acquitted themselves well - and to discover
which players really cared about playing for their
national team.

With the opposition coming mostly from the
lower reaches of the world's elite group,
assistant coach **Gary Stefan** declared: "The
determination and hard work of our players
showed we could play with Pool A countries."

BRITAIN's SENIOR PLAYER REGISTER 1989-2003
Forwards and Defencemen

ADEY Paul   b. 28-Aug-63

Club	Year	Comp	GP	G	A	Pts	PIM
Not	1995	OQ	3	1	0	1	0
Not	1996	WC	7	4	4	8	10
Not	1996	OQ	5	3	4	7	0
Not	1997	WC	7	5	1	6	4
Not	1998	WC	7	4	4	8	4
Not	1999	WC	7	3	3	6	2
Milan	1999	WCQ	4	0	0	0	0
Milan	2000	OQ	3	3	1	4	27
Milan	2000	WC	7	2	5	7	14
She	2001	WC	5	3	2	5	4
		Totals	55	28	24	52	65

BAILEY Chris   b. 05-Jan-82

Club	Year	Comp	GP	G	A	Pts	PIM
Car	2002	EC	9	0	0	0	20
Car	2003	WC	4	0	0	0	25
		Totals	13	0	0	0	45

BENNETT Ivor   b. 29-Jul-61

Club	Year	Comp	GP	G	A	Pts	PIM
Dur	1989	WC	4	0	1	1	2

BERRINGTON Paul   b.24-Jan-75

Club	Year	Comp	GP	G	A	Pts	PIM
Dun	2002	WC	5	1	1	2	6
Bas	2002	EC	12	2	3	5	28
Bas	2003	WC	5	1	2	3	2
		Totals	22	4	6	10	36

BIDNER Todd   b. 5-Jul-61

Club	Year	Comp	GP	G	A	Pts	PIM
Una	1993	OQ	4	1	1	2	4

BISHOP Mike   b. 15-Jun-66

Club	Year	Comp	GP	G	A	Pts	PIM
Hum	1995	OQ	3	0	0	0	0
Hum	1996	WC	7	1	1	2	22
Not	1996	OQ	5	1	3	4	12
Not	1997	WC	7	2	1	3	45
Not	1998	WC	7	1	0	1	12
Ayr	2000	WC	7	0	3	3	18
		Totals	36	5	8	13	109

BOBYCK Brent   b. 26-Apr-68

Club	Year	Comp	GP	G	A	Pts	PIM
Not	1999	WCQ	4	0	0	0	0
Not	2000	OQ	3	0	1	1	0
		Totals	7	0	1	1	0

BOE Vince   b. 23-Dec-70

Club	Year	Comp	GP	G	A	Pts	PIM
Ayr	1999	WC	7	0	2	2	16
Ayr	1999	WCQ	1	0	0	0	4
Ayr	2000	OQ	3	0	1	1	2
		Totals	11	0	3	3	22

BREBANT Rick   b. 21-Feb-64

Club	Year	Comp	GP	G	A	Pts	PIM
Car	1994	WC	6	1	0	1	8
Dur	1995	OQ	1	0	0	0	0
Man	1998	WC	7	3	5	8	10
Man	1999	WCQ	3	0	1	1	4
Lon	2000	OQ	3	1	2	3	42
Lon	2000	WC	7	4	4	8	14
She	2002	WC	5	1	1	2	0
		Totals	32	10	13	23	78

CAMPBELL Scott   b. 22-Jan-72

Club	Year	Comp	GP	G	A	Pts	PIM
Lon	1999	WCQ	4	0	0	0	2
Gui	2002	WC	5	0	1	1	31
New	2003	WC	4	0	0	0	27
		Totals	13	0	1	1	60

CHARD Chris   b. 22-Jun-71

Club	Year	Comp	GP	G	A	Pts	PIM
Bas	1995	OQ	1	0	0	0	0

CHINN Nicky   b. 14-Sep-72

Club	Year	Comp	GP	G	A	Pts	PIM
Car	1993	OQ	2	0	0	0	0
Car	1994	WC	6	0	0	0	0
Car	1995	WC	4	1	2	3	4
She	1995	OQ	1	0	0	0	0
She	1996	OQ	3	1	0	1	2
She	1997	WC	7	1	1	2	29
She	1998	WC	7	1	2	3	31
Car	1999	WC	7	2	3	5	39
Car	2000	OQ	3	0	0	0	4
		Totals	40	6	8	14	109

CLARKE David   b. 5-Aug-81

Club	Year	Comp	GP	G	A	Pts	PIM
Pet	2000	WC	7	0	0	0	2
New	2001	WC	5	2	0	2	6
Lon	2002	WC	5	0	1	1	10
Gui	2002	EC	6	2	1	3	18
Gui	2003	WC	5	0	0	0	8
		Totals	28	4	2	6	44

CONWAY Kevin   b. 13-Jul-63

Club	Year	Comp	GP	G	A	Pts	PIM
Bas	1992	WC	5	13	10	23	6
Bas	1993	WC	7	8	11	19	8
Bas	1993	OQ	4	1	0	1	6
Bas	1994	WC	6	2	1	3	6
Bas	1995	OQ	3	2	1	3	6
Bas	1996	WC	7	3	2	5	6
Bas	1996	OQ	5	1	0	1	6
Bas	1997	WC	7	2	3	5	0
Bas	1998	WC	7	0	2	2	2
New	1999	WC	7	1	3	4	8
		Totals	58	33	33	66	54

COOPER Ian   b. 29-Nov-68

Club	Year	Comp	GP	G	A	Pts	PIM
Car	1989	WC	4	4	4	8	8
Car	1990	WC	4	6	5	11	8
Dur	1991	WC	8	4	2	6	16
Dur	1992	WC	5	3	6	9	8
Car	1993	WC	7	4	4	8	6
Car	1994	WC	6	1	0	1	4
Car	1995	WC	2	1	0	1	2
Car	1995	OQ	3	0	0	0	2
Car	1996	WC	7	0	2	2	10
Car	1996	OQ	5	1	2	3	2
Car	1997	WC	7	0	0	0	12
Car	1998	WC	7	3	2	5	38
Lon	1999	WC	7	1	2	3	2
Lon	1999	WCQ	1	0	0	0	0
Gui	2000	WC	7	2	2	4	10
		Totals	80	30	31	61	128

COOPER Stephen   b. 11-Nov-66

Club	Year	Comp	GP	G	A	Pts	PIM
Car	1989	WC	4	3	4	7	4
Car	1990	WC	4	3	6	9	8
Dur	1992	WC	5	1	4	5	4
Car	1993	WC	7	0	4	4	6
Car	1993	OQ	4	1	0	1	2
Car	1994	WC	6	0	1	1	4
Car	1995	OQ	3	0	0	0	10
Car	1996	WC	7	0	3	3	6
Man	1996	OQ	3	0	0	0	4
New	1999	WC	7	0	0	0	2
Not	1999	WCQ	4	1	1	2	2
Not	2000	WC	7	2	4	6	2
		Totals	61	11	27	38	54

COTE Matt   b. 19-Jan-66

Club	Year	Comp	GP	G	A	Pts	PIM
Brk	1994	WC	6	0	0	0	8
Brk	1995	WC	7	0	1	1	4
Brk	1996	OQ	4	0	0	0	2
Brk	1999	WC	7	0	1	1	2
Brk	1999	WCQ	4	0	0	0	0
Brk	2000	OQ	1	0	0	0	0
		Totals	29	0	2	2	16

COWLEY Russell   b. 12-Aug-83

Club	Year	Comp	GP	G	A	Pts	PIM
Cov	2002	EC	3	2	0	2	2
Cov	2003	WC	5	0	0	0	0
		Totals	8	2	0	2	2

CRAIPER Jamie   b. 29-Jan-60

Club	Year	Comp	GP	G	A	Pts	PIM
Brk	1990	WC	4	7	5	12	0
Brk	1991	WC	8	4	1	5	9
Brk	1992	WC	5	1	2	3	25
		Totals	17	12	8	20	34

CRANSTON Tim   b. 13-Dec-62

Club	Year	Comp	GP	G	A	Pts	PIM
She	1993	WC	7	3	1	4	41
She	1993	OQ	4	1	1	2	8
She	1994	WC	6	0	0	0	4
She	1995	OQ	3	0	2	2	6
She	1996	WC	7	4	4	8	14
She	1996	OQ	5	2	2	4	10
She	1997	WC	7	1	3	4	8
		Totals	39	11	13	24	91

DIXON Paul   b. 4-Aug-73

Club	Year	Comp	GP	G	A	Pts	PIM
Dur	1995	WC	5	1	1	2	2
Dur	1995	OQ	2	0	0	0	0
Dur	1996	WC	7	1	1	2	14
New	1996	OQ	2	0	1	1	0
New	1997	WC	7	0	1	1	0
New	1998	WC	4	0	2	2	2
New	1999	WC	7	0	1	1	0
Gui	1999	WCQ	3	0	0	0	2
Gui	2000	WC	7	0	2	2	0
Gui	2001	WC	5	1	2	3	0
Gui	2002	WC	5	0	3	3	2
		Totals	54	3	14	17	22

DURDLE Darren   b. 15-Aug-67

Club	Year	Comp	GP	G	A	Pts	PIM
Ber	1996	OQ	2	0	1	1	2
Ber	1998	WC	6	0	1	1	10
Ber	1999	WC	7	1	0	1	12
Car	1999	WCQ	4	1	2	3	8
Car	2000	OQ	3	1	2	3	4
		Totals	22	3	6	9	36

EDMISTON Dean   b. 12-Feb-69

Club	Year	Comp	GP	G	A	Pts	PIM
Pet	1991	WC	8	2	1	3	13
Med	1992	WC	4	1	3	4	2
		Totals	12	3	4	7	15

ELLIS Mike   b. 21-May-73

Club	Year	Comp	GP	G	A	Pts	PIM
Bas	2000	WC	7	1	1	2	0
Bas	2001	WC	5	0	2	2	10
Bas	2002	WC	5	0	1	1	0
Bas	2002	EC	3	0	1	1	2
Bas	2003	WC	5	0	0	0	8
		Totals	25	1	5	6	20

FERA Rick   b. 13-Aug-64

Club	Year	Comp	GP	G	A	Pts	PIM
Bas	1993	WC	7	6	13	19	18
Tra	1993	OQ	4	0	2	2	12
Tra	1994	WC	6	1	2	3	4
		Totals	17	7	17	24	34

GALAZZI Mark   b. 15-Nov-77

Club	Year	Comp	GP	G	A	Pts	PIM
Gui	2002	EC	6	1	0	1	8
Gui	2003	WC	4	0	0	0	25
		Totals	10	1	0	1	33

GARDEN Graham   b. 2-Jul-70

Club	Year	Comp	GP	G	A	Pts	PIM
Hum	1995	OQ	2	1	0	1	0
Hum	1996	WC	3	1	0	1	4
Deg	1996	OQ	5	0	0	0	2
Deg	1997	WC	7	1	0	1	10
Not	1999	WC	7	2	5	7	10
Not	2000	OQ	3	0	0	0	2
		Totals	27	5	5	10	28

HAND Paul   b. 24-Nov-65

Club	Year	Comp	GP	G	A	Pts	PIM
Mur	1989	WC	4	5	0	5	8
Fif	1990	WC	4	1	3	4	13
Fif	1991	WC	8	1	2	3	14
Mur	1992	WC	2	0	0	0	6
		Totals	18	7	5	12	41

HAND Tony   b. 15-Aug-67

Club	Year	Comp	GP	G	A	Pts	PIM
Mur	1989	WC	4	6	12	18	2
Mur	1990	WC	4	5	8	13	0
Mur	1991	WC	8	9	12	21	12
Mur	1992	WC	5	6	12	18	4
Mur	1993	WC	7	6	8	14	2
Mur	1993	OQ	4	0	2	2	4
Mur	1994	WC	6	0	0	0	0
Ayr	1999	WCQ	4	1	0	1	6
Ayr	2000	WC	7	2	8	10	2
Ayr	2001	WC	5	3	13	16	0
Dun	2002	WC	5	2	4	6	2
		Totals	59	40	79	119	34

HARDING Mike   b. 24-Feb-71

Club	Year	Comp	GP	G	A	Pts	PIM
Man	1999	WCQ	4	1	1	2	0
Man	2000	OQ	3	0	2	2	4
		Totals	7	1	3	4	4

BRITAIN's SENIOR PLAYER REGISTER 1989-2003
Forwards and Defencemen

HOAD Jeff   b. 26-Jan-73

Club	Year	Comp	GP	G	A	Pts	PIM
Bel	2002	WC	5	3	1	4	6
Lon	2002	EC	6	3	1	4	2
Lon	2003	WC	5	2	2	4	4
		Totals	16	8	4	12	12

HOPE Shannon   b. 25-Nov-62

Club	Year	Comp	GP	G	A	Pts	PIM
Car	1992	WC	2	0	0	0	0
Car	1993	WC	7	0	2	2	4
Car	1993	OQ	4	0	0	0	2
Car	1994	WC	6	0	1	1	14
Car	1995	WC	6	1	1	2	14
Car	1995	OQ	3	0	0	0	6
Car	1996	WC	7	0	1	1	8
Car	1996	OQ	4	0	1	1	28
Car	1997	WC	7	0	2	2	10
Car	1998	WC	7	0	0	0	2
		Totals	53	1	8	9	88

HORNE Kyle   b. 30-Sep-80

Club	Year	Comp	GP	G	A	Pts	PIM
Fif	2001	WC	5	0	2	2	4
Fif	2002	EC	9	0	3	3	16
Fif	2003	WC	5	0	0	0	0
		Totals	19	0	5	5	20

HUNT Simon   b. 16-Apr-73

Club	Year	Comp	GP	G	A	Pts	PIM
Not	1995	OQ	3	1	0	1	2
Not	1996	WC	7	2	1	3	24
Not	1996	OQ	1	0	0	0	0
		Totals	11	3	1	4	26

HURLEY Darren   b. 14-Jun-73

Club	Year	Comp	GP	G	A	Pts	PIM
Man	1999	WC	7	1	1	2	8
Man	1999	WCQ	4	0	0	0	29
Car	2000	OQ	3	1	0	1	8
Car	2000	WC	7	1	3	4	32
Brk	2001	WC	5	2	2	4	12
Brk	2002	WC	5	4	0	4	39
Brk	2002	EC	3	0	0	0	31
Brk	2003	WC	5	0	2	2	10
		Totals	39	9	8	17	169

IREDALE John   b. 8-Oct-66

Club	Year	Comp	GP	G	A	Pts	PIM
Whi	1989	WC	4	5	4	9	4
Whi	1990	WC	4	0	1	1	4
Whi	1992	WC	5	1	0	1	4
Whi	1993	WC	7	0	3	3	0
Whi	1993	OQ	4	0	0	0	0
		Totals	24	6	8	14	12

JOHNSON Anthony   b. 4-Jan-69

Club	Year	Comp	GP	G	A	Pts	PIM
Dur	1990	WC	4	6	3	9	2
Hum	1991	WC	8	1	1	2	10
Hum	1992	WC	5	5	5	10	0
Hum	1993	WC	7	3	4	7	4
Hum	1993	OQ	4	0	0	0	4
		Totals	28	15	13	28	20

JOHNSON Shaun   b. 22-Mar-73

Club	Year	Comp	GP	G	A	Pts	PIM
Hum	1992	WC	4	1	2	3	2
New	2000	WC	7	0	1	1	0
Cov	2001	WC	5	1	4	5	4
		Totals	16	2	7	9	6

JOHNSON Stephen   b. 19-Jun-67

Club	Year	Comp	GP	G	A	Pts	PIM
Dur	1990	WC	4	2	6	8	0
Hum	1991	WC	8	4	3	7	2
Hum	1992	WC	4	1	0	1	0
Hum	1993	WC	7	3	3	6	4
		Totals	23	10	12	22	6

JOHNSTONE Jeff   b. 21-Sep-75

Club	Year	Comp	GP	G	A	Pts	PIM
Brk	1999	WC	7	4	2	6	4
Lon	1999	WCQ	4	0	1	1	0
Man	2000	OQ	3	0	0	0	2
		Totals	14	4	3	7	6

KENDALL Jason   b. 9-Jul-75

Club	Year	Comp	GP	G	A	Pts	PIM
Brk	2000	OQ	3	0	0	0	0

KELLAND Chris   b. 22-Dec-57

Club	Year	Comp	GP	G	A	Pts	PIM
Mur	1990	WC	4	3	5	8	0
Mur	1991	WC	7	3	2	5	22
Not	1992	WC	5	4	1	5	4
Not	1993	WC	5	0	0	0	4
She	1993	OQ	4	0	0	0	6
She	1994	WC	6	0	0	0	8
		Totals	31	10	8	18	44

KIDD John   b. 22-May-63

Club	Year	Comp	GP	G	A	Pts	PIM
Ayr	1989	WC	4	2	1	3	0

KINDRED Mike   b. 26-May-71

Club	Year	Comp	GP	G	A	Pts	PIM
Mil	1995	WC	5	0	1	1	2

KURTENBACH Terry   b. 14-Mar-63

Club	Year	Comp	GP	G	A	Pts	PIM
Rom	1993	OQ	4	0	1	1	2
Rom	1994	WC	6	1	1	2	2
Gui	1995	WC	7	0	4	4	2
Gui	1995	OQ	3	0	1	1	0
Gui	1996	WC	7	0	0	0	0
Gui	1996	OQ	2	0	0	0	0
		Totals	29	1	7	8	6

LAMBERT Dale   b. 9-Oct-59

Club	Year	Comp	GP	G	A	Pts	PIM
Sol	1993	OQ	4	0	0	0	4

LARKIN Bryan   b. 2-Feb-67

Club	Year	Comp	GP	G	A	Pts	PIM
Swi	1997	WC	7	0	1	1	6

LATTO Gordon   b. 18-Dec-58

Club	Year	Comp	GP	G	A	Pts	PIM
Vas	1976	WC	4	0	0	0	0
Fif	1977	WC	6	0	1	1	2
Fif	1981	WC	7	0	0	0	2
Fif	1989	WC	4	2	1	3	6
		Totals	21	2	2	4	10

LAWLESS John   b. 8-Jan-61

Club	Year	Comp	GP	G	A	Pts	PIM
Car	1990	WC	4	4	8	12	0
Car	1991	WC	8	1	2	3	22
		Totals	12	5	10	15	22

WORLD CHAMPIONSHIPS (WC/WCQ), **OLYMPIC QUALIFIERS** (OQ), **EURO CHALLENGE 2002-03** (EC)

BRITAIN's SENIOR PLAYER REGISTER 1989-2003
Forwards and Defencemen

LEE Phil — b. 22-Dec-65

Club	Year	Comp	GP	G	A	Pts	PIM
Sol	1989	WC	4	1	0	1	0
Sol	1990	WC	4	1	0	1	0
		Totals	8	2	0	2	0

LIDDIARD Neil — b. 7-Mar-78

Club	Year	Comp	GP	G	A	Pts	PIM
Pet	2000	OQ	3	0	0	0	0
Pet	2000	WC	7	0	0	0	0
Bas	2001	WC	5	2	2	0	4
Bas	2002	WC	5	0	0	0	8
Bas	2002	WC	8	2	2	4	43
		Totals	28	4	4	8	55

LINDSAY Jeff — b. 5-Jul-65

Club	Year	Comp	GP	G	A	Pts	PIM
Pet	1995	WC	7	0	0	0	10
Man	1995	OQ	3	0	1	1	4
Man	1996	WC	7	0	0	0	6
Man	1996	OQ	5	0	0	0	2
		Totals	22	0	1	1	22

LITTLE Richard — b. 16-Sep-66

Club	Year	Comp	GP	G	A	Pts	PIM
Bas	1996	OQ	3	2	1	3	4
Bas	1997	WC	7	3	1	4	14
		Totals	10	5	2	7	18

LONGSTAFF David — b. 26-Aug-74

Club	Year	Comp	GP	G	A	Pts	PIM
Whi	1994	WC	6	0	0	0	6
Whi	1995	WC	7	6	1	7	8
New	1995	OQ	1	0	0	0	0
She	1996	WC	7	1	2	3	10
She	1996	OQ	5	1	3	4	6
She	1997	WC	7	1	2	3	8
She	1998	WC	7	4	3	7	8
She	1999	WC	7	2	2	4	4
She	2000	OQ	3	0	1	1	2
She	2000	WC	7	2	3	5	14
She	2001	WC	5	3	7	10	4
Dju	2002	WC	3	1	4	5	2
New	2002	EC	3	0	3	3	4
New	2003	WC	5	3	6	9	2
		Totals	73	24	37	61	78

MacNAUGHT Kevin — b. 23-Jul-60

Club	Year	Comp	GP	G	A	Pts	PIM
Med	1990	WC	4	4	4	8	4
Med	1991	WC	8	3	7	10	10
Med	1992	WC	5	7	5	12	2
		Totals	17	14	16	30	16

MALO Andre — b. 10-May-65

Club	Year	Comp	GP	G	A	Pts	PIM
Bil	1993	WC	7	1	2	3	6
Not	1993	OQ	4	0	0	0	8
Not	1994	WC	5	0	0	0	6
She	1997	WC	7	1	3	4	4
She	1999	WC	7	0	2	2	16
She	1999	WCQ	4	0	0	0	0
She	2000	OQ	3	0	0	0	0
		Totals	37	2	7	9	40

MARSDEN Doug — b. 13-Nov-64

Club	Year	Comp	GP	G	A	Pts	PIM
Pai	1997	WC	7	0	1	1	8

MASON Brian — b. 1-Apr-65

Club	Year	Comp	GP	G	A	Pts	PIM
Slo	1990	WC	4	4	3	7	2
Slo	1991	WC	8	2	2	4	6
Slo	1992	WC	5	3	4	7	29
Mil	1993	WC	7	1	1	2	0
Slo	1993	OQ	4	0	0	0	0
Slo	1994	WC	6	0	0	0	0
		Totals	34	10	10	20	37

McEWEN Doug — b. 2-Oct-63

Club	Year	Comp	GP	G	A	Pts	PIM
Car	1993	WC	7	2	4	6	6
Car	1993	OQ	4	2	1	3	4
Car	1994	WC	6	1	2	3	0
Car	1995	OQ	2	0	0	0	4
Car	1996	WC	7	2	0	2	2
Car	1996	OQ	4	1	1	2	0
Car	1997	WC	7	2	0	2	8
Car	1998	WC	7	2	5	7	4
Pet	2001	WC	5	1	0	1	2
		Totals	49	13	13	26	32

MOODY Scott — b. 6-Sep-79

Club	Year	Comp	GP	G	A	Pts	PIM
Slo	2002	EC	8	0	0	0	0
Slo	2003	WC	4	1	0	1	2
		Totals	12	1	0	1	2

MORGAN Neil — b. 24-Dec-72

Club	Year	Comp	GP	G	A	Pts	PIM
Bla	1995	WC	7	1	2	3	2
Not	1995	OQ	2	0	0	0	0
Not	1996	WC	7	3	1	4	2
Not	1996	OQ	5	1	4	5	2
Not	1997	WC	7	0	1	1	6
Not	1998	WC	7	6	3	9	4
		Totals	35	11	11	22	16

MORIA Steve — b. 3-Feb-61

Club	Year	Comp	GP	G	A	Pts	PIM
Car	1995	OQ	2	0	0	0	0
Car	1996	WC	7	2	1	3	4
Car	1996	OQ	5	4	1	5	2
Car	1997	WC	7	4	2	6	4
Car	1998	WC	7	3	3	6	12
Car	1999	WC	7	2	1	3	2
Car	1999	WCQ	4	0	0	0	0
Car	2000	OQ	3	1	1	2	4
Car	2000	WC	7	6	4	10	2
		Totals	49	22	13	35	30

MORRIS Frank — b. 22-Mar-63

Club	Year	Comp	GP	G	A	Pts	PIM
Mur	1994	WC	6	0	0	0	8
Tra	1995	WC	7	1	1	2	2
		Totals	13	1	1	2	10

MORRISON Scott — b. 12-Aug-64

Club	Year	Comp	GP	G	A	Pts	PIM
Whi	1993	WC	7	10	4	14	2
Whi	1993	OQ	4	0	0	0	0
Whi	1994	WC	4	0	1	1	4
Hum	1995	WC	7	4	2	6	10
Bas	1995	OQ	3	1	1	2	0
		Totals	25	15	8	23	16

WORLD CHAMPIONSHIPS (WC/WCQ), OLYMPIC QUALIFIERS (OQ), EURO CHALLENGE 2002-03 (EC)

BRITAIN's SENIOR PLAYER REGISTER 1989-2003
Forwards and Defencemen

MULVENNA Glen   b. 18-Feb-67

Club	Year	Comp	GP	G	A	Pts	PIM
New	2000	WC	7	0	0	0	18

NEIL Scott   b. 1-Aug-62

Club	Year	Comp	GP	G	A	Pts	PIM
Mur	1981	WC	7	0	0	0	4
Mur	1989	WC	4	5	4	9	0
Mur	1990	WC	4	5	3	8	0
Mur	1991	WC	8	7	1	8	10
Mur	1992	WC	5	6	4	10	4
She	1993	WC	5	0	0	0	0
She	1993	OQ	4	0	0	0	0
		Totals	37	23	12	35	18

NELSON Craig   b. 8-Jul-76

Club	Year	Comp	GP	G	A	Pts	PIM
Dun	2002	WC	5	0	0	0	10

ORD Terry   b. 4-Dec-65

Club	Year	Comp	GP	G	A	Pts	PIM
Whi	1989	WC	4	0	1	1	0

O'CONNOR Mike   b. 12-Dec-61

Club	Year	Comp	GP	G	A	Pts	PIM
Dur	1992	WC	5	3	1	4	10
Dur	1993	WC	7	0	3	3	16
Hum	1993	OQ	4	1	1	2	14
Hum	1994	WC	6	0	0	0	12
		Totals	22	4	5	9	52

OWEN Greg   b. 19-Jun-81

Club	Year	Comp	GP	G	A	Pts	PIM
Mil	2002	EC	9	1	0	1	2
Mil	2003	WC	5	0	0	0	20
		Totals	13	1	0	1	22

PAYNE Anthony   b. 26-Jun-72

Club	Year	Comp	GP	G	A	Pts	PIM
Pet	1995	WC	6	1	0	1	0

PENNYCOOK Jim   b. 12-Jun-57

Club	Year	Comp	GP	G	A	Pts	PIM
Dun	1977	WC	5	1	0	1	0
Mur	1979	WC	7	3	4	7	0
Mur	1981	WC	7	3	1	4	4
Tay	1989	WC	4	3	4	7	0
		Totals	23	10	9	19	4

PENTLAND Paul   b. 11-Nov-64

Club	Year	Comp	GP	G	A	Pts	PIM
Mur	1989	WC	4	0	0	0	0

PHILLIPS Jonathan   b. 14-July-82

Club	Year	Comp	GP	G	A	Pts	PIM
Car	2002	EC	9	0	0	0	8
Car	2003	WC	5	0	1	1	6
		Totals	14	0	1	1	14

PICKLES Andy   b. 9-Jun-73

Club	Year	Comp	GP	G	A	Pts	PIM
IOW	2001	WC	5	0	1	1	2

PLOMMER Tommy   b. 26-Aug-68

Club	Year	Comp	GP	G	A	Pts	PIM
She	1995	OQ	3	0	0	0	4
She	1996	OQ	4	3	0	3	0
		Totals	7	3	0	3	4

POPE Brent   b. 20-Feb-73

Club	Year	Comp	GP	G	A	Pts	PIM
Sol	2002	EC	9	0	3	3	16
Sol	2003	WC	5	0	0	0	10
		Totals	14	0	3	3	26

POUND Ian   b. 22-Jan-67

Club	Year	Comp	GP	G	A	Pts	PIM
Sol	1995	WC	7	0	0	0	10

PRIEST Merv   b. 2-Aug-73

Club	Year	Comp	GP	G	A	Pts	PIM
Bas	1996	WC	7	1	0	1	4
Bas	1996	OQ	3	1	2	3	4
Car	1999	WC	7	1	2	3	10
Car	1999	WCQ	4	0	0	0	2
Car	2000	OQ	2	1	0	1	2
Car	2000	WC	7	2	3	5	8
		Totals	30	6	7	13	30

REID Alistair   b. 15-Jul-63

Club	Year	Comp	GP	G	A	Pts	PIM
Ayr	1989	WC	4	1	2	3	0

RHODES Nigel   b. 19-Jul-67

Club	Year	Comp	GP	G	A	Pts	PIM
Not	1989	WC	4	2	0	2	2

ROBERTSON Iain   b. 2-Jun-69

Club	Year	Comp	GP	G	A	Pts	PIM
Fif	1991	WC	8	0	1	1	2
Fif	1992	WC	5	2	2	4	0
Fif	1993	WC	7	1	0	1	0
Fif	1995	WC	7	1	0	1	0
		Totals	27	4	3	7	2

SAUNDERS Lee   b. 3-Jun-70

Club	Year	Comp	GP	G	A	Pts	PIM
Bas	1995	WC	7	0	1	1	0
Mil	1996	OQ	1	0	0	0	0
		Totals	8	0	1	1	0

SCOTT Patrick   b. 12-Nov-66

Club	Year	Comp	GP	G	A	Pts	PIM
Mil	1993	OQ	4	2	0	2	0
Mil	1994	WC	6	2	0	2	2
Mil	1995	OQ	3	0	1	1	0
Mil	1996	WC	7	1	4	5	2
Bas	1996	OQ	4	1	1	2	2
Bas	1997	WC	7	4	3	7	18
		Totals	31	10	9	19	24

SHIELDS Colin   b. 27-Jan-80

Club	Year	Comp	GP	G	A	Pts	PIM
Una	2001	WC	5	6	2	8	4
UoM	2002	WC	5	2	3	5	4
UoM	2003	WC	5	4	1	5	2
		Totals	15	12	6	18	10

SMITH Damian   b. 8-Oct-71

Club	Year	Comp	GP	G	A	Pts	PIM
Dur	1992	WC	4	2	2	4	0
Dur	1993	WC	4	1	1	2	0
Dur	1995	WC	6	0	1	1	10
		Totals	14	3	4	7	10

WORLD CHAMPIONSHIPS (WC/WCQ), **OLYMPIC QUALIFIERS** (OQ), **EURO CHALLENGE 2002-03** (EC)

BRITAIN's SENIOR PLAYER REGISTER 1989-2003
Forwards and Defencemen

SMITH David — b. 14-Feb-73

Club	Year	Comp	GP	G	A	Pts	PIM
Tra	1995	WC	5	1	0	1	0

SMITH Paul — b. 3-Jul-61

Club	Year	Comp	GP	G	A	Pts	PIM
Dur	1981	WC	7	0	0	0	11
Dur	1989	WC	4	0	1	1	2
		Totals	11	0	1	1	13

SMITH Peter — b. 29-Nov-61

Club	Year	Comp	GP	G	A	Pts	PIM
Pet	1989	WC	4	4	1	5	2
Pet	1990	WC	2	2	0	2	2
Car	1991	WC	8	1	1	2	6
		Totals	14	7	2	9	10

SMITH Stephen — b. 11-Apr-63

Club	Year	Comp	GP	G	A	Pts	PIM
Whi	1989	WC	4	2	1	3	2

STEFAN Gary — b. 23-Jun-59

Club	Year	Comp	GP	G	A	Pts	PIM
Slo	1990	WC	4	4	7	11	8
Slo	1991	WC	8	3	1	4	12
Slo	1992	WC	5	5	2	7	8
		Totals	17	12	10	22	28

STONE Jason — b. 30-Dec-72

Club	Year	Comp	GP	G	A	Pts	PIM
Car	1998	WC	6	0	0	0	0

STRACHAN Rick — b. 27-Mar-63

Club	Year	Comp	GP	G	A	Pts	PIM
Mil	1995	WC	7	0	0	0	2
Bas	1995	OQ	3	0	0	0	0
Bas	1996	WC	7	2	1	3	2
Bas	1996	OQ	5	1	1	2	2
Bas	1997	WC	7	1	4	5	2
Bas	1998	WC	6	0	2	2	2
Bas	1999	WC	7	1	0	1	0
Bas	1999	WCQ	4	0	0	0	2
Bas	2000	OQ	3	0	1	1	2
Bas	2000	WC	7	1	1	2	2
Car	2001	WC	5	0	0	0	0
Mil	2002	WC	5	1	0	1	4
Sol	2002	EC	3	0	0	0	2
		Totals	69	7	10	17	22

TAIT Ashley — b. 9-Aug-75

Club	Year	Comp	GP	G	A	Pts	PIM
Not	1995	WC	2	0	0	0	4
Not	1995	OQ	3	1	1	2	0
Not	1996	WC	7	1	1	2	10
Kin	1998	WC	7	2	0	2	4
Not	1999	WCQ	4	0	0	0	4
Not	2000	OQ	3	0	0	0	6
Not	2000	WC	7	3	4	7	10
Not	2001	WC	5	2	4	6	4
Not	2002	WC	5	1	1	2	0
Cov	2002	EC	3	1	1	2	2
Cov	2003	WC	5	0	3	3	0
		Totals	51	11	15	26	44

TASKER Michael — b. 10-Jul-73

Club	Year	Comp	GP	G	A	Pts	PIM
Cov	2001	WC	5	1	3	4	4
Cov	2002	WC	5	1	0	1	4
		Totals	10	2	3	5	8

THOMPSON Paul — b. 6-May-68

Club	Year	Comp	GP	G	A	Pts	PIM
Gui	1998	WC	6	1	1	2	8

THORNTON Steve — b. 8-Mar-73

Club	Year	Comp	GP	G	A	Pts	PIM
Car	1999	WC	7	2	1	3	0
Car	1999	WCQ	4	0	1	1	2
Car	2001	WC	5	2	8	10	6
Bel	2002	EC	3	1	0	1	4
Bel	2003	WC	5	1	9	10	0
		Totals	24	6	19	25	12

WAGHORN Graham — b. 31-Dec-72

Club	Year	Comp	GP	G	A	Pts	PIM
Not	1991	WC	8	0	2	2	10
Not	1993	WC	7	1	1	2	4
Not	1995	OQ	1	0	0	0	2
Not	1996	OQ	3	0	0	0	0
		Totals	19	1	3	4	16

WEAVER Jonathan — b. 20-Jan-77

Club	Year	Comp	GP	G	A	Pts	PIM
New	1998	WC	7	1	5	6	0
Man	1999	WC	7	0	2	2	2
USA	1999	WCQ	4	0	0	0	2
Ayr	2001	WC	5	7	2	9	0
Ayr	2002	WC	3	0	0	0	0
Fif	2002	EC	3	1	0	1	2
Fif	2003	WC	5	2	1	3	4
		Totals	34	11	10	21	10

WEBER Randall — b. 2-Sep-68

Club	Year	Comp	GP	G	A	Pts	PIM
Not	1998	WC	7	0	2	2	6

WILSON Rob — b. 18-Jul-68

Club	Year	Comp	GP	G	A	Pts	PIM
She	1998	WC	7	1	4	5	10
She	1999	WC	7	1	3	4	6
New	2001	WC	5	6	7	13	2
Man	2002	WC	5	1	2	3	4
Man	2002	EC	3	1	0	1	2
Man	2003	WC	5	2	3	5	6
		Totals	32	12	19	31	30

WISHART Gary — b. 28-Aug-81

Club	Year	Comp	GP	G	A	Pts	PIM
Fif	2002	WC	5	0	2	2	4
Dun	2002	EC	6	1	0	1	2
		Totals	11	1	2	3	6

YOUNG Scott — b. 26-May-65

Club	Year	Comp	GP	G	A	Pts	PIM
Ayr	1999	WCQ	4	0	0	0	10
Ayr	2000	OQ	3	2	1	3	18
Ayr	2000	WC	5	3	3	6	20
Dun	2002	WC	4	0	0	0	8
		Totals	16	5	4	9	56

WORLD CHAMPIONSHIPS (WC/WCQ), **OLYMPIC QUALIFIERS** (OQ), **EURO CHALLENGE 2002-03** (EC)

BRITAIN's SENIOR PLAYER REGISTER 1989-2003
Netminders

CAVALLIN Mark   b. 20-Nov-71

Club	Year	Comp	GP	GPI	Mins	GA	GAA
Sco	2002	EC	3	3	178	9	3.03
Sco	2003	WC	4	3	180	8	2.67
		Totals	7	6	358	17	2.85

COWLEY Wayne   b. 4-Dec-64

Club	Year	Comp	GP	GPI	Mins	GA	GAA
Not	1999	WCQ	3	0	0	0	0.00
Not	2000	WC	7	3	160	10	3.75
		Totals	10	3	160	10	3.75

FOSTER Stephen   b. 1-Jul-74

Club	Year	Comp	GP	GPI	Mins	GA	GAA
Dur	1995	WC	7	6	320	28	5.25
Dur	1995	OQ	2	0	0	0	0.00
Dur	1996	WC	5	3	180	11	3.67
New	1996	OQ	3	0	0	0	0.00
New	1997	WC	5	4	200	12	3.60
New	1998	WC	6	3	155	10	3.87
Ayr	2000	OQ	3	0	0	0	0.00
		Totals	31	16	855	61	4.28

GRAHAM David   b. 24-Oct-59

Club	Year	Comp	GP	GPI	Mins	GA	GAA
Not	1989	WC	4	3	150	12	4.80
Not	1990	WC	3	1	60	1	1.00
Not	1991	WC	3	2	120	5	2.50
		Totals	10	6	330	18	3.27

GRUBB Ricky   b. 3-Mar-77

Club	Year	Comp	GP	GPI	Mins	GA	GAA
Fif	1995	WC	1	1	40	5	7.50

HANSON Moray   b. 21-Jun-64

Club	Year	Comp	GP	GPI	Mins	GA	GAA
Mur	1989	WC	2	1	60	4	4.00
Mur	1991	WC	3	2	120	11	5.50
Mur	1994	WC	4	3	137	17	7.45
		Totals	9	6	317	32	6.06

HIBBERT Jim   b. 8-Feb-75

Club	Year	Comp	GP	GPI	Mins	GA	GAA
New	2000	WC	1	1	20	3	9.00

LYLE Stevie   b. 4-Dec-79

Club	Year	Comp	GP	GPi	Mins	GA	GAA
Car	1995	OQ	1	0	0	0	0.00
Car	1996	WC	3	1	60	2	2.00
Car	1996	OQ	2	0	0	0	0.00
Car	1997	WC	6	2	120	8	4.00
Can	1998	WC	5	4	205	12	3.51
Car	1999	WC	7	5	300	12	2.40
Car	1999	WCQ	4	4	240	5	1.25
Car	2000	OQ	3	3	180	8	2.67
Car	2001	WC	5	5	270	8	1.78
Man	2002	WC	3	2	120	8	4.00
		Totals	39	26	1495	63	2.53

McCRONE John "Bernie"   b. 26-Feb-63

Club	Year	Comp	GP	GPi	Mins	GA	GAA
Ayr	1989	WC	2	1	30	0	0.00
Ayr	1991	WC	4	4	240	9	2.25
Ayr	1992	WC	3	3	122	4	1.97
Fif	1993	WC	7	5	280	13	2.79
Fif	1993	OQ	3	3	180	13	4.33
Fif	1994	WC	4	3	105	18	10.29
		Totals	23	19	957	57	3.57

McKAY Martin   b. 27-Apr-68

Club	Year	Comp	GP	GPI	Mins	GA	GAA
Mur	1990	WC	2	2	120	4	2.00
Mur	1992	WC	3	1	60	2	2.00
Mur	1993	WC	3	1	60	0	0.00
She	1993	OQ	3	1	60	8	8.00
She	1994	WC	4	3	118	14	7.12
		Totals	15	8	418	28	4.02

MORRISON Bill   b. 27-Oct-64

Club	Year	Comp	GP	GPI	Mins	GA	GAA
Bas	1995	WC	6	1	60	2	2.00
Bas	1995	OQ	3	3	180	4	1.33
Bas	1996	WC	6	3	180	10	3.33
K/R	1996	OQ	5	5	300	11	2.20
Rat	1997	WC	3	2	100	2	1.20
Pai	1998	WC	3	1	60	5	5.00
Rod	1999	WC	7	2	120	4	2.00
		Totals	33	17	1000	38	2.28

MURPHY Stephen   b. 11-Dec-81

Club	Year	Comp	GP	GPI	Mins	GA	GAA
Fif	2001	WC	5	1	30	1	2.00
Dun	2002	WC	3	1	60	2	2.00
Dun	2002	EC	3	0	0	0	0.00
Dun	2003	WC	2	0	0	0	0.00
		Totals	10	2	90	3	2.00

O'CONNOR Scott   b. 3-May-69

Club	Year	Comp	GP	GPI	Mins	GA	GAA
Pet	1992	WC	4	3	118	4	2.03
Pet	1993	WC	3	2	80	0	0.00
Mil	1993	OQ	2	0	0	0	0.00
		Totals	9	5	198	4	1.21

SMITH Jeff   b. 11-Jul-63

Club	Year	Comp	GP	GPI	Mins	GA	GAA
Car	1990	WC	3	1	60	2	2.00

WATKINS Joe   b. 27-Oct-79

Club	Year	Comp	GP	GPI	Mins	GA	GAA
Bas	1999	WCQ	1	0	0	0	0.00
Bas	2000	WC	6	4	240	10	2.50
Brk	2002	WC	4	2	120	6	6.00
Brk	2002	EC	6	6	370	29	4.70
Brk	2003	WC	4	2	119	5	2.52
		Totals	21	14	849	50	3.53

WORLD CHAMPIONSHIPS (WC/WCQ), **OLYMPIC QUALIFIERS** (OQ), **EURO CHALLENGE 2002-03** (EC)

WORLD JUNIOR CHAMPIONSHIPS

U20 CHAMPIONSHIPS

Division II, Miercurea Ciuc, Romania, 6-12 January 2003.

Age limit is under 20 years on 1 January 2003

GROUP STANDINGS

Group A	GP	W	L	D	GF	GA	Pts
Estonia	5	5	0	0	62	8	10
Britain	5	4	1	0	64	7	8
Romania	5	3	2	0	34	26	6
Lithuania	5	2	3	0	21	31	4
South Africa	5	1	4	0	12	58	2
Bulgaria	5	0	5	0	5	68	0

Estonia promoted to Division I in 2004, Bulgaria relegated to Division III.

BRITAIN'S RESULTS

6 Jan	Bulgaria-Britain	0-19 (0-6,0-5,0-8)
7 Jan	Britain-Romania	9-1 (4-0,2-0,3-1)
9 Jan	Britain-S Africa	21-0 (7-0,9-0,5-0)
11 Jan	Lithuania-Britain	1-13 (0-3,0-5,1-5)
12 Jan	Britain-Estonia	2-5 (1-4,1-1,0-0)

BRITAIN'S POINTS SCORERS

	GP	G	A	Pts	Pim
Stephen Wallace	5	12	6	18	10
Matt Myers	5	8	9	17	4
Russ Cowley	5	7	7	14	2
Paul Moran	5	5	9	14	4
Ryan Lake	5	10	3	13	22
Danny Meyers	5	6	5	11	31
Matt Towalski	5	2	7	9	4
Adam Radmall	5	1	6	7	2
Adam Walker	5	4	2	6	4
Paddy Ward	5	0	6	6	0
Leigh Jamieson	5	2	3	5	2
Adam Carr	5	2	3	5	4
Lee Richardson	5	2	3	5	2
James Hutchinson	5	1	3	4	4
Michael Plenty	5	1	2	3	0
Nathan Hunt	5	0	3	3	16
Mark Richardson	5	1	1	2	0
Adam Brittle	5	0	2	2	0

BRITAIN UNDER-20

Richard Ashton BIL, Allan Levers COV, Stewart Rugg DUN; Adam Radmall COV, Paddy Ward EDI, Nathan Hunt HUL, James Hutchinson IOW, Leigh Jamieson MIL, Dan McIntyre MUR, Steve Duncombe SHE, Michael Plenty SLO; Matt Myers CAR, Russell Cowley, Lee Richardson COV, Adam Walker FIF, Ryan Lake HUL, Adam Carr IOW, Stephen Wallace NEW, Paul Moran NOT, Matt Towalski SLO, Danny Meyers SOL capt, Mark Richardson SWI, Adam Brittle TEL.
Head coach: Kevin King. *Manager*: Jim Laing.

Old story

Kevin King's team, well-stocked by names familar to fans of BNL hockey, iced a strong side and enjoyed a better overall goal difference than Estonia, the only other serious contenders.

But in the game between the two nations, with the obligatory finicky ref, the old British curse of taking too many penalties destroyed their chances of promotion from 'pool C'. Estonia scored four powerplay goals in just over 11 minutes of the first period and went on to record a decisive 5-2 victory.

Newcastle's STEPHEN WALLACE was voted the championship's Best Forward after ending as runner-up overall in the goal scoring and fourth in points.

BRITAIN'S NETMINDING

	GPI	Mins	SoG	GA	Sv%
Richard Ashton	1	31	2	0	100.O
Allan Levers	3	99	35	2	94.3
Stewart Rugg	5	170	43	5	88.4
GB TOTALS	5	300	80	7	91.2

U18 CHAMPIONSHIPS

Division I, Group A, Ventspils, Latvia, 23-29 March 2003.

Age limit is under 18 years on 1 January 2003

GROUP STANDINGS

Group A	GP	W	L	D	GF	GA	Pts
Denmark	5	4	0	1	31	12	9
Germany	5	4	1	0	34	8	8
Slovenia	5	3	2	0	24	27	6
Latvia	5	1	2	2	14	15	4
Japan	5	1	3	1	15	19	3
Britain	5	0	5	0	8	45	0

BRITAIN'S RESULTS

23 Mar	Britain-Germany	0-13	(0-3,0-5,0-5)
24 Mar	Latvia-Britain	6-2	(1-0,3-0,2-2)
26 Mar	Britain-Denmark	2-11	(1-3,0-4,1-4)
27 Mar	Slovenia-Britain	5-1	(0-0,3-1,2-0)
29 Mar	Japan-Britain	10-3	(5-0,1-2,4-1)

BRITAIN'S NETMINDING

	GPI	Mins	SoG	GA	Sv%
David Lawrence	4	175	177	24	86.4
Nathan Craze	4	125	116	19	83.6
GB TOTALS	5	300	293	43	85.3

BRITAIN'S POINTS SCORERS

	GP	G	A	Pts	Pim
Adam Brittle	5	0	4	4	0
Mark Richardson	5	3	0	3	0
Adam Walker	5	1	2	3	4
Scott McAndrew	5	2	0	2	4
Simon Butterworth	5	1	1	2	0
Leigh Jamieson	5	1	1	2	14
Alain Campbell	5	0	2	2	0
George Murray	5	0	2	2	2

UNDER-20 CHALLENGE GAME

2 Jan 2003 at Basingstoke
BASINGSTOKE BISON-GB UNDER-20   9-2
Michael Plenty and **Stephen Wallace** netted for Britain in this pre-championship warm-up against most of Bison's BNL squad. GB's Man of the Match was **Lee Richardson** while his younger brcther **Mark Richardson**, who was guesting for Basingstoke, was named their best player.

Up and down

Britain knew they faced a difficult task because many of their best players who helped the side finish third in last year's Division II were ineligble to compete at this level.

So it was an unpleasant shock when the IIHF told them they'd have to move up a division because they'd somehow allowed an extra nation, Bulgaria, into the group from Division III.

GB were out of their depth in Division I against the might of the Germans, the Danes and even the Japanese, with the shell-shocked goalies facing almost 60 shots a game.

Against this quality of opposition, scoring even one point amounted to a good performance and Telford's 17-year-old **Adam Brittle** and Swindon's **Mark Richardson**, 16, came out on top. Both of them played for English Premier League teams as did several more of the 22-strong squad. Most of the other members were on the fringes of their senior club sides with one playing in the Czech Republic.

BRITAIN UNDER-18

Nathan Craze CAR, David Lawrence SHE; Chad Reekie FIF, Kurt Reynolds GUI, James Day, Kevin Phillips (both HUL), Leigh Jamieson MIL, Bernie Bradford PET, Dale Howey WHI; Nicky Watt BAS, Andrew Thornton BIL, Joe Miller CAR, Adam Walker, Scott McAndrew (both FIF), David Pyatt HUL, Ben Burn NOT, Alain Campbell PAI, Simon Butterworth SHE, Mark Richardson SWI, Adam Brittle TEL, Dan (DJ) Good WHI, George Murray (Znojmo, CZE).
Head coach: Allan Anderson.
Manager: Michael Evans.

So next year Britain will be back where they were last year - and should have been this year - hopefully having learned some valuable lessons along the way. Fortunately, half this team will be eligible again next time.

☑ The small nation of Denmark proved the excellence of their youth development system as their under-18s joined their seniors among the world's elite.

GB UNDER-18S IN FRANCE

CHALLENGE
I6 Feb at Courchevel **France u18-GB u18   4-2**
TOURNOI DE LA VANOISE
18 Feb at Albertville **GB u18-Slovenia u18 1-4**
19 Feb at Courchevel **Austria u18-GB u18   7-5**
20 Feb at Meribel **France u18-GB u18 17-1**

CONTINENTAL CUP

The Continental Cup was established in 1997 as a replacement for the European Cup (inaugurated 1965). The name was changed to avoid confusion with the European League (1996-2000).

British teams have entered the competitions in every year since 1983.

Costs are kept down by gathering clubs together geographically as far as possible and allowing games to be played by groups of teams in one venue, rather than home and away.

Israel and Turkey were among the 44 clubs from 25 countries taking part in the 2002 competition which was played over three qualifying rounds in September, October and November, with an eight-team final round in January. In each qualifying round, the teams played a round-robin over three days.

Britain's representatives were Belfast Giants, the 2001-02 Superleague winners, and (Ayr) Scottish Eagles who were the runners-up. Eagles were seeded into the Second Round and Giants into the Third Round which they hosted.

We give below details of both British teams' cup groups.

SECOND ROUND

Group F in Rouen, France

	GP	W	L	D	GF	GA	Pts
Scottish Eagles	2	2	0	0	8	3	4
HC Rouen FRA	2	1	1	0	7	7	2
Storhamar NOR	2	1	1	0	3	3	2
Riga 2000 LAT	2	0		0	2	7	0

SCOTTISH EAGLES

Mark Cavallin, Eoin McInerney; Bob Quinnell, Paddy Ward, Stefan Bergkvist, Evan Marble; Jonathan Weaver, Xavier Majic, Sean Selmser capt, Mike Harding, Jeff Williams, Jason Bowen, Johan Astrom, Jeff Johnstone, Jonni Vauhkonen. *Manager-coach:* Paul Heavey.

Eagles qualified for the Third Round but their place was taken by Rouen after Eagles Hockey Ltd was wound up in November. The third games were cancelled as the ice was unfit.

RESULTS

18 Oct	Eagles-Storhamar	2-1 (0-0,1-0,1-1)
	Rouen-Riga	5-1
19 Oct	Storhamar-Riga	2-1
	Eagles-Rouen	6-2 (2-1,2-1,2-0)
20 Oct	Eagles-Riga	) not
	Rouen-Storhamar	) played

EAGLES' GAME SUMMARIES

18 October 2002, Patinoire Ile Lacroix, Rouen

EAGLES-STORHAMAR   **2-1 (0-0,1-0,1-1)**

Eagles' scoring:

Majic (Williams, Bowen)	32.24	(1-0)
Quinnell	42.34	(2-0)

Penalty minutes:
Eagles 28 (Selmser 10-misc.), Storhamar 6.
Eagles' man of match: Ward.
Netminding:

McInerney SCO	shots 36	save percent 97.2
Norgren STO	shots 27	save percent 92.6

Referee: Bachelet FRA.   *Attendance:* 775

19 October 2002, Patinoire Ile Lacroix, Rouen

EAGLES-ROUEN   **6-2 (2-1,2-1,2-0)**

Eagles' scoring:

Astrom	6.48 pp	(1-1)
Johnstone (Selmser, Majic)	18.53 pp	(2-1)
Johnstone (Marble, Astrom)	28.08 sh	(3-2)
Johnstone (Astrom)	35.26	(4-2)
Johnstone (Marble)	44.38	(5-2)
Majic (Astrom)	52.10	(6-2)

Penalty minutes:
Eagles 64 (Selmser, Vauhkonen, Marble 10-misc.)
Rouen 36 (Bourdeau 10-misc.)
Eagles' man of match: Johnstone.
Netminding:

McInerney SCO	shots 19	save percent 89.5
Raymond ROU	shots 36	save percent 83.3

Referee: Awizus KAZ   *Attendance:* 2,897

Eagles' finest hour before 'Dunkirk'

Eagles' game against their hosts ranks alongside some of their great performances, writes *Neil Hughes*. While it was hard to gauge Rouen's quality, for Eagles to achieve such a win when they had been together only a brief time was remarkable.

Moreover, the team were short-benched, a long way from home, in front of a full house of noisy opposing fans and up against a different style of refereeing. Only later did we discover that most of the players and their coach, **Paul Heavey**, had not been paid, either.

Despite this, they dominated the game when even-handed (not very frequently), killed off penalty after penalty, and in **Jeff Johnstone** had a player for whom the goal looked ten yards wide. Indeed, the GB international should have had a goal before his first, but by netting four times in a row he became only the second Eagle to achieve the feat against similar standard opposition. **Jamie Steer** was the other.

Rouen could not cope with the trickery of **Xavier Majic**, the pace of **Johan Astrom** and **Evan Marble**, the strength of **Sean Selmser** and **Jason Bowen** (when he wasn't in the box) and the pugilistic talents of **Jonni Vaukhonen**.

Though not the most talented bunch of players ever to have pulled on an Eagles' shirt, Heavey had them performing at a much higher level than the sum of their parts. He wanted the entire team to be awarded the man of the match but that must have broken an IIHF rule so Johnstone understandably got the nod.

This win and the almost equally convincing victory over Norway's Storhamar, were enough to secure Eagles' path into the next round. This was fortunate as a technical fault in the refrigeration plant (the technician forgot to flick the switch marked 'freeze' overnight) resulted in both the last day's games being cancelled.

• Eagles played only four league games after the Continental Cup before being forced to disband through lack of funding. Rouen, whom they had soundly beaten, replaced them in the next round.

• Three Eagles missed the Rouen weekend as their paperwork wasn't in order - new signings **Jason Rushton** and **Scott Campbell**, and Lithuanian **Dino Bauba** who had applied for UK citizenship but whose passport hadn't arrived in time for him to leave the UK. A fourth, **Dan Ratushny**, had concussion.

• The Rouen rink was strangely bereft of goal judges or goal lights. We understand the French manage without either in their domestic league games but the *Annual* thought this must contravene international rules.

When we asked the IIHF's tournament director, **Patrick Francheterre**, for an explanation, he told us: "We dodn't need them. The puck is either in or it's out." The IIHF's Swiss HQ failed to respond to our request for a clarification of this odd ruling.

• The games in Rouen, an historic port on the River Seine, were held in the main pad of the two-pad ice rink on an island in the Seine. Rouen is where William the Conqueror died in 1087 and where Joan of Arc was burned at the stake (by the Brits) in 1431.

THIRD ROUND
Group J in the Odyssey Arena, Belfast

	GP	W	L	D	GF	GA	Pts
Belfast Giants	3	3	0	0	16	3	6
EHC Linz AUS	3	1	1	1	10	10	3
Valerengen NOR	3	1	2	0	6	7	2
HC Rouen FRA	3	0	2	1	5	17	1

Giants qualified for the Super Final

RESULTS
22 Nov Rouen-Linz	4-4	(3-0,0-0,1-4)
Giants-Valerengen	3-0	(2-0,1-0,0-0)
23 Nov Linz-Valerengen	3-1	(1-0,2-1,0-0)
Rouen-**Giants**	0-8	(0-3,0-3,0-2)
24 Nov Valerengen-Rouen	5-1	(3-0,1-0,1-1)
Giants-Linz	5-3	(2-2,0-0,3-1)

GIANTS' GAME SUMMARIES
22 November 2002, Odyssey Arena

GIANTS-VALERENGEN 3-0 (2-0,1-0,0-0)

Giants' scoring:
Selmser (Ward, Matsos)	8.33	(1-0)
Stevens (Ward)	14.41	(2-0)
Bowen (Kruse, MacDonald)	23.59	(3-0)

Penalty minutes:
Giants 26 (Selmser 10-misc), Valerengen 12.
Giants' Man of Match: Ryder.
Netminding:
Ryder BEL   *shots* 31   *save percent* 100.00
Lund VAL   *shots* 30   *save percent* 90.00
Referee: Bergman. *Linesmen*: Staniforth, Hicks.

23 November 2002, Odyssey Arena

ROUEN-GIANTS 0-8 (0-3,0-3,0-2)

Giants' scoring
Riehl (Stevens)	3.42	(1-0)
Selmser (Sandrock)	9.29	(2-0)
Stewart (Riehl)	15.03	(3-0)
Sandrock (Riehl)	20.24	(4-0)
Ward	31.22 pp	(5-0)
Kruse (MacDonald, Bowen)	37.43	(6-0)
Kelman (Matsos, Schulte)	47.53	(7-0)
Schulte (Kelman, Kruse)	50.27	(8-0)

Penalty minutes: Rouen 12, Giants 10.
Giants' Man of Match: Ryder.
Netminding:
Raymond ROU   *shots* 33   *save percent* 75.76
Ryder BEL   *shots* 23   *save percent* 100.00
Referee: Mandioni. *Linesmen*: Folka, Staniforth.

24 November 2002, Odyssey Arena

GIANTS-LINZ 5-3 (2-2,0-0,3-1)

Giants' scoring:

Kruse (Stevens, Johnson)	16.14	(1-1)
Selmser (Stevens)	18.58	(2-2)
Sandrock (Kruse, MacDonald)	41.32	(3-2)
Stewart (Stevens, Kelman)	47.47	(4-2)
Bowen (Stewart, Selmser)	59.14	(5-3)

Penalty minutes: Giants 10, Linz 14.

Netminding:

Ryder BEL	shots 24	save percent	87.50
Nestak LIN	shots 33	save percent	84.85

Referee: Bergman.

Linesmen: Coenen, Staniforth.

Tournament Awards
Best Netminder - **Colin Ryder**
Best Defenceman - **Robby Sandrock**
Best Forward - **Paul Kruse**

Giants qualify for 'superfinal' despite Selmser controversy

Dave Whistle's Belfast Giants cruised through the Third Round of their Continental Cup group with only the Black Wings of Linz, Austria giving them any trouble.

Giants' players swept the awards with **Colin Ryder**, who was in cracking form all weekend, chalking up two shutouts in the first two games.

Belfast met Linz in the last game when they needed only a draw to go through to the Superfinal. Making a sluggish start, they were tied 2-2 at the end of the second period through skipper **Paul Kruse** and temporary forward signing **Sean Selmser**. But they sensed they had the measure of the Austrians and won the last period 3-1.

Robby Sandrock, whose blinding blueline shot was the goal of the series, and **Rob Stewart** gave Giants a 4-2 lead 12 minutes from time and though Linz pulled one back, **Curtis Bowen** iced the win with 47 seconds left.

▪ The IIHF decided to take no action over the Giants using former Scottish Eagles' captain **Sean Selmser** in the Third Round of the Cup.

The Austrian club, Linz, who were beaten into second place by Giants, complained to the governing body that Selmser's signing broke Continental Cup rule 6.3 which forbids 'speculative transfers for the duration of the Continental Cup tournament'.

Selmser, 28, was signed by Giants four days before the start of the tournament and scored in each of the games. The club's statement said he was needed as injury cover 'in [Whistle]'s bid to

ice a winning squad in this weekend's Continental Cup.'

The former Team Canada forward, who played for Eagles in the previous round, did not appear in any Superleague games for Giants as he accepted a better offer from Villach (another Austrian club) immediately after the Cup. Giants had no league games scheduled between 9 November and the start of the Third Round.

The IIHF told the Annual that they found no evidence that the transfer was speculative, adding that 'it definitely helped the Giants' cause that Selmser came from a team which folded'.

Even so, we bet there were a few sweaty palms round the Odyssey before the decision was handed down. Giants certainly broke the spirit of the rule, even if unintentionally.

SUPERFINAL

First Round
10 Jan in Milan

Jokerit Helsinki FIN-Slovan Bratislava SVK		5-2
Milan Vipers ITA-HC Keramin Minsk UKR		3-4

after OT and penalty shots

10 Jan in Lugano

HC Davos SWI-Lokomotiv Yaroslavl RUS	1-2
HC Lugano SWI-**Belfast Giants** GBR	2-0

Second Round
11 Jan in Milan

Slovan Bratislava-Milan Vipers	6-1
Jokerit Helsinki-HC Keramin Minsk	5-2

11 Jan in Milan

HC Davos-**Belfast Giants**	2-4
Lokomotiv Yaroslavl-HC Lugano	6-3

Final Round
12 Jan in Milan

HC Davos-Milan Vipers	2-0
Slovan Bratislava-**Belfast Giants**	4-3

12 Jan in Lugano

HC Lugano-HC Keramin Minsk	5-0
Lokomotiv Yaroslavl-Jokerit Helsinki	1-2

Jokerit Helsinki win the 2002 Continental Cup.

GIANTS' GAME SUMMARIES

10 January, Lugano

LUGANO-GIANTS 2-0 (0-0,1-0,1-0)

Penalty minutes: Lugano 10, Giants 12.

Netminding:

Rueger LUG	shots 36	save percent	100.0
Bach BEL	shots 38	save percent	94.7

Referee: Milan Minar. Attendance: 4,130

11 January, Milan

DAVOS-GIANTS	2-4	(0-1,1-1,1-2)

Giants' scoring:

Bowen (Johnson)	10.19	(0-1)
Karlander (Stevens)	37.13	(1-2)
Ward (Riehl, Karlander)	44.34 pp	(1-3)
MacDonald (Johnson)	59.25	(2-4)

Penalty minutes: Davos 2, Giants 16 (Ward 10-misc.).

Netminding:

Hiller DAV	shots 44	save percent 93.0
Bach BEL	shots 29	save percent 93.1

Referee: Roland Aumuller   *Attendance:* 1,170

12 January, Milan

BRATISLAVA-GIANTS	4-3	(2-1,2-1,0-1)

Giants' scoring:

Sandrock (Riehl, MacDonald)	17.18 pp	(1-1)
Matsos (Schulte, Johnson)	21.13	(3-2)
Bowen (Matsos, Kelman)	51.34	(4-3)

Penalty minutes: Bratislava 49 (Javin 2+10 check/behind, Kulha 5+game x-check), Giants 41 (Kuwabara 5+game board).

Netminding:

Ondrejka BRA	shots 23	save percent 87.0
Ryder BEL	shots 29	save percent 86.2

Referee: Thomas Anderson.   *Attendance:* 700.

GIANTS' LEADING SCORERS
(Third Round & Superfinal)

	GP	G	A	Pts	Pim
Rod Stevens	6	1	5	6	0
Curtis Bowen	6	4	1	5	8
Paul Kruse	6	2	3	5	2
Kevin Riehl	6	1	4	5	6
Doug MacDonald	6	1	4	5	10

GIANTS' NETMINDING

	GPI	Mins	SoG	GA	Sv%
Ryan Bach	2	120	67	4	94.03
Colin Ryder	4	240	107	7	93.46

BELFAST GIANTS
Ryan Bach, Colin Ryder; Rob Stewart, Shane Johnson, Robby Sandrock, Todd Kelman, Lee Sorochan; Curt Bowen, Dave Matsos, Doug MacDonald, Kory Karlander, Paul Kruse capt, Kevin Riehl, Colin Ward, Rod Stevens, Paxton Schulte, Ryan Kuwabara, Steve Thornton.
Coach: Dave Whistle.
Note: Bach, Kuwabara and Thornton did not compete in the Third Round. *Mark Cavallin* and *Sean Selmser* competed in the Third Round.

'Fun hockey'
Giants finished sixth in the eight-team Superfinal after being whitewashed 2-0 in their crucial first game against hosts, Lugano.

A later victory over Swiss A league champs, HC Davos, was satisfying, and they had two goals disallowed in their narrow defeat by Bratislava of Slovakia. But London Knights' silver medal in the 2000 Cup remains the high watermark of British clubs' achievements in this competition.

Giants' **Paul Kruse** told the *Daily Express*: "Overall we're happy with our performances. It was fun hockey to play, very quick and it was a good weekend for us and our fans."

The pace and skill of the crack Swiss clubs surprised Giants after they had romped through the cup's Third Round, but they had adjusted somewhat by the time they met Davos in game two. The 4-2 victory left coach **Dave Whistle** ecstatic. "This is one of the finest moments in my coaching career," he enthused to the *Belfast Telegraph*. "We've just beaten a very good Swiss side and I couldn't fault any player on my roster. They were absolutely terrific."

* Jokerit Helsinki, the Continental Cup winners, were scheduled to meet the NHL's Toronto Maple Leafs on 16 September in Helsinki's Hartwall Arena during a three-game exhibition series, NHL Challenge 2003, played by the Leafs in Scandinavia.

WHERE WERE THE BIG BOYS?
The organisers were very unhappy that three of Europe's major hockey playing nations - Russia, Sweden and the Czech Republic - snubbed the Continental Cup.

"For many years the Swedes have had this arrogant attitude that they don't have to play for any club titles and they still call their league the best in Europe.

"Well, if their teams are so good, why don't they come here and prove it? You want to brag? Show up and play or shut up. In the long run, the Swedes and the Czechs will lose by isolating themselves."
Larry Huras, HC Lugano's Canadian coach.

"We are battling with...the 'village mentality' which exists to such a high degree in European club hockey. Many clubs in the highest ranked leagues feel they are on top of the world if they beat their next door neighbour. It is the task of the IIHF to broaden the horizons of the people who run the leagues and the clubs. The real challenge lies in beating the best of the best." *Rene Fasel, president of the world governing IIHF.*

NORTH AMERICAN LEAGUES

NATIONAL HOCKEY LEAGUE
STANLEY CUP
Winners　　　　NEW JERSEY DEVILS
Finalists　　MIGHTY DUCKS OF ANAHEIM
Game scores

　　3-0h,3-0h,2-3ot-a,0-1ot-a,6-3h, 2-5a,3-0h
　　　　　　　　　(Devils shown first)
　　(All seven games won by the home team)
PRESIDENT'S TROPHY (*most league points*)
　　OTTAWA SENATORS (Eastern Conference)
Runners-up
　　　DALLAS STARS (Western Conference)

FIRST ALL-STAR TEAM
Goal　　　　**Martin Brodeur**, New Jersey
Defence　　　**Niklas Lidstrom**, Detroit
　　　　　　　Al MacInnis, St. Louis
Centre　　　**Peter Forsberg**, Colorado
Right Wing　　**Todd Bertuzzi**, Vancouver
Left Wing　**Markus Naslund**, Vancouver

AWARD WINNERS
Art Ross Trophy (Most Points)
Peter Forsberg, Colorado Avalanche
Maurice 'Rocket' Richard Trophy (Most Goals)
Milan Hejduk, Colorado Avalanche
Hart Memorial Trophy (Most Valuable Player)
Peter Forsberg, Colorado Avalanche
James Norris Mem'l Trophy (Best Defenceman)
Niklas Lidstrom, Detroit Redwings
Vezina Trophy (Best Goaltender)
Martin Brodeur, New Jersey Devils
William Jennings Trophy (Fewest Goals Against)
*Martin Brodeur New Jersey Devils/**Roman Cechmanek** & **Robert Esche**, Phil. Flyers
Lester B Pearson Trophy (Players' Player)
Markus Naslund, Vancouver Canucks
Calder Memorial Trophy (Rookie of the Year)
Barret Jackman, St. Louis Blues
Lady Byng Mem'l Trophy (Most Sportsmanlike)
Alexander Mogilny, Toronto Maple Leafs
Jack Adams Award (Coach of the Year)
Jacques Lemaire, Minnesota Wild
Conn Smythe Trophy (Playoffs MVP)
J-S Giguere, Mighty Ducks of Anaheim
Frank J.Selke Trophy (Defensive Forward)
Jere Lehtinen, Dallas Stars
Bill Masterton Memorial Trophy (Most Dedicated)
Steve Yzerman, Detroit Redwings
* shared

Old Warrior gets one hand on Stanley Cup

NORMAN de MESQUITA

In a season of surprises, one of the biggest was that former Whitley Warriors' defenceman, **Mike Babcock**, was not even a finalist for the Jack Adams Trophy as Coach of the Year.

In his first season behind an NHL bench, he masterminded the Mighty Ducks of Anaheim to an improvement from 69 points to a franchise-best 95 and then took the previous no-hopers (only two playoff appearances in nine years) to the Stanley Cup final.

Their success was based on a well-drilled defensive system and some superb goaltending by Jean-Sebastian Giguere. Even though the Ducks lost the final to the New Jersey Devils, Giguere won the Conn Smythe Trophy as playoff MVP, only the fifth player (four of them goalies) from the losing team to do so.

Because both the Ducks and the Devils rely on defence, it was hardly a final series to remember. There was always the feeling that if the Devils scored first, especially at home, they would win. They did indeed and it was the first final series since 1965 when all seven games were won by the home team.

"I thought we had stage fright early," said Babcock, when Ducks lost the first two games in the Meadowlands. But two overtime wins tied the series with Stockport-born veteran **Steve Thomas** netting the winner in game four, giving the Ducks their seventh overtime win in as many games.

The regular season was dominated by the Ottawa Senators in the east and the Dallas Stars in the west. The Senators filed for bankruptcy in January and there was some doubt as to whether the players would be paid. But it did not affect their play and, happily, they found a new owner.

Shortly after the season ended, **Patrick Roy**, thought by many to be the greatest goaltender the game has seen, announced his retirement after an 18-year career with Montreal and Colorado, winning four Stanley Cups, and the Conn Smythe and Vezina trophies three times. He posted a record 551 wins with 66 shutouts.

MINOR LEAGUES
PLAYOFF WINNERS
American League (AHL) - Calder Cup
Houston Aeros

East Coast League (ECHL) - Kelly Cup
Atlantic City

Central League (CHL) - President's Cup
Memphis

United League (UHL) - Colonial Cup
Fort Wayne Komets

West Coast League (WCHL) - Taylor Cup
San Diego

Atlantic Coast League (ACHL) -
Orlando Seals

*Canadian (Major Junior A) League (CHL)
Memorial Cup*
Kitchener Rangers

HALL OF FAME
The following were to be inducted into the Hockey Hall of Fame in November 2003:

GRANT FUHR
Won five Stanley Cups playing in goal for the Edmonton Oilers in the Eighties. Played 868 games for six NHL teams, plus 150 Stanley Cup playoff games. Won the Vezina Trophy in 1988. His 92 playoff wins are second all-time.

PAT LAFONTAINE
Scored 468 goals and 1,013 points in 865 NHL games, mainly with New York Islanders and Buffalo Sabres, before being forced into retirement due to injury, aged 33. Twice had 50-goal NHL seasons and scored 30 goals nine times. Played for the USA in two Winter Olympics.

MIKE ILITCH
Elected for building Detroit Red Wings into a powerhouse NHL club, winning three Stanley Cups, four conference titles, and nine division championships, since purchasing the team from the Norris family in 1982. He has been a lifelong supporter of junior hockey through his *Little Caesars* pizza chain.

BRIAN KILREA
With the major junior Ottawa 67s since 1974 as their coach and manager, winning more than 1,000 games.

MIKE BABCOCK
The coach of the Mighty Ducks of Anaheim, the surprising Stanley Cup finalists, played for Whitley Warriors in the 1987-88 British League, helping them to the runners-up spot in the Premier Division. Though not officially Warriors' coach - that was **Terry Matthews** who was voted coach of the year - the defenceman was widely recognised as the 'power behind the throne'.

Babcock, 40, (*pictured above courtesy of Ice Hockey Archives*) first came to prominence in Canada as coach of their national team in the 1997 World Junior Championships. As coach of Moose Jaw in the Western (Major Junior) League, he coached **Scott Allison, Marc Hussey, Joe Cardarelli** and **Andrew Milne**, who all subsequently played in Britain.

Quotes of the Year
"You must be a heck of a defensive coach. You're the first guy who was ever able to stop [Ducks'] **Paul Kariya** from scoring." *Barry Melrose, TV analyst, to Anaheim coach* **Mike Babcock.**

"I was so damn nervous, I dropped my stick. I didn't know what to do out there." *Ken Daneyko, a lifelong member of New Jersey Devils, who iced only in the final minute of game seven of the Stanley Cup final owing to injury.*

"You either get suspended, fined, or have to give your first-born child to the league." *Pat Burns, New Jersey Devils' coach, on upsetting the league with his comments on refereeing.*

"This is the greatest game in the world. I thank you for letting me play it." *Wayne (the Gent) Gretzky to NHL commissioner Gary Bettman, on having his jersey retired and hung in the rafters of Los Angeles' Staples Center.*

OBITUARIES

MAC COLVILLE

Mac Colville, who played on the New York Rangers' Stanley Cup championship team in 1940, died on 27 May 2003, aged 87.

Colville played right wing on a line with his older brother, Neil, and left wing **Alex Shibicky**. He spent nine years in the league and enjoyed his best season in 1940-41 when he had 14 goals and 17 assists for 31 points. He missed three seasons serving in the Canadian armed forces during World War II and finished his career with 71 goals and 104 assists.

His death leaves only four surviving members of the 1939-40 Rangers -- Shibicky, **Clint Smith**, **Dutch Hiller** and **Alf Pike**.

FATHER LES COSTELLO

Father Les Costello was the only professional ice hockey player to quit the NHL to go into the priesthood. He left simply because of his faith, not because his hockey career was going nowhere. On the contrary, his three seasons with Toronto Maple Leafs came when the team won two Stanley Cups and he made a major contribution to one of them.

On his debut in the spring of 1948, he scored two goals and four points, including the game winner over Boston Bruins, as the Leafs went on to beat Detroit Red Wings to win the Cup. But only 15 games into the following season he fell out with coach, **Hap Day**, who subjected him to a stern lecture during practice. He handed Day his gloves and stick and said: "If you're so good, you do it." His behaviour earned him a ticket to Leafs' farm team in Pittsburgh and it was while there that he began to worry that he might turn into a 'hockey bum'. Though he was called up for the playoffs in 1950 he played only one game of Leafs' third successive Cup-winning run before quitting to join the church.

But he did not entirely sever his connections with the sport. In 1962 he co-founded the Flying Fathers, a team of skating priests recruited from all over Canada. They played more than 1,000 exhibition games for charity and raised around $4 million for good causes.

Costello never had any doubts about the wisdom of his action. "I'd rather teach people to live with God than thrill them occasionally on Saturday nights," he told a Canadian magazine. "Days at the movies, nights at the rink. I thought there must be a better way to spend my life."

Leslie John Thomas Costello was born on 16 February 1928 at South Porcupine, now part of Timmins in northern Ontario. He was ordained in 1957 and said his first Mass at St Joachim's Church in South Porcupine. In 1979 he became priest at St Alphonsus parish at Schumacher, near Timmins, and was still the parish priest

there at the time of his death on 10 December 2002. He died on the ice with the Flying Fathers after injuring his head during the warm-up while stretching for the puck. He was not wearing a helmet.

Father Costello is survived by two brothers and a sister. His younger brother, Murray, also played in the NHL.

STEVE DURBANO

One of pro hockey's most villainous characters died of liver cancer in Yellowknife, a town in Canada's bleak Northwest Territories, a month short of his 51st birthday.

The stories of Durbano's wild undisciplined life, on and off the ice, are legendary. His NHL career in the Seventies, mostly with the St Louis Blues and Pittsburgh Penguins, brought him up against Penguins' biggest rivals, Philadelphia Flyers, in an era when the brawling team were known as the Broad Street Bullies.

"I remember one game against the Flyers," recalled his cousin in the *Toronto Sun*. "**Dave Schultz** jumped him and then **Bob Kelly** jumped him. But Steve didn't care who it was, he'd fight anybody. The arenas were electric then. Those are sounds you don't hear anymore."

The first round draft pick of the New York Rangers in 1971 was notorious for his love of fighting. "He was a character right out of *Slap Shot*," said former Toronto Maple Leafs' coach, **Mike Murphy**, who used to play with Steve in junior hockey. "You think those guys were invented? You didn't know Steve Durbano.

"He scared me when he played with me and when he played against me. He was very likeable, funny, friendly and genuine. But he used his stick in vile ways."

In 1983, three years after he retired, he was sentenced to seven years in prison for his part in a scheme to import $568,000 worth of cocaine. Some years later, he was caught taking five shirts from a clothes shop. He had $12 in his wallet at the time and claimed to be living on welfare.

Murphy remembered another incident in a junior playoff game in London, Ontario when Durbano, then a rough and ready teenager, was playing for the local team's hated rivals, the Toronto Marlboros. "On his first shift he speared **Darryl Sitler**, **Gordie Brooks** and **Gary Geldart**. There are these three guys, doubled over on the ice, lying there. The crowd just wanted to kill us. I think we won the series right there. It was scary to see. But that was Steve."

Some say he got his temper from his father, Nick, who once waited in the car park after a game and attempted to run the referee over.

Steve Shutt, another former Marlie, now in the Hockey Hall of Fame, recalled: "I don't know how many rinks we'd drive away from and have to go pick up Steve and get him out of jail. We'd play, he'd get arrested. We got used to that."

KEN MCKENZIE

The co-founder of *The Hockey News* of Toronto died on 9 April 2003, aged 79.

McKenzie was in his early 20s when he and his partner **Will Cote** got together and agreed it was time that hockey had its own weekly paper. The idea caught on. They used $383.81 in subscriptions to pay the printer and *The Hockey News* was born in Montreal in 1947.

At the time, McKenzie was the NHL's publicity director and as the league thought the paper would benefit the sport, they co-operated in getting it off the ground. He was a 'hands-on' publisher, always to be seen at games, while Cote was happy to stay in the background, taking care of the administration.

McKenzie was honoured by the Hockey Hall of Fame who gave him the Elmer Ferguson Award for excellence in journalism in 1997.

ROGER NEILSON

The NHL coach known as Captain Video for his innovative use of taped games, died at his home in Peterborough, Ontario on 21 June 2003. He was 69 and had been fighting cancer for four years. Neilson coached teams for 50 years and was head coach of several NHL clubs, starting in 1977 with **Harold Ballard**'s Toronto Maple Leafs and going on to Buffalo Sabres, Vancouver Canucks, Los Angeles Kings, New York Rangers, Florida Panthers, Philadelphia Flyers and Ottawa Senators. Senators recently gave him a game so he could reach his 1,000th.

Though unable to attend every Ottawa game during the 2003 playoffs, Neilson, frail from chemotherapy and radiation treatments, attended every pre-game meeting. His speech about getting second chances in life, before game five with the Senators down 3-1 in their series against New Jersey Devils, inspired Ottawa to win the next two games.

"Roger could do it all as a coach," said legendary Detroit coach **Scotty Bowman**. "He could prepare a team for games and practices, plus nobody could match lines the way that Roger could during games. He knew who to put on in the right situations. He was a really, really intelligent person. He coached 1,000 games behind the bench and there are not a lot of coaches in the league who can say that."

Neilson, who had legions of friends throughout the sport, was always dreaming up new ways to beat the opposition. He was the first to realise what a powerful tool video-tape is for analysing games, though he took a lot of ribbing when he insisted that his players sit down and watch the game they'd just played. Now every NHL club employs a video co-ordinator.

The league was forced to change some of its rules as he exploited some unexpected loopholes to get any advantage he could. Once when he pulled his goalie in the last minute of a game, he told the keeper to leave his stick lying across the goalmouth. Another time, after the opposing team were awarded a penalty shot, he replaced his netminder with a defenceman and told him to rush the shooter. And when he had two players in the penalty box, he sneaked on a fourth skater saying it didn't matter how many penalties he got because the rules say you can't have fewer than three on the ice.

The Towel Incident is probably the one thing for which Neilson will be best remembered by fans. During the 1982 Stanley Cup playoffs he became annoyed at the refs and waved a white towel stuck on the end of a stick in mock surrender. Ever since, NHL fans have waved white towels in a show of support for the home team. "I just wish I had the (towel) concession," he said. Something of a rebel, he hated the NHL's suit-and-tie 'uniform' behind the bench. His way of showing his sartorial independence was to wear the most outrageous ties he could find. When he coached his 300th NHL win in New York, the Rangers bought him 300 ties.

He was inducted into the Hockey Hall of Fame last year and awarded the Order of Canada, the country's highest honour, in May 2003.

CHARLIE 'CHUCK' RAYNER

Former New York Rangers goaltender **Charlie 'Chuck' Rayner**, who died on 9 October 2002 aged 82, won the Hart Trophy as the NHL's most valuable player in 1950. He played ten seasons with Rangers and was elected to the Hockey Hall of Fame in 1973.

'Bonnie Prince Charlie', as he was sometimes called, was the first goaltender in history to be credited with scoring a goal. While playing with a Royal Canadian Navy team against an Army side in Halifax, Nova Scotia in 1944, he skated all the way up the ice for the historic tally.

JACQUES RICHARD

The troubled life of the one-time 50-goal scorer ended tragically in a single vehicle car crash in October 2002. The former Quebec Nordique was 50. A junior scoring sensation with the Quebec City Remparts, Richard was drafted by the NHL's Atlanta Flames in 1972 and scored 52 goals for the Nordiques in 1980-81.

After retiring, however, he became a cocaine addict and once spent 14 months in prison for smuggling three kilograms of the substance in his golf bag on a flight home from Colombia. Police found five grams of cocaine in the remains of his car.

ROLL OF HONOUR
Modern Era

Winners and runners-up in all major domestic club competitions since the start of the Modern Era.
Compiled exclusively for the Annual by Gordon Wade with contributions from Martin Harris.
The Roll of Honour for the years before season 1982-83 is in The Ice Hockey Annual 1998-99.

SEASON	COMPETITION	WINNER	RUNNER-UP	NOTES
2002-03	+ Superleague Playoff Ch'ship	Belfast Giants	London Knights	Won 5-3 at Nottingham
	+ Superleague	Sheffield Steelers	Belfast Giants	Only five teams in league
	+ Challenge Cup	Sheffield Steelers	Nottingham Panthers	Won 3-2 at Manchester
	British Nat'l Lge Ch'ships	Coventry Blaze	Cardiff Devils	Won 5-3 on agg. (3-2a,2-1h)
	British National League	Coventry Blaze	Dundee Stars	Blaze lost only five games
	Findus Cup	Newcastle Vipers	Coventry Blaze	Won 3-0 at Newcastle
	Eng Nat'l Lge, Premier Div Ch'ship	Milton Keynes Lightning	Peterborough Phantoms	Won 16-4 on agg. (10-0h,6-4a)
	Eng Nat'l Lge, Premier Division	Peterborough Phantoms	Milton Keynes Lightning	12-team league
	Eng Nat'l Lge, Premier Cup	Peterborough Phantoms	Milton Keynes Lightning	Won 7-6 on agg. (2-4a,5-2h)
	Eng Nat'l Lge, Div. One Ch'ship	Basingstoke Buffalo	Altrincham Aces	Won 10-9 on agg. (4-5a,6-4h)
	Eng Nat'l Lge, Div. One North	Sheffield Scimitars	Altrincham Aces	Aces' last season
	Eng Nat'l Lge, Div. One South	Basingstoke Buffalo	Bracknell Hornets	
	Caledonian Cup	Fife Flyers	Dundee Stars	Won 9-7 on agg. (5-3h,4-4a)
2001-02	+ Superleague Playoff Ch'ship	Sheffield Steelers	Manchester Storm	Won 4-3 (ps) at Nottingham
	+*Sekonda* Superleague	Belfast Giants	Ayr Scottish Eagles	Giants' second season
	+ Challenge Cup	Ayr Scottish Eagles	Belfast Giants	Won 5-0 at Belfast
	British Nat'l Lge Ch'ships	Dundee Stars	Coventry Blaze	Won 8-7 on agg. (7-4a, 1-3h)
	British National League	Dundee Stars	Coventry Blaze	Stars' first season
	Findus Cup	Fife Flyers	Coventry Blaze	Won 6-3 at Nottingham
	Eng Nat'l Lge, Premier Div Ch'ship	Invicta Dynamos	Isle of Wight Raiders	Won 6-3 on agg. (2-1a, 4-2h)
	Eng Nat'l Lge, Premier Division	Invicta Dynamos	Solihull Barons	
	Eng Nat'l Lge, Premier Cup	Romford Raiders	Invicta Dynamos	Won 9-7 on agg. ((5-3h, 4-4a)
	Eng Nat'l Lge, Div. One Ch'ship	Whitley Warriors	Basingstoke Buffalo	Won on agg. 12-7 (6-6a, 6-1h)
	Eng Nat'l Lge, Div. One North	Whitley Warriors	Altrincham Aces	
	Eng Nat'l Lge, Div. One South	Basingstoke Buffalo	Flintshire Freeze	
	Eng Nat'l Lge, Cup	Whitley Warriors	Telford Wild Foxes	Won 10-8 on agg. (2-5a, 8-3h)
	Caledonian Cup	Dundee Stars	Fife Flyers	Won 8-4 on agg. (3-2a, 5-2h)
2000-01	+= Superleague Playoff Ch'ship	Sheffield Steelers	London Knights	Won 2-1 at Nottingham
	+ *Sekonda* Superleague	Sheffield Steelers	Cardiff Devils	Won by 19 points but censured for breaking wage cap.
	B&H Autumn Cup	Sheffield Steelers	Newcastle Jesters	Won 4-0 at Sheffield
	+Challenge Cup	Sheffield Steelers	Ayr Scottish Eagles	Won 4-2 at Belfast
	Findus British Nat'l Lge Ch'ships	Guildford Flames	Basingstoke Bison	Won 12-4 on agg. (7-2a, 5-2h)
	Findus British Nat'l Lge	Guildford Flames	Basingstoke Bison	
	Benson and Hedges Plate	Basingstoke Bison	Guildford Flames	Won 3-2 at Sheffield
	ntl Christmas Cup	Guildford Flames	Fife Flyers	Won 7-3 on agg. (4-1h,3-2a)
	Eng Nat'l Lge, Premier Div Ch'ship	Romford Raiders	Chelmsford Chieftains	Won 11-4 on agg. (7-2, 4-2)
	Eng Nat'l Lge, Premier Division	Swindon Phoenix	Chelmsford Chieftains	
	Eng Nat'l Lge, Premier Cup	Isle of Wight Raiders	Swindon Phoenix	Won 5-2 on agg. (3-2a, 2-0h)
	Eng Nat'l Lge, Div. One Ch'ship	Whitley Warriors	Billingham Eagles	Won 14-7 on agg. (4-6h,10-1a)
	Eng Nat'l Lge, Div. One North	Billingham Eagles	Whitley Warriors	
	Eng Nat'l Lge, Div. One South	Basingstoke Buffalo	Flintshire Freeze	
	Scottish Cup	Fife Flyers	Edinburgh Capitals	Won 7-4 at Kirkcaldy.

ROLL OF HONOUR

SEASON	COMPETITION	WINNERS	RUNNERS-UP	NOTES
1999-00	+= Superleague Playoff Ch'ship	London Knights	Newcastle Riverkings	Won 7-3 at Manchester
	+ Sekonda Superleague	Bracknell Bees	Sheffield Steelers	
	B&H Autumn Cup	Manchester Storm	London Knights	Won 4-3 (ps) at Sheffield.
	+Challenge Cup	Sheffield Steelers	Nottingham Panthers	Won 2-1 at London Arena
	British National Lge Ch'ship	Fife Flyers	Basingstoke Bison	Won best-of-five series 3-0.
	British National Lge	Fife Flyers	Guildford Flames	
	Benson and Hedges Plate	Basingstoke Bison	Slough Jets	Won 5-1 at Sheffield
	ntl Christmas Cup	Fife Flyers	Basingstoke Bison	Won 6-5 on agg. (3-3,3-2)
	Eng. Lge, Premier Div. Ch'ship	Chelmsford Chieftains	Swindon Chill	Won 7-4 on agg. (5-2,2-2)
	English Lge, Premier Div.	Chelmsford Chieftains	Isle of Wight Raiders	
	Data Vision Millennium Cup	Chelmsford Chieftains	Swindon Chill	Won 10-7 at Swindon.
	English Lge, Div. One Ch'ship	Whitley Warriors	Billingham Eagles	Won 14-10 on agg. (7-4,7-6)
	English Lge, Div One North	Billingham Eagles	Whitley Warriors	
	English Lge, Div One South	Haringey Greyhounds	Basingstoke Buffalo	
	Scottish Cup	Fife Flyers	Paisley Pirates	Won 9-4 at Kirkcaldy
1998-99	+=Superleague Playoff Ch'ship	Cardiff Devils	Nottingham Panthers	Won 2-1 at Manchester
	+Sekonda Superleague	Manchester Storm	Cardiff Devils	
	B&H (Autumn) Cup	Nottingham Panthers	Ayr Scottish Eagles	Won 2-1 at Sheffield
	+Challenge Cup	Sheffield Steelers	Nottingham Panthers	Won 4-0 at Sheffield
	British National Lge Playoffs	Fife Flyers	Slough Jets	Won 6-5 (ps) at Hull
	British National League	Slough Jets	Basingstoke Bison	
	Benson and Hedges Plate	Guildford Flames	Telford Tigers	Won 4-3 at Sheffield
	Vic Christmas Cup	Peterborough Pirates	Basingstoke Bison	Won 5-3 on agg. (2-1,3-2)
	Eng. Lge, Premier Div. Ch'ship	Solihull Blaze	Milton Keynes Kings	Won 5-3 on agg. (3-0,2-3)
	English Lge, Premier Div	Solihull Blaze	Milton Keynes Kings	
	English Cup	Milton Keynes Kings	Solihull Blaze	Won 13-9 on agg. (7-6,6-3)
	English Lge, Div. One Ch'ship	Whitley Warriors	Billingham Eagles	Won 14-10 on agg. (7-4,7-6)
	English Lge, Div One North	Billingham Eagles	Altrincham Aces	
	English Lge, Div One South	Cardiff Rage	Basingstoke Buffalo	
	Scottish Cup	Fife Flyers	Edinburgh Capitals	Won 6-4 at Kirkcaldy.
1997-98	+Superleague Playoff Ch'ship	Ayr Scottish Eagles	Cardiff Devils	Won 3-2ot at Manchester
	+Superleague	Ayr Scottish Eagles	Manchester Storm	
	B & H (Autumn) Cup	Ayr Scottish Eagles	Cardiff Devils	Won 2-1 at Sheffield
	+The Express Cup	Ayr Scottish Eagles	Bracknell Bees	Won 3-2 at Newcastle
	British National Lge Playoffs	Guildford Flames	Kingston Hawks	Won 5-1 at Hull
	British National League	Guildford Flames	Telford Tigers	
	Northern Premier League	Fife Flyers	Paisley Pirates	
	Southern Premier League	Guildford Flames	Slough Jets	
	Benson & Hedges Plate	Slough Jets	Telford Tigers	Won 4-3 at Sheffield
	Upper Deck Christmas Cup	Telford Tigers	Guildford Flames	Won 10-7 on agg. (5-5, 5-2)
	Eng. Lge, National Div Ch'ship.	Solihull Blaze	Chelmsford Chieftains	Won 18-6 on agg. (9-5,9-1)
	English Lge, National Div.	Solihull Blaze	Whitley Warriors	
	English Lge, Div One North	Solihull Blaze	Whitley Warriors	
	English Lge, Div One South	Invicta Dynamos	Chelmsford Chieftains	
	Scottish Cup	Fife Flyers	Paisley Pirates	Won 5-1 at Kirkcaldy
1996-97	+Superleague Playoff Ch'ship	Sheffield Steelers	Nottingham Panthers	Won 3-1 at Manchester
	+Superleague	Cardiff Devils	Sheffield Steelers	
	B & H (Autumn) Cup	Nottingham Panthers	Ayr Scottish Eagles	Won 5-3 at Sheffield
	Premier League Playoffs	Swindon IceLords	Fife Flyers	Won 5-0 at Manchester
	Northern Premier League	Fife Flyers	Paisley Pirates	
	(Southern) Premier League	Swindon IceLords	Solihull Blaze	
	English League Championship	Wightlink Raiders	Chelmsford Chieftains	Won 10-6 on agg. (5-2,5-4)
	English League, South	Romford Raiders	Chelmsford Chieftains	
	English League, North	Kingston Jets	Altrincham Aces	
	Scottish Cup	Paisley Pirates	Fife Flyers	Won 8-4 at Kirkcaldy
	British Jnr Championship	Sunderland Arrows	Fife Flames	Won 3-2 at Manchester

ROLL OF HONOUR

| --- | --- | --- | --- | --- |
1995-96	British Championship	Sheffield Steelers	Nottingham Panthers	Won on 2-1 PS (3-3ot) at Wembley.
	British League, Premier Div.	Sheffield Steelers	Cardiff Devils	
	British League, Div One	Manchester Storm	Blackburn Hawks	
	Promotion Playoffs	Manchester Storm	Milton Keynes Kings	Two playoff group winners
	B & H (Autumn) Cup	Sheffield Steelers	Nottingham Panthers	Won 5-2 at Sheffield
	English League Championship	Wightlink Raiders	Durham City Wasps	Won 15-8 on agg. (8-0,7-8)
	English League, South	Oxford City Stars	Wightlink Raiders	
	English League, North	Humberside Jets	Altrincham Aces	
	Autumn Trophy	Dumfries Border Vikings	Chelmsford Chieftains	Won 23-0, second leg not played.
	British Jnr Championship	Guildford Firestars	Fife Flames	Won 3-2 at Wembley
1994-95	British Championship	Sheffield Steelers	Edinburgh Racers	Won 7-2 at Wembley
	British League, Premier Div.	Sheffield Steelers	Cardiff Devils	
	British League, Div One	Slough Jets	Telford Tigers	
	Promotion Playoffs	Slough Jets	Whitley Warriors	Two playoff group winners
	B & H (Autumn) Cup	Nottingham Panthers	Cardiff Devils	Won 7-2 at Sheffield
	English League Championship	Wightlink Raiders	Sunderland Chiefs	Won 11-5 on agg. (7-2,4-3)
	English League, South	Wightlink Raiders	Peterborough Patriots	
	English League, North	Sunderland Chiefs	Nottingham Jaguars	
	Autumn Trophy	Solihull Barons	Swindon Wildcats	Won 19-16 on agg. (7-6,12-10)
	Scottish Cup	Fife Flyers	Paisley Pirates	Won 11-2 at Kirkcaldy
	British Jnr Championship	Fife Flames	Durham Mosquitoes	Won 5-1 at Wembley
1993-94	British Championship	Cardiff Devils	Sheffield Steelers	Won 12-1 at Wembley
	British League, Premier Div.	Cardiff Devils	Sheffield Steelers	Fife Flyers later placed 2nd
	British League, Div One	M Keynes Kings (N)	Slough Jets (S)	No playoff. Kings most points.
	Promotion Playoffs	Milton Keynes Kings	Peterborough Pirates	Two playoff group winners
	B & H (Autumn) Cup	Murrayfield Racers	Cardiff Devils	Won 6-2 at Sheffield
	English League Championship	Wightlink Raiders	Nottingham Jaguars	Won 17-7 on agg. (6-4,11-3)
	English League	Wightlink Raiders	Sunderland Chiefs	
	Autumn Trophy	Telford Tigers	Medway Bears	Won 11-7 on agg. (8-3,3-4)
	Scottish Cup	Fife Flyers	Murrayfield Racers	Won 6-5 at Kirkcaldy
	British Jnr Championship	Fife Flames	Swindon Leopards	1-1ot at Wembley. Trophy shared.
1992-93	*British Championship	Cardiff Devils	Humberside Seahawks	Won 7-4 at Wembley
	*British League, Premier Div	Cardiff Devils	Murrayfield Racers	
	*British League, Div One	Basingstoke Beavers	Sheffield Steelers	
	*Promotion Playoffs	Basingstoke Beavers	Sheffield Steelers	Two group winners
	B & H (Autumn) Cup	Cardiff Devils	Whitley Warriors	Won 10-4 atSheffield
	English League Championship	Solihull Barons	Guildford Flames	Won 16-13 on agg. (6-7,10-6)
	English League, Conference A	Solihull Barons	Bristol Bulldogs	
	English League, Conference B	Guildford Flames	Chelmsford Chieftains	
	BL Entry Playoffs	Trafford Metros	Chelmsford Chieftains	Also EL PO. Two group winners
	Autumn Trophy	Milton Keynes Kings	Solihull Barons	Won 11-4 at Sheffield
	Scottish Cup	Murrayfield Racers	Whitley Warriors	Won 8-7 at Murrayfield
	British Jnr Championship	Durham Mosquitoes	Fife Flames	Won 5-2 at Wembley
1991-92	*British Championship	Durham Wasps	Nottingham Panthers	Won 7-6 at Wembley
	*British League, Premier Div.	Durham Wasps	Nottingham Panthers	
	*British League, Div One	Fife Flyers	Slough Jets	
	*Promotion Playoffs	Bracknell Bees	Fife Flyers	Two group winners
	Autumn Cup	Nottingham Panthers	Humberside Seahawks	Won 7-5 at Sheffield
	English League	Medway Bears	Sheffield Steelers	No championship playoff.
	BL Entry Playoffs	Medway Bears	Sheffield Steelers	Also EL PO. Two group winners.
	Autumn Trophy	Swindon Wildcats	Milton Keynes Kings	Won 3-2 on PS (5-5ot) at Sheffield.
	Scottish Cup	Whitley Warriors	Ayr Raiders	Won 7-4 at Murrayfield
	British Jnr Championship	Fife Flames	Durham Mosquitoes	Won 3-2 at Wembley

ROLL OF HONOUR

SEASON	COMPETITION	WINNERS	RUNNERS-UP	NOTES
1990-91	*British Championship	Durham Wasps	Peterborough Pirates	Won 7-4 at Wembley
	*British League, Premier Div.	Durham Wasps	Cardiff Devils	
	*British League, Div One	Humberside Seahawks	Slough Jets	
	*Promotion Playoffs	Humberside Seahawks	Bracknell Bees	Two group winners
	Norwich Union (Autumn) Cup	Durham Wasps	Murrayfield Racers	Won 12-6 at Whitley
	English League	Oxford Stars	Milton Keynes Kings	First Division
	BL Entry Playoffs	Lee Valley Lions	Milton Keynes Kings	Also EL PO. Two group winners.
	Autumn Trophy	Chelmsford Chieftains	Oxford City Stars	League format.
	Scottish Cup	Murrayfield Racers	Ayr Raiders	Won 9-4 at Murrayfield
	British Jnr Championship	Fife Flames	Romford Hornets	Won 5-0 at Wembley
1989-90	*British Championship	Cardiff Devils	Murrayfield Racers	Won 6-5 PS (6-6 ot) at Wembley.
	*British League, Premier Div.	Cardiff Devils	Murrayfield Racers	
	*British League, Div One	Slough Jets	Cleveland Bombers	
	*Promotion Playoffs	Cleveland Bombers	Slough Jets	Div One top four
	Norwich Union (Autumn) Cup	Murrayfield Racers	Durham Wasps	Won 10-4 at Basingstoke
	English League	Bracknell Bees	Romford Raiders	First Division
	BL Entry Playoffs	Basingstoke Beavers	Romford Raiders	Also EL playoffs
	Autumn Trophy	Humberside Seahawks	Bracknell Bees	Won 23-17 on agg. (15-9,8-8)
	Scottish Cup	Murrayfield Racers	Cardiff Devils	Won 13-4 at Murrayfield
	British Jnr Championship	Nottingham Cougars	Fife Flames	Won 3-1 at Wembley
1988-89	*British Championship	Nottingham Panthers	Ayr Bruins	Won 6-3 at Wembley
	*British League, Premier Div.	Durham Wasps	Murrayfield Racers	
	*British League, Div One	Cardiff Devils	Medway Bears	
	*Promotion Playoffs	Cardiff Devils	Streatham Redskins	Premier winner v last in Div One.
	Norwich Union (Autumn) Cup	Durham Wasps	Tayside Tigers	Won 7-5 at NEC, Birmingham
	English League	Humberside Seahawks	Bracknell Bees	First Division
	Autumn Trophy	Cardiff Devils	Medway Bears	Won 15-8 on agg. (9-4,6-4)
	Scottish Cup	Murrayfield Racers	Ayr Bruins	Won 9-5 at Murrayfield
	British Jnr Championship	Durham Mosquitoes	Dundee Bengals	Won pen shots at Wembley (5-5)
1987-88	*British Championship	Durham Wasps	Fife Flyers	Won 8-5 at Wembley
	*British League, Premier Div.	Murrayfield Racers	Whitley Warriors	
	*British League, Div One	Telford Tigers (S)	Cleveland Bombers (N)	Won 21-14 on agg. (12-10, 9-4)
	Promotion Playoffs	Peterborough Pirates	Telford Tigers	Premier winner v last in Div One
	British League, Div Two	Romford Raiders	Chelmsford Chieftains	
	Norwich Union (Autumn) Cup	Durham Wasps	Murrayfield Racers	Won 11-5 at Kirkcaldy
	Autumn Trophy	Cardiff Devils	Trafford Metros	Won 11-10 on agg. (7-5,4-5)
	Scottish Cup	Murrayfield Racers	Fife Flyers	Won 9-6 at Murrayfield
	British Jnr Championship	Nottingham Cougars	Fife Flames	Won 4-2 at Wembley
1986-87	*British Championship	Durham Wasps	Murrayfield Racers	Won 9-5 at Wembley
	*British League, Premier Div.	Murrayfield Racers	Dundee Rockets	
	*British League, Div One	Peterborough Pirates	Medway Bears	
	British League, Div Two	Aviemore Blackhawks	Cardiff Devils	Won playoff 10-9 at Cardiff
	Norwich Union (Autumn) Cup	Nottingham Panthers	Fife Flyers	Won 5-4ot at NEC, Birmingham
	Scottish Cup	Murrayfield Racers	Dundee Rockets	Won 7-6 at Kirkcaldy
	British Jnr Championship	Durham Mosquitoes	Murrayfield Ravens	Won 11-1 at Wembley

ROLL OF HONOUR

SEASON	COMPETITION	WINNERS	RUNNERS-UP	NOTES
1985-86	*British Championship	Murrayfield Racers	Dundee Rockets	Won 4-2 at Wembley
	*British League, Premier Div.	Durham Wasps	Murrayfield Racers	
	*British League, Div One	Solihull Barons	Lee Valley Lions	
	British League, Div Two	Medway Bears	Grimsby Buffaloes	Won playoff 26-4 at Medway
	Norwich Union (Autumn) Cup	Murrayfield Racers	Durham Wasps	Won 8-5 at Murrayfield
	Scottish Cup	Dundee Rockets	Murrayfield Racers	Won 7-3 at Dundee
	British Jnr Championship	Streatham Scorpions	Fife Flames	Won 7-0 at Wembley
1984-85	*British Championship	Fife Flyers	Murrayfield Racers	Won 9-4 at Wembley
	*British League, Premier Div.	Durham Wasps	Fife Flyers	
	*British League, Div One	Peterborough Pirates	Solihull Barons	
	British League, Div Two	Oxford Stars	Aviemore Blackhawks	Won playoff 6-1 at Oxford
	Bluecol Autumn Cup	Durham Wasps	Fife Flyers	Won 6-4 at Streatham
1983-84	*British Championship	Dundee Rockets	Murrayfield Racers	Won 5-4 at Wembley
	*British League, Premier Div.	Dundee Rockets	Durham Wasps	
	*British League, Div One	Southampton Vikings	Crowtree Chiefs	
	British League, Div Two	Whitley Braves	Streatham Bruins	Won playoff 14-9 on agg (6-7, 8-2)
	Autumn Cup	Dundee Rockets	Streatham Redskins	Won pen shots at Streatham (6-6)
1982-83	*British Championship	Dundee Rockets	Durham Wasps	Won 6-2 at Streatham
	British League Section A	Dundee Rockets	Murrayfield Racers	)
	Section B	Durham Wasps	Cleveland Bombers	)Div One - interlocking schedule
	Section C	Altrincham Aces	Blackpool Seagulls	)
	British League, Div Two	Solihull Barons	Grimsby Buffaloes	Won Play-off 8-5 at Solihull

= Sponsored by Sekonda * Sponsored by Heineken   + All-professional competition

GOVERNING BODIES

ICE HOCKEY UK LTD

Chairman: Stuart Robertson.
Administrator: Gill Short, 47 Westminster Buildings, Theatre Sq, Nottingham NG1 6LG.
Tel: 0115-924-1441. **Fax:** 0115-924-3443.
e-mail: hockey@icehockeyuk.co.uk
website: www.icehockeyuk.co.uk
The Board of Directors of the sport's national governing body are: **Stuart Robertson** (chairman & SIHA), **Danny Carroll** (treasurer), **Neville Moralee** (vice-chairman & EIHA), **Bob Wilkinson** (EIHA), **Alan Gray** (SIHA), **John Lyttle** & **Andy Gibson** (NIIHF), **Gary Stefan** (BNL) & **Tom Muir** (BNL), **Warren Rost** (players rep).

BRITISH NAT. ICE HOCKEY LGE LTD

Chairman: Tom Muir.
General Manager: Gary Stefan.
Secretary: To be appointed.
e-mail: admin@britnatleague.co.uk
website: www.fbnl.co.uk

ELITE ICE HOCKEY LEAGUE LTD

Chairman: Eamon Convery.
Secretary: To be appointed.
Address: EIHL Ltd, Phoenix House, Mansfield Road, Sutton-in-Ashfield, Nottingham NG17 4HD.
Tel: 01623-551150. **Fax:** 01623-440483.
website: www.eliteicehockey.co.uk

ENGLISH ICE HOCKEY ASSOCIATION

Chairman: Ken Taggart.
Gen Secretary: Bill Britton, 7 Laughton Avenue, West Bridgford, Notts NG2 7GJ.
Tel/Fax: 0115-923-1461
website: www.eiha.co.uk
The EIHA is managed by an Executive Committee comprising: **Ken Taggart** (chairman), **Tony Oliver** (deputy chairman), **Bill Britton** (secretary), **Neville Moralee** (treasurer), **Bob Wilkinson, Alan Moutrey, Irene Jones**.

N IRELAND ICE HOCKEY FED.

Chairman: John Lyttle.
Secretary: Lorna Taylor.

Address: 1st floor, 201 Upper Newtownards Road, Belfast BT4 3JD.
Tel: 012890-654040. **Fax:** 012890-651700.

SCOTTISH ICE HOCKEY ASSN.

President: Frank Dempster.
Secretary: Mrs Pat Swiatek, 71 Prestwick Road, Ayr KA5 7LQ.
Tel/Fax: 01292-284053
website: www.siha.net
SCOTTISH NATIONAL LEAGUE
Secretary: Adeline Andrews, 3 Hollybank, Viewpark, Ayr KA7 3PN. **Tel:** 01292-265800.
e-mail: Aand55@aol.com.

WOMEN'S ICE HOCKEY LEAGUE

Chairman: Bill Britton.
Secretary: Sylvian Clifford, 14 Windrush Drive, Springfield, Chelmsford CM1 7QF.
Tel/Fax: 01245-259181.
e-mail: sylvian.clifford1@btopenworld.com
website: www.eiha.co.uk

ICE HOCKEY PLAYERS ASSOCIATION (GB)

Executive Director: Joanne Collins, 25 Caxton Ave, Addlestone, Weybridge, Surrey KT15 1LJ.
Tel: 01932-843660. **Fax:** 01932-844401.
e-mail: ihpa@virgin.net
website: www.ihpa.co.uk

USEFUL ADDRESSES

BRITISH ICE HOCKEY WRITERS' ASSN

Chairman: Stewart Roberts.
Secretary (acting): Stewart Roberts, 50 Surrenden Lodge, Surrenden Road, Brighton BN1 6QB. **Tel/fax:** 01273-597889.
e-mail: stewice@aol.com
website: www.bihwa.co.uk

GB SUPPORTERS CLUB

Secretary: Annette Petrie, 65 Leas Drive, Iver, Bucks SL0 9RB. **Tel/Fax:** 01753-710778.
e-mail: gbsc@blueyonder.co.uk.
website: www.gbsc.co.uk/

CLUB DIRECTORY 2003-04

ABERDEEN

Rink Address: Linx Ice Arena, Beach Leisure Centre, Beach Esplanade, Aberdeen AB2 1NR.
Tel: 01224-655406/7. **Fax**: 01224-648693.
Ice Size: 184 x 85 feet (56 x 26 metres).
Spectator Capacity: 1,200
Club Secretary: Carol Hogan, 326 Holburn Street, Aberdeen AB10 7GX.
Tel: 01224-594900.
e-mail: donaldo.northstar3@btinternet.com

AYR/PRESTWICK

Rink closed at press-time.
Arena Address: Centrum Arena, Ayr Road, Prestwick KA9 1TR.
Tel: 01292-671600. **Fax**: 01292-678833.
Ice Size: 200 x 103 feet (61 x 31.5 metres).
Spectator Capacity: 2,745.

BASINGSTOKE

Rink Address: Planet Ice Basingstoke Arena, Basingstoke Leisure Park, Worting Road, Basingstoke, Hants RG22 6PG.
Tel: 01256-355266. **Fax**: 01256-357367.
Ice Size: 197 x 98 feet (60 x 30 metres)
Spectator Capacity: 1,600.
Senior Teams: Bison (Elite League) and Buffalo (Eng Nat Lge South).
Bison's contact: Steve Moria at the rink.
Tel: 01256-346159. **Fax**: 01256-357367
Bison's Colours: *home*: White, Red & Silver; *away*: Red & Silver.
website: www.bstokebison.co.uk

BELFAST

ODYSSEY ARENA
Address: Queen's Quay, Belfast BT3.
Tel: 02890-766000. **Fax**: 02890-766044.
Ice Size: 197 x 98 feet (60 x 30 metres).
Spectator Capacity (for ice hockey): 7,100.
Team: Giants (Elite League).
Communications to: Rob Stewart.
Club Address: Belfast Giants Ltd, Unit 3, Ormeau Business Park, 8 Cromac Avenue, Belfast BT7 2JA.
Tel: 028-9059-1111. **Fax**: 028-9059-1212.
e-mail: office@belfastgiants.co.uk
Colours: *home*: White, Red & Teal; *away*: Teal, White & Red.
website: www.belfastgiants.co.uk

DUNDONALD INTERNATIONAL ICE BOWL
Address: 111 Old Dundonald Road, Dundonald, Co Down, N Ireland.
Tel: 02890-482611. **Fax**: 02890-489604.
Ice Size: 197 x 98 feet (60 x 30 metres).
Spectator Capacity: 1,500.
Junior and recreational teams only 2003-04

BILLINGHAM

Rink Address: Billingham Forum Leisure Centre, Town Centre, Billingham, Cleveland TS23 2OJ. **Tel/Fax**: 01642-551381.
Ice Size: 180 x 80 feet (55 x 24 metres)
Spectator Capacity: 1,200.
Senior Team: Bombers (Eng Nat Lge North).
Club Secretary: Brian McCabe, 7 Cranstock Close, Billingham, Cleveland TS22 5RS.
Tel/Fax: 01642-534458.
e-mail: bmccabe_1@hotmail.com
Colours: *Home*: White, Red & Black; *away*: Black & Red.

BIRMINGHAM

Rink closed following fire. Re-opening date unknown at press-time.

Rink Address: Planet Ice Birmingham Arena, Pershore Street, Birmingham B5 4RW
Tel: 0121-693-2400. **Fax**: 0121-693-2401
Ice Size: 180 x 80 feet (55 x 24 metres)
Spectator Capacity: 300

CLUB DIRECTORY

BLACKBURN

Rink Address: Blackburn Arena, Lower Audley, Waterside, Blackburn, Lancs BB1 1BB.
Tel: 01254-668686. **Fax:** 01254-691516.
Ice Size: 197 x 98 feet (60 x 30 metres)
Spectator Capacity: 3,200.
Senior Team: Hawks (English Nat Lge North)
Club Secretary: Mark Halliwell c/o the arena.
e-mail: mark@blackburnicearena.co.uk
Colours: Pacific Teal, Grey, Black & White.

BRACKNELL

Rink Address: John Nike Leisuresport Complex, John Nike Way, Bracknell, Berks RG12 4TN.
Tel: 01344-789006, **Fax:** 01344-789201.
Ice Size: 197 x 98 feet (60 x 30 metres)
Spectator Capacity: 3,100.
Senior Teams: Bees (British National League) and Hornets (English Nat Lge South).
Bees' Club Secretary: Jane McDougall c/o rink.
Tel: 01344-789209. **Fax:** 01344-789222
e-mail: bracknellbees@nikegroup.co.uk
Bees' colours: *home:* White, Gold & Black; *away:* Black, Gold & White.
website: www.beesprohockey.co.uk

BRADFORD

Rink Address: Great Cause, Little Horton Lane, Bradford, Yorks BD5 0AE.
Tel: 01274-729091. **Fax:** 01274-778818.
Ice Size: 180 x 80 feet (55 x 24 metres)
Spectator Capacity: 700.
Senior Team: Bulldogs (English Nat Lge North).
Club Secretary: Phil Lewis, Glendair, Gawthorpe Drive, Bingley, W Yorks BD16 4DH.
Tel/fax: 01274-567735.
e-mail: phil_l@btopenworld.com
Colours: White, Green & Black.

BRAEHEAD (GLASGOW)

Arena Address: Braehead Arena, Kings Inch Road, Glasgow, G51 4BN
Tel: 0870 444 6062.
Ice Size: 197 x 98 feet (60 x 30 metres).
Spectator Capacity (for ice hockey): 4,000.
No senior ice hockey 2003-04.

BRISTOL

Rink Address: John Nike Leisuresport Bristol Ice Rink, Frogmore Street, Bristol BS1 5NA.
Tel: 0117-929-2148. **Fax:** 0117-925-9736.
Ice Size: 180 x 80 feet (55 x 24 metres).
Spectator Capacity: 650.
Club Secretary: Mary Faunt, c/o the rink.'
Juniors only 2003-04.

CAMBRIDGE UNIVERSITY

No home ice 2003-04
Communications to: Prof Bill Harris, Dept of Anatomy, Cambridge University, Downing St. Cambridge CB2 3DYUK.
Phone: 01223-333772. **Fax:** 01223-333786.
e-mail: harris@mole.bio.cam.ac.uk
Colours: Light Blue & White.
website: www.cam.ac.uk/societies/cuihc
Recreational.

CARDIFF

Rink Address: Wales National Ice Rink, Hayes Bridge Road, Cardiff CF1 2GH.
Tel: 02920-397198, **Fax:** 02920-397160.
Ice Size: 184 x 85 feet (56 x 26 metres).
Spectator Capacity: 2,700.
Senior Team: Devils (Elite League).
Communications to: Shannon Hope at the rink.
Tel: 02920-396669. **Fax:** 02920-396668
e-mail: info@wnir.co.uk
Colours: *home:* White, Red & Black; *away:* Red, Black & White.
website: www.thecardiffdevils.com

CHELMSFORD

Rink Address: Riverside Ice & Leisure Centre, Victoria Road, Chelmsford, Essex CM1 1FG.
Tel: 01245-615050. **Fax:** 01245-615056.
Ice Size: 184 x 85 feet (56 x 26 metres).
Spectator Capacity: 1,200.
Senior Team: Chieftains (Eng Premier Lge).
Club Secretary: Ollie Oliver, Kings Ridden, Chelmsford Road, High Ongar, Essex CM5 9NX.
Tel: 01277-822688. **Fax:** 01277-364055
e-mail: ollie@highongar7.fsnet.co.uk
Colours: *home:* White, Blue & Red; *away:* Blue, White & Red.

COVENTRY

Rink Address: Planet Ice at Skydome Arena, Skydome Coventry, Croft Road, Coventry CV1 3AZ. **Tel:** 02476-630693. **Fax:** 02476-630674
Ice Size: 184 x 92 feet (56 x 28 metres)
Spectator Capacity (for ice hockey): 2,616.
Senior Team: Blaze (Elite League).
Communications to: Coventry Blaze IHC, The Hockey Locker, Co-op Extra Superstore, Queen Victoria Road, CoventryCV1 3LE.
Tel/fax: 02476-631352
e-mail: grantcharman@coventryblaze.co.uk
Colours: *Home:* White & Navy Blue; *away:* Navy Blue & White.
website: www.coventryblaze.co.uk

DEESIDE

Rink Address: Deeside Ice Rink, Leisure Centre, Chester Road West, Queensferry, Clwyd CH5 5HA.
Tel: 01244-814725. **Fax:** 01244-836287.
Ice Size: 197 x 98 feet (60 x 30 metres).
Spectator Capacity: 1,200.
Senior Team: Flintshire Freeze (English National League).
Club Secretary: Mike Welch c/o the rink.
e-mail: mike_welch@flintshire.gov.uk
Colours: *home:* White, Purple & Green; *away:* Green, Purple & White.

DUMFRIES

Rink Address: The Ice Bowl, King Street, Dumfries DG2 9AN.
Tel: 01387-251300, **Fax:** 01387-251686.
Ice Size: 184 x 95 feet (56 x 29 metres).
Spectator Capacity: 1,000.
Senior Team: Solway Sharks (Scot. Nat. Lge).
Communications to: Sandra Edgar, 5 St Anne's Road, Dumfries DG2 9HZ. **Tel:** 01387-264010.
e-mail: sedgar5701@aol.com
Colours: Blue, White & Green.
website: www.solwaysharks.co.uk

DUNDEE

Rink Address: Camperdown Leisure Park, Kingsway West, Dundee.
Tel: 01382-608060. **Fax:** 01382-608070
Ice Size: 197 x 98 feet (60 x 30 metres).
Spectator Capacity: 2,400.
Senior Teams: Dundee Stars (British National League) and Camperdown Stars (Scottish National League).
Club Secretary: Steve/Marie Ward, 223 Clepington Road, Dundee.
Tel: 01382-832244. **Fax:** 01382 884248
website: www.dundeestars.co.uk
Colours: *home:* White, Red & Blue; *away:* Blue, Red & White.
Senior Team: Dundee Tigers (Scot. Nat. Lge.).
Club Secretary: Joe Guilcher, 9 Merton Avenue, Clement Park, Dundee DD2 3NA.
Colours: *home:* White, Gold & Black; *away:* Black, Gold & White.

EDINBURGH

Rink Address: Murrayfield Ice Rink, Riversdale Crescent, Murrayfield, Edinburgh EH12 5XN.
Tel: 0131-337-6933, **Fax:** 0131-346-2951.
Ice Size: 200 x 97 feet (61 x 29.5 metres).
Spectator Capacity: 3,800.
Senior Team: Capitals (British National League and Scottish National League).
Communications to: Scott Neil at the rink.
Tel/fax: 0131-313-2977.
e-mail: edcapitals@aol.com
Colours: *Home:* White, Red & Blue; *away:* Red, White & Blue.
website: www.edinburgh-capitals.com

FIFE

Rink Address: Fife Ice Arena, Rosslyn Street, Kirkcaldy, Fife KY1 3HS.
Tel: 01592-595100. **Fax:** 01592-595200.
Ice Size: 193.5 x 98 feet (59 x 30 metres).
Spectator Capacity: 3,280.
Senior Teams: Flyers (British National League) and Kirkcaldy Kestrels (Scottish Nat. League).
Communications to: Tom Muir c/o the arena.
Tel: 01592-651076. **Fax:** 01592-651138.
e-mail: tom@britnatleague.co.uk
Colours: Flyers - *Home:* White, Gold & Blue; *away:* Blue, White & Gold.
Website: www.fifeflyers.co.uk

CLUB DIRECTORY

GILLINGHAM

Rink Address: The Ice Bowl, Ambley Road, Gillingham Business Park, Gillingham, Kent ME8 0PP.
Tel: 01634-388477. **Fax:** 01634-374065.
Ice Size: 184 x 85 feet (56 x 26 metres).
Spectator Capacity: 1,500.
Senior Teams: Invicta Dynamos (English National League South)
Club Secretary: Jackie Mason, 17 Beckenham Drive, Maidstone, Kent ME16 0TG.
Tel: 01622-671065. **Fax:** 01622-754360.
e-mail: Jackie.Mason@Invictadynamos.co.uk
website: www.invictadynamos.co.uk
Dynamos' colours: *Home:* White, Red, Blue & Black; *Away:* Blue, White, Black & Red.

GOSPORT

Rink Address: Forest Way, Fareham Road, Gosport, Hants. PO13 0ZX.
Tel: 02392-511217. **Fax:** 02392-510445.
Ice Size: 145 x 73 feet (44 x 22 metres).
Spectator Capacity: 400.
Club Secretary: Peter Marshall, 15 Islands Close, Hayling Island, Hants PO11 0NA.
Tel: 02392-466809.
e-mail: peter.marshall@havant.gov.uk
Senior Team: Solent Sharks (English National League South).
Colours: Black & Red.
website: www.solenticehockey.co.uk

GRIMSBY

Rink Address: The Leisure Centre, Cromwell Road, Grimsby, South Humberside DN31 2BH.
Tel: 01472-323100. **Fax:** 01472-323102.
Ice Size: 120 x 60 feet (36.5 x 18 metres).
Spectator Capacity: 1,300.
Senior Team: Buffaloes (English Nat Lge North)
Club Secretary: Allan Woodhead, Weelsby Park Riding School, Weelsby Road, Grimsby, South Humberside DN32 8PL.
Tel/Fax: 01472-346127.
Colours: *Home:* Red & White, *away:* Black, White & Red.

GUILDFORD

Rink Address: Spectrum Ice Rink, Parkway, Guildford GU1 1UP.
Tel: 01483-444777. **Fax:** 01483-443311.
Ice Size: 197 x 98 feet (60 x 30 metres).
Spectator Capacity: 2,200.
Senior Team: Flames (British National League).
Communications to: Rob Hepburn at the rink.
Tel: 01483-452244, **Fax:** 01483-443373.
e-mail: rob@guildfordflames.com
Colours: *Home:* Gold, Red & Black;
away: Black, Red & Gold.
website: www.guildfordflames.com

HARINGEY (LONDON)

Rink Address: The Ice Rink, Alexandra Palace, Wood Green, London N22 4AY.
Tel: 0208-365-2121. **Fax:** 0208-444-3439.
Ice Size: 184 x 85 feet (56 x 26 metres).
Spectator Capacity: 1,750.
Senior Team: Racers (Elite League/English Premier League).
Club Secretary: Roger Black, Haringey Racers IHC, 13 New North Street, London WC1N 3PJ.
Tel: 020 7420 5900. **Fax:** 020 7420 5911.
e-mail: roger@racershockey.com
website: www.racershockey.com
Colours: *Home:* Gold & Blue;
away: Blue & Gold.

HULL

Rink Address: The Hull Arena, Kingston Park, Hull HU1 2DZ.
Tel: 01482-325252. **Fax:** 01482-216066.
Ice Size: 197 x 98 feet (60 x 30 metres).
Spectator Capacity: 2,000.
Senior Teams: Stingrays (British National Lge) and Kingston Jets (English Nat Lge North).
Communications to: Mike/Sue Pack.
Tel/fax: 01908-317029 .
e-mail: info@hullstingrays.co.uk
Colours: Stingrays - *Home:* White, Purple & Black, *away:* Purple, Black & Silver.
Website: www.hullstingrays.co.uk

IRVINE

Rink Address: Magnum Leisure Centre, Harbour Street, Irvine, Strathclyde KA12 8PD.
Tel: 01294-278381. **Fax:** 01294-311228.
Ice Size: 150 x 95 feet (45.5 x 29 metres).
Spectator Capacity: 750.
Club Secretary: Jennifer Wilson, 18 Woodfield Road, Ayr KA8 8LZ. **Tel/Fax:** 01292-263739.
Junior and recreational teams only in 2003-04

ISLE OF WIGHT

Rink Address: Planet Ice Ryde Arena, Quay Road, Esplanade, Ryde, I of Wight PO33 2HH. **Tel:** 01983-615155. **Fax:** 01983-567460.
Ice Size: 165 x 80 feet (50 x 24 metres)
Spectator Capacity: 1,000.
Senior Team: *Wightlink* Raiders (English Premier League).
Club Secretary: Mavis Siddons, 6 Port Helens, Embankment Road, St Helens, Isle of Wight PO33 1XG. **Tel:** 01983-873094.
e-mail: mave@twin2.plus.com
Colours: *Home:* White, Red & Black; *away:* Red, Black & White.
website: www.wightlinkraiders.com

KILMARNOCK

Rink Address: Galleon Leisure Centre, 99 Titchfield Street, Kilmarnock, Ayr KA1 1QY. **Tel:** 01563-524014. **Fax:** 01563-572395.
Ice Size: 146 x 75 feet (44.6 x 23 metres)
Spectator Capacity: 200
Club Secretary: Caroline Norwood.
Address: 12 Cunningham Drive, Giffnock, Strathclyde G46 6EP. **Tel/fax:** 0141-577-6946.
Team: Avalanche (Scottish Nat. League).

LEE VALLEY

Rink Address: Lee Valley Ice Centre, Lea Bridge Road, Leyton, London E10 7QL.
Tel: 0208-533-3156. **Fax No:** 0208-446-8068.
Ice Size: 184 x 85 feet (56 x 26 metres).
Spectator Capacity: 1,000.
Communications to: Mike Smith at the rink.
Juniors only 2003-04.

MANCHESTER

Arena Address: *Manchester Evening News* Arena, 21 Hunts Bank, Victoria Exchange, Manchester M3 1AR.
Tel: 0161-950-5000. **Fax:** 0161-950-6000.
Ice Size: 197 x 98 feet (60 x 30 metres).
Spectator Capacity (for ice hockey): 17,250.
Senior Team: Phoenix (Elite League).
Communications to: Andy Costigan, Manchester Phoenix IHC, Communications House, 126-146 Fairfield Road, Droylsden, Manchester M43 6AT.
Tel: 0161-301-6851 **Fax:** 0161-301-1571.
e-mail: info@fomih.co.uk
Colours: *Home:* White, Purple & Black; *away:* Black, Purple & White.
Website: www.manchesterphoenix.co.uk

MILTON KEYNES

Rink Address: Planet Ice Milton Keynes Arena, The Leisure Plaza, 1 South Row, (off Childs Way H6), Central Milton Keynes, Bucks MK9 1BL.
Tel: 01908-696696. **Fax:** 01908-690890.
Ice Size: 197 x 98 feet (60 x 30 metres)
Spectator Capacity: 2,200.
Senior Teams: Lightning (English Premier Lge) and Thunder (Eng Nat Lge South).
Lightning's Club Secretary: Harry Howton, Oldbrook House, Boycott Avenue, Oldbrook, Milton Keynes.
Tel: 01908-696993. **Fax:** 01908-696995.
e-mail: howtons.ltd@btinternet.com
Lightning's Colours: *Home:* White, Gold & Black; *away:* Black, White & Gold.
website: ww.mk-lightning.com

NEWCASTLE

Arena Address: *Telewest* Arena, Arena Way, Newcastle-on-Tyne NE4 7NA.
Tel: 0191-260-5000. **Fax:** 0191-260-2200.
Ice Size: 197 x 98 feet (60 x 30 metres).
Spectator Capacity (for ice hockey): 5,500
Senior Team: Vipers (British National Lge).
Communications to: Clyde Tuyl at the Arena.
Tel: 0191-242-2420. **Fax:** 0191-260-2328
e-mail: kbsvipers@wwmail.co.uk
Colours: *Home:* White, Gold & Black; *away:* Black, Gold & White.
website: www.newcastlevipers.com
Senior Team: Sunderland Chiefs (English Nat League North).
Communications to: Mike Hendry, 4 Floral Dene, South Hylton, Sunderland SR4 0NW.
Tel: 0191-534-7219. **Fax:** 0191-564-2695.
e-mail: mikehendry@tynetubepallion.co.uk
Colours: *Home:* White, Red & Blue; *away:* Blue, Red & White.

NOTTINGHAM

Rink Address: National Ice Centre, Lower Parliament Street, Nottingham NG1 1LA.
Tel: 0115-853-3000. **Fax:** 0115-853-3034.
Ice Size: 197 x 98 feet (60 x 30 metres).
Spectator Capacity (for ice hockey): 6,500.
Senior Teams: Panthers (Elite League) and Lions (English Nat League North).
Panthers' office: Gary Moran, 2 Broadway, The Lace Market, Nottingham NG1 1PS.
Tel: 0115-941-3103. **Fax:** 0115-941-8754. .
e-mail: info@panthers.co.uk
Panthers' colours: *Home:* White, Gold & Red; *away:* Black, Gold & Red.
Website: www.panthers.co.uk

CLUB DIRECTORY

OXFORD

Rink Address: The Ice Rink, Oxpens Road, Oxford OX1 1RX.
Tel: 01865-467002. **Fax**: 01865-467001.
Ice Size: 184 x 85 feet (56 x 26 metres).
Spectator Capacity: 1,025.
Senior Team: City Stars (Eng Nat Lge South)
Club Secretary: Gary Dent, 42 Westfield Way, Wantage, Oxon OX12 7EW.
Tel/fax: 01235-763264.
e-mail: oxfordcitystars@aol.com
Colours: *Home*: Red & White, *away*: amarillo.
website: www.oxfordstars.com

OXFORD UNIVERSITY

Home Ice: The Ice Rink, Oxpens Road, Oxford OX1 1RX (details above).
Communications to: Chris Pettengell.
Tel: 07939-502703.
e-mail: christopher.pettengell@exeter.ox.ac.uk
Colours: Dark Blue and White.
website: www.ouihc.org/home.asp
Recreational.

PAISLEY

Rink Address: Lagoon Leisure Complex, Mill Street, Paisley PA1 1LZ.
Tel: 0141-889-4000. **Fax**: 0141-848-0078.
Ice Size: 184 x 85 feet (56 x 26 metres).
Spectator Capacity: 1,000.
Senior Team: Pirates (Scottish Nat League).
Communications to: Gil MacDonald at the rink.
e-mail: macdonal@fish.co.uk
Colours: Black & White
website: www.paisleypirates.net

PETERBOROUGH

Rink Address: Planet Ice Peterborough Arena, 1 Mallard Road, Bretton, Peterborough, Cambs PE3 8YN.
Tel: 01733-260222. **Fax**: 01733-261021.
Ice Size: 184 x 85 feet (56 x 26 metres).
Spectator Capacity: 1,500.
Senior Teams: Phantoms (English Premier League) and Islanders (Eng Nat Lge South).
Phantoms' contact: Phil Wing, Manor Farm, Great North Road, Stibbington, Peterborough.
Tel/fax: 01780-783963
e-mail: phil.wing@peterborough-phantoms.com
Phantoms' colours: *Home*: White, Black, Silver & Red; *away*: Black, Silver, White & Red

ROMFORD

Rink Address: Rom Valley Way, Romford, Essex RM7 0AE.
Tel: 01708-724731. **Fax**: 01708-733609.
Ice Size: 184 x 85 feet (56 x 26 metres).
Spectator Capacity: 1,500.
Senior Team: Raiders (English Premier Lge).
Club Secretary: Karen Bartlett, 282 Collier Row Lane, Romford RM5 3NL
Tel: 01708-766046. **Fax**: 01708-501909.
e-mail: gm@romfordraiders.org.uk
Colours: *Home*: White, Gold & Blue; *away*: Blue, Gold & White.
website: www.romfordraiders.co.uk

SHEFFIELD

Hallam FM ARENA
Address: Broughton Lane, Sheffield S9 2DF.
Tel: 0114-256-5656. **Fax**: 0114-256-5520.
Ice Size: 197 x 98 feet (60 x 30 metres).
Spectator Capacity (for ice hockey): 10,000.
Senior Team: Steelers (Elite League).
Communications to: Betty Waring at Arena.
Tel: 0114-242-3535. **Fax**: 0114-242-3344.
e-mail: sheffsteel@freeuk.com
Colours: *Home*: White, Blue, Orange & Teal; *away*: Black, Blue, Orange & Teal.
website: www.steelersihc.co.uk.

iceSHEFFIELD
Address: Coleridge Road, Sheffield S9 5DA.
Tel: 0114-223-3900. **Fax**: 0114-223-3901.
e-mail: info@icesheffield.com
Spectator Capacity: 1,500 (main rink).
Senior Team: Sheffield Scimitars (English Nat Lge North)
Club Secretary: Dave Lawrence, 103 St Paul's Parade, Ardsley, Barnsley South Yorks S71 5BU.
Tel/fax: 01226-212754.
e-mail: lolhock@hotmail.com
Colours: *Home*: White, Black & Blue; *away*: Black, White & Blue.

CLUB DIRECTORY

SLOUGH

Rink Address: The Ice Arena, Montem Lane, Slough, Berks SL1 2QG.
Tel: 01753-821555. **Fax**: 01753-824977.
Ice Size: 184 x 85 feet (56 x 26 metres).
Spectator Capacity: 1,500.
Senior Team: Jets (English Premier League).
Club Secretary: Pauline Rost, 37 Monks Avenue, East Molesey, Surrey KT8 0HD.
e-mail: pauline.postie@virgin.net or woz@sloughjets.co.uk
Colours: *Home*: White, Blue & Red; *away*: Blue, White & Red.
website: www.sloughjets.co.uk

SOLIHULL

Rink Address: Hobs Moat Road, Solihull, West Midlands B92 8JN.
Tel: 0121-742-5561. **Fax**: 0121-742-4315.
Ice Size: 185 x 90 feet (56 x 27 metres).
Spectator Capacity: 1,500.
Senior Team: Kings (English Premier Lge).
Communications to: Jon Rodway c/o the rink.
e-mail: enquiry@solihullkings.co.uk
Colours: Information not available.
website: www.solihullkings.co.uk

STREATHAM

Rink Address: 386 Streatham High Road, London SW16 6HT.
Tel: 0208-769-7771. **Fax**: 0208-769-9979.
Ice Size: 197 x 85 feet (60 x 26 metres).
Communications to: Adam Goldstone.
Address: 155 Grange Road, London SE25 6TG.
Tel: 0208-771-1427
e-mail:adam@streathamicehockey.com
Senior Team: Redskins (English Nat Lge South).
Colours: *Home*: White & Red; *away*: Black & Red.
Website: www.streathamicehockey.com

SUNDERLAND

Crowtree Leisure Centre closed in June 2000 and it is uncertain when it will re-open. The Chiefs are playing at the Telewest Arena in Newcastle-on-Tyne. See entry under Newcastle.
Rink Address: Crowtree Leisure Centre, Crowtree Road, Sunderland, Tyne & Wear SR1 3EL.
Ice Size: 184 x 85 feet (56 x 26 metres).
Spectator Capacity: 1,200.

SWINDON

Rink Address: Link Centre, White Hill Way, Westlea, Swindon, Wilts SN5 7DL.
Tel: 01793-445566. **Fax**: 01793-445569.
Ice Size: 184 x 85 feet (56 x 26 metres).
Spectator Capacity: 1,650.
Senior Team: Lynx (English Premier Lge).
Club Secretary: Andrea Brathwaite (director).
Address: 6 Audley Close, Grange Park, Swindon SN5 6BT **Tel/fax**: 01793-424040 .
e-mail: andrea.brathwaite@swindonlynx.com
Colours: *Home*: White, Blue, Silver & Gold; *away*: Blue, White, Silver & Gold.
website: www.swindonlynx.com

TELFORD

Rink Address: The Ice Rink, St Quintens Gate, Town Centre, Telford, Salop TF3 4JQ.
Tel: 01952-291511. **Fax**: 01952-291543.
Ice Size: 184 x 85 metres (56 x 26 metres).
Spectator Capacity: 2,250.
Senior Team: Wild Foxes (Eng Premier Lge).
Club Secretary: Mrs Jen Roden, 12 Dee Close, Wellington, Telford TF1 3JH
Tel/fax: 01952-405506.
e-mail: telfordwildfoxes@blueyonder.co.uk
Colours: *Home*: White, Orange & Black; *away*: Orange, Black & White.
website: www.telfordwildfoxes.co.uk

WHITLEY BAY

Rink Address: The Ice Rink, Hillheads Road, Whitley Bay, Tyne & Wear NE25 8HP.
Tel: 0191-291-1000. **Fax**: 0191-291-1001.
Ice Size: 186 x 81 feet (56.5 x 24.5 metres).
Spectator Capacity: 3,200.
Senior Team: Warriors (Eng Nat Lge North).
Club Secretary: Doreen Flynn c/o the rink.
e-mail: icerink@ukonline.co.uk.
Colours: *Home*: White, Gold & Maroon; *away*: Maroon, White & Gold.
website: www.warriors-online.com

LEGEND

The abbreviations used in the *Annual* are -

LEAGUES

ISL   Ice Hockey Superleague Ltd
BNL   British National Ice Hockey League
EPL   English Premier League

SCORERS

GP	-	Games Played
G	-	Goals
A	-	Assists
Pts	-	total Points
Pim(s)	-	Penalties in minutes
N	-	Netminder
Ave		Points per Games Played

NETMINDERS

GPI	-	Games Played In
Mins	-	Minutes played
SoG	-	Shots on Goal
GA		Goals Against
SO	-	Shutouts
Sv%-		Save percentage

TEAMS

S	-	Seasons
W	-	Win
RW		Win in regulation time (60 Mins)
OW	-	Win in overtime
RL		Loss in regulation time
OL		Loss in overtime
D	-	Draw
GF	-	Goals For
GA	-	Goals Against
Pct	-	Points gained as a percentage of total games played.

PLAYERS

*		British born and trained (ISL only)
I		ITC holder (BNL & EL)
WP		Work Permit holder

TIE BREAKERS

The system for deciding league places varies between each league/competition (you know it makes sense). The various systems are -

Superleague
- total number of points
- total number of wins
- overall goal difference
- goals scored

British National League
English Premier League
as per IIHF Rule Book

WORK PERMIT HOLDERS
Work permits are required by players from outside the European Union area who do not qualify for an EU passport. Such players will normally also require an ITC.

ITC - INTERNATIONAL TRANSFER CARD
A signed International Transfer Card (ITC) is required by any player who has been a member of another national federation. There are two types of ITC - 'limited' for one season, and 'unlimited' for players who intend to remain in this country. Ice Hockey UK only keeps records for players needing 'limited' cards and these are the ones shown in the *Annual*.

SAVE PERCENTAGE - CALCULATION METHOD
Shots on goal less goals against, divided by shots on goal, multiplied by 100.
Example: 100 shots less 10 goals scored, equals 90, divided by 100, equals 90 per cent.